pg 21
79
85
87
90
93
94
95

PROPHECY
2000

PROPHECY 2000

DAVID ALLEN LEWIS

New Leaf Press

First Printing, May 1990
Second Printing, June 1990
Third Printing, October 1990 (Expanded Edition)
Fourth Printing, February 1991 (Expanded Edition)
Fifth Printing, June 1992 (Expanded Edition)
Sixth Printing, August 1993 (Expanded Edition)
Seventh Printing, February 1995

Library of Congress Catalog Number: 90-60310
ISBN: 0-89221-179-2

Contents

1

Prophecy 2000

2000! It is like magic. You see it everywhere, like a universal logo! While flying to Rome on Alitalia Airline, I was given a copy of the Italian language magazine *Ulisse 2000*. One intriguing article was headed, "Futuro 2000 + Quanti Seremo?" It expressed concern over the burgeoning world population. That is just one of the monumental problems that scientists, politicians, and sociologists would like to solve by the year 2000, lest the human race plunge into extinction, victimized by its own greed, selfishness, and carelessness.

In the fall of 1989 the front cover of *Life* magazine was bannered, "The Future and You—2000 and Beyond." A lead article in *Life*, "2000—Visions of Tomorrow," reflects the thinking of thousands of secular and New Age futurologists who are making a capital business of prophesying the future. Foretelling the future is a growth industry for the 1990s. The World Future Society makes projecting a picture of the world of 2000 and beyond its major enterprise.

At this moment a photograph of U.S. President George Bush sits in front of me, President Bush is standing in front of a huge banner. The enchanting number 2000 fills the banner, looming like an open portal to—what? The news magazine projects itself into the future—beyond 2000—and asks, "Looking Back From 2000—What Did Bush Do?" Bush himself had said earlier that it would be from the

OLLIE NORTH'S $100,000 WEEKENDS ▪ EARTHQUAKES: WHY THEY HAPPEN

FEBRUARY 1989/$2.95

LIFE

THE FUTURE AND YOU

A 30-PAGE PREVIEW: 2000 AND BEYOND

VISIONS OF TOMORROW

COVER

We await its arrival with the same anticipation we had as children watching the odometer on the family's old Chevy turn to a row of zeros. But when it rolls around less than 11 years from now, will we know how to greet it? Will we call it two thousand, twenty hundred, or perhaps resort to the lingo of the '80s and just say 20-something?

A more serious question looms ahead. Can the next century possibly live up to our expectations for a better tomorrow? Much of the future looks promising. We will eat better and live longer. We will work less and stay home more. Tech-

nology will befriend us, freeing us of boring tasks and linking us still closer to the world at large. Our newest neighbors may be extraterrestrial, our next platoon of soldiers robotic. As we become increasingly aware of the fragility of the earth, we will have to treat it more kindly.

On the following pages, after consulting experts in fields ranging from demography to industrial design to medicine to interstellar travel, LIFE previews the changes that will follow the zeros on our calendar. Welcome to the first pictures and dispatches from 20-something.

ULISSE2000

ON BOARD:

Giulietta Masina   Tomaso Poggio   Mike J. Murphy
Maurizio Beretta   Omar Sharif   Alfredo Pieroni
Gino Gullace   Stephen King   Roger Moore   Shirley Temple

63

copia omaggio per voi   your complimentary copy   GIUGNO 1989

BOUTIQUE ALITALIA
PAG. 175

SPEDIZ. IN ABB. POSTALE GRUPPO 1/70 – BERGAMO

OCTOBRE 1999. N°244. 3,5 ECU

ACTUEL

1999

L'histoire des anés 90 en 200 fotos

Le premier journal en **nouvèle ortografe**

retrospective view in 2000 that his present political programs would be evaluated.

In the secular realm, major corporations and multinationals are picking up the 2000 logo for use in advertising campaigns that span the globe. Wherever you are coming from the looming number 2000 will be before your eyes in increasing importance every day that goes by!

2000! Where will you be? Will there be a peaceful new millennium? Or will a dark age of doomsday be thundering in upon us? Will the Church still be here? What about the Second Coming? Will there be a rapture of the believers as taught by Hal Lindsey, J. Dwight Pentecost, John Walvoord, and most Evangelicals? Or is the Rapture a cruel hoax, a false interpretation of Scripture? Is Dominionist David Chilton right when he proclaims that Christ cannot return for a minimum of forty thousand years and that it will probably be hundreds of thousands of years before He comes back? Will the decade of the 90s be even further characterized by confusion in the religious ranks?

ANNO DOMINO 2000—WHITHER THE CHURCH?

In the church world the lure of 2000 is powerful. Some are inspired to set a date for the earthly return of Jesus Christ (ignoring the traditional teaching of the potential imminence of His return). Date setters are drawn to 2000 as particles of steel are pulled to a magnet.

Other Christian groups project ambitious plans for the fulfilling of the Great Commission, to finish the task of preaching the gospel to the entire human race by the year 2000. Associate editor Robert Walker wrote a tract in *Charisma* titled "The Christian World: Gearing Up for the Year 2000." *Christianity Today* offered an essay, "AD 2000—Racing the Calendar."

An ecumenical (largely Roman Catholic) Charismatic group published a magazine, *AD 2000—Together*. Their announced objective is to win over half the world's population to the Church. One article in this publication refers to "The 20th century Pentecostal Charismatic renewal in the Holy Spirit with its goal of world evangelism." Some believe that the Church may dominate the world or a significant part of it by the year 2000.

Cautious Evangelicals and Pentecostals question the definition of evangelism used by the writers of *AD 2000—Together*. They want to know if this evangelism is merely a call to church membership or a challenge to a born-again experience. Some churchmen would like to take dominion over the world political system. They speak of discipling the nations as a fulfillment of the Great Commission. This usurps the

To Bring the Majority of the Human Race to Jesus Christ by the End of the Century ...

AD2000 *together*

VOLUME 3, NUMBER 2   NORTH AMERICAN RENEWAL SERVICE COMMITTEE   MAY-JUNE 1989

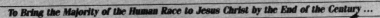

Aglow

Jane Hansen
of
Women's
Aglow

Women Are God's *Secret Agents*

primary goal of reaching lost souls with the gospel of salvation.

For some Christian extremists 2000 is the portal to a future world featuring a church-run theocratic world government. It will not be necessary for Christ to return to bring this to pass. The Church will do it. Democracy will be abolished. Pluralism will no longer be tolerated. Many "incorrigibles" will simply have to be executed or imprisoned in detention camps in order to bring about this more perfect society.

Dominionism is a revival of the postmillennial system launched by Rev. David Whitby in the 1700s. While the postmillennial concept thrived in some churches for almost two hundred years, it almost died out after the First World War. The idea that Jesus would return after the Kingdom is established (postmillennialism) was almost entirely replaced in evangelical circles by the teaching of premillennialism. It declares that Jesus will come back first and then establish the visible manifestation of the kingdom of God on earth. This was the view held by the early church for the first two hundred years of her existence.

2000! Its magical bells toll out a message—but what is that message? At any rate, for now, the religious world speaks of this decade of destiny or the decade of harvest. Some church groups have set up very legitimate goals with a view to completing the task of preaching the gospel to the world by the year 2000.

NEW AGE MOVEMENT SETS ITS SIGHTS—2000

In 1975 powerful leaders in the New Age movement declared the "Tri Millennial Countdown." A paradigm shift in the very manner in which humanity perceives reality must be effected by the year 2000. Then the world will enter into the age of Aquarius, the New Age. Globalsim will flourish. National boundaries will blur. Mankind will realize its own divine "godhood." We are told that our planet is already a living sentient being and is now in contact with the ancient ascended masters of the hierarchy of the universe. By the year 2000 all humanity will enter into harmonic convergence and communication with the masters.

One hundred years earlier, in 1875, Helena Petrovna Blavatsky, a Russian noblewoman, launched the Theosophical Society which many look upon as the grandmother of the current New Age movement. One can confirm this perception by looking in Encyclopedia Britannica under the entries "Blavatsky, H.P." and "Theosophy." Britannica credits the society, which today headquarters in Wheaton, Illinois, with being the major force in popularizing Eastern mysticism in western Christian civilization. It would be overly simplistic to see Theosophy as the only root of the New Age movement, but most researchers would grant that it was one of the major factors in the process.

One New Age analyst claims that the movement has branched out into politics, education, entertainment, media, health care, motivational courses, environmentalism, religion, and a host of other realms. Now there are upwards of fifteen thousand organizations in the U.S.A. and Canada. They comprise a loosely knit network which has no central control but shares a general philosophy embracing globalsim, the concept that man is god, psychic humanism as a synchretical world religion, and the need for a world economic system.

The New Age movement did not emerge into full blown existence from nowhere. It was a long time in development, and when awareness was heightened in recent times, almost a billion humans found a comfortable shelter under the newly declared New Age umbrella. For example, Hindus and other Eastern religionists found immediate identity with the New Age movement. Sharp promoters lifted the New Age from the status of mom and pop storefront businesses and gave it a multinational corporate image. Liaisons and covenants were established and corporate takeovers effected in the realm of the paranormal, the metaphysical and the mystic.

Anthropologist Margaret Mead and U.N. Assistant Secretary General Robert Mueller were the two key people responsible for inauguration the 1975 Tri Millennial Countdown. One of the principal functions of the T.M.C. was the organizing of an annual December 31 prayer meeting. This Day of Planetary Healing features hypnotic prayers, and a host of bizarre rituals. The annual event is also called Instant of World Cooperation and various other titles. Does it surprise you to learn that some Evangelicals naively participate in the occultic exercise?

This 7 a.m., December 31 (EST) prayer meeting was kicked into high gear in 1986 by such New Age luminaries as Barbara Marx Hubbard (author of *Evolutionary Journey* and *Happy Birthday Planet Earth*) and John Randolph Price of the Quartus Foundation, and the Planetary Commission. The activity is to be repeated until the year 2000 when the New Age "Earth Celebration" will be fulfilled. Flowing in the same vein Jose Arguelles, of Harmonic Convergence fame, said, "What EC2000 is all about is articulating the power…the Earth itself…first as an image and then, as a living breathing being we all depend on" (*Planet Earth* magazine, Vol. 9 No. 1, p. 6). I attended the New Age December 31, 1986 prayer meeting in Kansas City, Missouri. Robert Muller was the principal speaker. The meeting was held at the downtown

Kansas City Municipal Auditorium. Much of our research into the New Age is done "on location," in order to insure accurate reporting. Both we and our researchers have continued this type of on-the-spot observations.

Lucis Trust, headquartered in New York City, was founded by Alice Bailey as the Lucifer Publishing Company in the early 1920s. It is an offshoot of Blavatsky's Theosophical Society. Lucis Trust is a chief promoter of the annual December 31 event.

While the New Agers make frequent use of the words love, peace, brotherhood, and cooperation, there is an ominous side to their aspirations. The not-too-subtle warning is "don't get in the way of our plans." Those who resist the paradigm shift in the year 2000 will be construed as "bad seed" and will have to be dealt with or eliminated. Guess whose hit list that puts you on!

BIBLE PROPHECY—2000

After recent and continuing date-setting disasters and debacles, it is a wonder that the biblical message gets a hearing at all. But Bible prophecy is alive and well. On the other hand we know that as we approach the year 2000, the date-setters will have a heyday. You cannot believe how many books will be published "proving" that Christ must return in the year 2000. Actually, I believe He could come today. But if He has not come by the year 2001, we will still offer the biblical message as valid then as it is now. What if Jesus has not returned by the year 2007? What is your contingency plan? Read on, friend, read on.

Yes, in spite of self-anointed, card-carrying (we joke not) "prophets" who, in the churches, substitute their personal prophetic pronounce-ments for real Bible prophecy, there are still those who uphold the dignity, magnificence, and accuracy of the prophecies of the Bible. This is your sure guide to the future.

We grant the reality of the gift of prophecy, visions and dreams for our times, but these things must meet the standard of the Bible. We cannot force the Bible to conform to our personal revelations.

The year 1999 will be like a madhouse with frenetic date-setting activity bursting all around us. You will hardly know what to believe or who to listen to. It will not be an easy time, and if you think the Rapture 1988 error was damaging to our cause, what will it be like in 1999 (if Jesus doesn't come before then)?

Setting a date destroys the concept of potential imminence, which implies that Jesus could come today. One who understands the concept of imminence will not be taken by surprise when the Lord returns.

We expect Him at any time. Nor will the idea of His coming make an escapist out of a well-informed Bible-believing Christian. If you persuade me that Jesus is coming in 2000 and if He comes tomorrow, then you have deceived me and the event truly would take me by surprise.

Make plans for the future. Be ready to go today. Be prepared to stay around for the rest of a natural lifetime. Living responsibly on the edge of time and eternity has always been the practical and blessed hope of God's people. Whether we go or stay, these are exciting times to be living in. Here we are right now in the midst of the greatest fulfillments of prophecy since the first coming of Jesus almost 2000 years ago. We are indeed living the latter days, the end-times, the final era.

In spite of all warnings mentioned, let those of us who adhere to conservative principles of interpretation of the Bible not go into a retreat and defeat mode. Set biblical goals for the future. Strive to attain those goals. Let this be the greatest decade of harvest even known to the Church. Let the Gospel go to the four corners of the earth fulfilling the Matthew 24:14 prophecy, "And this gospel of the kingdom shall be preached in all the world for a witness unto all nations; and then shall the end come."

IN THE ARENA

Far from practicing escapism, we move aggressively into the arena of spiritual warfare, rescuing the souls of men and women from the powers of deception and darkness in the last days. It is refreshing to see Evangelical, Pentecostal, and Charismatic groups who are staying true to the Word refusing to live like hermits, but rather going forward for God, doing exploits in the name of the Lord. Exciting times indeed. How happy the circumstances which have promoted the setting of legitimate goals for world evangelization with the target date of 2000 standing as a challenge before us!

Elijah lamented to the Lord that he was the only one left with the true message. God reproved him, informing the prophet that there were still thousands in Israel who had not bowed their knees to Baal. I want my prophecy chart to be right, but that is not enough. I also want my actions to be right. "Faith without works is dead" counsels the apostle James. How terrible it would be if I were right in my doctrines, but failed to win souls from eternal loss. How awful if prophecy becomes a bag of mind tricks or mere intellectual exercises while good works in the Master's service are ignored or sacrificed.

What in the world is coming next? Here are developments to watch in years to come if Jesus tarries.

INCREASE OF KNOWLEDGE

"And they that be wise shall shine as the brightness of the firmament; and they that turn many to righteousness as the stars for ever and ever. But thou, O Daniel, shut up the words, and seal the book, even to the time of the end: many shall run to and fro, and knowledge shall be increased" (Dan. 12:3,4).

The following quote speaks for itself:

"*The New York Times* weighs about 4-1/2 pounds and contains some 500,000 words. To read it all, at an average reading speed of 300 words per minute, would take almost 28 hours. Not only would your Sunday be shot, but also a good part of the rest of the week, too.

"Take television, a powerful and pervasive medium; Television didn't replace radio or newspapers or magazines. Each of the three older media is bigger and stronger than it ever was.

"Television is an additive medium. And the amount of communication added by television is awesome.

"Ninety-eight percent of all American homes have at least one television set. (A third have two or more.)

"The average American family watches television more than seven hours a day. (More than 51 hours a week.)

"Down the halls at the Pentagon, copy machines crank out 350,000 pages a day for distribution throughout the Defense Department. That is equal to 1,000 good-sized novels.

"Consider this: The Lord's Prayer contains 56 words; the Gettysburg Address, 266; The Ten Commandments, 297; the Declaration of Independence, 300; and a recent U.S. government order setting the price of cabbage, 26,911.

"At the state level, over 250,000 bills are introduced each year. And 25,000 pass the legislatures to disappear into the labyrinths of the law.

"Ignorance of the law is no excuse. Ignorance of the lawmakers apparently is. Our legislators continue to pass thousands of laws that you can't possibly keep track of. And even if you could, you couldn't possibly remember how a law might differ from one of our 50 states to another.

"There's a traffic jam on the turnpikes of the mind. Engines are overheating. Tempers are rising." (From *Positioning—The Battle for Your Mind* by Al Ries and Jack Trouth. *Positioning* is a secular book on advertising.)

In the next ten years we will witness a knowledge and technology explosion. But that is not all. Read Daniel 12:3,4 in the Amplified Translation. It indicates that the knowledge of God and His purposes shall increase. We will understand more about prophecy and God's purposes every day and month that goes by! That is, provided we study the document He has given us—the Bible.

FASCINATING JOURNEY

In our fascinating journey through the biblical prophecies of the end-times, we will be gazing upon a wide variety of subjects and scenarios. We will ponder the meaning of the monumental changes in Europe and the evolutionary revival of the Roman Empire. A Jewish scholar in Jerusalem remarked to me, "David, Hadrian is alive in the world today." I asked him if he meant that literally. He replied, "No not literally. The spirit of the Roman Emperor Hadrian is alive. The Roman Empire is coming back to life. It will seem good to Israel for a while but it will finally be an evil thing and destructive to us all." I showed my friend how this was parallel to Christian eschatological anticipations.

WILL PERESTROIKA SURVIVE TILL 2000

We are now, in 1990, seeing the breakdown of the Communist world and its system of errors and abuses. My phone rings daily, church leaders, pastors, and lay persons ask, "Will glasnost last? Will perestroika work? Will the ruler of Russia be the Antichrist?"

When Gorbachev met with the pope in 1989, the whole world wondered what this unprecedented meeting could mean. When the head of an atheistic government met with the leader of the largest Christian body in the world, we asked, "What accommodation and compromise were these men endeavoring to achieve? Was this not a major trend toward globalism and the final one-world government? Is perestroika New Age Marxism? How near to the coming of Christ does this place us?"

Will perestroika (restructuring) last? Will the Soviets lose more and more ground? Could a harsh regime come into power once again, even worse than the evil Stalinist machine? We will ponder what desperation will come upon Russia to pressure her into making the bold, though ill-fated, invasion of the Middle East, as is prophesied in Ezekiel 38, 39 (Gog and Magog).

WINDS OF DOCTRINE

Strange winds of doctrine are blowing through the Evangelical and Charismatic fellowships. We have long been used to the theological liberalism and modernism in the old-line denominations, but not in our own ranks. Now we have our own modernists and liberals. Some of our brethren are denying the inerrancy of the Word of God, which is even worse than denying the literal interpretation of the inerrant Word of the Almighty. A spirit of compromise prevails in the religious world. This too is prophesied in Scripture. The Book of Revelation speaks of a harlot religious system that comes to full stature in the Tribulation period. Diverse groups will join hands to form a one-world religion. That religion is ultimately overthrown by the Antichrist as he exalts himself above all that is called God or that is worshipped (2 Thess. 2:3,4).

CHURCH AND POLITICS

Christians should penetrate every realm of society. Christian men and women should have places in government, education, politics, and all of the legitimate professions. The purpose, however, is not to dominate and take over the world system, but to carry the witness of the gospel of Jesus Christ and Christian influence into every segment of human endeavor.

Some churchmen, however, have a different vision. They see the Church conquering the world, setting up the Kingdom, and then welcoming Jesus back after the task of political domination is completed. The Dominion teachers are vigorous and on the move. The neo-Kingdom preachers are sweeping the Charismatic realm. Evangelicals and Pentecostals see their churches infiltrated and taken over in some cases.

WHO IS RESPONSIBLE?

How unfortunate for us that many of our Bible colleges and seminaries have abandoned the teaching of eschatology (end-time Bible prophecy). A vacuum has been created in the Church. Many pastors seldom if ever preach messages on the Second Coming or teach the Book of Revelation. This gives the Dominionists, the neo-Kingdom, the Apostles and Prophets, the Manifest Sons, and the Theonomists a field day. They promote their radicalism with great success. Our people are easy prey simply because they are untaught, not that our interpretation of the Bible is indefensible, or that they are gullible.

If the pure message of Bible prophecy and the premillennial concept of Christ's return is to be restored to its justified prominence in the Church, we must again have a generation of pastors who will begin to study and preach the whole Word of God. They cannot sweep certain truths under the rug because they were told at some Kingdom or Dominion conference that these doctrines are divisive.

WORLD ECONOMY

Your financial future is at stake. Does it matter? Frankly I don't care if you do or do not get a fancier automobile, a bigger house, or a finer wardrobe. I must, however, think of the role that finance plays in our stewardship of world evangelization. Is there anything we can do to protect ourselves from the coming crash that scores of economic advisors predict is upon us? The analysts predict a major depression before the year 2000. We believe, as we will explain later, that there are things that we can do to protect our families, the Church, and to maintain our stewardship role.

We believe that the church corporate, through intercession, can come against the powers of chaos even in the realm of world and national economy. While we know that worldwide economic Babylon will crash in the Tribulation, we do not believe that we are helpless or without authority in this present time frame. It is important that Christians understand this.

2

East Europe—Political Earthquake

"**O**h, east is east and west is west and never the twain shall meet" (Rudyard Kipling, "The Ballad of East and West").

Wonder of wonders, before our very eyes, in our very lifetime, the twain have now met. In 1989, the Berlin Wall comes down!

Mikhail Gorbachev, the ruler of Russia, launches perestroika (restructuring) for his nation and for the world. His book by that title had become a best-seller in the United States as early as 1987!

An article by George F. Will appears in *Newsweek* (November 20, 1989, page 90) headlines, "EUROPE, SECOND REFORMATION."

Will wrote, "Today, Gorbachev watches almost helplessly as the Soviet Union is riven by national ethnic, religious, linguistic and cultural differences—all those things that Marx knew, simply had lost their saliency. The Evil Empire, those who took such strong exception to that characterization have fallen silent; [it's about time] is going the way of the Ottoman and the Austro-Hungarian empires. Czechoslo-vakia—a dagger pointed at a continent of supermarkets—cannot for long resist the tides lapping around it. Soon those tides may surge south and engulf even Europe's most brackish backwaters, Bulgaria and Rumania.

"Only the reformation is remotely comparable to today's gale-force intellectual winds and loud cracking of institutional foundations. No

---

23

year, even in the 16th century, ever swept so many people or such complex societies into a vortex of change."

I am holding in my hand a copy of *Newsweek* magazine. The front cover is headlined "Super Partners, An Ambitious Game Plan for a News Era." A smiling Gorbachev and a smiling George Bush are pictured on the cover. Just think of that: here is an ambitious game plan for a new age for planet earth and the leaders of the most powerful nations of the world are joining hands, saying they are going to make things work for this new global system. Peace on earth and good will toward all men is the goal before us today.

POPE JOHN PAUL II AND GORBACHEV REASON TOGETHER

" 'This is the Holy Father,' said Soviet leader Mikhail Gorbachev, introducing his host to his wife, Raisa. 'We are aware we are dealing with the highest religious authority of the world, who is of Slavic origin as well.' To which a smiling John Paul II replied: 'Yes, I'm the first Slavic pope, but I'm sure providence prepared the way for this meeting with Mr. Gorbachev—and Mrs. Gorbachev as well.'

"Thus concluded the historic summit at the Vatican last week, signaling a dramatic reversal of relations between the Soviet Union and the Roman Catholic Church.

"As tokens of their unprecedented visit, the Gorbachevs gave the pope two 14th-century books written in church Slavonic, the language of the Russian Orthodox liturgy. From the pope, Raisa received a mother-of-pearl rosary. For the leader of the Communist Party and the Soviet chief of state there was an early Christian mosaic of St. Peter's tomb with a relief of Christ. It bore a scriptural message in Latin, one that Gorbachev may have recognized from his Christian childhood: 'I am the way, the truth and the light. All those who believe in me shall live' " (*Newsweek*: December 11, 1989).

What's happening in the world today? Are we seeing prophecy fulfilled in our times? We recently saw the most remarkable of occurrences: the head of the Kremlin visited with the pope in the Vatican. The USSR comes to Rome! Many people are saying this is but a precursor or forerunner to a joint alliance that will lead to a world government. We think, however, that it may be premature to draw this conclusion at this time.

AT THE HOUSE OF DEMONS

Something truly remarkable was launched in the island nation of

Iceland in the capital city of Reykjavik, when President Ronald Reagan met with Soviet leader Mikhail Gorbachev at their first summit conference. While in Iceland for meetings in the Filadelfia Churches, I was being escorted throughout the city by Pastor Haflidi Kristinsson.

One day I asked Haflidi to show me the place in Reykjavik where President Reagan met with Gorbachev. "Oh, you mean the house of demons," he replied.

I said, "What are you talking about?" It was explained that the Icelanders believe the grand house is infested with "ghosts." No one wishes to live there, although it was used for various official functions. I also noted that tourist guidebooks make mention of this as well.

PERESTROIKA

Defined, perestroika means restructuring. Fully recognizing that communism has failed, Mikhail Gorbachev has launched a system of reforms designed to restructure the political and economic sectors of his nation. This may seem like good news to many, but there are those who have serious questions, as to Gorbachev's sincerity and his credibility. Many political analysts would inject yet a further doubt and that is whether or not it is too late in the day for the communist regime to reform itself and to solve its very deep economic problems and political woes.

G. Karlov of Moscow writes in a recently published article, "I am amazed by the Western euphoria over the phenomenon known as *perestroika*." He is amazed that the West should prove to be so naive as to think that *glasnost* and *perestroika* have the slightest degree of authenticity in the Soviet Union. He then asks the existential questions, "What have we, the Soviet people—more than three years after the proclamation of *perestroika*—gotten out of it?" The answer he gives is, "empty shelves in our stores. We wonder whether the West can understand that having something to eat must precede the various (political) freedoms. Those of us fated to live under *perestroika* do not share the euphoria or even the joy of those who view our lives from afar."

Political columnists Evans and Novak noted: "...veteran party leader Andre Gromyko may have summed up Gorbachev best in 1985, when he nominated him for General Secretary: 'Comrades, this man has a nice smile, but he's got iron teeth.'

"But when Gorbachev talks about correcting the mistakes of the Stalin era, he does *not* mean correcting the underlying socialist system. Gorbachev is not proposing a pluralistic, Westernized society, but a Marxist-Leninist system that works. Capitalism, he insists, quoting

25

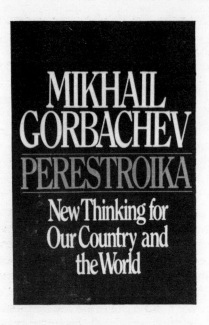

MIKHAIL
GORBACHEV
PERESTROIKA
New Thinking for
Our Country and
the World

Marx, remains a 'hideous, pagan idol.' We visited Alexander Ioffee, a prominent Jewish mathematician and dissident...who said 'Things are changing here, but we are cautious. We can't be sure, because Gorbachev is still only polishing the facade' " (*Reader's Digest*, October 1987).

Foreign correspondent Hilaire DuBerrier stated graphically, "Soviet Russia's prime aim is to advance by new means an old policy."

Another writer, Khenn Arak, informs us in the West that "the edifice we [the Russians] inherited is the one that Stalin built. Nowadays the Soviet leaders suggest that we renovate the edifice." This renovation, classified as reconstruction, is failing. Sergei Grigoryants states that the attempts to reconstruct the ruined edifice halted last year (1988). To demonstrate his point, he reports the decree of April 11, signed by Gorbachev, which "provides a prison sentence of up to ten years for 'public calls for the overthrow of the Soviet state and social system.' " Another section assures citizens of a three-year sentence for any "public insult or defamation of the USSR's supreme organs of state power."

BEWARE OF KREMLIN'S ILLUSION MACHINE

Joseph Puder, executive director of Americans for a Safe Israel, wrote the following in a special to *The Courier Post* (September 14, 1987): "Natan Scharansky is a man who should know the Kremlin well, warns that a dangerous complacency is engulfing the U.S. Jewish community.

"He pointed out at a recent meeting in Manhattan with Jewish leaders that Gorbachev's 'glasnost' has blinded America, preventing otherwise thinking Americans from realizing that the tokenism exercised by Moscow is a cover up for a tougher policy which intends to limit to a minimum the desired mass emigration of Soviet Jews."

I met with Scharansky in the Israeli Embassy in Washington and he expressed himself very similarly to Puder on the matter of glasnost.

I bought a copy of Gorbachev's book, *Perestroika*, when it first came on the market in the U.S. I was anxious to find out exactly what the man was saying. I read the book through very carefully, on three different occasions. In the book, I found that Gorbachev recognized the terrible problems that are facing the Soviet Union at the present time. He frankly speaks of the need for reform or restructuring—perestroika—in the Soviet Union. He sees the perestroika concept as applying to the entire world as well. It seems that Gorbachev is saying, "We are going to change our tactics for pragmatic reasons at the present time."

However, throughout the book he continually says that the Soviets are not abandoning Marxist-Leninst principles or ideals or goals. We know that Leninism and Marxism teach the absolute inevitability of conquest of the whole world by the system of communism by one means or another. This could be accomplished through negotiation, by infiltration, or by open warfare. Gorbachev is a Marxist leader who frankly admits to Marxist views and is saying, "We are going to cooperate with you now, but we will get you in the end."

On page 132 of *Perestroika*, Gorbachev writes:

"The process of perestroika in the Soviet Union holds out fresh opportunities for international cooperation.

"We are saying openly for all to hear: we need lasting peace in order to concentrate on the development of our society and to cope with the tasks of improving the life of the Soviet people. Ours are long-term and fundamental plans. That is why everyone, our Western partner-rivals included, must realize that our international policy of building a nuclear-weapon-free and non-violent world and asserting civilized standards in interstate relations is equally fundamental and equally trustworthy in its underlying principals."

Is Gorbachev describing those fundamental and underlying principles when he writes:

"The theory we call scientific socialism says that human society passes certain stages in its development. There was primitive society, then the slave-owning system and then feudalism. Feudalism gave way to capitalism and the twentieth century saw the birth of socialist society. We are convinced that these are natural steps on one historical ladder. This is the inevitable evolution of the world. Let the West think that capitalism is the highest achievement of civilization. It's their prerogative to think so. We simply do not agree with this. And let history decide who is right" (*Perestroika*, p. 151).

PERESTROIKA—IT WON'T WORK

Even if we give Gorbachev the highest marks possible for being well-intentioned, we must recognize that perestroika is not going to work. We have always said that communism will not rule the world. We have taught through the decades of our ministry that it is not the Leninist dream that will be fulfilled. It will be an entirely different system that will lead to a globalist society or one-world government. That ruling force will be of short duration before Jesus Christ returns and establishes the truly successful and workable world system, which we Christians call the Millennium. Communism is a total failure. The walls are crumbling and the people are revolting against tyrants who have betrayed them over and over again. Instead of fulfilling the basic needs of the masses of the communist-dominated countries, that system has held them in political, spiritual and economic slavery and bondage. Perestroika is the last-ditch stand as communist leaders try to preserve their position and dominance.

An excellent illustration of the failure of communism is seen in the plight of the housewife in Moscow. She has to spend from four to six hours daily shopping for groceries to have barely adequate supplies to feed her family. Walking down the street, the lady searching for food sees a line of people before a shop. She does not question what is being sold, but first gets into line and then begins to question. The simple fact is that if there is anything available, you stand in line as long as necessary and buy the maximum amount of the product that is available to you. How strange inasmuch as the Soviet union has some of the richest farmland in the world. If the Soviet agricultural system were working properly, it could produce enough wheat and other grains so that the Soviet Union could be a food exporting nation. The sad failure of communism is that without importing wheat from Australia, Canada,

World events are moving so rapidly! Since this text was written we have seen our predictions of the fall of communist power come to pass in many East European nations.

BUSH VS. NORIEGA
Next, the Legal Tug of War

Newsweek

ROMANIA

The Last Days of a Dictator

A Violent End to a Year of Revolution

TIME

WHEN TYRANTS FALL

RUMANIA
A Firing Squad
For Ceausescu

PANAMA
End of the Line
For Noriega?

The Economist

YUPPIE WELFARE
JAPAN'S PROPERTY GRAB
KNOW-HOW FOR THE POOR
SACHS'S PERESTROIKA

Gorbachev's bolshie republics

and the U.S., the people of the Soviet Union would starve. In every realm this failure is seen. Now the people are rebelling.

The United States has been bailing out the Communist regime from the time of the revolution in 1917. If we had not undergirded their economy in a thousand ways and a thousand times over, the system would have long since failed and a genuine revolution would have brought in a more democratic society. The economic troubles of the East Bloc Communist nations run so deep that there is no way the system is going to be healed at this late date. The simple fact is that the United States also is in such deep economic trouble that we can no longer afford to bail out Moscow to keep the Communist regime afloat as we have been doing for over seventy years.

THE EIGHTIES A DECADE OF CHANGE

At the beginning of the 1980s, for the first time we heard about AIDS. Now in America over a million people are infected with the virus and another five million worldwide are also infected.

Famine took the lives of hundreds of thousands in the country of Ethiopia. People worldwide responded—for awhile—then the commitment waned. At this writing, without a miracle, hundreds of thousands more will soon die of starvation.

Earthquakes of enormous proportions killed thousands, hurricanes, and tidal waves did the same. It appears that the world is indeed shaking at its very core. Could the coming of the Lord be very near?

The 1980s appeared to be good for democracy. It began in Poland when Lech Walensa led the strike at the Lenin Shipyard for lower food prices. We knew, however, that the Poles were really bidding for more control of their lives.

The Polish military, fearing Soviet intervention, declared martial law. Solidarity was outlawed and its leaders arrested or driven undergound.

In the Soviet Union, the 1980s would bring about changes no one had dreamed of, Mikhail Gorbachev wanted change as his nation was slipping toward a third world status. He called for the economy to be restructured *perestroika*. He made it easier for people to emigrate and called for a new openness—*glastnost*.

The movement for change in China was under way when Gorbachev went to China to pay a visit and toasted the first Sino-Soviet summit in thirty years. The students in Tiananmen Square, however, wanted democracy. They even unveiled a statue that looked like the Statue of Liberty and called her the Goddess of Democracy. The world was shocked as the iron fist of old-line communism came down and many

31

of these students were killed or taken prisoners.

In other parts of the world there were also struggles for freedom which often ended in despair or death. The people of the Philippines called it the People Revolution. It was a struggle, but eventually, the people drove Marcos from power and elected Corazon Aquino. Two years and six coup attempts later, she is simply surviving.

The idea of freedom was everywhere in the 1980s; Argentina, Haiti, Korea, Pakistan, and in Chile. In Eastern Europe, which the Soviets have held by force since World War II, has changed, Gorbachev loosened the reigns and said that Moscow would no longer interfere.

As a result, today in Poland, Solidarity leads the government with a non-Communist majority. Then Hungary began to break up the Iron Curtain. Tens of thousands of East Germans saw it on West German television. They headed for those openings in "the curtain" between Hungary and Austria and then they headed for the West German embassy in Czechoslovakia. The pressure of East Germans fleeing in such numbers forced the East German government to make one concession after another. The pressure was too much and the Communist leadership succumbed. Travel restrictions were lifted and that became a decision of monumental proportions.

For the first time since 1961, the East Germans made a hole in the Berlin Wall. There was no stopping freedom for them after that and they left by the tens of thousands.

In Romania the iron fisted Nikolai Ceausescu, who had gunned down his own people to stay in power, fell. The people then took him and his wife out of the palace and executed them.

Czechoslovakia's people brought down the Communist party there in less then four weeks.

Lithuania also wants its freedom and is nearing that goal.

In Azerbaijan the people are angry at Russia and are threatening secession. Some are calling it Gorbachev's Civil War. Azerbaijan is providing yet another test on Mikhail Gorbachev's nerves and political skill. When diplomacy failed, the Soviet leaders used force. Only time will give us the outcome.

At the end of the 1980s so many walls were coming down it was difficult to keep up with all of the happenings. It appeared that democracy was winning, but was it?

There is no way of telling whether the Iron Curtain has been broken or whether it will merely be a passing phase. But we Christians need not be afraid, we can look up and rejoice for surely our redemption draws near.

Newsweek

The Wall Comes Down

DER SPIEGEL

DAS VOLK SIEGT

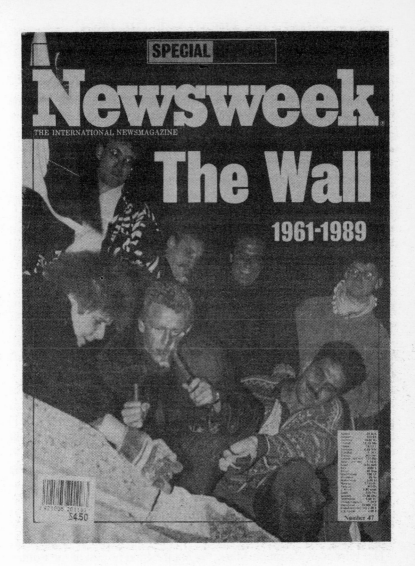

WHAT LIES AHEAD FOR THE USSR
AND EASTERN EUROPE?

Bible prophecy does not give us all the details of next month's newspapers. We can read the headlines, and as we go through the process of prophecy being fulfilled in our times, details are filled in. In some cases it is acceptable to offer a conjectural scenario of what the future holds. Certainly God does not want us to turn our minds off and not try to figure out what forces are at work determining our destiny until the Lord Jesus Christ returns. Prophecy teachers get in trouble only when they offer their theories and conjectures as dogma. What follows is my theoretical scenario of what could happen and what I think most likely will happen in Eastern Europe and the world.

Communism is not going to rule the world. The Bible reveals that there will be a ten-nation federation which we can conveniently call the Revived Roman Empire. This is clearly outlined in Daniel, chapters 2 and 7 and Revelation, 13-19. In the 13th chapter of the Book of Revelation, we see the Antichrist beast arise. In the ensuing passages, we see a ten-nation federation over which he rules. This is but a rephrasing of what we had already discovered in Daniel, chapters 2 and 7. The defeat of the beast and the federation that he rules is pictured in Revelation 19, when Jesus Christ comes back with the raptured, glorified Church in His entourage.

In the days to come, we will likely see movement toward a closer relationship between the Western nations and the Eastern Communist nations. As it becomes more and more obvious that perestroika is coming apart at the seams, this alliance will be short-lived. It may not be formally dissolved, but in all practical aspects it will cease to function. Some East Bloc countries could remain in alliance with the West, further isolating the USSR.

THE REVIVED ROMAN EMPIRE
AND THE COMMON MARKET

The European Common Market is not the final revival of the Roman Empire, but there will be a revival of the Roman Empire. The European Common Market is one of the major forces that will bring revived Rome to life in our times. We are actually seeing these ancient prophecies being fulfilled in their embryonic form in this day in which we live. I do not pretend to know what final ten nations will form the Revived Roman Empire, the original regime of the Antichrist, but it is over these ten nations that the Antichrist will first reign, before he moves out to establish a shaky world government that will last for a period of only three-and-a-half years.

When the rapture of the Church takes place, the restraining power of the Holy Spirit ceases to function in the manner that it does now as described in 2 Thessalonians 2. When the Church is gone, all hell breaks loose on the earth. The Antichrist comes forward and becomes the ruler of the ten nations of the Roman Empire revived in our times. One of the diabolical actions of the Antichrist as he comes to power shortly after the Rapture is that he will force a covenant or treaty upon the nation of Israel. It is this event alone that marks the time parameters of the period we know as the seven years of Tribulation, a time of global trauma. The covenant-signing marks the beginning of the seven years (see Dan. 9:24-27). The Antichrist will reign over the ten nations and perhaps over other areas as well for the first three-and-a-half years of the seven year Tribulation.

GOG AND MAGOG

The prophet Ezekiel spoke of a great invasion against the land of Israel that would take place in the last days. The account of this is found in Ezekiel 38-39. We find that the invasion out of the land that is to the extreme north of Israel takes place at a time when Israel is at rest and has peace. That certainly does not describe the condition that exists in the Middle East at the present time. It is apparent, therefore, that the Magog-Russian invasion of Israel will take place during the first three-and-a-half years of the Tribulation when Israel enjoys the protection of the new United Europe. This Magog battle could not be in the last three-and-a-half years because the Antichrist will defile the temple, an event that is referred to by Daniel and Jesus as the abomination of desolation (see Dan. 9:24, and Matt. 24:15-22). The apostle Paul also refers to this event in 2 Thessalonians 2:3,4, where he describes the man of sin entering the temple of God and declaring himself to be divine. When this abomination of desolation has been accomplished, there will be a time of unprecedented trouble for the Jewish people.

IDENTIFYING MAGOG AS RUSSIA

Are we justified in identifying Magog in Ezekiel 38 as Russia? Yes we are. Josephus, a contemporary of Jesus, says in his *Antiquities and Wars of the Jews* that in ancient times the Magog tribes settled north of the Caucasus Mountains which are in Russia.

Gesenius, over a hundred years ago, before Russia became a world power, interpreted the words of Ezekiel in this fashion. Gesenius was a famous Hebrew scholar and lexicographer.

Many modern translations include the word ROSH (not found in the KJV) as a proper noun. It is so translated in the Amplified, Jerusalem Bible, New English, etc. Here is how the verse appears in the Jewish-English translation, published by the Hebrew Publishing Company of New York:

"And the Word of the Lord came unto me, saying, Son of man, set they face against Gog, the land of Magog, the prince of Rosh, Meshech and Tubal, and prophesy against him, And say, Thus saith the Lord God; Behold I am against thee, O Gog, the prince of Rosh, Mesech, and Tubal: And I will turn thee back and put hooks into thy jaws" (Ezek. 38:1-4).

"Therefore, thou son of man, prophesy against Gog, and say, Thus saith the Lord God: Behold, I am against thee, O Gog, the prince of Rosh, Mesech, and Tubal: And I will turn thee back, and lead thee astray, and will cause thee to come up from the north parts" (Ezek. 39:1,2).

The geographic identity leaves no doubt that the identity of Magog is Russia. Over and over it stated that it is the land to the north; one translation of Ezekiel 39:2b translates "north parts" as the "extreme north." Only Russia would have the power to attempt an invasion from the north against Israel! A reading of chapters 38 and 39 will persuade you.

It is interesting to note that many Jewish rabbis and authors interpret these passages exactly as we do. One recent example is the book *Settings of Silver, an introduction to Judaism* by Rabbi Stephen M. Wylen. In that book he says, "The end is preceded by times of terrible upheaval in the world. The forces of lawlessness and evil will become powerful, and the Jews will suffer terrible oppression. Many people will be killed or will fall away from the Torah during that time.

"The forces of evil will gather together into a great army, the army of Gog and Magog."

Of course, as a Christian theologian, I have certain differences in my interpretation of prophecy and point of view compared to the rabbinical writings. It is interesting to note how closely parallel their point of view is to that of Christian literal interpreters of the Bible. Rabbi Stephen M. Wylen sees the Gog and Magog battle as the beginning of worldwide unrest and warfare the culmination of which he describes as the final battle called Armageddon. Wylen continues:

Elijah heralding the Messiah who is entering Jerusalem through the Golden Gate. Above the gate is a warrior symbolizing the war of Gog and Magog. *Mantua Haggadah*, Mantua, 1560. Jerusalem, J.N.U.L.

Illustrates Jewish understanding of Ezekiel 38 is similar to ours!

"Then God will send the Messiah Ben David, the Messiah descended of King David, who will miraculously turn the tide of battle and bring together defeat to the forces of evil."

This, in fact, is exactly what is going to happen. The battle of Gog and Magog, about the middle of the Tribulation or three-and-a-half years into the Tribulation, brings about the intervention of God and the destruction of the communistic system known as Magog. Out of the ashes of ruin and war the expanded world reign of Antichrist develops. As Ezekiel says, the Magog battle will set off a global conflict. It is also seen in the sixth chapter of Revelation pictured by the going forth of the red horse and his rider, who has the power to take peace from the earth. At that time one-fourth of the world's population is going to perish in a terrible time of war. The world will be in a more desperate condition than ever before. Jesus said there will be a time of tribulation such as never before has been upon the earth or ever shall be (Matt. 24). The Antichrist is then able to extend his government worldwide. Even so it is a shaky world coalition and there are sporadic uprisings against the Antichrist during these last three-and-a-half years of his reign, before his defeat at the hand of Christ at Armageddon.

WILL ANTICHRIST RULE THE WHOLE WORLD?

There has been some question as to whether the Antichrist would actually rule over the whole world. I think the answer is apparent in Revelation 13 and other passages. John writes: "...all the world wondered after the beast" (Rev. 13:3).

"...Power was given him over all kindreds, and tongues, and nations. And all that dwell upon the earth shall worship him, whose names are not written in the book of life of the Lamb slain from the foundation of the world" (Rev. 13:7,8). "And he [antichrist, beast] causeth all, both small and great, rich and poor, free and bond, to receive a mark in their right hand, or in their foreheads; and that no man might buy or sell, save he that had the mark, or the name of the beast, or the number of his name" (Rev. 13:16,17).

Incidentally, one matter needs to be clarified: Who are the saints in verse seven against whom the Antichrist has power to make war? This would include the Jewish remnant, the 144,000, and the multitude of Gentiles who are going to be converted as we read in Revelation 7:9, "After this I beheld, and, lo, a great multitude, which no man could number, of all nations, and kindreds, and people, and tongues, stood before the throne..." The saints of God simply means the people on earth at any given time who are living for God and have a salvation-redemption relationship with our Lord Jesus Christ.

The objection has been made that the terminology "all the earth" has been used in a limited capacity in at least one passage. In writing to the Corinthians, Paul does say that the gospel has been preached in all the world. Since we know historically that this refers to the Church's reaching the known world, or the Roman Empire of that period of time, with the gospel of Jesus Christ, therefore, any reference to "all the world" must refer to the Roman Empire only. The conclusion is then drawn by a few expositors that the Antichrist will never rule anything more than the Revived Roman Empire. This is an absolutely unacceptable manner of interpreting the Scripture. The context certainly puts a limitation on the use of "all the world" in Corinthians, as we know that Paul and the early Church didn't preach in North and South America as well as other yet undiscovered parts of the world. Nevertheless, "all the world" can be used in another context very literally. Beyond this there is the fact that it says the Antichrist will rule over all the world. Revelation 13 also uses the terms "all that dwell upon the earth," meaning this entire physical planet. Note the reference in Revelation 13 to all kindreds, and tongues, and nations.

I would further observe that if the terminology "all the world" is to be limited to the Roman Empire, then we have no business preaching the gospel in North and South America, Africa, or Australia, for Jesus said, "Go ye into all the world and preach the gospel to every creature." Certainly he meant more than the Roman Empire. This is a proof that the terminology "all the world" can be used in an inclusive manner.

Finally, if "all the world" in Paul's day meant to him the known world of that time, then "all the world" and "all the earth" in Revelation must mean the known world of the future projected in this prophecy. Yes, the Antichrist will reign worldwide. His power will not be as great in some areas as in others. There will be rebellions against him. He will not have the authoritarian power that some have pictured him as having on an entire worldwide basis, but he does have a worldwide coalition of nations which he heads up. He leads all the nations of the world in the great conflict known as Armageddon. At that time Jesus Christ will appear and defeat the powers of Antichrist. This prepares the way for the judgment of the living people comprising the nations of all the earth. This is to determine who will be allowed to enter the glorious millennial reign. And that Millennium is what we are looking forward to with high anticipation, not as a perfect age, but as an idyllic age. The Millennium, after all, is God's inauguration to the eternity of eternities "wherein dwelleth righteousness." There shall never again be any rebellion against God. Eternity, following the Millennium, is the time of perfection.

3

World Peace—
World Government

The only hope for lasting world peace is for some kind of a World Government to be established. Few would disagree with this statement. The great German scholar and Bible teacher Erich Sauer wrote, "Amid the triumphant shouts of heavenly hosts the gospel entered the arena of the earthly world. 'Glory to God in the highest, and on earth peace, good will to men' (Luke 2:14). This rang out at that hour of the night in the fields of Bethlehem-Ephratah " (Erich Sauer, *Triumph of the Crucified*, p. 11). How and when will an era of peace and good will come to mankind?

There will ultimately be a World Government and there will be peace on this earth. The big question is, "How will this World Government come into existence, and who will rule over the world when it is established?" There are many opinions confronting humanity. Will some hidden conspiracy bring it to pass? Will it come into being through political maneuvers? Will some Christian plot for world domination be the answer? Could the Bible literalists be right? If the latter is so then there will be a short-lived attempt at world domination by the Antichrist. He will be defeated upon the visible return of Jesus Christ. Jesus will then set up the truly peaceable Kingdom. Many conservative Bible scholars call this the Millennium.

ILLUMINISM AND ITS SPAWN

In 1776 Adam Weishaupt, an apostate Roman Catholic, who had been raised by Jesuits, launched an organization, the theories of which still linger and are manifested in a multitude of groups and philosophies today. Mother Basalea Shlenk, founder of the Evangelical Sisterhood of Mary, wrote,

"On May 1, 1776, Adam Weishaupt, a professor of Canon Law, founded the Order of the Illuminati in Ingolstadt, Bavaria. Five years before that he was initiated into alchemy and witchcraft and under the cover of the Freemason Lodge in Munich he carried out occult practices. However, the Order of the Illuminati that was established as an atheistic institution not only practiced occultism and Satanism, but also pursued political goals. The members of his order were, for instance, Voltaire, Mirabeau, and Robespierre. In France the most fanatical group of Freemasons, the Jacobins, joined the Illuminati. They were the instigators of the gruesome French Revolution" (*On the Eve of Persecution* by M. Basalea Shlenk).

The Illuminists stated several preliminary goals:
1. The abolition of private property.
2. The abolition of the family structure.
3. The abolition of religion.
4. The abolition of national governments.
5. The abolition of inheritance rights.
6. The abolition of capitalism.

The Illuminists saw these accomplishments as necessary for the establishing of their concept of a New World Order. Of course the leadership of the Illuminati would become the rulers of the New Order.

In 1927 Vivian Herbert wrote,

"This was the secret entrusted to the adepts of the intermediary category, but hidden carefully from the initiates. The Areopagites or twelve disciples of Weishaupt alone knew what the aim of the society was—to establish their own world dictatorship after clearing out established institutions" (*Secret Societies Old and New*, 1927, Vivian Herbert).

In 1979 I wrote, "It seems it is very possible that the Illuminati still exists.

"The general theory is that the philosophy of Weishaupt has various manifestations, but is secretly guided by a small group of powerful, wealthy men throughout the world. Only this small group is aware of the unity of purpose behind the many manifestations of the Illuminati" (*The Todd Phenomenon—Fact or Fantasy?* 1979, David Lewis and Daryl Hicks).

Scores of books have been written, examining the Illuminati conspiracy concept. I think that what we wrote in 1979 was an oversimplification. We know from documented history that the Illuminati did exist. Its philosophy is alive today. But to see one conspiracy alone leading to World Government is too simple. The fact is (as we pointed out in 1979) there are multiple conspiracies for world domination. The most visible today is the New Age movement.

ANTICHRIST AND WORLD GOVERNMENT

In Scripture antichrist is both a spirit and a man. The mystery of iniquity already works, declared the apostle Paul. John says there will be many antichrists and a final Antichrist. He will have a shaky world government, but it is short lived, lasting on a worldwide level for only forty-two months, and even then he does not have total control as evidenced by the fact that there are uprisings against him. Not understanding the prophetic structure and plan of the Bible could lead people with good intentions to accept the Antichrist.

THE NEW AGE MOVEMENT

I have no doubt that the Illuminists were an early manifestation of the New Age movement. The New Age movement really is not new. It simply heralds the coming of a New Age. (See my booklets, *The New Age Movement* and *New Age Confusion,* Menorah Press.)

The leaders of the New Age movement profess themselves to be the vanguards of a New World Order. Since there is such great diversity in the New Age movement, we hear varying opinions. One thing is sure: while there is infighting for dominance, nevertheless they agree that there must be a United World governing body, for the sake of peace, of course. It could be pointed out here that Gorbachev's "perestroika" is nothing more or less than New Age Marxism.

THE COMMUNISTS, GORBACHEV, PERESTROIKA = UNCHANGING GOALS

The Communists following the teachings of Marx, Lenin, and Engles have given the modern world a dialectic of materialism. They claim that the laws of social science (class struggle, warfare of the proletariat) demand that the world someday be a Communist world. Conquest by one means or another, or by all means is inevitable.

Make no mistake about Gorbachev. He is a Marxist-Leninist. Having read his much heralded book, *Perestroika,* I know he has not abandoned the original vision of the Bolshevik Communist Revolutionaries. Only the tactics have changed. In his mind the outcome is sure. Since it is "inevitable" anyway, he can afford a change of tactics for his own advantage. A world socialist government is inevitable. Gorbachev says,

"In accordance with Marxist theory, the future belongs to a society where there is no exploitation of man by man and no national and racial oppression [capitalism banished, communism is supreme]. The future belongs to a society governed by principles of social justice, freedom and harmonious development of the individual."

While he disclaims any wish to force Marxism on any other nation, he nevertheless believes it will come. He cites Marx and Lenin to justify his change of methodology, noting that Marx said, "The victorious proletariat cannot impose on any other nation its own ideal of a happy life without doing damage to its own victory."

Although disclaiming any desire to export the Communist Revolution, and even quoting Marx and Lenin to substantiate his fantastic claims, we know the record of history shows the opposite. The Communists have promoted violent revolution wherever they could get away with it. Afghanistan was their first failure. Gorbachev says, "This is the inevitable evolution of the world. Let the West think that capitalism is the highest achievement of civilization. It's their prerogative to think so. We simply do not agree with this. And let history decide who is right" (*Perestroika,* p. 151).

Communism is only one dream of world conquest. For now it seems to have fallen on hard times. But candidates for the office of Antichrist will have to stand in line, and the line is growing longer. (See 1 John 2:18.)

4

Western Europe and the Revived Roman Empire

In 1992, the European Common Market, the Council of Europe, and the European Parliament plan to forge the first form of a new European Federation, or a United States of Europe.

Recently, a brilliant researcher, who was referred to me by Dr. Isaac Rottenberg of the Dutch Reformed Church, called with some important information. In the span of our four-hour telephone conversation, he commented on the weighty meaning of the new European Unity Movement. He remarked that the formation of a United Europe would have profound social, political, and historical ramifications for the whole world. The new bloc of nations would wield the power of a four to six trillion dollar annual economy, would involve 330-400 million population, and would undoubtedly raise the standard of living in Europe (at what cost to the U.S.A.?).

The researcher referred to here, being Jewish, has a special interest in the potential relationship between Israel and the future United Europe. Not only do the Jewish people have an interest in the remarkably developing situation, but we Christians also have a great curiosity concerning the unfolding scenario of prophecy (Rev. 13-17 and Dan. 2, 7, 9, etc.).

During September 1989, the *Jerusalem Post* ran an entire magazine section—consisting of 24 pages—about Israel's entering the European

Common Market. The headline carried the twelve stars of New Europe in a flag that is being flown all over Europe. They placed an arrow containing the Magen David (the Star of David) to represent Israel's effort to penetrate the European Common Market. The feature article is by Shlomo Maoz and is titled, "Entering Europe's Charmed Circle."

ENTERING EUROPE'S CHARMED CIRCLE
Shlomo Maoz

The post 1992 European Community will, irony of ironies, be an imitation of what most Europeans like to hate - the United States of America. The idea, if not the execution, of the 1992 scheme is simple, to forge a huge domestic market from the EC's 12 member countries that will give them the economies of scale a single economic unit yields. The EC's transformation into an economic United States of Europe will be consumated once it has adopted a single currency.

America is not the EC's only role model. Japan has taught America that the principle of unfettered competition in business can't hold its own against the joint ventures and close co-operation that the Japanese engage in. Thus the Europeans have already begun encouraging their firms to join ranks as the only means of creating the home markets, rationalization and research and development budgets needed to cope with the

U.S. and Japan. Airbus Industrie, the French, German, British and Spanish consortium, has already won itself a big chunk of the civilian aircraft market - once an American monopoly - and now the Europeans are scurrying to develop the next-generation TV.

Thus 1992 aims to create a new economic superpower of 330 million people that can match the big two - the U.S and Japan - on even terms.

Continued on page XXI

Israel's desire to enter the common market is illustrated in the Jerusalem Post.

"Japan has taught America that the principle of unfettered competition in business can't hold its own against the joint ventures and close cooperation in which the Japanese engage. Thus the Europeans have already begun encouraging their firms to join ranks as the only means of creating the home markets, rationalization and research and development budgets needed to cope with the U.S. and Japan. Airbus Industries, the French, German, British and Spanish consortium, has already won itself a big chunk of the civilian aircraft market—once an American monopoly—and now the Europeans are scurrying to develop the next-generation TV.

"Thus 1992 aims to create a new economic super power of 330 million people that can match the big two—the U.S. and Japan—on even terms."

The following are important dates leading to the complete projection of the evolution of the European Common Market:

April 18, 1951: The Treaty of Paris establishes the European Coal and Steel Community.

March 25, 1957: The signing of the Treaty of Rome establishes the European Economic Community, or EEC, also known as the Common Market. The original members were Belgium, Luxembourg, the Netherlands, France, Italy, and West Germany.

1962: The Common Agricultural Policy (CAP) is established.

1968: All internal tariffs are eliminated and a common external tariff imposed.

January 1, 1973: The Six become Nine as the UK, Denmark, and Ireland join.

1975: Israel and EEC sign a Free Trade Agreement (FTA) under which both sides undertake to phase out tariffs on each other's exports of goods.

1979: The European Monetary System comes into effect, reducing exchange rate volatility between member currencies. Britain has consistently refused to join.

1981: The Nine become Ten, with the entry of Greece to the EEC.

April 1989: The Delors Report calls on the EEC to undertake a three-stage program aimed at achieving full economic and monetary union. The program was adopted in June, despite fierce opposition from British Prime Minister Margaret Thatcher.

1990s: Austria, Cyprus, Turkey, Malta are all in the process of seeking membership. Speculation also extends to Hungary, Norway, Sweden, and Switzerland.

December 31, 1992: The target date for eliminating all trade barriers within the EEC.

This is not the final form of the Revived Roman Empire. This is one of many things moving toward the Roman Empire. The interest that we have here is expressed on a *Jerusalem Post* headline, "Why Should Israel Care?" That's a question that we are going to have to leave to the Israelis to settle for themselves. Naturally, we would assume that a treaty with the European Common Market would be a security measure for Israel as well as an economic boon.

The four-nation Arab council founded by North Yemen, Jordan, Egypt, and Iraq met in Sanaa on September 24, 1989, with King Hussein of Jordan, President Mubarak of Egypt, and President Hussein of Iraq. They launched what in essence is an Arab Common Market like the EEC in Brussels. Its declared aim is a free-trade market for their eighty million people. But also like its Brussels counterpart, the group will expand and become political. And here may be the solution for Arab unity that until now has escaped them.

Once the Sanaa group, which will eventually be based in Cairo or Alexandria, becomes a power to be reckoned with, there is no reason why it should not merge with Brussels, as the moderate Communist states are preparing to do. At that time Tel Aviv, like the rest of the West, will confront a power not as toothless as the UN with each member at the mercy of fanatic Moslem minorities. So much for the bleak picture of the Middle East with its internal quarrels.

The Bible says in Daniel 9:24-27 (the seventy weeks vision) that there will be a covenant between the Antichrist and leaders of Israel. People have sometimes faulted Israel because of the fact that they are going to enter into a covenant with the Antichrist. One thing that we need to recall from our studies of Scriptures is that the Antichrist deceives the West world nations, forms his European Bloc of power and has influence throughout the Gentile world before he enters into a covenant with Israel. It is interesting to note that the only thing that marks the beginning of the seven-year Tribulation in the Bible is the signing of that covenant. That sets the parameters of the seven-year Tribulation, or the seventieth week of Daniel. (In this vision each of the seventy weeks represents seven years.) So the seventieth week is a seven-year period of time characterized by Jesus as a time of Tribulation. It is called "the time of Jacob's trouble" in other passages.

I had a very interesting conversation with the late Rev. Zeev Kaufsman, pastor of Messianic Assembly of God in Jerusalem. The assembly was on the corner of King George and Gershon Agron Streets, not more than a half-block from the Great Synagogue and the Hechel Shlomo, which houses the chief rabbinate of Israel. This property was sold by the Assemblies of God to a conservative Jewish foundation.

In conversation with Kaufsman, on many different occasions, we discussed Bible prophecy. I found him to be a scholarly man. In 1969, he said to me: "David, right now Israel is the darling of the West, popular and enjoys an aura of security. But, as we have defensive war after defensive war and wars of attrition in the years that lie ahead of us, if Jesus tarries, the popularity of Israel is going to be eroded."

I hope that is not true. I especially hope it is not true that America would abandon Israel, because the Bible says that God will bless those who bless Israel and curse those who curse the seed of Abraham, through the chosen line of Jacob, who became Israel.

Old city of Jerusalem—the Citadel of David.

Kaufsman said, "It is almost inevitable. The world is going to grow tired of us. The Jew always ends up being a scapegoat in times of difficulty or trouble. The day is going to come when the Antichrist will be in power over the ten nations. He will come to the leaders of Israel and say, 'All right, you Jews, we've had it. War, the intifada, the uprising, your stubborn refusal to cede more territory, for peace!' "

Kaufsman's view was that the treaty, or seven-year covenant was not going to be so much sought by Israel, although I'm certain there are some who would seek it even now, as it would be a logical thing to want alliances. It is likely, however, that the treaty will be literally shoved down the throats of the Israelis. They will be forced to take the conditions or be abandoned and destroyed by their neighbors. It is a point of view that is worth considering that Israel won't be so much seeking the covenant, but it will be forced upon them by the Western world.

The current conflict is tragically interesting. It began in the fall of 1987 with riots in the streets and Arab men, women, and children throwing rocks and molotov cocktails at the Israelis. In the Arab world, if anyone started a riot, the government would go out with a show of force that would be absolutely unbelievable. Israel, striving to be a democratic nation, has taken its lumps in the press for responding the way they have. The fact is that they have been remarkably restrained. In contrast to this remember when Syria had a political uprising in the town of Hama a few years ago. They sent the army in and killed 20,000 people in three days. That's how Syria handled their political protest.

Israel has actually used great restraint, if you measure it by any normal standard. What did we do in Philadelphia? We bombed a house because there was a cultic organization there. In Los Angeles when riots broke out in Watts, we sent police in with live ammunition. Many people were killed. Israel has been restrained, yet criticized by governments and media for over-reacting to the deadly rocks and bombs.

Kaufsman saw in 1969 that there would be continuous trouble between Israel and her neighbors. When the covenant comes from the Antichrist and the Western world, Israel will be forced to accept conditions that are self-destructive. But for the sake of survival, they will accept them.

In the *Jerusalem Post* there was an article by Benjamin Netanyahu, whom I have known for many years. He was the ambassador of Israel to the United Nations. He presently serves as deputy foreign minister in Israel and has a bright political career before him. Netanyahu says, "Regarding the Middle East, those positions may not necessarily be always to our liking. It is no secret that in the past 20 years we have invested a major political effort in our relations with the U.S. and not without significance. But it is also true that in that same period pro-Arab views have made headway among European opinion leaders. And it will not do just to brush aside the unfavorable voices. As Europe's political and economical clout grows, so will its stature in world affairs, and its influence will be felt in the policies of other nations.

"Israel must therefore focus on Europe politically as well as economically. We can enhance and deepen our relations with the leaders of European governments. We can broaden our contacts with European parliaments, where we already have many friends.

"In the last 40 years, Europe has proven that cooperation and peace can replace belligerence and wars even between age-old enemies.

"Europe can help in the quest for peace in the Middle East by using its considerable influence in the Arab world toward these ends. Israel is prepared for a serious dialogue with Europe, because we believe that Europe can make a difference."

CHINA CONFRONTS EUROPE

With all that is transpiring in China and the Far East we cannot overlook the coming clash between China and Europe as foreseen through the pages of the Book of Revelation.

This really fits the Bible prophecies of Armageddon. Two principal forces converge at Armageddon: the European nations, or the Revived Roman Empire, and the Kings of the East.

Revelation 16:12-16 reads, "And the sixth angel poured out his vial upon the great river Euphrates; and the water thereof was dried up, that the way of the kings of the east might be prepared. And I saw three unclean spirits like frogs come out of the mouth of the dragon, and out of the mouth of the beast, and out of the mouth of the false prophet. For they are the spirits of devils, working miracles, which go forth unto the kings of the earth and of the whole world, to gather them to the battle of that great day of God Almighty. Behold, I come as a thief. Blessed is he that watcheth, and keepeth his garments, lest he walk naked, and they see his shame. And he gathered them together into a place called in the Hebrew tongue Armageddon."

I am sure that many prophecy watchers will see this as a foreshadowing of conditions that will exist and make possible the covenant between the powerful leaders of the West Bloc nations and the state of Israel. It is the signing of that covenant which begins the seven-year period of time known as the seventieth week, the time of Jacob's trouble or the Tribulation.

JJSS - MYSTERY MAN OF FRANCE

These things were predicted years ago by Jean-Jacques Servan-Schreiber, first in his book *The American Challenge* (1968) and later in his profound statement in the book *The World Challenge* (1981), upon which I have commented in past years.

Briefly, JJSS, in his 1981 writing, begins by describing a conference of world leaders he had attended in Taif, Saudi Arabia. He chaired the meeting which was attended by Naohiro Amaya, Minister of MITI of Tokyo; President Leopold Senghor, described as the soul and the mind of Black Africa; Professor Seymour Papert; Ambassador James Akins; Sheik Ahmed Zaki Yamani; Ali Khalifa al-Sabah; and Abdulatif al-Hamad. These latter three have had power over much of the world's energy supply. Along with them was a collection of power barons from Europe. JJSS noted that the three-day conference was directed toward "the birth of a new united world" (*World Challenge,* pp. 5,6).

BRILLIANT DEDUCTIONS

While I cannot agree with the philosophy or goals set out by JJSS and his associates, I admire his analysis of world affairs as being nothing less than brilliant. Naturally, as a globalist, he makes observations such as, "At a time when the world is trembling at the thought of a fundamental crisis, scientific and human ways of forging a common future are now appearing."

His grasp of the computer revolution and its impact on the world society is the most incisive I have ever read. JJSS cites the president of the Kiel Institute who spoke of "gathering the courage and the will to act to pave the way for the renaissance of a unified world" (*World Challenge,* p. 262).

This author, JJSS, does not overlook the enormous power of Islam in today's world. With total candor, he reports, "After devoting twenty years to gaining control over oil and its revenues—and succeeding—the 'Yamani committee' had reached a new agreement for a 'leap forward' toward a world economic policy.

"The ministers ended the session. With these weighty problems resting on their shoulders, they had the feeling that the course of world events for years to come would be tied to the 45 pages of the Taif Report and to the 'international order' it described. As the sun was setting behind the mountains in Taif most of them left on a pilgrimage to Mecca" (*World Challenge,* p. 71).

INTELLIGENCE REPORT FROM MONTE CARLO

Recently, from Monte Carlo, Monaco, we received an intelligence report from Hilare Du Berrier. This particular source of information has been invaluable to us over and over. Commenting on the current European Movement, Du Berrier notes that Walter Hallstein, early president of the European Economic Community (EEC), candidly told a London audience that they should get it out of their heads that what was afoot was a mere set of economic measures. He said, "We are in politics." He further noted that the political aim was nothing more nor less than to expand from a regional group into a world federation.

When *Time* magazine (July 4, 1969) predicted a ten-nation economic entity in Europe, Hallstein more boldly declared, "We may fully expect the great fusion of all economic military and political communities together into the United States of Europe."

On May 28, 1979, Greece became the tenth member nation of the EEC. The ten nations were Belgium, Denmark, France, West Germany, Ireland, Italy, Luxembourg, Netherlands, United Kingdom (Britain), and Greece. Shortly thereafter, I was standing on the shores of the Mediterranean near Caesarea Maritima in Israel. Our television crew was in place, the cameras rolling, as I commented that I did not see these ten as the final form of the Revived Roman Empire, that undoubtedly there would be more nations joining the pact. I offered that probably Spain and Portugal could become the next member nations. That is exactly what took place. I further think that while the EEC, the European Parliament, and the Council of Europe are moving toward a ten-nation federation, more changes, drop-outs and additions could be made. I cannot conjecture as to what will be the final ten. Some think that because the U.S.A. was originally of European stock, we are an extension of the old Roman Empire and could be a part of the final ten. Time will tell.

In 1965, Du Berrier had pointed out the plan: "The European seed group was to strip Europe's nation states of their identity and bind them together in a federal package. There was nothing new about it. Austria's Weiner Freie Press printed an article by Walter Rathenau on December 24, 1912, in which he stated, 'Three hundred men who knew each other and constantly select those who will succeed them direct the economic destinies of the world.' The one-worlders were already working to control the economics of nations that they might impose a single government and a single money on the world."

---

of the certificate upon demand. You could take one paper dollar and nineteen copper pennies to any U.S. mint and exchange it for one ounce of silver dust. Our coins were made of real silver so our currency had real value. Our money was worth something. The old saying, "it's as sound as a dollar" had meaning, but in 1964 we went off the silver standard. That was the beginning of the dollar's demise.

JUST PAPER

Today's paper money is worthless. There is nothing of real value backing it up. Its seeming value could be wiped out in a moment's time by government decree or financial upheaval. Paper currency has always been nothing but a symbol. When the symbol could be exchanged for something of real value, silver or gold, it was worth something. Now the only reason the currency is still working is because people still have some degree of confidence in the government. That is fast eroding. Only if people have confidence in the fellows at Foggy Bottom (Washington, D.C.) will the currency work.

WHEN THE CHIPS ARE DOWN

Silicon chips in electronic computers are fast replacing paper and metallic money. For every paper dollar that exits, there are fifteen electronic dollars that exist only in the electric memory of computer chips. Here is how it works: You go to the bank with ten one hundred dollar bills and deposit them in your account. Now the bank has a thousand dollars, and the computer account shows that you too have a thousand dollars, but there are only one thousand physical paper dollars in existence backing those figures. John Farbish goes into your bank and borrows a thousand dollars. Now he has a thousand, and the bank has another electronic thousand in the loan file in the computer. And so on it goes. These imaginary dollars only show up on a computer screen and in receipts or forms you have in your possession.

If all the computers failed to function tomorrow, it would be chaos. The brain of the computer is the silicon chip. Silicon, next to oxygen, is the most abundant substance on earth, for silicon is made from sand. Jesus told of a man who built his house on the sand. When the storms came, it fell and great was the fall of it. Our whole economy is resting on a foundation of sand. When world wide commercial Babylon falls, the rich men of earth will lament, "Alas, Babylon...so great riches is come to naught in one hour's time."

Kitchener-Waterloo Record

Business

MONEY MATTERS – by Mike Grenby

Electronic banking on way

Are you drowning in the flood of bills the mail carriers have been unloading on you following the postal strike? And remember the hassle you had trying to pay those bills while the strike was still on?

Well, electronic banking will solve all these problems. It will even reduce much of the pain in dealing with monthly bills when the mail is being delivered.

Of course, electronic banking will also produce problems of its own, but more about that later, I asked Jim Grant, the Royal Bank's vice-president for strategic planning in retail banking, to gaze into his crystal ball to see what lies ahead for ordinary people in banking.

"We should recognize we are on the edge of a technological revolution which will have an impact on our lifestyles as great as that of the radio, car, television and airplane combined," he said.

You will use a home computer terminal hooked up to your TV to transfer money between accounts, pay bills, reconcile your accounts and perhaps even send money to individuals. However, many bills will be paid automatically. You will authorize a utility company, for example, to transfer the amount of your bill from your account to its account.

When you go shopping or otherwise spend money, you will use special plastic identification card sometimes called a debit or bank card. Instead of cash. The computer will transfer the amount of your purchase from your account to the merchant's.

You will carry an "electronic instead of cash. This will be a plastic card with a small computer embedded in it. You will fill in your bank and ask to have, for example, $100 put into the wallet from your account. As you...

located where you live, work and spend.

You will do almost all your banking through your home TV and will store your bank package with you or have a year to plan your budget, arrange credit needs, get financial planning advice and so on.

Family payment card...

You will have a pocket computer which holds your total financial records. Plug the pocket computer into it and get personal and you have an individual bank branch.

Cash will be virtually unnecessary. You will carry the debit card and

spending.

Banks will compete with each other both on the price and speed of the various services they offer.

Electronics will certainly simplify part of your financial life. I'm sure you won't miss those once-hour lineups at the bank on payday, for example. And a computer can make financial planning more efficient, too.

But problems bring both problems and comforts. You will...

The loss of individuality in the world of mass finance and impersonal...

The situation with computer breakdown and mistakes. Delaying and receiving delays. What will be lost when...

The U.S. Has A Date With Electronic Banking

All-electronic banking is on its way. have to make room in your wallet for a debit card. All-electronic banking is on its way.

...reaches into her purse, ...money and hands it to ...checkout counter ...shoves it into ...That night the manager counts up the cash, makes out his deposit slips, gets into his car and takes the proceeds to the bank's night depository. If he doesn't get robbed, the day's business is done.

That's in 1978.

Now it's 1990.

The shopper hands a card to the checkout person who inserts it into a computer terminal and the transaction is over. No money-counting, no handling of bills, no deposits to make. That card actuated an electronic impulse that transferred the price of the groceries from the customer's ac...

around the clock. Some individuals and businessmen will object to the absence of physical evidence of a transaction when checks are not retained. But they will be mollified by improved retrieval systems (who likes to look through a batch of year old returned checks for the needed one?) and by the availability, in effect of after-hours banking.

The concept of electronic banking is not new. There was plenty of talk about the forthcoming imminent perhaps society ten years ago. But this was ahead of its time. The public has been slow in accepting the change from receipts and checks to hand to a summary statement prepared by some faceless, cardless machine.

The other problem, also one of psychology, not technology, is that...

banks as well as commercial banks have terminals in supermarkets, but in the street and at offices and factories. Full customer acceptance is likely by the end of this year when BankAmericard and Master Charge will be promoting their patron with debit cards.

After that it will be possible for a resident of Atlanta to go to a cooperating organization, perhaps a grocery store, in Oregon and withdraw money from his Georgia account. This is not far-fetched. It is already being done on a local level to dozens of states and hundreds. In addition, National Bank of Atlanta Inc. will be the All-time Teller machines to draw a depositor's balance, take cash or hand cash payments for individual advances. First National was fourth to enter this field in the city...

MONEY IN BIBLE PROPHECY
THE NEW SYSTEM

"And he causeth all, both small and great, rich and poor, free and bond, to receive a mark in their right hand, or in their foreheads; and that no man might buy or sell, save he that had the mark, or the name of the beast, or the number of his name. Here is wisdom, Let him that hath understanding count the number of the beast: for it is the number of a man: and his number is Six hundred threescore and six" (Rev. 13:16-18).

This describes the new economic system introduced by the Antichrist. It features a new identity system and a new redistribution of earth's wealth and resources. It speaks of absolute totalitarian control over all humans. He who controls money controls the people. It is by controlling the new financial system that the beast rules the world for his brief, dark hour.

MARK OF THE BEAST

The word "mark" has a specific meaning. In the original Greek the word is *charagma*. This unique word only appears in the last book of the Bible (Rev. 13:16,17; 14:9,11; 15:2; 16:2; 19:20; and 20:4). It only refers to the "mark of the beast." It is not symbolic. The Greek word *charagma* is very specific. It is translated, "physical mark, or insignia, a scratch or etching."

"And he [antichrist] causeth all...to receive a mark in their right hand or in their foreheads. And that no man might buy or sell, save he that had the mark or the name of the beast, or the number of his name."

This passage establishes the following:

1.) Antichrist will promote a new economic system.

2.) No one can buy or sell unless he cooperates and receives a special mark.

3.) The mark or number is placed on the individual's forehead or hand.

We conjecture the following possibilities:

1.) At first the mark could be a painlessly applied invisible laser tattoo that would show up under ultra violet light at the bank, the check out counter of the store, or any place of financial transaction. It could merely be a symbol or the number 666. This would only prove that the individual bearing the "mark" is cooperating with the system. Rebels who refuse to follow the beast will be shut out of the normal world of commerce. The means of earning a living and carrying out the normal

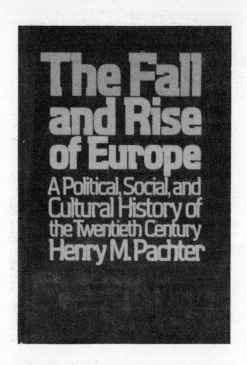

The Fall
and Rise
of Europe
A Political, Social, and
Cultural History of
the Twentieth Century
Henry M. Pachter

IRON LADY DIGS IN HER HEELS—CAN SHE SURVIVE?

On May 29, 1989, former conservative British Prime Minister Edward Heath attacked the current prime minister, Margaret Thatcher, before the Belgian Royal Institute of International Affairs because of her defense of British sovereignty. Mrs. Thatcher has suffered attacks from varied quarters ever since and has seen her political popularity wane in Britain.

Nevertheless, the "iron lady" stood firm and undaunted, and carried her demands to the front lines of the European political theater. *The Detroit News* (June 28, 1989) reveals that "European Economic Community leaders reached a compromise Tuesday with British Prime Minister Margaret Thatcher on a strategy for creating a unified monetary system for the 1990s."

While Thatcher could not stop the move, her efforts had the effect of slowing it down. The article datelined Madrid, Spain, (*Detroit News*) continued, "Under the compromise, Great Britain agreed to a starting date of July 1, 1990, for the first phase of monetary union. That phase calls for the currencies of all twelve EEC nations to be linked in a system that restricts exchange rates within a narrow margin."

U.S.A. AND THE COMMON MARKET

Another meeting was held in Bruges on October 17, in the same place where Margaret Thatcher fought for national sovereignty in September, 1988, and touched off a storm designed to wreck her and devalue the pound. Instead of concentrating on his plan for a single money and a single central bank, at the October 17 meeting, President Jacques Delors of the EEC Commission outlined his "vision of a rapid rapprochement between the two halves of Europe." To pave the way for strengthening the socialist hold on Western Europe by Polish and Hungarian membership in the EC, Mr. Delors and France's minister of foreign affairs, Mr. Roland Dumas, announced they were going to Budapest and Warsaw.

The political dialogue had already started, Mr. Delors told his colleagues at Bruges, and the European Community had been given a mandate to fulfill its responsibility in Eastern Europe. A mandate by whom? Opposition to communism in Hungary and Poland might be sincere, but they are being used to convince the West that no Warsaw Pact nation constitutes a danger. Some political analysts hold a view that differs from my own. Taking the long view, giving Mr. Gorbachev's

Russia full rights in the European Community could be a more real menace than Krushchev's threat to bury us. Russia was then working openly from without. Now the EEC is implementing trade agreements with Hungary, Czechoslovakia and Poland, and a $200 million (294 million pounds) loan to Poland and Hungary is being finalized. President Bush stated in the Netherlands last June that "a stronger Europe, a more united Europe is good for my country," but he was not seeing what the Europe of 1992 has in store for the United States. Once the drivel is removed, in only a few spots is the news good.

NEW EUROPEAN MONETARY PLAN DELAYED— NOT CANCELED

"Leaders of the EEC agreed to delay the second and third phases of the monetary plan, which calls for the formation of a European Central Bank and a unified currency unit. *The Detroit News* calls it a victory for Thatcher. However, it is a bitter victory, which will cost her dearly.

"Americans have been warned for years that a group of international financiers, politicians, and Utopian dreamers were plotting to turn the world into a super-state from which there would be no escaping. The public scoffed and called it a conspiracy theory.

"Now only a miracle can save America from what is already happening in Europe. Bumper stickers, giant posters in department store windows, paintings on the sides of buildings and automobile license plates proclaim rejection of allegiance to flag or country. Drivers traversing Europe pass huge blue billboards bearing gold stars for what once were nations and facing them is an announcement that they are entering a European community instead of the city of a sovereign country.

"In recognizing a boundaryless Europe as their country, Europeans are repudiating their attachment to everything their forefathers died for. In the beginning they were told they were building an economic community to do away with passports and customs barriers. But as soon as it was on its feet, it was turned into a constituent assembly with all the powers of government, which were never included in the 1957 Treaty of Rome. Schools have sprung up in which professors run an eraser over the blackboards of history and traditions, teaching that rootlessness and loyalty to no flag or country will bring Utopia" (HDB Reports 9/89).

The prophetic significance of the European movement is notable. Chapters 2 and 7 of Daniel (the Image and the Four Beast Visions) foresee a final form of the fourth great empire (Rome) being revived in the last days. Out of this proceeds the "Little Horn," the Antichrist. This visionary foreview is enlarged in Revelation, chapters 13-18. (See John Walvoord's commentaries on Daniel and Revelation and J. Dwight Pentecost's *Things to Come* for detailed studies.)

TWENTIETH CENTURY MYTHOLOGY
HOLY GRAIL—ANTICHRIST IDEOLOGY

A few years ago, while in Toronto, I purchased a book titled *Holy Blood, Holy Grail* (1982, by Michael Baigent, Richard Leigh, and Henry Lincoln). It had taken Europe by storm and was then appearing in North America. A recent sequel to *Holy Blood, Holy Grail* is a book titled *The Messianic Legacy.*

The blasphemous movie, *The Last Temptation of Christ*, created a furor in the Evangelical community, but really had little effect (in my estimation) on anyone. The Don Wildman-led boycott of the movie was evidently successful, since it was a financial flop. However, what the movie represents in dream-like visionary impression, these books present as fact.

The three authors adequately documented that there is a mysterious, powerful, well-funded organization known as the Priory of Zion or the Prieure de Sion. It is headquartered in France, but has offices throughout Europe and extending to North America. It secretly works for European Unity (a revival of the Roman Empire) by the mid-1990s and finally, a world government. It seems the Priory was founded by the European Crusaders group known as the Knights Templar, in the middle ages, founded around the twelfth century A.D.

The central and most bizarre aspect of the books is the claim that Jesus did not die on the cross, but survived, married Mary Magdalene and fathered several children. The leaders of the Prieure de Sion organization claim to possess the records of the actual physical descendants of Jesus. Presently, Pierre Plantard de Saint-Claire heads the organization.

ANTICHRIST CANDIDATE, GO TO THE BACK OF THE LINE

In the thinking of some evangelical authors such as Rev. J. R. Church, this makes him a prime candidate for the office of the Antichrist! In early 1988, we published a booklet titled, *False Messiah, Unholy Blood, Satan's Grail*. It both exposes and refutes the theories of the Priory of Zion. It is illustrated with pictures of Pierre Plantard de Saint-Claire and many other things connected to this story. In its pages you will journey by word and pictures to the village of Rennes-le-Chateau in France, where the first clues to this mystery were uncovered by the authors Baigent, Leigh, and Lincoln. The contents of our booklet are included in a later chapter of this book.

NO USE FOR EVANGELICALS OR THEIR RAPTURE CONCEPT

The authors of these two strange books have an absolute loathing of Evangelical Christians. Especially in *Messianic Legacy,* they attack the concept of the Rapture of the Church and the return of the real Jesus Christ as being a fantasy not worthy of consideration. It seems that since the writing of the first book, they "discovered" us. No wonder, since I—and my colleagues—have spared no effort to expose and refute their wild theories about our Saviour.

Actually there are many who seem to be candidates for the Antichrist position. While the theories of the books by Baigent, Leigh, and Lincoln may sound foolish, they are having a disproportionate influence in some political and New Age circles and should not be ignored.

5

The Beast Arises

These are strange and changing times. In the marketplace of ideas, humanity is confronted with a veritable smorgasbord of concepts that set the mind reeling. The new and the weird are mingled with the old and the bizarre. Like the witches' black kettled brew in Shakespeare's Macbeth, one hardly knows what will bubble up next.

The year the European Common Market was formed, 1957, Henri Spaak, Belgium's foremost modern statesman, remonstrated, "We do not want another committee: we have too many already. What is needed is a man of sufficient stature to hold the allegiance of all people and to lift us out of the economic morass into which we are sinking. Send us such a man and, be he god or devil, we will receive him."

Some time ago TV show host Morton Downey, Jr. stood before his highly controlled and manipulated studio audience shouting, "I love Jesus... but..." But...it was apparent that the "Jesus" he loves has absolutely no relationship to the Christ of the Bible. The program for the evening was a discussion of the blasphemous movie, *The Last Temptation of Christ*. Morton Downey, Jr. was defensive of the movie. It seems to me that he accepted the fiction as potential fact. Then he made the outlandish claim that, after all, the Bible is probably fiction too, since Matthew, Mark, Luke, and John never met Jesus either and that the Gospels that bear their names were written long after Jesus (and the original disciples) were gone.

Never has blasphemy against Christ been so blatant, so widespread, and expressed in so many forms.

The book *Holy Blood, Holy Grail* by Baigent, Leigh and Lincoln, was mentioned earlier. It advances a devilish theory—one that, incidentally, is getting a growing acceptance, and is not totally unlike the content of the movie *The Last Temptation of Christ*.

Baigent, Leigh, and Lincoln, authors of the two books *Holy Blood, Holy Grail,* and *Messianic Legacy,* suggest that Jesus Christ did not die on the Cross. He survived the Cross, got married, and had several children, and His descendants are alive and known in the world today. It is claimed that a mystery organization hopes to put one of Jesus' descendants on the throne of a revived Holy Roman Empire before the turn of the century.

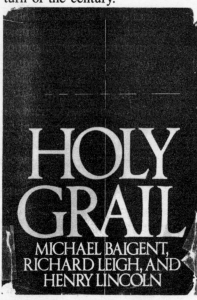

Holy Blood, Holy Grail by Baigent, Leigh, and Lincoln was first published in 1982. It became a best seller in Europe and America.

Messianic Legacy is the sequel to *Holy Blood, Holy Grail.* After the first book was released, it is obvious that negative reaction from Evangelicals came to the attention of the authors. In this second book they heavily criticize Bible-believing Christians. Their scorn for Bible truths relating to prophecy knows no bounds.

The three authors mentioned are not the only ones to suggest the existence of the priory and its claims. A Swiss writer, Mathieu Paoli, wrote *The Undercurrents of a Political Ambition*. This book also grew out of an investigation of the Priory of Zion. Paoli is now dead, having been shot by an Israeli "hit team" as a spy for selling secrets to the Arabs.

It is my opinion that the secular world is open to these mad ideas and that you can look for greater manifestation of them as the days go by.

Since people around you are accepting these ungodly notions, it is good for you to have a basic knowledge of the ideas that are influencing your families, neighbors, and those you work with. And don't be too sure about your clergyman if you are in a modernistic liberal church.

Will Pierre Plantard de Saint Claire rule the world? Is he still the master of the Priory of Zion? Are the Knights Templar still in existence? Are the members of the Priory of Zion Jews or deluded Gentiles? When did the priory actually begin?

UNHOLY BLOOD, SATANIC GRAIL, FALSE MESSIAH

The marketplace is flooded with unhealthy books and movies that are leading people to ask, "Did Jesus really die on the Cross? Did He survive and marry Mary Magdelene? How many children did they have? Are the physical descendants of Jesus alive in the world today? Are they known?"

You can see that the devilish theories about Jesus go even beyond the wicked movie *The Last Temptation of Christ*.

In 1982 a book authored by Michael Baigent, Richard Leigh, and Henry Lincoln, *Holy Blood, Holy Grail*, was published by Jonathan Cape Ltd. in Great Britain and by Delacort Press in the U.S.A. It is commonly available in Canada and the U.S.A. and has been on various bestseller lists.

Seldom in a lifetime do students of Biblical prophecy see written works coming from our opponents that tend to confirm our views relating to the end-times in such a vivid manner.

Baigent, Leigh, and Lincoln are bitterly anti-fundamentalist and spare no words in condemning those who take the Bible literally. Their scorn of the rapture of the Church knows no bounds. Isn't that an interesting factor?

They propose a theory, based on years of extensive research, that, if a certain part is true, has deep significance for we who are evangelical in our belief, biblical in our orientation.

But, "if it is true," I refer to the following claims made by the three authors: First, they say that there exists a mysterious organization, the Priory of Zion (Prieure de Sion-French).

Secondly, this conspiratorial group claims that Jesus did not die on the Cross. He survived and married Mary Magdelene with whom He had several children.

Thirdly, the Prieure de Sion claims to know the identity of the physical descendants of Jesus, and that many of them are living in France and other parts of Europe today.

Fourthly, the leaders of the Priory assert that one of their own will rule a new Holy Roman Empire by the 1990s. That ruler will be a physical descendant of Jesus.

Of course we deny the validity of these wild ideas, except for the fact that the Priory exists and that they do hold to these fantastic views. This the authors Baigent, Leigh, and Lincoln capably document.

The views of these authors were (in part) reflected in the blasphemous movie *The Last Temptation of Christ*. (Universal Studios, Hollywood).

Further we believe that the claim of the Priory of Zion, that it is the House of David, thus Jewish, is utterly false. Later in this chapter we will discuss who we think these people really are.

HOLY BLOOD? UNHOLY LIES!

If the three authors' research is accurate, it simply proves that there is a secretive organization which strives for a United States of Europe. The Priory hopes to herald a Messiah-like leader who will lead this Revived Roman Empire, who ultimately could rule the entire world. Interesting? Yes, but that is the slightest part of this whole weird concept.

A new book by the same authors, *The Messianic Legacy* (by Baigent, Leigh, Lincoln; Henry Holt & Co., New York) adds information that almost makes the word bizarre lose its significance. According to this new book a new Messiah could soon take the stage in a United Europe and even gain worldwide acceptance by the year 2000.

The original concept in *Holy Blood, Holy Grail* is that a secret organization, the Prieure de Sion, exists in France and exerts influence throughout many European nations and the U.S.A. The purpose of the group is to restore the Merovingian line of royalty to power. The Merovingian blood line is supposed to be directly descended from Jesus Christ who did not die on the Cross, but lived, married and had children. The Prieure de Sion (Priory of Zion) allegedly kept alive the knowledge of who is of that bloodline.

It is claimed that the bloodline includes prominent and powerful people living on earth today. When *Holy Blood, Holy Grail* was written, the head of the clandestine group was Pierre Plantard de Saint-Clair. He is pictured in the book along with his young son, Thomas, in a photo taken in 1979. Plantard supposedly resigned his position, but authors Baigent, Leigh, and Lincoln think that this may simply be misinformation. They indicate that he continues to head the Prieure. If not, it is uncertain who presently heads the organization.

The authors indicate that while the Prieure may be trying to hide its existence, it is even more active than before. They stated, "Following M. Plantard's resignation, the Prieure de Sion became, in effect, invisible...Nevertheless, it had become increasingly clear that the Prieure de Sion did have interests, and did conduct activities, in a somewhat murky sphere—a sphere where Christian Democratic parties of Europe, various movements dedicated to European unity, royalist cliques, neo-chivalric orders, freemasonic sects, the CIA, the Knights of Malta and the Vatican swirled together, pooled themselves temporarily for one or another specific purpose, then disengaged again..." (*Messianic Legacy*, pp. 272-273).

How did this information come to the attention of Baigent, Leigh, and Lincoln? Herein lies a mystery they are happy to share in their two large volumes.

Pierre Plantard de Saint-Clair, head of the Priory of Zion for many years. Baigent, Leigh, and Lincoln indicate that he probably is still their leader.

THE PRIEURE DE SION

In 1891 mysterious documents were found in a strange church in Rennes-le-Chateau, a village in France. The discovery was made by a Roman Catholic priest, Berrenger Sauniere, the pastor of the church. These documents supposedly told of all these strange ideas about Jesus Christ, the lineage of His true descendants and more.

Allegedly these documents described the history and activity of the Priory of Zion. It was knowledge of this recent discovery that started the three authors on their research, and finally led to their incredible conclusions.

Pictures of the village and the church are shown in the book *Holy Blood, Holy Grail*. There is a strange inscription on the church. One can clearly see on the church the Latin motto: Terribilis Est Locus Iste (This Place Is Terrible).

The village of Rennes-le-Chateau in France.

Why had the original builders of the church put such a negative epitaph on their place of worship? Or was it added at some later date? What horrified the priest Sauniere was that the documents he discovered while renovating the church alleged that Jesus survived the Cross, married Mary Magdaline, had several children, and lived to a ripe old age. Upon his death Mary Magdaline, some of the children, and a couple of the original apostles moved to what is today the country of France. The claim is made that the Priory of Zion was established in the late first century A.D. The purpose was to keep track of the blood descendants of Jesus.

The mystery deepens, as Baigent, Leigh, and Lincoln tell a tale of how the pauper priest Sauniere suddenly became an extremely wealthy man after discovering the horrible documents. Did he sell the documents? Were they purchased by friends of the Vatican who would have reason to suppress the very knowledge that they existed? Is there yet another barely conceivable answer?

Actually, the existence of the Prieure de Sion can only be traced to the twelfth century. It may have been started by the Knights Templar at that time. That it had any existence prior to that is sheer conjecture.

That the Prieure actually does exist today the authors prove admirably. They do not claim to believe all that the Prieure says about its early origins, but one gets the impression that the authors may be believers in the myth. The second book, *The Messianic Legacy,* makes this impression even stronger in spite of the writers protests that they are not interested in forwarding the aims of the Prieure de Sion. I wonder, in my own mind, what might the motivation of these authors actually be?

THE ULTIMATE CONSPIRACY THEORY

Herein is a tale that involves the Knights Templar, the Albigenses, the Merovingians, the Crusaders, the Roman Church, the Freemasons, the French Revolution, the Cathars, modern day leaders (many of whom are named), British and French intelligence agencies, and the American CIA. Here is a sort of ultimate conspiracy theory that tops them all.

Not for one moment do we believe the blasphemous concepts set forth in these books. Here in these two books is a denial of the authority of the Word of God, the atoning death of our Saviour, and the deity of Jesus. Furthermore they hold out the promise of a humanistic messiah, physically descended from Jesus. He would thus be of the House of David, and as the authors point out could be a reconciliation point for Christians "*Other Than Fundamentalists*" and the Jewish people. (Emphasis ours.)

The authors believe that the Israelis would accept a descendant of a purely human Jesus as their latter day humanistic or New Age Messiah. As ruler of the Revived Roman Empire (United States of Europe) they could easily make a covenant with him.

TREASURES OF THE TEMPLE

The Prieure de Sion claims to have possession of the lost treasures of the Temple of Israel. This would include the ark of the covenant. They are supposedly hidden somewhere in France, but could be returned to Israel under the proper circumstances and at an opportune time (*The Messianic Legacy,* p. 322).

IS IT REALLY ZION?

Who, actually, are the men of the Prieure de Sion? I believe that they are deluded gentiles thinking themselves to be of the House of David and Judah. This is but another weird twist of an old and evil theory like that of the ten lost tribes of Israel being white Ayrian Europeans and Americans.

Think of the possibility of a gentile antichrist "messiah" posing as a descendant of Jesus of the House of Judah! Lost temple treasures returned to Israel! The temple rebuilt only to be defiled by the man of sin, that son of perdition, the very beast of Revelation! (See 2 Thess. 2:3,4.)

In *The Messianic Legacy* it is stated, "Aided by the techniques of modern public relations, modern advertising and modern political packaging, the Prieure could thus present to the modern world a figure who by the strictest scriptural definition of the term, could claim to be a Biblical Messiah. It may seem preposterous. But it is no more preposterous, surely, than the conviction of tens of thousands of Americans who are prepared to be 'raptured' upwards from their cars at various points on the freeway between Pasadena and Los Angeles" (p. 323).

The book asks, "What, for example, would be the implications for modern Israel, as well as for both Judaism and Christianity, if—on the basis of records or other evidence issuing from the Temple of Jerusalem—Jesus stood revealed as the Messiah? Not the Messiah of later Christian tradition, but the Messiah expected by the people of Palestine two thousand years ago—the man, that is, who was their nation's rightful king, who married, sired children and perhaps did not die on the Cross at all. Would it not rock the foundations of two of the world's major religions and possibly the foundations of Islam as well? Would it not, at a single stroke, eradicate the theological differences between Judaism and Christianity, and at least some of the antipathy of Islam?"

Yes, and the Antichrist will be the great false reconciler and maker of deceptive peace. Of the Antichrist Daniel prophesies that "by peace will he destroy many."

PARALLEL TO THE NEW AGE VISION OF CHRIST

This whole diabolical theory could, of course, aid and abet the aims and vision of the New Age movement. The New Age also envisions and heralds the coming of a Christ who specifically is not Jesus. For more information on the "New Age Second Coming" see *The Armageddon Script*, by Peter Lemesurier; St. Martin's Press, New York.

The idea of the coming of a "new" Christ was promoted in the late 1800s by Helena Petrovna Blavatsky, founder of the Theosophical Society and grandmother of the New Age movement, by Annie Besant, her successor, by Alice Bailey (Lucis Trust), and a host of other New Agers including Robert Muller, author of *New Genesis*. Until his recent retirement, Muller was the assistant secretary general of the United Nations.

ATTACK ON BIBLE-BELIEVING CHRISTIANS

Baigent, Leigh, and Lincoln attack and scorn Bible-believing Christians. Their savage and repeated attacks on those who believe in the Rapture, the return of the historical Jesus Christ of the Bible, knows no bounds. See *The Messianic Legacy*, pp. 7, 18, 19, 120, 121 (Reagan and Armageddon), 144, 155, 161, 182, 193 (claims Jesus was a failure), 194, 195, 323, etc.

THE FINAL WORD

Baigent, Leigh, and Lincoln leave no doubt as to their opposition to biblical Christianity. Here are the very last words, the summation of their latest book: "We would prefer to see a mortal Messiah presiding over a united Europe than a supernatural Messiah presiding over Armageddon. The Prieure de Sion cannot provide a Messiah of the sort which that word has come erroneously to connote for, say, American fundamentalists. We question whether anyone other than the special effects department of Hollywood studio can provide that. But if we are correct in our assessments, it would seem that the Prieure de Sion can provide a Messiah of the kind that Jesus Himself, as an historical personage, actually was" (*Messianic Legacy,* p. 326).

WORLD DIVIDED

The world is polarized into two camps today. Where are you standing? It is either Christ or Antichrist. You are either saved or lost. Either you believe the Word of God or you don't.

Are you in the camp of the "modern" Evangelicals and Charismatics who deny that there will be a Rapture, a literal Millennium, and that national Israel will play a role in the economy of God? Do you agree with the Kingdom Now teachers that there will not even be a personal antichrist? What a perfect way for people to be prepared to accept the humanist antichrist leader when he appears! Persuaded that there will be no antichrist, they will not recognize him.

If you have accepted these errors and denials of God's Word, you are in the bad company of the New Agers and the secular blasphemers. No, I do not say you are lost. No, I do not say you are a New Ager. But, why are you in bed with them? Why do you agree with their false teachings? When will you return to basic Christian New Testament teaching relating to end-time prophecy?

Are you one of those Christians who says that prophecy is not important? Are you a pastor who never deals with prophecy because it is controversial? I plead with you. Please do not throw away our most effective weapon in the fight against end-time deception! We must declare all of God's truth to prevail against the massive error campaign being waged today.

It must not be supposed that we think we have located the *final* antichrist. We have located one of the *many* antichrist plots of this age. John's first Epistle tells us that while there will be a final antichrist, there are many forerunners, each an antichrist in his own right (1 John 2:18).

For more information relating to the end-time warfare and our victory potential, read *Smashing The Gates of Hell in the Last Days* by David Allen Lewis (New Leaf Press, Green Forest, Arkansas).

6

The World Economy
Your Financial Future

I do not have to be a mind reader to know that sometime today you thought about money. You put a quarter in the parking meter or paid $1.39 for a hamburger at McDonalds. Money was paid out for groceries, rent, car payments, repairs, clothing, or the telephone bill.

Does our paper currency still have value?

ROOT OF ALL EVIL?

On a "Family Feud" television show the participants were asked, "If you could have one wish, what would it be?" The number one answer was, "I wish I had more money." Following that there were wishes for happiness, peace, family, and love. But money came first with this set of people.

The Apostle Paul counseled young pastor Timothy saying that, "the love of money is the root of all evil: which while some coveted after, they have erred from the faith, and pierced themselves through with many sorrows" (1 Tim. 6:10).

Money is only a symbol. It represents the ability to acquire and accomplish in this natural, physical world. Money cannot buy happiness or salvation, but it can buy mansions, Rolls Royces, a woman's or a man's body, a slave, a Rolex President watch, a hamburger sandwich, and a toy. In other words money simply represents the things of this physical world, be they good or evil. Paul's words mean, "the love of this material world is the root of all evil." We do not deny the physical world. It is ours to properly use and enjoy, but we keep things in place and keep our priorities straight.

Not money itself, but the love of money is the root of all evil. Gold is neither good nor evil. In the first book of the Bible we read the words of God as He surveys His creation and says, "the gold of that land is good."

GOLD AND SILVER

Precious metals have been the most universally accepted form of money throughout most of history. At one time the U.S.A. was on a gold standard. Our paper currency was backed by actual wealth in the form of gold bullion. Following our golden era we went on a silver standard for a period of years.

Why is gold precious? Because of its rarity. If all the gold that has ever been mined out of the earth were gathered and formed into a cube, then placed beside the Washington Monument, it would look like an ice cube beside a Coke bottle. It would be dwarfed by the monument. There just isn't a lot of gold in the world.

Fernando Rojas, a sixteenth century Spanish author wrote, "There is no place so high in the world that an ass laden with gold cannot reach it." Money talks. It gets you where you want to go. It obtains for you whatever you want as far as the natural things of earth are concerned.

The United States Bullion Depository, Fort Knox, KY.

One day, thank God, our whole perspective on what is truly valuable is going to change. Gold means little to God. He has prepared an eternal city, New Jerusalem. Gold is so common there that the streets are paved with it. We will walk on earth's most valuable commodity (Rev. 21:21). One day we will understand what is truly valuable. In the meantime we have to cope with the realities of this present realm, and here we find that it is hard to get by without what gold represents—money.

When the gold standard was in effect, paper currency could be exchanged for real gold coins at any bank. A ten dollar bill brought you a gold piece of a certain weight, worth a real ten dollars. The gold standard was ended by our government in 1933. Suddenly it was illegal to own gold, except for jewelry, teeth fillings, and as numismatic (coin collector's) curiosities. The government confiscated the citizen's gold and stored it in the National Treasury at Fort Knox, Kentucky. Our gold resources are now drastically depleted. We have no way of knowing (the government won't reveal figures) how much gold there is left in Fort Knox. Some people think that it is nearly all gone.

Still, our paper currency had some real value. We went on a silver standard. Silver is much more plentiful than gold. Our paper money was imprinted with a guarantee that silver would be paid to the bearer

activities of buying and selling will be denied them. This emergency measure is enforced due to chaotic conditions existing as the Antichrist is solidifying his power and authority. It is presented as a necessary measure during the time of restructuring the world's government and economy.

2.) As the system is refined following the initial period of chaos early in the Tribulation, every person will be ordered to accept a personal number. The person becomes a living credit or debit card.

3.) Only Antichrist himself will possess the personal number 666.

Verse 17 can be translated, "And that no man might buy or sell, save he that had the mark, or the name of the beast or the number of his [own] name." This is possible because the phrase "or the number of his name" is a dangling phrase in the sentence structure and can refer back to or modify the original subject—the "man" in "no man might buy or sell..." Further, of the number 666 we are told it is the number of "a" man, the Antichrist. It is not the number of every man.

Of course, it is possible that 666 could be a prefix to each person's personal number as a symbolic enhancement.

Why would the Antichrist choose 666 as his personal number? Wouldn't that be a dead giveaway as to what and who he really is? Quite the opposite. He will deliberately select the diabolical cipher as a show of his opposition to God. He "opposeth...all that is called God or that is worshiped..." (2 Thess. 2:4; also Dan. 11:36; Rev. 13:6). The psychic humanist beast will denounce all religions except the deification of man as outmoded superstitions. When he announces the selection of 666 as his personal number, he will make it clear that he has done this deliberately as a token of his rejection of all the old "gods"—including Jehovah.

4.) Why is the mark placed on the hand or the forehead of the recipient? We take this statement to be as literal as the mark itself.

Years ago the president of the American Banking Association wrote in the *ABA Magazine* that the cashless society is ready. We have both the hardware and software to make it work. What is lacking is a foolproof identification system so no one could fraudulently use a lost or stolen identity card. Revelation 13 gives the answer, but what does it mean? Why the right hand or the forehead?

In addition to the number, there is need for a secondary system to corroborate identification of the individual. It would not do for someone to change or tamper with his number.

The human body has several foolproof identity systems, the most commonly recognized being our fingerprints. In addition each person

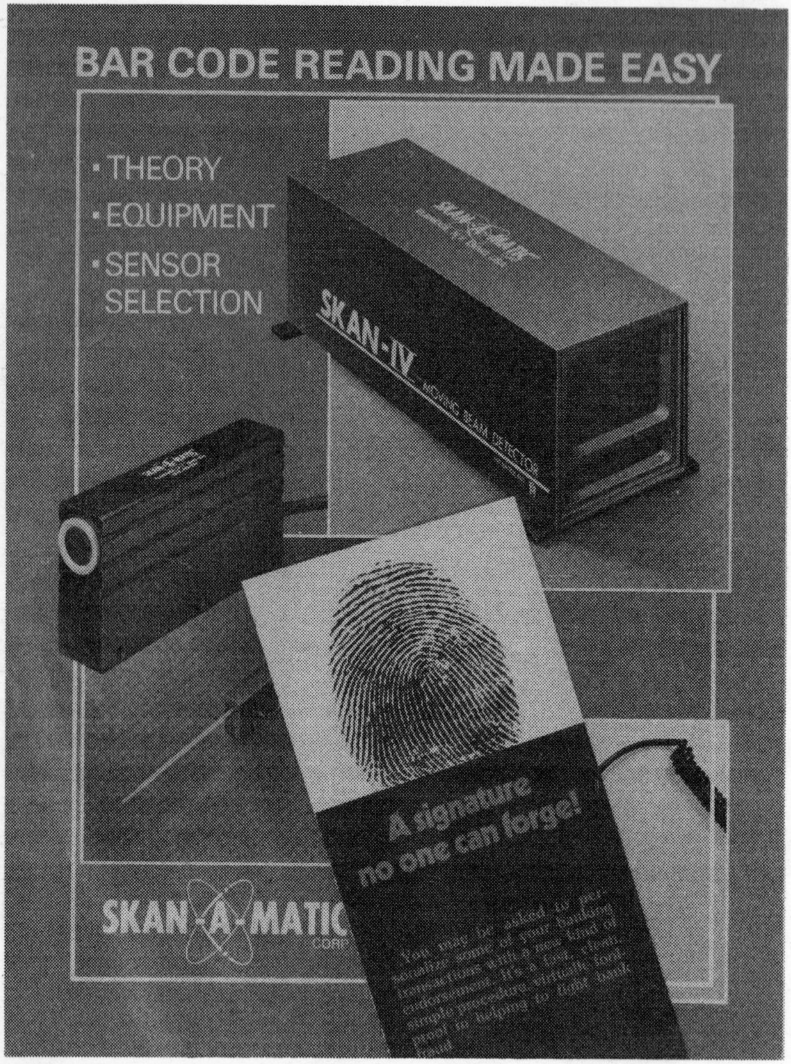

BAR CODE READING MADE EASY

- THEORY
- EQUIPMENT
- SENSOR SELECTION

SKAN-IV MOVING BEAM DETECTOR

SKAN-A-MATIC CORP.

A signature no one can forge!

has an individual gene code, retina formation, and voice pattern. The gene code is too complicated and takes too long to determine. A voice scanner could be fooled by a tape recording of the real owner of the card number. Fingerprints and retina patterns are the most likely to be used. We have photographs from news magazines showing a retina scan device. One looks into the scanner and identity is established. In the Revelation 13 context, the number in the forehead is read simultaneously with the retina scan and identification is established. The computer then accepts and records the financial transaction immediately removing credits from your computer account and transfers them (credits) to the account of the recipient of the funds. A number on the right hand is verified by a fingerprint scanner. Both of these devices are already in limited use in defense installations and other sensitive security situations. Both types have been shown in popular news magazines.

STATE OF THE ART—FOR NOW

It has already been stated that the four categories of information above are "conjectural." When we mention laser tattoos and scanning devices, we are simply evaluating the present "state of the art" technology available at the time of this writing. Next month, or by the time you read this, there may be a whole new technology. Maybe implanted scannable computer chips will be used.

As more and more sophisticated scientific advances are made, everything we say here could be obsolete, except for the biblical fact that some such numbering and identification system will exist. Also, it will be used to expedite the new world money system. Of these facts we are absolutely sure.

WHEN WILL THE MARK APPEAR?

Probably the mark of the beast will not be enforced until the beast (Antichrist) has a power base from which to operate. He first rules the ten nations of Revived Rome, later the whole world. In the meantime a physical, scannable mark could be offered by various banks or governments. Most likely in free nations it would be suggested as a convenient option. Take it or leave it. My advice? Do not accept a physical identity mark on your body (especially your right hand or forehead). This does not apply to a temporary invisible ink rubber stamp mark for passage in and out of Disney World or Six Flags over Texas.

666 = KISSINGER, ETC.

If A = 6; B = 12; C = 18; — continue adding six to each letter of the alphabet as follows:

A=6, B=12, C=18, D=24, E=30, F=36, G=42, H=48, I=54, J=60, K=66, L=72, M=78, N=84, O=90, P=96, Q=102, R=108, S=114, T=120, U=126, V=132, W=138, X=144, Y=150, Z=156.

Many people believed that this system confirmed that Henry Kissinger is the Antichrist.

K=66, I=54, S=114, S=114, I=54, N=84, G=42, E=30, R=108, TOTAL: 666

Using this system my daughter and I found fifty-two names in the "A" section of the Detroit phone directory equaling 666 before we got bored with the project! The word computer also equals 666, and the name of one of my wife's sisters equals 666. One could use tricky numbering systems like this and get a huge variety of possible candidates for the role of the beast.

Poor Henry, and he didn't even know he had been nominated!

A gentleman approached me following a church meeting I spoke for in Brockville, Ontario a few years ago. Handing me a slip of paper with the numbering system shown above, he asked if I knew what it meant. Not wishing to get into a big discussion I simply replied, "Well, people in the U.S.A. think it proves that Kissinger is the Antichrist." All bent out of shape he hotly responded, "You Yankees are a selfish lot, always wanting everything for yourselves! I can hardly abide your arrogance. It is not Kissinger! It is P. E. Trudeau, the prime minister of Canada." He proceeded to demonstrate that the system worked to make P. E. Trudeau equal 666.

Putting my tongue in my cheek, I said, "Look, I know you Canadians have your national pride like anyone else. Since we have so many candidates for the office of the Antichrist in the U.S.A., I am satisfied to let you have this one." Walking away, he kept looking back over his shoulder at me.

A lot of Canadians bought into that one. Trudeau must have heard about it and having a marvelous sense of humor, he had a vanity license plate made for his personal automobile that had the identity number "PET-666." That fairly well proved the case for some of my Canadian colleagues, but when Trudeau fell upon hard times politically the idea fell by the wayside, sharing the fate of all of these silly systems.

BUT IT REALLY IS COMING

The Antichrist is going to take advantage of the technology that will exist when he comes on the scene. He will seize the reigns of the world economy. Under the guise of a more equitable distribution of the wealth of the world, the same old drama is played out. The rich get richer and everybody else is manipulated. For three-and-a-half years there will be relative prosperity, followed by a major worldwide economic collapse that will bomb the fortresses of super capitalism and all other financial bases. The wrath of God will be poured out in a variety of ways. It will be the time of the Great Tribulation.

Many secular futurologists see the need for a world government and a new world economy. In 1976 the Canadian Institute of International Affairs published an article by J. Gordon King, "The New International Economic Order." King stated, "The new international Economic Order is the most striking Utopian concept to catch the imagination of the post-war world. For the militant leaders of the nations of the Third World, it represents the essential and inevitable goal towards which a global revolutionary movement is heading. To the liberal internationalist, it signifies an advance toward an orderly world society called for by the interdependent character of the modern international community."

New world order! The Bible prophesies it. The secular economic analysts predict it. The New Age is sure of it. Globalist politicians work for it. A new economic system will soon emerge!

Christians who are applying themselves to studying the Bible, our handbook to the future, see a sinister side to the developing world monetary system. The very symbols of Revelation give us strong clues. The "whore" of "Babylon" rides on the back of the "beast." She drinks from the golden cup of abominations.

"And there came one of the seven angels which had the seven vials, and talked with me, saying unto me, Come hither; and I will shew unto thee the judgment of the great whore that sitteth upon many waters. With whom the kings of the earth have committed fornication and the inhabitants of the earth have been made drunk with the wine of her fornication" (Rev. 17:1).

Isaiah cries out as he sees this latter day dual fulfillment of the fall of Babylon, "And behold here cometh a chariot of men with a couple of horsemen. And he answered and said, Babylon is fallen, is fallen" (Isa. 21:9).

———

MYSTERY BABYLON

Mystery Babylon, which permeates the whole world in the end days is seen in three notable modes:

First, there is political Babylon, the regime of the Antichrist.

Secondly, there is religious Babylon, the ecclesiastical aspect of Babylon. It is too simplistic to say that the whore is the Roman Church. That is too narrow. It is a provincial view. No, the whore represents all apostates whether they be Protestant, Roman, Orthodox, Evangelical, Fundamentalist, Charismatic, or Pentecostal.

The whore rides on the back of the beast. Some have thought that this could only mean that religion dominates the political sphere. If the neo-Kingdomists and the Dominionists have their way, then this would be an accurate picture. But the dreams of the new postmillennialists will not be fulfilled. Another possibility is simply that the political beast is carrying the whore for his own nefarious purposes. She gets a free ride until the beast is through using her. Then he destroys her and rends her to pieces.

Thirdly, there is the economic Babylon. Altogether these three form a hellish partnership and they set out to rule the world. They may seem to succeed for a short while, but they are doomed to failure. The "merchants of the earth [super rich multinationals] are waxed rich with the abundance of her delicacies." When the economic system finally collapses, the super cheaters of mankind will get their due. "Alas, alas, that great city Babylon, that mighty city! For in one hour is thy judgment come. And the merchants of the earth shall weep and mourn over her; for no man buyeth their merchandise any more...In one hour so great riches is come to nought...In one hour is she made desolate" (Rev. 18:10,11,17,19).

No wonder the Antichrist is called a "raiser of taxes." The greed mongers of the Capitalist, Socialist, and Communist nations have put an almost unbearable tax burden on humanity to support their monstrous greed for power and control. The rich with their tax avoidance schemes get richer; the poor are ground into the dirt and poor middle class Charlie pays the bills and gets it in the neck.

"Go to now ye rich men, weep and howl for your miseries that shall come upon you. Your riches are corrupted...Your gold and silver is cankered; and the rust of them shall be a witness against you, and shall eat your flesh as it were fire. Ye have heaped treasure together for the last days. Behold, the hire of the laborers who have reaped down your fields, which is of you kept back by fraud, crieth; and the cries of them which have reaped are entered into the ears of the Lord of

Sabbath. Ye have lived in pleasure on the earth, and been wanton; ye have nourished your hearts, as in a day of slaughter" (James 5:1-4). God is already not pleased with the economic situation on earth, and under the regime of the beast it will get worse. This demands the outpouring of the wrath of the Almighty!

FOUR HORSEMEN OF THE APOCALYPSE

We hear the thundering hoofbeats of the four horsemen of the Apocalypse as they ride roughshod over all the earth. Deception! War! Famine! Pestilence! "And when he had opened the third seal, I heard the third beast say, Come and see. And I beheld, and lo a black horse; and he that sat on him had a pair of balances in his hand. And I heard a voice in the midst of the four beasts say, A measure of wheat for a penny, and three measures of barley for a penny; and see thou hurt not the oil and the wine" (Rev. 6:5,6). What we are seeing and hearing in the world today is but a mere shadow of the future tribulation fulfillment of these awesome prophecies. "A choinix of wheat for a denarion!" A pint of wheat for a day's wages! In the time of earth's worst economic collapse, a day of hard labor will only purchase bare subsistence for one person.

HORROR OF FAMINE—TIMES OF DESPERATION

We know little about hunger and next to nothing about famine in the U.S.A. and Canada. The Episcopal archbishop of Juba, Sudan wrote, "We are dying like animals, without being counted." So terrible is the famine in Africa!

Another missionary wrote, "The people are like walking skeletons—stick figures moving about slowly, trying to find a scrap of food. The children, lined up to receive a handful of porridge or gruel cradle their tin feeding bowls with weak little arms. Their eyes look huge in their sunken faces. They stare quietly as the food is handed out. Sometimes they cry. They never speak.

"There are so many deaths from starvation that no one knows how many have died. We do know that we're losing children at a rapid rate—as many as 500 a day in this famine-stricken region! The little ones who still have strength left in their bodies eat boiled grass to stave off their hunger. Their parents can do nothing. Civil War, floods, plagues of locusts, water-borne disease—all have destroyed the resources of this terribly poor country."

According to relief officials this famine, at the beginning of the final

The legendary phoenix rises from the ashes of a ruined world economy. "The Economist" advises "Get Ready For a World Currency."

decade of the twentieth century, is even worse than the Ethiopian famine of 1984!

A time of famine for the whole world is coming, worse than ever seen before. It will come for sure in the Tribulation. It could come before if we live by the rule of fatalism, if we fail in our prayers and our tasks.

Desperation will force the world to accept the Antichrist's proposals. A cover of the international magazine *Economist* carried a graphic piece of artwork captioned, "Get Ready For A World Currency." The artwork showed burning currencies in an ash heap. Out of the ashes rises the legendary phoenix. The editors see a coming worldwide financial disaster, and out of the chaos emerges a new money system.

OUR PRESENT ECONOMIC WOES

The world is in a state of economic turmoil. The Western nations are practically bankrupt. The U.S.A. is skating on the thinnest of ice. Perestroika is not going to solve the even deeper problems of the East Bloc nations. Leadership is going in circles, not because they are inept, but because we have never before faced problems of this magnitude.

Back in 1989 economists in the U.S.A. looked with horror on the failure of the savings and loan institutions. The government manipulated a 300 billion dollar bail out. That money did not fall out of thin air. By printing currency and pumping it into the economic stream, by taxation both hidden and direct, it cost every man, woman, and child in the U.S.A. one thousand dollars per person to save the financial institutions. Not to have saved them could have triggered a domino effect that could have toppled the whole banking system. But the government did not pay for the succor of the savings and loans. You and I paid that bill. It could be the beginning of the end, the proverbial last straw that broke the poor camel's back. In the months ahead we will see what will be the result of this debacle and other fiascoes that have followed it up until more recent times.

NOW THEY SPEAK WITH ONE ACCORD

In the middle of the 1980s I noted that the independent economic newsletters were about divided in opinions regarding the economy. One said buy, another said sell. One said bull, another bear. One said good times, another hard times and recession, and so on. Now the independent economic analysts are mostly saying that in the next year or so we will likely have a massive depression. This kind of warning across the board started showing up in 1989 and has gotten stronger as time has gone by.

Panic descended on "Black Monday" October 19, 1987. The stock market went into a crashing slide actually worse than the crash of 1929 that brought on the Great Depression.

Futurologist Alvin Toffler, author of the books *Future Shock* and *The Third Wave*, wrote a lesser-known book, *The Coming Eco-Spasm*. He predicted a worldwide economic disturbance out of which would proceed something altogether different than we had ever witnessed before. He stopped short of defining what the "final" form of the world economy would take.

Financial analyst Louis Cabrini said, "Paper money is losing its value throughout the world. In America inflation will not be checked. We can expect to see rampant runaway inflation or crushing depression within the next six years."

Franz Pick, another well-known economist said, "The U.S. dollar will be wiped out and if the currency doesn't work, the country cannot work. The destiny of the currency will be the destiny of the nation. The U.S. dollar is going to be wiped out shortly."

Economy & Business

The Gathering Storm

Debtor countries meet to set strategy for their confrontation with bankers

"We hear the far-off thunder of violent drums. We feel the winds of storms," warned Colombian President Belisario Betancur last week in a chilling speech to government ministers of his Latin American neighbors. His rousing rhetoric referred not to war or natural disaster but to something equally momentous: Latin America's $350 billion debt burden. Since the beginning of the year, the pressure on both the borrowers and the American banks that lent them much of the money has grown sharply. A 2% jump in interest rates has hit Latin countries with a potential increase of $5 billion in annual interest payments. Meanwhile, big-city banks in the U.S. have taken a beating on Wall Street as investors grow more worried about whether the Latin debts will ever be repaid. Says

Latin restiveness could hardly be concealed. In his opening speech President Betancur compared Latin America's financial burden to the crushing debt and reparations problems after World War I, which helped wreck the international economy in the 1930s and laid the foundation for World War II. Said he "It is no exaggeration to say that the solution to Latin America's debt crisis is an essential ingredient for world peace."

IN THE HOLE
Total external debt at year-end in billions of dollars

$93
$90

After two days of talks, the ministers decided to set up two new groups. One will try to arrange talks with private banks and institutions like the International Monetary Fund (see following story). The debtors will tell them that the conditions set by the IMF for new loans should be aimed at fostering continued economic growth rather than austerity. The Latin Americans also agreed to propose a working group in the World Bank to deal with the global aspects of the debt crisis. The ministers plan to meet again just before next fall's IMF meeting. The next session will be held in Buenos Aires, which will put hard-lining Argentina in a diplomatically stronger position. The group last week also produced 24 proposals for easing the cost of their debt, ranging from longer periods of repayment to reduced interest rates. One plan, suggested by Mexican Finance Secretary Jesús Silva Herzog, calls for Latin borrowers to pay a

Over dinner my friend Willard Cantelon recalled the horrible inflation that debilitated Germany following the First World War. "David," he said, "It's coming to North America. It is only a matter of time." Willard is the author of the best selling book *The Day The Dollar Dies*.

I asked him, "Willard, I know a worldwide economic collapse is prophesied in the Book of Revelation. Do you think it has to come before the rapture of the Church?"

For a long moment he looked into my eyes and then slowly said, "David, we have some serious choices to make in the Church, don't we?" We were on the same wavelength. I knew what he meant.

Hans Webber, Swiss banker and director of the Foreign Commerce Bank, commented on the horrible inflation that hit Germany in the 1920s. He wrote, "Germany, after the first world war...things got to the point that it took a billion Deutsche Marks to buy one loaf of bread. One day people in the Western nations will have to have gold bullion or gold coins just to buy food for their families."

How bad can inflation get? It got so bad in Germany that they no longer looked at the numbers on the money. They weighed it by the pound. So many pounds of paper currency would buy a loaf of bread or a pound of butter. Workers were paid daily. They would load their money in carts or wheel barrows and run to the stores to buy whatever was available. Merchandise was marked up hourly.

Actual photo of German workers with a cart loaded with paper money representing a man's wages for a day's work. The year is 1922.

The German Deutsche mark was worth less than the paper on which it was printed. In 1914 one could buy a pound of butter for one and a half marks. By 1918, the price had doubled to three marks. By 1922 a pound of butter cost 2,400 marks. By mid-summer of 1922 the price of butter went to 150,000 marks per pound, and by fall of the same year it hit the astronomical figure of six billion marks.

Western nations are being ravaged by this inflationary monster. You won't notice it so much when the price goes from $1.50 to $3.00 for a loaf of bread, but when that loaf of bread costs six billion dollars ($6,000,000,000) you will know that the black horse is trampling you.

We have to face the fact that money that is not backed by silver or gold simply is not money. The only value it has is the confidence governments can generate, and we know how fragile that is.

In 1963 a generous man came to me saying, "David, you travel all the time, but you need a home for your family, a place you can come to and both work and rest up. I have a nice house that I will sell you for $12,000. Pay it off at $100.00 per month. I will not charge you any interest." Our young family was so financially strapped, our income so low that we had to regretfully decline his offer. It was a mistake. I should have taken a step of faith, but I did not.

If we were to buy that house today, it would cost about $75,000 or more. In 1963 we were still on the silver standard. A paper dollar could be exchanged for a real silver dollar. Almost any real silver dollar can now be sold for $7.00 (if the spot price of silver is around $6.00 per ounce). Today 12,000 silver dollars would buy that house, but it would take $75,000 in today's unsecured paper currency to buy the same dwelling.

Dr. Ravi Batra, a professor at Southern Methodist University, wrote back in 1989 in his book *The Great Depression of 1990* that a major depression is almost inevitable sometime during the 1990s. Dr. Geoffry F. Abert wrote *After the Crash* relating to the "depression of the 1990s" and Harry Browne's book *The Economic Time Bomb* is another financial doomsday warning for this decade. *Crash* is the title of Avner Arbel and Albert E. Kaff's book offering. They write of the October 19 Black Monday Stock Market slide—Ten Days In October...Will It Strike Again?

Various economic newsletters such as the *Kondratieff Report*, and journals by Howard Ruff, McMasters, Gary North, McKeever, Harry Shultz, and a host of others are all sounding the same kind of warnings.

You may have noticed that not only the independent financial analysts, but also the mainstream publications like *Forbes, Fortune, Time, Business Week, U.S. News and World Report, The Wall Street Journal,* and *Barrons* are beginning to carry articles with similar, if somewhat toned down reports. In their pages we have read that it is "crunch time," that there is a "gathering storm," "Third World debt's due now." Barton Biggs, Wall Street advisor, wrote in *Fortune* that there will be a final upsurge on the stock market this year and then "the party will be over."

WHAT CAN WE DO?

Are we victims of fate? Is there no hope? Can Christians do anything about the conditions under which they live? Are we of all people most helpless? Does faith still stand for anything? Does God still answer prayer? Can we know and pursue His will?

I believe that if about one percent of God's people band together in intercession, we can hold off the major economic collapse that is slated for sure to take place after the Rapture, in the Tribulation. I base this on the Gideon principle. Gideon, a judge in ancient Israel, became a deliverer of the nation. Faced by a huge enemy military force, he had a small army of 32,000 men. There was no way they could win. Gideon applied the fear test. "Anyone who is afraid can go home now." 22,000 left him. Then he applied the apathy test, telling the remaining 10,000 to take a drink of water. Most of the soldiers stuck their faces down to the surface of the water. Three hundred scooped water in their hands and drank, all the time keeping their eyes on the horizon, watching for the enemy. Gideon sent 9,700 men home and retained only the 300. With trumpets, the cover of night, and lights hidden under earthen pitchers, they surrounded the enemy camp. At a given signal they sounded the trumpets, uncovered the lamps, and made a great shout. In confusion the enemy soldiers rose from sleep and fought against each other.

Gideon won the battle with less than one percent of his forces on the front lines. If we can just get one out of a hundred Christians alerted, in intercession, waging spiritual warfare, I believe we can win battles in these end-times. But we need the one percent. If we listlessly drift along with the tide of fatalism and apathy, we could see really hard times, the drying up of missionary funds, and a general financial crippling of the Church's literature and foreign mission preaching and teaching outreach. Do you have any idea what it costs to keep a missionary on the foreign field for a year? The price is enormous, but due to the prosperity we have enjoyed in America and Canada, Christians there have been able to fund about ninety percent of the world missions and evangelism outreach. Is that base worth preserving?

One sure thing, if there is a depression, we will have to call most of the missionaries home. Does God still want Matthew 24:14 fulfilled? Are we seeking to know and cooperate with His will?

I am not asking God to stabilize the economy so we can have bigger automobiles, fancy vacations, luxury boats, entertainment units for our homes, and better wardrobes. We have a legitimate basis to pray for a preserved economy only if we wish to be good stewards in carrying out the work of the Kingdom of God. I am glad to see God's people prosper, but if you abuse what God has granted you then you will lose it. We are all skating on very thin ice right now. As Willard Cantelon said, "David, we have some serious choices to make in the Church, don't we?"

THE CYCLES OF HISTORY

What will be will be. What goes around comes around. History repeats itself. That is one way of looking at history and contemporary events. It is best called fatalism. This mind set snugly fits the Eastern mystical religions such as Hinduism with its doctrine of reincarnation. But this kind of thinking is foreign to the Bible. No matter how much history may repeat itself and run in cycles, Christians know the cycles of doom can be broken by the intervention of God. Christian faith is dynamic. It challenges the patterns ordered by a fallen humanity. Jesus said that the thief (Satan) comes to kill and destroy. But Jesus came to bring abundant life (see John 10:10).

Most universities now offer courses in historiography which deal with the methods by which we interpret the events of history. The linear method is a normal examination of the known facts of history, presented in an orderly fashion. The spiral method sees everything in the framework of an upward, evolutionary spiraling effect. The cyclical method of interpretation is what we have described in the paragraph above. History repeats itself. There are inevitable economic cycles. We are fated to have depressions on a regular cyclical basis.

Clement Juglar, a French physician, made a name for himself by publishing his views on economic cycles. Perhaps the best-known was the Russian economist, Nikolai Kondratieff. He claimed to demonstrate that the Western nations go through economic cycles that brought about massive depressions every fifty to sixty years. It is inevitable according to Kondratieff.

I do not accept these theories, first of all because history does not bear them out. For an examination of the accuracy of the cycle theory, read the entry "Business Cycles" in Encyclopedia Britannica. Further, various cycle theories contradict each other. Finally, God always encourages His people to intercede to bring His mercy upon the land. Abraham prayed for Sodom for Lot's sake. God agreed that if ten righteous men could be found, He would spare Sodom. Even when ten righteous could not be found, for Abraham's sake, God evacuated Lot and his family before destroying Sodom. God commanded the children of Israel to pray for the peace of Babylon when they were in captivity there that they might dwell in peace themselves (Jer. 29:7).

DON'T BE OVERCONFIDENT

Please don't assume anything about your financial future. It is all in a state of flux. There is a lot of ebbing and flowing. Strange forces with strange agendas are at work. Satan wants to destroy the Church, Israel, and finally all humanity. God guarantees a preserved remnant of all three in the final days. But our choices are going to determine the quality of life we live in the days ahead. Intercession and positive action can turn things around. Apathy and inactivity is the best way to guarantee ruin.

MANIPULATORS

The dangers we face are very real. The power mad super rich capitalists and Communists both strive to manipulate the world. We look to them like tiny pawns on the world's geo political chessboard.

During the oil crisis of the 1970's I drove into a Gulf Oil station in Texas. A sign said, "Out of gas." I asked the attendant if that meant that the storage tanks were empty and they were really out of gas, or if it meant they had sold their allotment. He looked at me strangely and said, "The tanks are almost full. We have sold all we are allowed to sell for this week."

Somebody was manipulating us. The super manipulators are never at rest. They are always active, plotting, prowling, conspiring (oh, dreaded word). There never was an energy crisis. There is none now. So many alternative energy sources exist that we could easily stop using fossil fuels, except for the fact that the wealthiest and most powerful people in the world have a vested interest. Let the environment be damned, we will accumulate our dollars, dinar, yen, lira, and francs.

Who are these manipulators? *Fortune* magazine occasionally lists all the billionaires of the world. Look over the list, you will have a good idea of who is jerking us around. Now these are not your ordinary neighborhood variety of rich folks, like the chap from my hometown who became a millionaire selling Amway. He could lose his shirt overnight.

Ordinary millionaires are commonplace. I was once preaching in a church where I observed a poor looking fellow who came to service barefooted, wearing a ragged shirt, and torn jeans. Feeling sorry for him I discreetly asked the pastor if there was a way I could buy him some clothes without hurting his feelings. The pastor laughed, "That man is a millionaire. He owns a seagoing vessel, a lumber yard, a construction company, and keeps a hundred thousand dollars in his personal checking account. He just likes to poor mouth it." In a church where I served as pastor many years ago there was a farmer who came to church in ragged bib overalls, wearing shirts with frayed cuffs. The man was a millionaire. He had rich deposits of coal and minerals in his land. By the standards of the billionaires of the world these are not the rich, but merely the middle class.

There are about two hundred super-rich men from various countries who have more power than all the politicians put together. They buy and sell politicians every day of the week. Contrary to popular mythology only a few of them are Jewish. Not one billionaire is listed for Israel. No Rothschild is listed in the *Fortune* billionaire list anymore. The wealth of the world is largely in gentile hands. We only mention this to dispel a myth that suits the mentality of anti-Semites.

The richest men of earth sit on interlocking boards, are active in globalist organizations, have promoted the continual financial bail-out of the communist world, ordered assassinations, sponsored revolutions, supplied arms, winked at terrorism, and literally run the world, all the while sneering at or even ignoring the existence of the rest of us.

WHY A LOOMING MONETARY CRISIS?

The super rich, the multinationals, and the international bankers thrive on chaos. In a time of depression the poor and the middle class lose fortune, property, farm, and home. Mortgages are foreclosed. The rich get richer and the poor get poorer. The cycle starts over again.

It is also interesting that many New Age movement leaders look for a worldwide crisis out of which they envision a more equitable system for distributing earth's resources emerging. That is a marijuana pipe dream! But the New Agers are busy promoting and predicting the coming collapse. They should know that the collapse that is coming is the great judgment of God being poured out during the Tribulation.

We have to be wary and prayerful lest Satan manipulate a collapse and chaos before the season of the final upheaval. The spirit of the beast (Antichrist) is actively promoting chaos now, hoping for control before the restraint is removed (2 Thess. chapter 2). Satan knows that economic chaos would hurt the cause of missions. He is working in every way possible to get the Church off television and radio. He is prowling around in the local church trying to promote division and destruction.

THE WAY TO VICTORY

In my book *Smashing the Gates of Hell in the Last Days* we explain how the Church can attain high level victory in the last days. Three essentials are intercession, information, and action.

Through intercessory prayer we give God the avenue through which to intervene in our world's affairs. God answers prayer, but He only answers prayers that are prayed (with certain notable exceptions, discussed in *Smashing the Gates of Hell*). We are not interested in changing or thwarting the will of God, but we are interested in knowing the will of God and then praying and working to implement His will.

Basic and adequate information is essential. God says that His people can be "destroyed for a lack of knowledge."

"Faith without works is dead." A program of action is essential if we are to succeed in fulfilling God's will in the Kingdom. First of all, let me give you some practical advice on how to protect the well-being of your family. These bits of advice also promote good results that spill over for the benefit of the Church and society in general.

A PLAN OF ACTION FOR YOU

Here are things you can do to protect your future, your home and family. I am going to start with a tough one, but you are going to have to accept it or there is no hope for your financial future.

First, you must now enter into a tithe covenant with the Lord. The prophet Malachi says that the person who does not first take out a tithe (ten percent) of his income and give it to God's work is cursed with a curse. On the other hand God promises the faithful tither that He will pour out a blessing so lavish you cannot contain it. God says He will rebuke the devourer for your sake. He will cancel Satan's assignments against you (see Mal. 3:8-11).

Tithing takes faith. It offends the rationale of a carnal unregenerate person. How can nine-tenths of your wealth go further than the whole? That with God all things are possible is our simple yet incredibly deep answer. We know it works. Millions of us have tried it, live by this standard, and testify to the fact that it is practical.

Second, I advise you to get out of debt. Then if there is a collapse, no one can take your home, business, or farm.

Start with your personal credit cards. Stop using them unless you have enough self-control to pay them off every thirty days before you have to pay the outrageous rates of interest the banks charge. Go on a cash basis. If you can't pay for it, don't buy it.

Paying off your house loan is difficult for many. Liquidate any assets you can and pay it on your mortgage, with the clear understanding that all you pay beyond the regular monthly payment goes on the principle. Get it in writing. If you can do no more, you can at least make one extra house payment each year. That will save you thousands and perhaps tens of thousands of dollars in interest. When you buy a house on credit, for the first few years almost all the money you pay is for interest. For average people a paid for home is security. If a crash comes you will at least have a roof over your head. Your children may lose their homes, but you can crowd up together and survive. Debt is a curse. "The borrower is slave to the lender."

Third, "Pray for the peace of Jerusalem." (This will seem strange unless you are a born-again believer.) In Psalm 122 the Lord gives this command, promising "they shall prosper that love thee." Root out every vestige of anti-Semitism that lies within you. Even cleanse your terminology. Why say, "He's a real shylock," or, "I Jewed him down on the price." Why not say that you Englished him or Germaned him down on the price? Don't even copy the self-hating, self-detrimental terminology of your assimilated Jewish friend who uses such terminology as a defensive cover. Develop a genuine love for the Jewish people and for Israel. This is a key to prosperity. God's Word promises it.

Fourth, pray for the peace of Babylon. Now I know you must think I have taken leave of my senses, but I am only sharing with you principles I have found in the Word of God. Some say that New York or Rome is the Babylon of end-time prophecy, but that view is too restricted. The whole world is gripped by the Babylonian spirit of the end-times. Everyone is now in Babylon. When the children of Israel were going into the Babylonian captivity six hundred years before Christ, Jeremiah the prophet commanded them to "seek the peace of the city whither I have caused you to be carried away captives, and pray unto the Lord for it: for in the peace thereof shall ye have peace" (Jer. 29:7). Always pray for the leaders of your nation. Pray that peace and tranquility will prevail, pray for the defeat of evil, violent, criminal and disruptive forces, so that the gospel message may thrive under favorable conditions (see 2 Timothy 1-4).

DESTINY OF THE U.S.A. AND CANADA

Satan hates the U.S.A., Canada, and Israel above all the nations, and he hates everyone. Even his subjects are objects of his insane wrath. The devil is well-called the destroyer. Why does the devil specifically hate the U.S.A. and Canada?

The prophecy that is close to the heart of God is Jesus' prediction that the gospel will be preached for a witness to all nations before the end comes (the end in view here is Armageddon, at the end of the times of the Gentiles).

Christians in the U.S.A. are funding 85% of the missions and gospel outreach of the whole world. Canada, our northern neighbor, has only 10% of the population the U.S.A. has. Christians in Canada supply about 10% of the funds for world missions. Two countries with less than 8% of the world's population shelter the Christians who are paying 95% of the bill for world evangelization. No wonder the devil would like to ruin us, close down our churches, take our tax benefits away, raise up a persecution against clergy and laity alike! The devil wants to wreck our economy and bring us down in the dust of ruin. He is trying to corrupt the Church and nation from within and batter us from without. God! Send a revival of righteousness and true holiness! Let us renew our vows of stewardship!

Satan loves chaos. That is why God commands, "Submit yourselves therefore to God, resist the devil and he will flee from you" (James 4:7).

PRAYER CHANGES THINGS

We say this glibly, almost like a motto, but what does it mean? Prayer changes things. Prayer does not change the past. The ink is dry on the pages of yesterday. The present is not static. It will not hold still. The present is the doorway through which the future continuously flows into the past. If prayer changes anything it is the future! Prayer controls the course of future events, by bringing God's intervention down to earth. God intervenes when invited (with certain notable exceptions). Prayer will not change the course of previously prophesied events, but there are a thousand details of life that are not yet formed. This biblical concept has been explained in detail in several chapters of the book *Smashing the Gates of Hell in the Last Days.*

Prayer literally changes the course of future events. The fatalists say an economic collapse is imminent and inevitable. We say it is very possible and even likely if no one does anything about it. Who will do anything other than those concerned Christians who see what a drastic price we will pay in souls if our last days' outreach is hampered by a lack of funds? The Pentecostal Assemblies in Canada calls the 1990s the "decade of destiny" and has a vigorous call for repentance, restoration of biblical doctrine, and an outreach for lost souls. The Assemblies of God in the U.S.A. calls it the "decade of harvest" and has set ambitious goals for missions at home and abroad. Will it be a decade of harvest or disaster? The choice is yours. The decision is in your hands. God wants to save souls. He wants to pour out His Spirit upon all flesh. He has chosen to use human instrumentality to bring His purposes to pass. It is not just finance at stake. This is just a small part of the picture. But it is a vital concern. Here is a model prayer. Read this prayer to God often. Elaborate upon it as the Holy Spirit guides you:

PRAYER

Heavenly Father, we come to You in the name of the Lord Jesus Christ, submitting to Your will. Thy will be done in earth as it is in heaven. We would not pray for anything that is contrary to Your will.

Forgive us our sins as we forgive those who have sinned against us. Send a revival of true holiness to all believers in the Church.

Our nation has sinned and done great evils in Thy sight. We confess the sins of our nation. Your Church has sinned and fallen far short of the mark. Cleanse Your Church and make it powerful once again. Purify our motives for Jesus' sake.

Please prosper faithful men and women in Your Church. Give us the means to continue sending the Gospel to the whole world until Jesus comes and brings to us the visible kingdom of God on earth.

Grant that Your faithful servants will continue to be employed. Do not allow the enemy to steal their homes and businesses. Rebuke the devourer for the sake of those who faithfully serve You with their substance. We pray for prosperity with a purpose—to faithfully win souls and build Your Church until Jesus comes.

Lord, rebuke Satan. We join You in rebuking him. Father in heaven, we repudiate the devil's evil doctrine of fatalism. Lord Jesus, please break Satan's cycles of chaos. God, loose Satan's hold on the economy of this nation. Force mammon to bow down and do service to God and His purposes. Reprove and smite those who abuse riches, oppress the poor and hinder the preaching of the Gospel. As Jesus taught us, we pray, deliver us from evil. Deliver us from the evils of an economic depression or chaos.

Again, we pray, Thy will be done in all things. Thank You for the Word that tells us that when we pray, You answer according to Your will. Amen.

BIBLE PROMISES

"Blessed is the man that walketh not in the counsel of the ungodly, nor standeth in the way of sinners, nor sitteth in the seat of the scornful. But his delight is in the law of the Lord; and in his law doth he meditate day and night. And he shall be like a tree planted by the rivers of water, that bringeth forth his fruit in his season; His leaf also shall not wither and whatsoever he doeth shall prosper. The ungodly are not so: But are like the chaff which the wind driveth away" (Ps. 1:1-4).

"Beloved I wish above all things that thou mayest prosper and be in health even as thy soul prospereth" (3 John 2).

"But seek ye first the kingdom of God and His righteousness; and all these things shall be added unto you" (Matt. 6:33).

"The thief cometh not, but for to steal, and to kill, and to destroy: I am come that they might have life, and that they might have it more abundantly" (John 10:10).

"Elijah was a man subject to like passions as we are, and he prayed earnestly that it might not rain; and it rained not on earth by the space of three years and six months. And he prayed again, and the heaven gave rain, and the earth brought forth her fruit" (James 5:17-18).

BASEBALL'S GOLDEN ARMS
Pitchers Make a Striking Start

Newsweek.

BONFIRE
OF THE
S&Ls

How Much You Will Pay

Are the Banks Next?

7

Young Lions of Tarshish

Vladimir Sakharov, former Russian-Mideast expert in the USSR, brought us some startling revelations in 1980. His book *High Treason* (published by G. P. Putnam's Sons) clearly gives warning relating to Soviet intentions for the Middle East.

In our own book *Magog 1982 Canceled* we outline Russia's plan to invade Israel and take over the entire middle east by August 1982. The Israeli invasion of Lebanon and subsequent discovery of massive deposits of Soviet weapons there put a delay on the Russian plans. We strongly urge you to read this incredible book. It was my privilege to testify before the Senate Foreign Relations Committee in Washington, D.C. At that session I was questioned about the book.

Now residing in the United States, Sakharov tells in detail the plans the Soviet Union has for Israel, the U.S.A., and the Arab world. It is his claim that all Soviet diplomats, officials in Russian embassies, consulates, and foreign trade missions are under the direct control of the KGB (Russian Secret Police). Sakharov says, "All are soldiers who wage political, ideological, and economic warfare against the capitalist countries and their imperialist sponsor, the United States."

Sakharov recalls a conversation with one of his Russian instructors in which the teacher said, "When Russia invades Israel the United States will take Israel's part and Russia will be on the other side—the Arab side." He said, "This is the side Russia is on now. We'll support them all the way against the Jews. Gradually they will take control of oil production and America will be isolated. In the mid-seventies oil prices will skyrocket and by 1980 a recession or maybe an economic depression will hit the Western World. I'd say between 1985 and 1990 the capitalistic system will collapse." (This conversation took place in the mid-1960s. Quoted in the *Saturday Review,* April 12, 1980.)

An Israeli Consul general from Houston told me, "The only thing that stops Russia from sweeping into the Middle East and taking over from the Persian Gulf to the Mediterranean is the existence of the nation of Israel and its peculiar relationship to the United States of America." In recent visions of venerable rabbis in Israel the prophecy of a Russian invasion of Israel plays a prominent role. The rabbis believe their dreams and visions signal the soon coming of the Messiah.

The rise of Russia as a world power and the emergence of Israel as a nation set the stage for the fulfillment of the Gog and Magog prophecy of Ezekiel.

UNLIKELY PROPHECY

One hundred years ago the entire fulfillment of Ezekiel 38 and 39 seemed very unlikely. As early as the seventeenth century Dr. Increase Mather, an early president of Harvard University, wrote an essay outlining that the prophecies concerning the Jews would be fulfilled literally. He was scorned for espousing such an unlikely viewpoint. Others, through the years, wrote of the power north of Israel invading a re-established nation of the Jews. But there was no Israel to be attacked until May 14, 1948.

The budding of the fig tree, Israel, (Joel 1:6,7; Jer. 24:1-10; and Matt. 24:32-34) as cited in Jesus' Olivet discourse is the greatest single sign indicating that we are living in the final era leading to the rapture of the Church and the earth-shattering events that follow. Further, Russia was the boondocks of Europe—the hinterlands of nowhere in the nineteenth century. It was looked upon scornfully by other Europeans as the one nation of Europe totally bypassed by the renaissance, the industrial revolution, and the Protestant reformation. The Arabs seemed to have disappeared from the geopolitical arena of the world and were a threat to no one. Who had heard of petrodollar power?

Now the entire Middle East picture has changed. All the pieces are in place for the final moves on the chess board of the end-times!

A PUZZLE IN PROPHECY

One verse has been a puzzler in the Ezekiel 38 prophecy—the mention of the nations which protest against the invasion of Gog into the Mideast. "Sheba, and Dedan, and the merchants of Tarshish, with all the young lions thereof, shall say unto thee, Art thou come to take a spoil?" (Ezek. 38:13). Here are the nations that protest against Russia's move against Israel. There is little difficulty in determining that Sheba and Dedan are Arab nations. They could be ancient names for Saudi Arabia and Jordan.

TARSHISH

Conservative scholars who interpret the Ezekiel passage literally have tended to identify Tarshish as Great Britain. The young lions thereof would be the English-speaking nations of the world such as the U.S. and Canada.

Scholars have recently come up with facts and theories that give interesting and broader insight into the identity of Tarshish. It now seems evident from history and archaeology that the Phoenicians (modern Lebanon) had widespread colonization of Mediterranean countries. Phoenician scholar Sabatino Moscoti traces Phoenician colonies in Spain as far back as the ninth century B.C. He states, "Tarshish (Tartessus) was probably to the north of Cadiz, at the source of the Guadalquivir. The identification of Tarshish with Tartessus leads us to believe that we can ascribe Phoenician settlements in Spain in the tenth century if not to the traditional date" (dates are B.C.). He quotes the poet Stesichorus who wrote in 600 B.C. and who spoke of the city of Tartessus in Spain (From *World of Phoenicians,* by Moscoti).

The great German scholar and writer Gerhard Herm comes to the same conclusion and adds that the Phoenicians also settled trading colonies in the British Isles. He notes that while the *Mayflower* had a displacement of a hundred eighty tons, in the third century B.C. the Romans had ships with a displacement of over a thousand tons, and the ships of Tarshish were probably not much smaller. All of this leads us a wider notion of Tarshish than merely identifying it as the British Isles. The prophecy then indicates that Western European powers could protest the Russian invasion.

Druids in Vermont? Phoenicians in Iowa before the
time of Julius Caesar? The first major
work to penetrate the mystery of America's remote past.

"A stunning book . . . an authentic landmark
destroys the premise of every previous text."—Peter Tompkins,
author of Secrets of the Great Pyramid

AMERICA B.C.

Ancient Settlers in the New World
by Barry Fell

79079-X $3.95

THE U.S. IN PROPHECY

This leads us to the next exciting conclusion—that this is the one prophecy of the Bible that can be identified with the U.S.

Dr. Barry Fell, professor at Harvard University, boldly asserts that recent archaeological discoveries prove that the Phoenicians had colonies in North America as early as 1000 B.C. His famed book *America B.C.* (condensed in the *Reader's Digest,* February, 1977) offers fascinating proof that these colonies existed in West Virginia, Texas, Iowa, New Hampshire, and many other areas as early as 1000 years B.C. Dr. Fell tells of an inscription found at Union, New Hampshire, reading "Voyagers From Tarshish This Stone Proclaims."

So the young lions of Tarshish would definitely refer to the North American colonies as well as the European colonies, and hence bring the U.S. into this prophecy as one of the nations that will strongly protest the Russian invasion of Israel in the last days.

It is not specified in the prophecy whether the protesting nations merely protest verbally or whether they rise to arms in defense of Israel. Some time ago I witnessed a Marine Corps demonstration of weapons and troop maneuvers in a California desert. I turned to an officer and said, "This desert reminds me of the Middle East, especially the Negev in Israel." He looked at me, startled, and responded, "Well, I guess this is a dress rehearsal. We know the Middle East is where everything is going to end up."

In the defeat of Russia God will manifest His mighty power. He will be known in the eyes of all nations. However, one phrase speaks of human instruments used in the defeat of Russia. God says, "I will call for a sword against him" (Ezek. 38:21). The Scripture is not clear as to who will bear that sword. Does this refer to secret weapons in Israel's arsenal? (They have some.) Or is the sword in the hand of the United States? We can give no final answer to this question for the Bible does not say who will bear the great sword that helps to defeat Gog on the mountains of Israel.

One thing is sure: the Lord is coming back, and in these end-times we will keep an eye on the world developments that set the stage for the battle of Gog and Magog, and then for the Battle of Armageddon at the close of the Tribulation. We cannot read all the fine type in the newspaper of the future, but we can see the headlines. Greater illumination on the prophecies can be expected as we progress toward the end of the age. Meantime, with Paul, we must admit, "We know in part and we prophesy in part" (1 Cor. 13:9).

The Soviet's enormous recent losses in East Europe could be the factor that would drive them to such a desperate move—the invasion of the Mid-East!

David Lewis, and colleagues testify before the U.S. Senate Foreign Relations Committee in favor of Israel.

8

U.S.A. IN PROPHECY

What is the role of the United States of America in end-time Bible prophecy? Is there no hint concerning this major world superpower in divine revelation? Russia is seen in the Gog and Magog prophecy of Ezekiel. The European Unity movement is linked with the prophecies in Daniel and Revelation concerning the ten-nation, Revived Roman Empire. China may be identified with the "kings of the east" in the Apocalypse. Where then is the U.S.A.?

Attempts have been made to identify the U.S.A. with the unknown nation of Isaiah 18. The late Reverend I. E. Aide carefully expounded this passage in such fashion, and he is joined by a number of contemporary authors of like mind.

Others are more comfortable identifying the U.S.A. with the "young lions of Tarshish." There is, however, a specific prophecy that can be linked to the destiny of the U.S.A. It is more definite than any other.

The spread of the gospel to all nations in the end-times is a prophecy of major importance in Scripture. Jesus said, "This gospel shall be preached in all the world for a witness unto all nations; and then shall the end come" (Matt. 24:14). If one could locate a nation that God is using primarily in the fulfillment of this prophecy then we will have located a nation of destiny, fulfilling a major prophecy. The consequence of that prophecy's being fulfilled would be greater than that of the Gog and Magog prediction of Ezekiel 38 and 39.

That nation is the United States of America. Statistics of various mission boards give varying estimates that 80 to 85% of all the finance for world missions and evangelization come from churches in the United States. About 80% of all the missionaries come from the U.S.A.

Surely it is not that the Christians in other nations are less generous than Americans. The Evangelicals in Europe are few and most nations other than the U.S.A. and Canada have severe restrictions that prohibit the churches from sending funds in any large amount out of the country. This is especially true of some of the socialistic nations in Europe. But the liberality of the U.S. Government and the level of affluence God has allowed this nation to reach combine to afford the churches here the opportunity of supporting a tremendous worldwide outreach of the gospel.

The U.S. government allows its citizens to give a sizable percentage of their income to the church and count is as a tax deduction! There is no restriction on sending funds to the mission field.

The atmosphere of religious freedom in this country, which has prevailed for two hundred years, contributes to the fulfillment of Jesus' prophecy. No other nation in history has ever seen two hundred continuous years of religious toleration. It should be noted here that the modern missionary movement was born in the nineteenth century America. Since America, with the liberality of its government and churches, has been the major instrument in the hands of God, fulfilling the prophecy of Matthew 24:14, it follows that the U.S.A. enjoys a *most exalted position* in the scheme of events that lead up to the end of this age.

The story of God's dealing with America in past centuries is an exciting saga of modern history. Is it possible that there is a special divinely-appointed destiny for our nation? If this is found to be true, what challenge does this present for the Church today? What role should we play in fulfilling the prophecy of the last days?

CHRISTOPHER COLUMBUS

Perhaps the earliest indication that God has a special plan for America can be discovered in the life, philosophy, and religious beliefs of Christopher Columbus.

In his personal journal, after three trips to the New World, Columbus tells of how God spoke clearly to him, reminding him that he had been specifically chosen to be the man to bring the light of Jesus Christ to the New World.

Columbus authored a volume titled *Book of Prophecies*. Large portions of this book were translated by August Kling and quoted in the *Presbyterian Layman* in October, 1971. He wrote, "It was the Lord who put into my mind (I could feel His hand upon me) the fact that it would be possible to sail from here to the Indies. All who heard of my project rejected it with laughter, ridiculing me. There is no question that the inspiration was from the Holy Spirit, because He comforted me with rays of marvelous inspiration from the Holy Scriptures....

"I am a most unworthy sinner, but I have cried out to the Lord for grace and mercy, and they have covered me completely. I have found the sweetest consolation since I made it my whole purpose to enjoy His marvelous presence. For the execution of the journey to the Indies, I did not make use of intelligence, mathematics, or maps. It is simply the fulfillment of what Isaiah had prophesied.

"No one should fear to undertake any task in the name of our Saviour, if it is just and if the intention is purely for His holy service."

God had chosen Columbus, a man of prayer and vision, to lift the curtain on the New World.

THE PILGRIMS

The Pilgrims, fleeing persecution in England, seeking religious freedom, landed on these shores at Plymouth on November 11, 1620, believing that God had led them to a new promised land.

The unutterable suffering they endured in the seven weeks' journey on the *Mayflower,* coupled with jeering and persecution from the crew of the ship, had driven this band of Christians closer together in covenant with God and each other as a body of Christian believers.

The Pilgrims produced a document unique in the annals of history that is indeed the cornerstone of the concept of this Republic of the United States of America. Under the God-inspired leadership of men like William Bradford, they composed the Mayflower Compact. The compact contains the line, "In the name of God, amen....Having undertaken, for the glory of God and the advancement of the Christian Faith...do by these presents solemnly and mutually in the presence of God and of one another, covenant and combine ourselves together into a civil body politic...."

This was the first time in history that free and equal men had the opportunity to organize their own civil government. Truly the Lord was doing a new thing.

THE PURITANS

The Puritans had tried to reform the corrupt church in England, but finally persecution forced them to follow the route of the Pilgrims. John White formed the New England Company and started the exodus of tens of thousands of Puritans from England to the New World. More than any other factor, it was the influence of the Puritans that prepared the way for America to become a Christian country, "One nation, under God."

The Puritans set sail from England in 1629. On board the *Talbot,* one of their five ships, John Higginson wrote: "We go to practice the positive part of church reformation, and to propagate the gospel in America." Governor John Winthrop preached on the deck of the flagship *Arbella*: "The Lord will be our God and delight to dwell among us, *for we consider that we shall be as a city upon a hill, the eyes of all people are upon us*" (Italics mine).

Like the Mayflower Compact of the Pilgrims, "The Model of Christian Charity" penned by John Winthrop stands as a rock of strength supporting the foundation of our American Republic.

What does it all mean? I believe that God's purpose for the nation was to provide a haven for the Church and a base from which the whole world could be evangelized in the last days. Indeed, the fact that the U.S. has afforded her citizens two hundred years of absolute religious freedom is unprecedented in all the history of nations.

SHORT OF THE MARK

The missions outreach of the Church in the U.S. is an encouraging account of victories won, yet we feel we are far short of the mark. The task is not ended, only begun. We look at the pagan society about us, continually exercising diabolical influence in spite of the resurgence of Evangelical Christianity and we wonder, "What is wrong with the nation?"

It is essential that we recognize that we are in an end-time, last-ditch battle with the forces of Antichrist which have always tried to defeat the Church. The combined forces of human greed, pride, and carnal rationalism are woven into a web of satanic intrigue which is designed to offset the plan of God.

Like Israel of old, the Church in America has gone through periodic cycles of revival and apostasy. The spiritual life of the nation seemed so low at times that it seemed Satan had won the war. But God has periodically sent renewal and with it the opportunity for the Church and the nation to fully realize God's planned destiny.

THE SECOND GENERATION

As the early Puritans prospered, their children did not have to endure the hardships their parents had suffered. It was these very hardships that had driven them to a dependence on God. The second and third generation descendants of the early founders began to drift far from God and His Church. Religion became formal. Many pulpits were filled by unsanctified men who were not committed to the authority of God's Word. The true ministers of God lamented this sad condition, and a reading of their sermons is like reading the Lamentations of Jeremiah for backslidden Israel. Michael Wigglesworth's thirty-one verse poem, "God's Controversy With New England," was much quoted by these faithful ministers of God:

"Our healthful days are at an
   end and sicknesses come on
From year to year, because our
   hearts
away from God are gone."

THE AWAKENING

As the faithful cried out to God, the Lord heard their pleas and saw the hunger of their hearts. Between the days of the dying embers of Puritanism and before the Revolutionary War, there was a period known as the "Great Awakening." The impact of this period on our national destiny can hardly be measured.

The fires of revival were lit in 1734 in Northampton, Massachusetts. God used the anointed preaching of Jonathan Edwards to kindle those flames. However, it was George Whitefield who had the greatest impact for God in that era. Through his preaching, the Great Awakening began around 1740. Whitefield did not mince words when he laid the blame for apostasy squarely at the door of the lukewarm clergy: "I am persuaded (that) the generality of preachers talk of an unknown and unfelt Christ. The reason why congregations have been so dead is because they had dead men preaching to them. How can dead men beget living children?" Whitefield's revivals cut across all denominational barriers. He was the first to accomplish a true ecumenicity of the Spirit. By the time the Constitution was framed the nation was gripped by the concept of the equality of all men. The stage was also being set for the Declaration of Independence of 1776: "We hold these Truths to be self-evident, that all Men are created equal....We therefore the representatives of the *United States of America*...with a firm Reliance on the Protection of Divine Providence...."

THE DECLARATION OF INDEPENDENCE

Thomas Jefferson drafted the Declaration of Independence and strenuously objected to the inclusion of the phrases referring to God, but the Congress prevailed over his objections. Jefferson was not a Christian. He was a humanist who described himself as an enlightened rationalist. Thank God the forces of humanism did not prevail in the framing of this document.

It is hard for us, after two hundred years, to realize how radical the words "all men created equal" seemed in that distant time. No government in the history of man had ever asserted, let alone actually believed in, the equality of man. And never before had God planted a body of believers (Pilgrims, Puritans) in a land that had no existing civil government. Due to the Great Awakening, God had many ministers of deep spiritual perception scattered throughout the land. The revivalist influence had never been greater than in the period before the Revolutionary War. Their preaching united the people within the forming nation.

The governors of the colonies were appointed by the king of England. One of these wrote to the Board of Trade in England: "If you ask an American who his master is, he will tell you he has none, nor any governor but Jesus Christ." The cry throughout the land, taken up by the people and echoed by the Colonial Committees of Correspondence was, "No King But Jesus Christ."

THE REVOLUTIONARY WAR

On March 23, 1775 Patrick Henry spoke to the Virginia House of Burgesses. He gave an impassioned call to arms against the forces of tyranny: "An appeal to arms and to the God of Hosts is all that is left us!

"They tell me we are weak, but shall we gather strength by irresolution? We are not weak. Three million people, armed in the holy cause of liberty and in such a country, are invincible by any force which our enemy can send against us. We shall not fight alone. God presides over the destinies of nations, and will raise up friends for us. The battle is not to the strong alone, it is to the vigilant, the active, the brave....

"Is life so dear, or peace so sweet, as to be purchased at the price of chains and slavery? Forbid it, almighty God! I know not what course others may take, but as for me, give me liberty or give me death."

On April 19, 1776 war broke out when the British forces fired on colonial minutemen at Lexington. On June 17, 1776 at the Battle of Bunker Hill the British losses were proportionately the heaviest ever sustained by English forces (almost 50% of their forces were lost). It seemed like an impossible war for the weak American colonies, with their pitiful volunteer citizen army arrayed against the world's mightiest empire of the time. But time and again the hand of God intervened.

The account of divine intervention on the side of the Americans has been carefully documented by a host of authors.

THE CONSTITUTION

May 14, 1787 saw the opening of the Constitutional Convention. The final peace treaty had been signed in 1783. America desperately needed a stable form of government. Again the hand of God is seen in the framing of the Constitution as the very basis of the republic. Can we not see divine intervention in the fact that two powerful agnostics, Jefferson and Paine, who could have exerted the wrong influence, were in Europe at the time of the convention?

The convention was a scene of chaos and bitter argument. The formation of a meaningful government seemed impossible. Only the dignity and presence of George Washington preserved any semblance of order. When it seemed that the meetings would end in shambles, Benjamin Franklin, at that time eighty-one years of age, rose feebly to speak. Franklin was an enigma. His philosophy seemed to fluctuate through the years. Never a Christian, many saw him as a veritable antichrist. However on this occasion he said, "In the beginning of the contest with Britain, when we were sensible of danger, we had daily prayers in this room for divine protection. Our prayers, sir, were heard, and they were graciously answered. All of us who were engaged in the struggle must have observed frequent instances of a superintending Providence in our favor...And have we now forgotten this powerful Friend? Or do we imagine we no longer need His assistance?

"I have lived, sir, a long time, and the longer I live, the more convincing proofs I see of this truth: that God governs in the affairs of men. And if a sparrow cannot fall to the ground without His notice, is it probable that an empire cannot arise without His aid?

"We have been assured, sir, in the Sacred Writings that except the Lord build the house, they labor in vain that build it.

"I therefore beg leave to move that, henceforth, prayers imploring the assistance of heaven and its blessing on our deliberation be held in this assembly every morning before we proceed to business."

Franklin's appeal marked the beginning of a new unity, a more agreeable climate in which our Constitution could be framed and accepted.

The Constitution with its recognition of human weakness and with its checks and balances of government was the outgrowth of Puritan teaching which recognized the fallen nature of man. The Constitution simply recognizes the scriptural truth that men are motivated by self-interest and self-love. This has to be checked; hence were conceived the three branches of government: the legislative, judicial, and the executive.

One of England's greatest prime ministers, William Gladstone, said that the Constitution was "the most wonderful work ever struck off at a given time by the brain and purpose of man." He failed to see that it was not merely the purpose of man, but the purpose of God. The Constitution has endured for two hundred years and is the oldest existing constitution still in use in the world today.

OUR FIRST PRESIDENT

After the Constitutional Convention, George Washington, who had been commander-in-chief of the armed forces during the Revolution, was elected the first president of the United States of America in 1789. History indicates that God, who "raises up kings and puts them down" appointed that the new nation "under God" should have a true Christian leader. Washington wrote a little book titled *Daily Sacrifice.* It contains many of his written prayers.

Washington prayed, "Direct my thoughts, words and work, wash away my sins in the immaculate Blood of the Lamb, and purge my heart by Thy Holy Spirit...daily frame me more and more into the likeness of Thy Son Jesus Christ....

"Thou gavest Thy Son to die for me; and hast given me assurance of salvation, upon my repentance and sincerely endeavoring to conform to His holy precepts and example."

During the war, as commander-in-chief, Washington had called for church services to be conducted for the troops each Sunday. He said, "To the distinguished character of a Patriot, it should be our highest glory to add the more distinguished character of a Christian."

Pastor Henry Muhlenberg, a Lutheran minister and contemporary of Washington, stated in a sermon, "His Excellency General Washington...does not belong to the so-called world of society, for he respects God's Word, *believes in the atonement through Christ,* and bears himself in humility and gentleness. Therefore, the Lord God has also singularly, yea, marvelously, preserved him from harm in the midst of countless perils, ambuscades, fatigues, and has hitherto graciously held him in His hand as a *chosen vessel."*

THE NEW APOSTASY

The eight years of Washington's presidency were also years of satanic attack on the new nation. An opposing spirit of humanism was rising in the land. Apostasy again reared its ugly head, even in the churches. Unitarianism (encouraged by Jefferson) was coming into being and grew rapidly. Agnostics like Thomas Paine bitterly and continuously attacked our Christian founding father, George Washington.

History testifies that the witness of the Church was once more corrupted. Seminaries began to produce ministers who seemed to specialize in unbelief.

But God is faithful to His chosen nation. In the nineteenth century revivalists like Lyman Beecher, Charles Finney, and Dwight L. Moody are remembered as shining stars that God used to bring renewal and awakening to the Church.

MISSIONS

Our premise is that God intended America to be a base from which the Church could evangelize the whole world in the end-times. It was in the nineteenth century that the modern missionary movement was born. It was also during this period that most of the modern Evangelical and Fundamentalist churches came into existence as a protest against the modernism of the older churches.

The missionary movement of the end-times was born right here in America. Adoniram Judson set sail for India and later became the Apostle of Burma and is noted to be the father of the modern missionary movement, which is largely an American phenomenon. The churches of Europe, at that time, showed little interest in world evangelization.

THE PENTECOSTAL MOVEMENT

Toward the end of the last century as the forces of modernism and humanism continued to battle the faith of our fathers, those of a godly spirit became ever more hungry for a New Testament outpouring of the Holy Spirit. They began to cry out to God for a new revival.

God's answer to their cries was another fulfillment of prophecy, and in the early twentieth century the Pentecostal revival was born. Without singular human leadership it was actually born of the Spirit. People of all denominations received the endument with power from on high. Most of them had no intention of leaving the churches they were in, but the churches could not tolerate them. Hence the Pentecostal fellowships such as the Assemblies of God, the Church of God, and The

Open Bible Standard came into being. Most of these fellowships were created for the giving of credentials to ministers and the stabilization of doctrine, but supremely for the promotion of establishing world missions and winning lost souls all over the world.

CHARISMATIC MOVEMENT

In 1952, while I was a student at Central Bible College in Springfield, Missouri, I heard Bob Walker, editor of *Christian Life* magazine, speak in the CBC chapel. He prophesied that the seeds of a mighty "Charismatic" revival had been planted by the Assemblies of God and other Pentecostals. He stated that soon this revival would break out in all denominations. It has come to pass. We are now seeing the end-time outpouring of the Spirit.

Satan is raging. We are at war. But the prophet said that when the enemy comes in like a flood, the spirit of God will raise up a standard against him. One of the greatest dangers facing the Evangelicals, Pentecostals, and Charismatics is a rejection of our biblical heritage and radical changes of our views on the end-times. The neo-Kingdomists and Dominionists are examples of this. New and extreme winds of doctrine seem to blow around us with gale force. Nevertheless many stand firm and proclaim God's truth for these last days. Indeed, we are "set for the defense of the gospel" and shall "earnestly contend for the faith."

HOPE FOR OUR NATION

Though we have fallen far short and the battle is intense, yet our hopes are high. We now see clearly the destiny desired by God for our nation. This knowledge should enable us to more intelligently cooperate with the plan of God, to realize the potential of His grace and power that are available to us for the completion of the end-time task of world evangelization.

A strong and revived Church is vitally important for these end-times. As powers of Antichrist wax strong throughout the world, preparing for the coming Tribulation, we must be alert, informed, and strong to resist the enemy through God's authority and through intercessory prayer coupled with good works.

It is no wonder Satan hates America. America, America, *God shed His grace on thee.* These are not mere pious words of a song—they are a statement of truth. Now may we do our part so the Lord can again shed His grace on our land and rescue us from the evil calamities that seem to loom before us.

_____

IS THE U.S.A. IN BIBLE PROPHECY?

There are three reasons why God has blessed the U.S.A. There are three reasons why the devil hates the U.S.A. Jesus made three predictions in the New Testament that are of vital importance to our nation in these end-times. First, the prophecy of Matthew 16. Jesus predicted, "I will build my church and the gates of hell shall not prevail against it." That is God's iron clad guarantee that the Church will not be destroyed. We shall prevail over the power of darkness. The U.S.A. is unique in that here the Church has found a safe haven for over two hundred years. No nation in the world has given the Bible-preaching Church two centuries of freedom of worship and freedom to preach the gospel without interference. We may be seeing these freedoms being eroded—but it is not too late to do something about it.

Second, Jesus prophesied that the gospel would be preached for a witness to all nations (Matt. 24:16). We have noted the American role in missions.

Thirdly, Jesus predicted that Israel would play an important role in end-time prophecy. The fig tree sign in Matthew 24:32-34, 44 is the key to understanding the era of time we live in. The fig tree is always Israel in Bible symbolism. God promised to bless those who bless Israel and curse those who curse Israel. This promise was made not only to Abraham in Genesis 12, but was repeated concerning Jacob in the book of Numbers. Again, the U.S.A. plays a key role in end-time prophecy as we have noted over and over in our newspaper, the *Jerusalem Courier.*

Friends, we must strengthen the Church and continue fulfilling the Great Commission and blessing Israel. If we do there is every reason to claim revival and spiritual renewal throughout our nation until the very end of this age.

9

Israel—
The Prophets Spoke

The very existence of the nation of Israel is a miracle. This fact needs to be emphasized over and over for several reasons:

First, the devil hates Israel and wants to destroy the nation. Why? Because God has made unbreakable promises to Abraham concerning his seed's possessing the land, and God will not break His Word regardless of what mankind may do.

Secondly, the world hates Israel and the Jewish people and works for their destruction. No one can deny the long centuries of anti-Semitism and the toll that has been taken. No sensible person can deny the Nazi Holocaust that in modern times, in a Christian nation, took the lives of six million Jewish people. Who would be so foolish as to think that, given a chance, evil men would not again raise up a "final solution" to eradicate the very memory of Israel off the face of the earth? The vicious attacks on Israel in the United Nations is a clear manifestation of this continued Gentile hatred of the Jewish people.

The third factor is the most startling of all. This should alarm out and cause you to rise up in active protest. I am referring to anti-Semitism (Jew hatred) in the Church. We have become accustomed to this evil in the older churches. The younger Evangelical, Fundamentalist, Pentecostal, and Charismatic fellowships, however, have been favorable to Israel because of a recognition of the validity of God's promises in

His Word. That is, until recent times, when there is a straying from God's clear mandate concerning our attitude toward Israel, which is the "apple of His eye."

The New Wave theologians, New Kingdomists, Dominionists, Reconstructionists, and Theonomists are vehemently promoting anti-Israel doctrine. They even say that the existence of the nation of Israel has no meaning at all. It is not a fulfillment of prophecy. They accuse anyone who teaches as I do of being a heretic.

I was in a major leadership conference a few months ago. A Charismatic leader asserted, "The identity of Israel is the major issue facing the Church today." His idea is that the Church has totally replaced Israel and that national Israel has no more role to play in God's economy. I was denied a voice in this conference. Although the "unstructured" meeting was advertised to be an open exchange of ideas among Christian leaders, my colleagues and I were effectively silenced. Those who have opposed us in their publications, specifically because of our stance on Israel, prophecy, and the Kingdom, were given ample time to express their views. No effective rebuttal was allowed.

COVENANTS, OLD AND NEW

Much is made of the idea that the new covenant abolishes the old covenant. The most that can be said from New Testament writing is that the Mosaic Covenant involving the sacrifice of animals is no longer in force. Never is a word said about any repudiation of the Abrahamic Covenant.

Can more than one covenant be in force at one time? Yes, of course they can. The covenant God made with all humanity after the flood, the Rainbow Covenant, is still in effect. It signifies God's promise never to destroy the world in a universal flood again. Further Paul writes of God's covenants (plural) with Israel (natural Israel, not the Church) in Romans 9:4.

A covenant is an agreement or a contract. It can be conditional or unconditional. The Abrahamic Covenant concerning the land of Israel was a unilateral, unconditional covenant. Its fulfillment rests on God's faithfulness alone, not on man's deeds. The fact that this covenant exists has nothing to do with the salvation of the individual. That is based on a personal relationship with God. Evangelicals, for the most part, believe that salvation, under the new covenant is solely through Jesus Christ. This does not demolish the unconditional promise of God to natural Israel. By His sovereign determination God is bringing His purposes to pass. The prophecies relating to Israel show the Jewish people returning to restore the nation and the land before the major spiritual awakening that will take place when Messiah appears. The 36th and 37th chapters of Ezekiel express this foreview. There are many other passages that show the same thing.

"And I scattered them among the heathen, and they dispersed through the countries: according to their way and according to their doings I judged them.

"And when they entered unto the heathen, whither they went, they profaned my holy name, when they said to them, These are the people of the Lord, and are gone forth out of his land.

"But I had pity for mine holy name, which the house of Israel had profaned among the heathen, whither they went.

"Therefore say unto the house of Israel, Thus saith the Lord God; I do not this for your sakes, O house of Israel, but for mine holy name's sake, which ye have profaned among the heathen, whither ye went.

"And I will sanctify my great name, which was profaned among the heathen, which ye have profaned in the midst of them; and the heathen shall know that I am the Lord, saith the Lord God, when I shall be sanctified in you before their eyes.

"For I will take you from among the heathen, and gather you out of all countries, and will bring you into your own land.

"Then will I sprinkle clean water upon you, and ye shall be clean: from all your filthiness, and from all your idols, will I cleanse you.

"A new heart also will I give you, and a new spirit will I put within you; and I will take away the stony heart out of your flesh, and I will give you a heart of flesh" (Ezek. 36:19-26).

REDEMPTION OF ISRAEL

The Bible does speak of the future redemption of Israel as a miraculous accomplishment! Zechariah 3:9 declares that God will remove iniquity from the land in one day's time—in the day of Messiah. The Book of Romans confirms this in a New Testament setting.

"For I would not, brethren, that ye should be ignorant of this mystery, lest ye should be wise in your own conceits; that blindness in part is happened to Israel, until the fulness of the Gentiles be come in.

"And so all Israel shall be saved: as it is written, There shall come out of Zion the Deliverer, and shall turn away ungodliness from Jacob:

"For this is my covenant unto them, when I shall take away their sins" (Rom. 11:26-27).

When the fullness of the Gentiles, also called the "times of the Gentiles" by Jesus in the Olivet discourse, is completed then there is

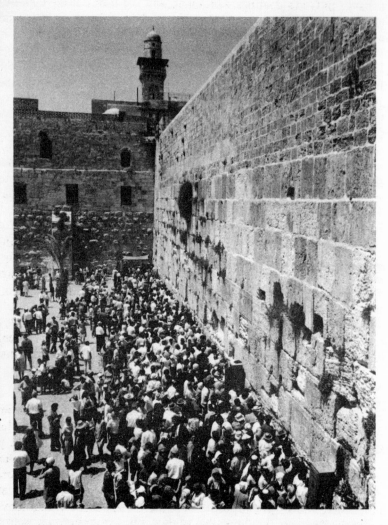

Western Wall—Jerusalem. Behold the chosen people, gathered from the four corners of the earth.

a change in God's dealings with mankind. The times of the Gentiles has nothing to do with the Church, which is the hidden mystery and has its own course to run.

As the prophets foretold, the day the Messiah comes, God will save the whole house of Israel. This cannot refer to people redeemed under the new covenant (the Church). The phrase "and so all Israel shall be saved" has to do with a future event. Evangelicals teach that believers are saved right now. Therefore the phrase has to do with God's future mercy to natural Israel.

Some people complain about our friendship with Israel and the Jewish people. They say that the Jews not only refuse Jesus, but they are not very religious even in the light of Judaism. For some reason our opponents, the religious anti-Semitics, think we should withdraw our friendship from Israel because of this.

It is not a problem to me that the Word of God is accurate. The prophets foresaw a time when the Jews would be scattered among the heathen. In the latter days they would be regathered in the land. They would return in unbelief, hardness of heart, and bitterness. Isaiah says they will return having passed through a "furnace of fire." The rabbis agree that this speaks of the Holocaust.

It is *after* the physical, national restoration that the Messianic Age comes and affects the spiritual revival of Israel. How can anyone deny that God's Word is being fulfilled exactly as declared by the prophets?

RECLAMATION OF THE LAND

Mark Twain described the treeless desolation of the land of Palestine (as it was called under the Turkish mandate) in the 1800s. He called it a "blistering, naked, treeless land" (*Innocents Abroad, Vol. II,* p. 234). He spoke of the villages as "ugly, cramped, squalid, uncomfortable and filthy" (*Ibid.,* p. 260), and "solitude to make one dreary...unpeopled deserts...rusty mounds of barrenness, that never, never, never do shake the glare from their harsh outlines...this stupid village of Tiberias, slumbering under its six funereal plumes of palms; yonder desolate declivity where the swine of the miracle ran down into the sea, and doubtless thought it was better to swallow a devil or two and get drowned into the bargain than have to live longer in such a place" (*Ibid.,* p. 266).

Incredible! You see, Twain was describing the area around the beautiful Sea of Galilee whose surrounding hills today are covered with trees. He was speaking of a desolate Tiberias that today is a modern, comfortable city.

The glorious Mount of Olives which "is before Jerusalem on the east."

Twain described the Palestine of his day accurately. Your local library will have a copy of *Innocents Abroad,* and reading the chapters on Palestine is quite an experience. Today the scene has changed and due to the tree planting projects, forests abound.

OTHER AUTHORS WITNESS

Nachmanides visited the land in 1267 and described Jerusalem as "Deserted and laid waste and that Judea was more destitute than Galilee."

George Sandys reported in 1610 that the "land was bare of trees. The country is a vast empty ruin."

Colonel C. R. Condor wrote in 1877 that "Palestine is empty. The population is not large enough to till the land."

M. Russell wrote in his book *Palestine the Holy Land* that "Jericho, once famous for its palm and balsam trees, is treeless and almost deserted."

TRANSFORMATION OF THE LAND

One author counted the trees in Palestine in the 1800s and reported that there were less than a thousand. Today there are over three hundred million fully grown, mature trees, half of them forest trees, half of them for fruit. Isaiah prophesied, "Israel shall blossom and bud and fill the face of the earth with fruit" (Isa. 27:6). Today Israel exports around eighty percent of her fruit and vegetable harvest. Growing and exporting citrus fruit is the number two industry of the country.

In the day of Israel's restoration the trees of the land are also to be restored:

"But thou, Israel, art my servant, Jacob whom I have chosen, the seed of Abraham my friend.

"Thou whom I have taken from the ends of the earth, and called thee from the chief men thereof, and said unto thee, Thou art my servant; I have chosen thee, and not cast thee away.

"Fear thou not; for I am with thee: be not dismayed:

"I will open rivers in high places, and fountains in the midst of the valleys: I will make the wilderness a pool of water, and the dry land springs of water.

"I will plant in the wilderness the cedar, the shittah tree, and the myrtle, and the oil tree; I will set in the desert the fir tree, and the pine, and the box tree together:

"That they may see, and know, and consider, and understand together,

"Israel shall fill the face of the earth with fruit." (Isaiah 27:6). Eighty percent of Israel's fruit harvest is now exported.

that the hand of the Lord hath done this, and the Holy One of Israel hath created it" (Isa. 41:8-10; 18-20).

CHRISTIANS WHO LOVE AND SUPPORT ISRAEL

There is a long history of Christian involvement in biblical Zionism, that is the idea that God owns the land, has given Israel to the Jewish people, and that Christians should be supportive of God's plan and should do all they can to implement the purposes of God. Biblical Zionism does not imply a total agreement with the policies of any one political system in or out of Israel. It rather implies an acceptance of the literal statements of the Bible relating to Israel.

In the mid-1600s Oliver Cromwell recognized the Bible prophecies indicating that the Jews would own the land of Israel.

In 1655 a German Protestant author, Paul Glegenhauver wrote of "The permanent return of the Jews to their own country eternally bestowed upon them by God through the unqualified promise to Abraham, Isaac, and Jacob."

Lord Anthony Ashley Cooper, the seventh earl of Shaftsbury, wrote an article in 1839 titled "The State of the Prospects of the Jews." He spoke of the Jews as having an exalted role in God's plan for the future and urged that they be allowed to have the land of Palestine. As a result of his teaching and efforts William Young, a devout Evangelical, became the first British consul to Jerusalem in 1839.

In 1845 Charles Henry Churchill, British staff officer serving in the Middle East, wrote to Sir Moses Montefiore (one of the Jewish restorers of Jerusalem): "I cannot conceal from you my most anxious desire to see your countrymen endeavor once more to resume their existence as a people. I consider the object to be perfectly obtainable."

Before Theodore Herzl held the first Zionist Congress in Basel, Switzerland, in 1897, it can be historically noted that the principal advocates of Zionism were Bible-believing Christians.

Herzl himself wrote more of one man than any other in his diaries. That man was Reverend William Hechler, an Evangelical clergyman, who was a primary source of encouragement to Herzl in the founding of Zionism. Hechler simply recognized the validity of God's Word, its promises, and prophecies.

WE URGE CHRISTIANS TO REAFFIRM
SUPPORT FOR ISRAEL

Some of our pastors have been intimidated by highly visible and highly charismatic personalities in the Church who are loudly calling for a rejection of our literal interpretation of the Bible. We are threatened, called heretics, and intimidation is attempted. But they have not shut us up in this ministry and they will not. Our commitment is firm. Some of our friends have stopped supporting us because they have been intimidated. They have been told that our ideas are an impediment to the unity of the body of Christ. That may be so for I do not believe in artificial unity at the cost of compromise in important areas of Bible truth.

Don't allow the new, modernistic Evangelicals to dictate to you and demand that you abandon the Word and abandon Israel. I call on you to stand firm and God will bless you for it. He will still curse those who curse Israel and bless those who bless Israel. I am glad that one person on the platform of the "Washington for Jesus" rally raised his voice to protest the absence of an Israeli flag among all the other flags of the nations. I am thankful that this one person dared to raise his voice to protest that while just about every other issue was dealt with and prayed about, the issue of Israel's survival was ignored.

This is not a minor issue. Literal Bible interpretation is not an option. I hope you will read the new book by Dr. Amos Millard: *Literal Interpretation of the Jewish and Christian Scriptures.* You could also read *The Controversy of Zion* by Claude Duvernoy and *Israel in Prophecy,* Louis Hauf. Prophecy must not be relegated to the realm of obscurity. It is a noble and powerful message and can bring vitality back to a compromising church that has lost its way.

"Behold, the days come, saith the Lord, that the plowman shall overtake the reaper, and the treader of grapes him that soweth seed; and the mountains shall drop sweet wine, and all the hills shall melt.

"And I will bring again the captivity of my people of Israel, and they shall build the waste cities, and inhabit them; and they shall plant vineyards, and drink the wine thereof; they shall also make gardens, and eat the fruit of them.

"And I will plant them upon their land, and they shall no more be pulled up out of their land which I have given them, saith the Lord thy God" (Amos 9:13-15).

Israeli prime minister Yitzhak Shamir has led his nation through
troubled times. Dr. Lewis, left; Mrs. Ramona Lewis, right.

Israel has known only a state of war since her founding in 1948. "Judah also shall fight at Jerusalem" (Zechariah 14:14).

An elderly Jew preparing for Succot (The Feast of Tabernacles).

Sound the Shofar! Call the wanderers home to the land of promise.

10

Temple of the Jews
Ancient Secrets Rise From the Dust

The temple of Israel will be rebuilt. Of that we have no doubt whatsoever. Scriptures that demonstrate this truth are found in both the Old and New Testaments:

"And he shall confirm the covenant with many for one week: and in the midst of the week he shall cause the sacrifice and the oblation to cease, and for the overspreading of abominations he shall make it desolate, even until the consummation, and that determined shall be poured upon the desolate" (Dan. 9:27).

"And arms shall stand on his part, and they shall pollute the sanctuary of strength, and shall take away the daily sacrifice, and they shall place the abomination that maketh desolate" (Dan. 11:31).

"And from the time that the daily sacrifice shall be taken away, and the abomination that maketh desolate set up, there shall be a thousand two hundred and ninety days" (Dan. 12:11).

Daniel's words concerning the abomination or defiling of the temple cannot be seen as fulfilled in the works of Antiochus Epiphanes (166 B.C.) or the Roman destruction (70 A.D.) at the hands of Titus. Jesus' prediction clarifies that the abomination of desolation is yet future from His time.

"And Jesus went out, and departed from the temple: and his disciples came to him for to shew him the buildings of the temple.

131

"And Jesus said unto them, See ye not all these things? Verily I say unto you, There shall not be left here one stone upon another, that shall not be thrown down.

"And as he sat upon the mount of Olives, the disciples came unto him privately, saying, Tell us, when shall these things be? and what shall be the sign of thy coming, and of the end of the world?" (Matt. 24:1-3).

John's words in Revelation finalize this clarification:

"And there was given me a reed like unto a rod: and the angel stood, saying, Rise, and measure the temple of God, and the altar, and them that worship therein.

"But the court which is without the temple leave out, and measure it not; for it is given unto the Gentiles: and the holy city shall they tread under foot forty and two months" (Rev. 11:1,2).

Jesus' prophecy of the destruction of the temple was fulfilled in 70 A.D., twenty years before John wrote the Revelation. This demonstrates that Revelation 11:1,2 looks forward to a future temple.

There remain several questions to be dealt with: When will it be rebuilt in relation to eschatological (end-time) events? Will there be one or two future temples? Is it to be built on the original site; if so where is that location? Is the temple under construction at the present or are materials being stockpiled for the rebuilding of the temple?

THE TEMPLE OF GOD

Some have committed the error of calling the next temple "the Antichrist temple." That borders on blasphemy since the Bible speaks of the temple that exists during the future time of trouble (Tribulation), the "temple of God" (Rev. 11:1,2).

The Antichrist will defile and profane the temple. That is what Daniel and Jesus refer to as the "abomination of desolation" (Dan. 9:27; Matt. 24:15-22). Paul refers to the man of sin sitting in the temple of God defying God and declaring himself to be the deity (2 Thess. 2:3,4). How in the world could the Antichrist defile the temple if it was already profane? Let this be a warning to anyone who says that God is through with the Jews. God honors the third (future) temple as a holy place (Matt. 24:15—the words of Jesus!).

A CHRISTIAN OBJECTION

We have heard some Christians object to the temple being rebuilt because it would be disruptive to their doctrine. It has been said that "If the temple is rebuilt and sacrifices reinstituted, it would nullify the atoning work accomplished by Christ on the Cross."

We answer by simply saying that nothing could nullify a genuine work of God, and further it is God's own Words which predict the building of the temple.

Christian theologians would view any future sacrifices, such as in the millennial temple, as commemorative in nature—like the partaking of communion in a Christian context. In other words, future sacrifices will be memorial, not redemptive.

THE FIRST TEMPLE

King David was crowned king of Israel in Hebron, but conquered Jerusalem from the Jebusites and made it his capital. David longed to build the temple, but was forbidden by God to do so. He compiled the materials and made some plans for the building, but it was his son King Solomon who built the temple. It was a magnificent building dedicated in 953 B.C. The holy ark of the covenant containing the two tablets of the Law was placed in the temple. The first temple was destroyed by the Babylonians about 586 B.C. and the Jews went into captivity in Babylon. After the "seventy years of the desolations of Jerusalem" (Dan. 9:1-3), the Jews returned to the land.

THE SECOND TEMPLE

After the return the Jews began to rebuild the temple. Sheshbazzar laid the foundations two years after the release from captivity (Ezra 3:2 and 5:16). It is often called the Temple of Zerubbabel since it was built under his leadership. This temple stood until 20 B.C.

In the eighteenth year of Herod's reign, reconstruction of the second temple began. It is argued whether Herod's Temple should be called the second temple (rebuilt) or the third temple (built in its place). For the sake of convenience we shall simply call it Herod's Temple. It was still under construction when Jesus started His ministry. Jesus was accustomed to teaching daily in the courts of the temple (Matt. 27:55; Mark 12:35; Luke 10:1; John 7:14; 18:20, etc.). Jesus prophesied the destruction of the temple saying that not one stone would be left standing on another (see Matt. 24:1-3). This was literally fulfilled in 70 A.D. when the Romans captured Jerusalem and destroyed the temple.

THE WAILING WALL

If you ask an uninformed person what the Wailing Wall is, you will probably be told that the proper name of it is the "Western" Wall and that it is the only remains of the temple destroyed by the Romans. However, the Wailing Wall was not part of the temple. It was an outer courtyard and earth-retaining wall. Where you stand at the Wailing Wall today is fifty-three feet above the level of Christ's time. The destructions of Jerusalem have filled in the area with that much debris. We will come back to the Wailing (Western) Wall later.

THE DOME OF THE ROCK

The "golden" dome of the Moslem shrine that stands on Mount Moriah, the Temple Mount, was constructed in the seventh century A.D. It is a place very holy to Islam, superceded in importance only by Mecca and Medina, both in Saudi Arabia. Many theorize that the Dome of the Rock must be destroyed for Israel to build the temple there. There is an alternate point of view, however. By the way, it is *not* the "Mosque of Omar." Further, it is not a mosque, but a shrine. The dome is not a "golden" dome, but is covered with gold colored anodized aluminum. It is considered to be one of the most beautiful buildings in the world. I heard the renowned scholar Ralph Harris describe it as being surpassed in beauty only by the Taj Mahal in India.

For many years I have said that I did not think that the temple stood on the exact location of the Dome of the Rock. The *Jerusalem Post* recently had a very interesting article about the theories of a scientist, Dr. Asher Kaufman. His research indicates that the temple stood about one hundred yards north of the Dome of the Rock. This gives rise to a possible conclusion (also based on analysis of Rev. 11:1,2,3) that the next temple could (as an appeasement) co-exist with the Dome of the Rock.

AN INTRIGUING CONVERSATION

One day as I came down from the upper room on Mount Zion, I walked through the courtyard of Yeshiva Diaspora (a Bible college for young men who are studying to be rabbis). A lively conversation was taking place between two groups of students. One group contended that Israel must build the temple soon and this would bring the Messiah to Israel and begin the age of world redemption. The other faction disagreed saying, "No, we must work for the spiritual rebirth of Israel and that will bring the Messiah. He will command the building of the temple." But there was no disagreement that Messiah would come and that the temple would be rebuilt on Mount Moriah.

A VISIT WITH AN ISRAELI ARCHITECT

The late Meyer Ben Uri lived in Kiryat Schmuel (Village of Samuel) suburban to Haifa. He was an architect of world renown. Religious buildings were his specialty.

I had gone to him to discuss his scientific theories concerning the ark of Noah and the great flood. While in his studios, I noticed his oil painting of King David dancing and rejoicing before the ark of the Lord, being brought back to Jerusalem. Later I noticed a small model of the ark of the covenant, made of copper and wood. When I inquired about it he asked, "Are you also interested in the ark of the covenant, and the rebuilding of our holy temple?" I assured him that I most certainly was interested. He showed me various models of the furnishings of the temple including a full-size menorah (seven-branched lampstand) made of papier-mache and plaster. Ben Uri commented that when the real thing was produced it would be made of pure hand-beaten gold. We discussed his plans for the temple. He said that certain details for the construction would have to be given by revelation from the Almighty. He expressed *no doubt that the temple would be built on Mount Moriah.* He expressed a hope of being chosen as the designer. "It will not be a Hollywood temple—it will be a biblical temple—it will be a reconstruction of the Temple of Solomon the Magnificent."

A RIVAL ARCHITECT?

Some have conjectured that Moshe Safde could well be chosen to build the temple. Safde designed the world famous Habitant condo-village at the 1967 Montreal World's Fair. The new construction near the Temple Mount in the revitalized Jewish quarter of the old city of Jerusalem reflects his ability to create modern structures that blend in with ancient surroundings.

An elderly rabbi from Safed has also drawn plans for the next temple. Among other periodicals, this fact was registered in an article in *Saudi Report!*

AT SETTLEMENT OPHRA

We took one of our tour groups to visit the Village Ophra, one of the so-called "illegal" settlements on the West Bank near Bethel. Ophra is near biblical Bethel and Shiloh. Rabbi Borer serves these communities and often speaks to our tour groups about the biblical significance of the area. He has been a great source of information for us all.

In the dining room of the Ophra community there is a large picture.

It is an aerial photograph of Jerusalem. However, there is a peculiar feature incorporated into it. Someone has airbrushed out the Moslem shrine, the Dome of the Rock, and has replaced it with an artist's concept of the ancient Temple of Israel. This indicates a belief on the part of the artist that the mosque will be removed before the temple is built. More recent scholarship (the findings of Dr. Asher Kaufman) indicates that the temple did not stand where the Dome of the Rock is. Rather, it stood about one hundred yards to the north of the Dome. Some conjecture (based on Rev. 11:1, 2) that as a compromise measure, the temple and Moslem shrine could stand side by side on Mount Moriah. Only time will tell which of these views is correct.

The Temple picture at Settlement Ophra.

AN OUTSTANDING ARTIST

Artist Nahum Arbel was the first Jew to move into the Old City after its capture in June, 1967. He says that his art is simply an expression of his quest for God. His mystical paintings frequently feature a temple standing on Mount Moriah. Another theme he frequently deals with is the New Jerusalem coming down from heaven and meeting with the old Jerusalem.

THIS RELIGIOUS CENTRE
THE SEAT OF THE CHIEF RABBINATE OF ISRAEL
ERECTED TO THE GLORY OF GOD AND HIS HOLY TORAH
WAS DEDICATED TO THE MEMORY OF THE LATE
SHLOMO AND NECHA SARAH WOLFSON
BY THE WOLFSON FAMILY
LONDON ENGLAND

Plaque at the Hechel Shlomo—by the Great Synagogue of Jerusalem.

IS THE TEMPLE UNDER CONSTRUCTION?

For some time we have read various theories that the temple is under construction, either on the west side of Jerusalem (the new city) or underground. I think the latter can be dismissed without too much comment. After our underground explorations and inquiries at the Temple Mount in May, 1981, with our TV crew, we can report that the temple is *not* under construction under Mount Moriah.

THE HECHEL SHLOMO

There is a persistent rumor that the temple is the Great Synagogue next door to the Hechel Shlomo, or palace of Solomon. Hechel does not mean "temple" as some have said (1 Kings 21:1). The word is consistently translated *palace* throughout the Old Testament. Nor is the Solomon (Shlomo) the Solomon of the Bible. The building was built with contributions from the wealthy Wolfson family and named in honor of Shlomo Wolfson. Actually the Hechel Shlomo is the religious headquarters of the Orthodox Jewish faith. Here both the chief rabbis of the Ashkenazi and the Shephardic communities have their offices.

The *Great Synagogue* of Jerusalem is *not* the temple. When the temple is built it will be on Mount Moriah since it is recognized and honored by God in its designated location.

137

MATERIALS COMPILED?

I find it hard to believe (there is no hard evidence, only unfounded rumors) that stones cut in Bedford, Indiana, have been shipped to Israel for the building of the temple. Anyone who has been to Israel is well aware that stone is one thing Israel does not have to import! It is a most plentiful commodity! It is altogether possible that precut stones are ready to be put in place, but we have no primary evidence. I conjecture from some comments I have heard that there is truth to this, but we cannot be positive. It would be no surprise to find out that the temple could be built within a couple of months.

WHEN WILL THE TEMPLE BE REBUILT?

There is no revelation in the Scripture as to whether the temple could be built before the Rapture or Tribulation, or in an interim between the Rapture and the onset of the Tribulation. Or it could be during the first part of the Tribulation. All we know for sure is that it is in existence at the middle of the seven years, for that is when it is profaned by the Antichrist.

INTERESTING DISCOVERIES AT THE TEMPLE SITE

In 1968 I was able to get back under the area where the "digs" were beginning. Now there is an arch cut into the wall that is perpendicular to the Wailing Wall. One can go into a large vaulted room that has been emptied of debris of centuries. The Wailing Wall continues on north for some distance, under the built-up area. As you follow the wall you come to a grating in the floor. It covers a shaft dug down fifty-three feet to the original level of the time of Jesus and Herod. It is the opinion of some that the massive underground stones below the ground level could be a remnant of the Temple of King Solomon. This must be taken as conjecture at this time.

WHEN YOU SEE THIS...

At the south end of the wall around the Temple Mountain (extension southward of the Wailing Wall), there is a large stone covered with glass for protection. This stone was uncovered within recent years. It has an inscription from Isaiah 66:14 chiseled upon it. Isaiah 66:14 is prefaced by the words "ye shall be comforted in Jerusalem..." (vs. 13). Then the words of verse 14: "And when you see this, your heart shall rejoice, and your bones shall flourish like an herb...." Perhaps some pious Jew chiseled these words as the temple was in flames, urged by the Spirit to do so. Then the stone was covered with rubble, only to be uncovered in recent times. Some of the rabbis of Israel express the opinion that the stone is a sign that the coming Messiah is near at hand. Who could deny it?

When the Messiah comes He will superintend the building of the final (fourth) Millennial Temple seen in vision by the prophets (see Ezek. 40-48 and Zech. 6:12).

TIME FOR THE TEMPLE

In previous times people touring Israel asked their Holy Land guides and new Israeli friends, "Will Israel rebuild the temple?" One could count on getting a stock answer. The answer was, "No. Israel has no need for the temple. The spirit of the nation is the only temple we need." Even deeply religious people would dodge the issue. The issue was too hot politically. Everyone assumes that the building of the temple demands the destruction of the Moslem shrine, the Dome of the Rock, which allegedly stands on the very site of the ancient temple of the Jewish people.

Today we see more and more Israelis willing to speak of their aspirations to have the temple rebuilt. Not only the religious Jewish communities are showing an interest in the rebuilding of the temple, but even the liberal *Jerusalem Post,* a secular newspaper, has carried several articles about the possibility of the rebuilding of the temple. I quote from an article they published on February 11, 1989, *"A Place for the Lord"* written by Pinchas H. Pell:

"The modern Jew found it difficult to face the binding obligation to rebuild the sanctuary, combined with the great dreams linked with it. He has suppressed the demands they make on him.

"He was hesitant to use religious language to describe the historic return to Zion and to national sovereignty. There are indeed a few exceptions to this, as for example, 'the third Temple,' once used by Ben-Gurion (in 1957) or the excessive use of the prophetic terminology of the 'ingathering of the exiles' during the years of mass aliya.

"Far beyond the formal commandment, the yearning to behold an actual concrete expression of a central religious and national focal point permeates all Jewish history.

"Another argument is that the rebuilding as postulated by Maimonides requires a certain order of events: 1) coming to the land; 2) appointment of a king from the house of David; 3) blotting out the descendants of Amalek; and only then 4) the building of the Temple. The counter-

This beautiful jigsaw puzzle depicts Jerusalem and its surroundings. Created for Jewish children and young people, it is now catching attention of Christians who are interested in the temple and biblical prophecy.

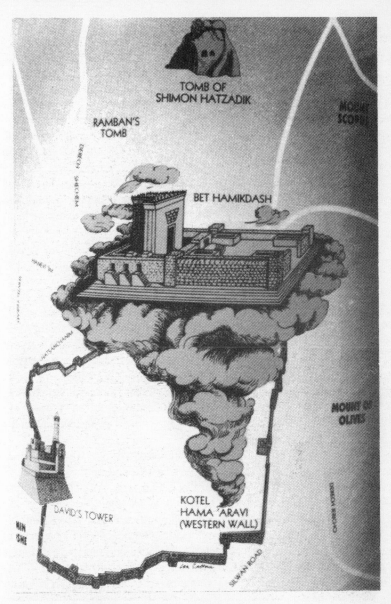

The production of this puzzle by Mr. Freidman in New York is
further indication of growing Jewish interest in the temple. The
puzzle shows the temple on a cloud above the Temple Mountain.

argument claims that, while this is indeed the ideal order of events, the events themselves are not necessarily mutually interdependent and one must carry out whichever is possible at the time."

Non-religious publications such as *Time* magazine are beginning to pay attention to the Jewish aspirations for the building of the temple. The October 16, 1989, edition carried an article titled, "Time for a New Temple?" The article is not entirely accurate in saying that "Next week, Israel's Ministry of Religious Affairs will sponsor a first-ever conference of Temple research." Several conferences have already taken place in years gone by. We have a poster in Hebrew announcing such a conference a few years ago. It is possible, however, that *Time* was indicating that this would be the first conference officially recognized by Israel's Minister of Religious Affairs. Here is the quotation from the *Time* article:

"Next week Israel's Ministry of Religious Affairs will sponsor a first-ever Conference of Temple Research to discuss whether contemporary Jews are obligated to rebuild the Temple. However, several small organizations in Jerusalem believe the question is settled. They are zealously making preparations for the new Temple in spite of the doctrinal obstacles and the certainty of provoking Muslem fury.

"Two Talmudic schools located near the Western (Wailing) Wall are teaching nearly two hundred students the elaborate details to Temple service. Other groups are researching the family lines of Jewish priests who alone may conduct sacrifices. Former Chief Rabbi Shlomo Goren, who heads another Temple Mount organization, believes his research has fixed a location of the ancient Holy of Holies so that Jews can enter the Mount without sacrilege.

"No group is more zealous than the Temple Institute, whose spiritual leader, fifty-year-old Rabbi Israel Ariel, was one of the first Israeli paratroopers to reach the Mount in 1967. 'Our task,' states the institute's American-born director, Zev Golan, 'is to advance the cause of the Temple and to prepare for its establishment, not just talk about it.'

"One difficulty is the requirement (as in Numbers 19:1-10) that priests purify their bodies with the cremated ashes of an unblemished red heifer before they enter the Temple. Following a go-ahead from the Chief Rabbinate, institute operatives spent two weeks in August scouting Europe for heifer embryos that will shortly be implanted into cows at an Israeli cattle ranch.

"But historian David Solomon insists that a new Temple is essential: 'It was the essence of our Jewish being, the unifying force of our people...but sooner or later, in a week or in a century, it will be done.

142

On the trail of the holy cow

IT HAS ALL the makings of a so-Hasidic thriller. A young Tora scholar in Jerusalem enlists the help of a prominent geneticist in Bell Dagan, an ex-Southern Baptist minister from Texas, and a veterinarian in Sweden to unlock the secret of ritual purification for worship in the Holy Temple.

But Menahem Burstin, a scholar who specializes in the Temple service, insists that his search for the rare red heifer is not a swashbuckling adventure: it is serious research aimed in part at taking the fear out of such practices as animal sacrifices.

"My father taught me kodashim and tohorot [orders of the Mishna dealing with the Temple service] when I was a child, so for me these subjects were natural," Burstin said last week in his time-bomb-lined

Even if reports of a herd of pure red cows in Sweden prove unfounded, scholar Menahem Burstin is convinced that genetic engineering can produce a kosher red heifer required for Temple services. His worldwide search is part of his attempt to demystify the ritual of animal sacrifice, reports JOEL REBIBO

apartment in Jerusalem's Ramema quarter. "But when I lectured about the Temple — to ultra-Orthodox, national-religious, Neturei Karta,

kibbutz youth — I found that people were scared by the idea of sacrifices and consequently scared of the rebuilding of the Temple."

On the advice of leading rabbinical figures like Rabbi Zvi Yehuda Kook and Rabbi Eliezer Schach, Burstin began researching the more "esthetic" aspects of Temple service, like incense offering.

He consulted with botanists and painstakingly gathered herbs and spices from all over the world to find the ingredients required by the Tora for such offerings.

Later, his studies led him to explore the mystery of Techelet, a bluish [some say violet] dye that was used in the Temple and that was also prescribed for the fringes of the tzitit. After nearly 14 years of researching the dye, which is produced by a sea-creature called the hilazon, Burstin published a book on the subject last year.

At the same time, he began a worldwide search for the red heifer, used during Temple times to "purify" those who had become ritually unfit through contact with the dead.

THE REASONS for the mitzva of the red heifer are not clear – King Solomon said of it: "I thought I would have wisdom but it is far from me" – but the specifications for such a cow are quite explicit: it must be pure red [even two black hairs render it unfit], must have no blemishes, and must never have borne a yoke.

During his search, Burstin came across two herds of red heifers. A

guess God's plans for a Temple. "I don't have to do thinking for Him," says Burstin who teaches at Mercaz Harav in Jerusalem. "But I have obligation to study all the laws Tora, including those relat Temple service. This func research is exciting because it to life all the verses and the and talmudic literature Temple service.

According to that literatu red heifer is burned togethe etz erez, ezuv and tola'at [cedar-wood, hyssop and s Burstin is convinced that accurately identified these the scarlet, for instance, is a

The goal is

Science Helping Hunt For Pure-Red Heifer

Tel Aviv (JTA) -- What does the scientific breeding of cattle in Israel have to do with building the Third Temple?

A great deal, say officials of the Temple Institute in Jerusalem, who concern themselves with preparations for the coming of the Messiah.

Last week, they persuaded the Sephardic chief rabbi,

ed with water can purify anyone who has become unclean by, for example, contact with a corpse.

To be suitable for the sacrifice, the cow must be pure red, without a single hair of another color. So far, none has been found.

But the Temple Institute is intrigued by the breeding experiments going on at the G and G. Ranch owne Danny Greenberg explaine

143

This photo appears in the Temple Institute. The red cow is on a secret farm location in Sweden. Attempts are being made to "clone" her in order to obtain a red heifer.

And we will be ready for it.' He adds with quiet urgency, 'Every day's delay is a stain on the nation.' "

TREASURE OF THE TEMPLE

We found in the Jewish quarter of the old wall city of Jerusalem an institution that has been established for research on all of the implements and furniture of the temple. They also do further research on the nature of the garments of the priests and the high priests of the Temple of Israel.

The woman who lectured to us about the temple implements and the garments of the priest said, "These are not examples, nor models. These are the actual objects that we will soon be using in our new temple for the worship of the Lord." Following are pictures of several of the temple implements, each with a caption briefly explaining what it is. You must understand that these are only a few of the objects that we saw while at the Temple Institute in the Old City. Also, let me clarify another matter. These are not ancient implements that have been discovered by archaeologists that have been digging through the layers of history. These are merely manufactured objects that have been brought into production at the Institute after years of arduous study from many sources as to what the implements should look like and what their size should be and how they should be used in temple worship. These are very serious people and it was never their intention to merely have a display of items for Christian and Jewish pilgrims to observe. That is simply a sideline from their research. Here are some photographs of the implements of the temple. I made these photographs on my first visit to the Institute.

The Temple Institute. This is where the implements of the temple can be seen.

The lottery box was used to decide which goat was sacrificed and which was sent into the wilderness, on Yom Kippur, The Day of Atonement.

Jewish lecturer speaks to our tour group on the lots (she is holding up the lots).

Tiara (crown) for the priest, worn during certain services in the temple.

David's Harp (Kinor David) built to Talmudic specifications for use by the Messiah. On loan to the Temple Institute until the Messiah's arrival.

Silver trumpets in wood case—in the precision of their resemblance to those of old, a symbol of our return to Zion. Just as we left—we have returned! Each trumpet is one meter (3 ft.) of sterling silver; one is inlaid with gold.

Container on cart for removal of the ashes of a completed sacrifice.

Loom for weaving linen for the priest's garments.

Linen emerges from the loom.

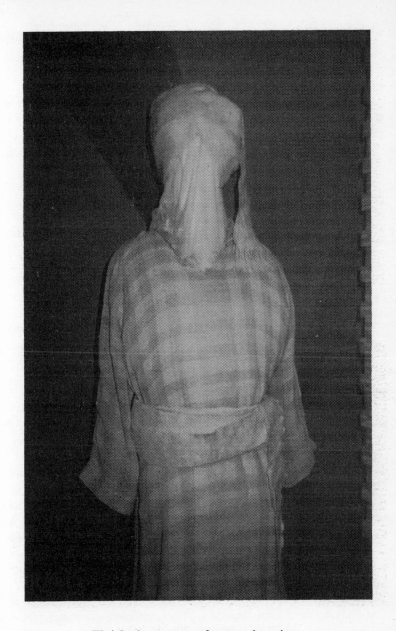

Finished garment of a temple priest.

The Temple Institute is located at 24 Misgav Ladakh St. in the Jewish quarter of the old walled city of Jerusalem. Research and development of the furniture, garments, and utensils used in the temple is undertaken there. The facility is open to the public (small admission charge) and every tour group should go there and request a lecture. A short video is also shown. For advance information, the mailing address is P.O. Box 31876, Jerusalem, Israel; telephone: 02-894-119. Be sure to call for an appointment as the place is small and many groups want to get in to observe these wonders.

AN AMAZING STORY

The December 1981 issue of *Hadassah* magazine, which is published by a Jewish ladies' organization by that same name, had an article titled, "Getting Ready—A Very Special Yeshiva." It tells of a school in Old Jerusalem that teaches young Levites and Cohanim to prepare for the building of the temple, for the coming of Messiah, and for the performance of the rites of temple worship. *Hadassah* tells the story:

"In a delapidated stone building tucked away in a corner of the old city of Jerusalem, a small group of young scholars huddles around a massive oak table, preparing for the end of the world as we know it.

"They are ready at a moment's notice—tomorrow, tonight, now—to rush out and usher in the Messianic era in the traditional manner prescribed by normative Judaism.

"It is certainly a time-honored Jewish tradition that the Messiah will come, perhaps even 'tomorrow,' but, asks Motti Hacohen, one of the young scholars, 'What is the sense in asking for the Messiah to come if we are not really ready to meet Him?' Motti is getting ready.

"Hacohen, barely 25, did not always plan for the future so assiduously. He knew he was a kohen (a priest), but that never affected his life very much. Until, that is, the day he looked up from his opened Talmud while he was studying at the Ramat Hamagshimim Yeshiva on the Golan Heights and espied a friend poring over a tractate dealing with the laws of the temple and the priesthood.

" 'Why in the world,' Hacohen asked, 'are you studying such obscure laws?'

" 'Why,' shot back his friend, 'aren't you? I'm not even a kohen and I'm studying these laws. You, as a kohen, should be doubly interested in regulations that apply specifically to you.' Motti accepted the challenge, and it changed his life."

It is a fact that the Levites and Cohanim know their tribal identity beyond doubt. This was demonstrated to me in a long conversation

An article in *Hadassah* led us to the School of the Levites.

with a Jewish college professor and other Jewish friends. Our *Audio Prophecy Digest* previously told this story. *Hadassah* next tells of Hacohen's search for a school. (Yeshiva = a Jewish seminary where young men are trained to become rabbis in the Jewish ministry.)

SEARCH FOR A YESHIVA

"Hacohen searched throughout Israel for a yeshiva that could provide a crash course in matters pertaining to the rebuilding of the Temple. He needed to study the order of the priests' services, associated rituals, and other subjects not immediately applicable to Jewish life in 1981, but indispensable for the coming of the Messianic era. Hacohen found only one such yeshiva, but it had a pronounced anti-Zionist bent and he could not in good conscience enroll there. The dilemma led him to think about forming a new house of learning—Torat Kohanim."

I, too, had searched for such a school, because I was intrigued with the very concept that young men were training for the priesthood. It could be no less than that. For a whole day our brilliant guide, Avigdor Rosenberg, along with Ramona, my wife, and Sandy, my daughter, searched and inquired throughout the Mea Sherim quarter where many of the Orthodox Jews live.

A book about end-time Bible prophecy had sparked our interest in the school, named Yeshiva Avodas Hakodesh. After a day of searching we found some leads but nothing substantial. Finally we decided that we were chasing shadows and that the author was merely fantasizing the whole thing. The book had included a photograph that purported to be a picture of the building the school was located in, but we could not find anything like it.

After reading the article in *Hadassah* we decided that our rejection of the Yeshiva in the Mea Sherim idea might be premature. Hacohen *found* a school but could not accept it because it was anti-Zionist. The Neturi Karta sect in the Mea Sherim quarter is anti-Zionist. We had talked to one of their leaders that we thought was going to tell us momentarily that school existed and was in operation. Then the rabbi became evasive. The area was plastered with anti-Israel signs and slogans. Think of it! Anti-Zionist Jews! One report is that one of these radical groups actually invited the PLO to invade Israel, offering to help them. After reading the *Hadassah* article about Hacohen's search for a school, it makes me think he found the one we failed to locate (anti-Zionist, etc.).

HACOHEN DECIDES TO START A SCHOOL

"One Friday, several Israeli newspapers printed a small ad modestly announcing a seminar on the priesthood and the Holy Temple. Hacohen had placed the ad before he had even secured a place for the event; he had no way of knowing if anyone would respond or if the affair would ever come off.

"Maybe, Hacohen figured optimistically, twenty or thirty people would express a tentative interest. He was amazed when he received three hundred fifty replies.

"The seminar, Hacohen decided, would have to take place in Jerusalem; and since the temple figured prominently in the discussion he envisioned, it should naturally be in the Old City during Passover. He went to existing institutions, only to find them too small, or unwilling, or not available on the dates he requested. He began exploring ideas that others brought him, and one such suggestion led to the wife of Rabbi Nahman Kahane who had a key to a building in a predominantly Muslim section.

"Somewhat skeptical about the notion of holding Jewish classes in a Muslim neighborhood, Hacohen changed his mind when he saw the building. It had served as a yeshiva until 1936 (the school's fifty-year-old name, Torath Hayim, was still visible over the doorway), and it contained a huge assembly hall which would suit his purposes. When he entered into negotiations with the self-appointed Arab caretaker,

This is the school Hacohen found in the Moslem Quarter of Old Jerusalem.

Hacohen learned that this particular Muslim had been living in the rickety building and caring for it since the expulsion of the Jewish populace from the area in 1936.

UNUSUAL STATEMENT BY MOSLEM CARETAKER

"The Arab had ensured the sanctity not only of the building itself, but of the more than twenty thousand Bibles and siddurim (prayer books) inside as well. How, asked the incredulous Hacohen, had the man managed to prevent harm from coming to the yeshiva during decades of war, riots, and concerted Jordanian destruction of Jewish buildings? 'I didn't watch over the building,' the caretaker said. 'It watched over me.' "

Hacohen had found books vital to the starting of his school. The Arab caretaker had felt that he was an instrument of destiny in the hands of God. Strange things—but not so strange when you think of the exciting things happening in the realm of fulfilled and soon-to-be-fulfilled prophecy. We believe the temple will be rebuilt and it may be very soon. The Bible does not indicate whether it will be before or after the Rapture of the Church. But it will be in existence in the time of the seventieth week. See Daniel 9:24-27; Matthew 24:15 and following; 2 Thessalonians 2:3,4; Revelation 11:1,2 etc. Now, more information from *Hadassah:*

REBUILDING THE TEMPLE—SUCCESSFUL SEMINAR

"Arrangements were made to use the hall during Passover 1978, and the seminar was so successful that a second one was held the following Sukkot. The seminars have continued on these two holidays ever since, attracting as many as fifteen hundred participants, including the Sefardic Chief Rabbi of Israel.

"At the second seminar, Aaron Bier, a popular Israeli tour guide and author, told Hacohen about another building, not far away, to which he had access. Hacohen and his nucleus of devoted scholars could, suggested Bier, live there while studying. Eli Gorodetzer, formerly of Brookline, Massachusetts, and now public relations chief for Yeshiva Ateret Cohanim, recalls Bier's offer:

"Bier was talking about the Moghrabi Building, which was built in 1850 by David Ben Shimon and housed Moroccan Jewish families until they were ousted in the 1936 Arab riots. It contains twenty rooms in a three-story complex. Fifty years ago, there were ten thousand Jews in that vicinity. Separated from the main Jewish Quarter, they formed their own communal institutions—schools, hospital, orphanage, even a free kitchen. The kitchen had a huge communal pot of cholent from which every family would take their Shabbat lunch.

"A half-century earlier, Bier had been one of those ten thousand Jews who was forced to flee. He now presented Hacohen with a demand, not a request: 'There will be ten people living here next week.' After Hacohen had accepted Bier's offer, a prominent Jerusalem attorney contacted him. His tone was supportive but critical: 'It's good you're having a seminar on the temple, but think a minute. Do you want your Cohanim and Levites to go out to greet the Messiah through this dirty, neglected area? Surely, they should have a more fitting path.' "

TEMPLE MODELS—TEMPLE PICTURES

Today, the yeshiva has many regular students, most of them Cohanim or Levites. Over fifty people live in the various buildings and study elsewhere. And there is a list of thirty additional families who are waiting for the basic repairs that will enable them to move in.

Every morning, classes are held similar to those of countless other Torah-learning centers. Afternoons and evenings are devoted to those portions of the Talmud and works by Maimonides dealing with the Bet Hamikdash, the Holy Temple. The students have built a model replica of the ancient temple based on their studies of its construction and dimensions. Almost every student has a framed photo in his room with a rendering of the temple as it might have appeared in its days of glory.

Scholars at work at the School of the Levites.

Rabbi Hacohen shows temple model to our tour group.

PREPARING FOR MESSIAH

The men and women of Ateret Cohanim are preparing. They believe as fervently in the hope of the future as in the glory of the past. So far, their faith has rebuilt several buildings, created two new yeshivas, and involved thousands of students, seminar participants, and tourists.

Perhaps, as one student said wistfully to a visitor, "If more of us believed, we could bring the Messiah that much faster. We could rebuild the temple and make the world a better place in which to live."

This lengthy article in *Hadasseh* is another indication that there is a growing Messianic consciousness in Israel. There is an increasing sense that we are living in the end-times. Christians have believed and preached this. Now our words are strengthened by the words and deeds of our Jewish friends. The *Hadassah* article was written by Charley J. Levine, formerly director of Zionist Affairs for *Hadassah* in New York and now a resident of Jerusalem.

I have just returned from my forty-sixth trip to the land of Israel. The things that we discovered on this last trip were so remarkable that it would take volumes to share in its entirety. Here is an interesting development. Whereas we have reported to you about the School of the Levites, we now can report that there are three well-established

Yeshivas (religious schools) for the training of the Levites and the priests of the new and future temple of Israel. Never before has there been such a high level of interest in the re-establishing of the Holy House of God on Mount Moriah among the Jews themselves as there is in our day.

EZEKIEL STONES

The atmosphere of Jerusalem seems to be filled with mystery and intrigue. Some of the strangest stories that I have ever heard have come to me from sensible, well-established people in the land of Israel. Many years ago, I met a man named Yehuda. He began to tell me unusual things and shared with me information about strange archaeological artifacts. Finally he told me that in a secret, highly secured room on the west side of Jerusalem there were sixty-four marble and four basalt tablets about fourteen inches square. Written upon these stone tablets was the Book of Ezekiel in the original Hebrew language. Later Yehuda showed me pictures of the mystical Ezekiel stones. To say the least, I was intrigued by what this might mean. How old were these stones? Where did they come from? Who found them? How did they arrive in the land of Israel? I asked these and many other questions of my friend Yehuda. Slowly in visit after visit, he eked out information to me as follows:

The stones were taken by grave robbers out of the tomb of Ezekiel, which is very near the site of ancient Babylon in the modern day country of Iraq. This, of course, is where Ezekiel, along with the exiles, spent the period known as the Babylonian Captivity of the Jews and there wrote his book of prophecy.

Finally, after some years had gone by, Yehuda decided to let me come along to see and to photograph the Ezekiel stones. To my amazement, they were unlike any stones with words upon them that I had ever seen. When you look at a gravestone, or a monument of any kind, you expect to see the words etched into the stones. However, the Ezekiel stones are totally different. The letters on the Ezekiel tiles leap out from the stone or stand away from the stone in bas-relief fashion. As far as I have been able to discover so far, there is no other example of any extensive ancient writing that uses this style of carving. As a matter of fact, Yehuda says that it is a mystery to the researchers working on the Ezekiel project as to how this unique feature was accomplished.

The Ezekiel stones were carried by the grave robbers to Syria and the stones were purchased by a well-to-do Christian Arab lady living in the Syrian city of Damascus. She told a religious authority about the stones. He was eager to examine them. Upon examination, he said that these stones have the Book of Ezekiel written on them in Hebrew and that he thought they were something very important. In the 1940s, before the war between the Arabs and Israel, a Jewish man by the name of Davida Hacohen heard about the stones. He was able to travel to Damascus, Syria. When he finally saw the stones, he was totally amazed and tried to purchase them. However, his attempts were refused. He was able to offer a very large sum of money for the stones, but the lady and the clergyman (both negotiated with him) finally decided to refuse his offer, regardless of how large it might be.

When the war broke out in May of 1948, after Israel declared her independence, a messenger came from Syria to Davida Hacohen, saying that they wanted him to purchase the stones for the last amount of money mentioned—with one extra provision. There were 250 Arab orphan children in an orphanage in Haifa. He had to provide them safe transportation to Beirut, Lebanon, where their people would pick them up and carry them to safety in Damascus. There were many more details, but without compromising the security of certain individuals, even at this late date, we cannot go into an explanation of how the gold bullion was obtained and transported for the purchase of the Ezekiel stones. Nor am I free at this time to give a full explanation as to how the children were transported out of the war zone and into Beirut, Lebanon.

Suffice to say that the stones fell into the hands of Davida Hacohen, who later gave them to his friend, Mr. Izhak Ben-Zvi, who ultimately became the president of the state of Israel. Ben-Zvi kept the stones stored in his home until someone indicated that they should be put into a safety deposit vault. Later, my friend Yehuda Oppenheim gained permission to examine the stones. He was amazed at some of the things that he discovered. Yehuda obtained funds from a Jewish sponsor to build the small room where the stones are currently standing on a rack available for study by scientists, archeologists, historians, and linguists. Yehuda told my fascinated group of Christian pilgrims why he believed that this was the original Book of Ezekiel not a copy of it but direct from the hands of a prophet.

If Yehuda and his associates are ever able to prove their theory concerning the originality of the stones, it will be one of the greatest, if not *the* greatest, archaeological discovery of all time. Remember that our Bibles today are based on copies of copies of copies. No original manuscript of any book of the Bible is in existence as far as we know, unless it is these Ezekiel stones.

Part of our tour group listening to the lecturer on the amazing Ezekiel stones.

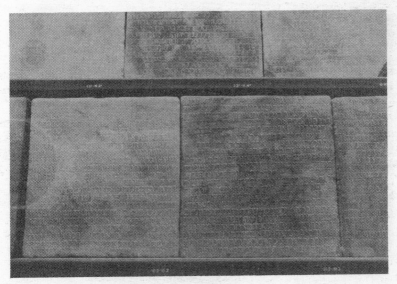

Part of the Book of Ezekiel on marble tablets.

Note the bas relief lettering on the stones. The raised lettering mystifies scholars. How was it accomplished?

Sixty-four of the stones are marble. The rest are made of basalt stone.

Interestingly enough, there are hidden messages that I am not at liberty to disclose at this time, within the stones themselves and by the manner in which the letters are arranged on the stones. I have carefully guarded the confidentiality that Yehuda requested of me throughout the years. What I am telling you now is as much as he has given me permission to release. I think that later on, we will be able to give you the complete story of the Ezekiel stones, and truly the world is going to be amazed at some of the things that will be revealed at that time. When asked by one of my friends accompanying me on a tour group a few months ago, whether or not they didn't want more people to come and see the stones, one of the associate directors of the institution where they are stored said in shocked horror, "No, please don't send any other groups, we do not receive tour groups."

My friend asked, "Why are we here today?"

He said, "The only reason that you are here is due to our friendship and trust in Dr. Lewis, but please do not send us any tour groups. We are not prepared to receive them and we do not wish to talk quite so openly as we have talked to you today."

It is my opinion that the researchers, Yehuda, and his friends have decided to talk to me and in a sense use our tour groups as a means of leaking information to the general public so that they can watch public reaction to their story. Truly, when Yehuda and his associates decide to publish their findings and theories concerning the Ezekiel stones, it is going to rock the world. Do you remember when the Dead Sea Scrolls, including the Book of Isaiah, were found in the 1940s? I know that you have heard about it. The oldest possible date that can be placed on the Scroll of Isaiah is about 200-250 years B.C. That means that the Isaiah Scroll is a copy that was produced about five hundred years after the original was written. So important was the finding of the Dead Sea Scrolls that there is hardly a month that goes by, even today, that there is not an article in some scientific or general publication or a book published about the amazing Dead Sea Scrolls. Just imagine if the marble and basalt tablets are the very original Book of Ezekiel. It is going to be the greatest find of all time unless the ark of the covenant should be discovered in the meantime, before the proof of Yehuda Oppenheim and his associates is offered publicly and to the scientific world and archaeological world in general.

Grant Jeffery, author of best selling prophecy books, was inspired to do his research on the Ezekiel stones at a camp meeting in Canada where Dr. Lewis showed pictures and spoke about the stones.

Dr. Stanley Horton is one of the leading Hebrew language experts. He has examined our pictures of the Ezekiel stones and has listened to taped lectures by Oppenheim. Concerning the claim that this is the original Book of Ezekiel he says, "It is a strong possibility (although not yet proven)."

LOCATION OF THE TEMPLE

In 1968, I visited the Temple Mountain for the very first time. I walked into the Moslem shrine, The Dome of the Rock, with my Israeli guide, Pinhas Komorosky from Netanya, Israel. I looked in amazement at the As-sakrah, the rock upon which it is said that Abraham was prepared to offer up Isaac on the Mount of Sacrifice, Mount Moriah. It was my impression at that time that the Rock of Sacrifice was in or under the Holy of Holies in the ancient Temple of Israel. I understand now that there is a difference of opinion among scholars on that question. There is a solid body of scholarship indicating that this idea is accurate. At any rate, I said, "Komorosky, how big is that rock of sacrifice?" He replied, "Oh, it's about forty by sixty-five feet."

I said, "Komorosky, the temple never stood here on the site of the Dome of the Rock."

He looked at me in amazement said, "You know, that flies in the face of all tradition and all scholarship."

I said, "Well, I don't know about tradition and don't know how much scholarship there is behind it, but I don't believe the temple ever stood here."

I went outside and walked around in the Temple Mountain. After a while I asked the twenty-five people who accompanied me on my first Holy Land tour to come over and look at something about a hundred yards north of the Dome of the Rock. There was a small cupola that stands about twenty-two feet high. As I looked at this structure, I was filled with a sense of knowledge that here was the place where the temple actually had stood. As far as I know, no one had ever given out that point of view prior to 1968. I could, however, be wrong about that or simply lacking in knowledge concerning previous ideas on the matter. At any rate, I certainly didn't find anyone at that time who agreed with my idea or who had had that particular concept presented to them. Komorosky thought that it was completely off the wall, and I can certainly understand why he reacted as he did.

A couple of years later, Dr. Asher Kaufman, a professor at Hebrew University, announced his scientific, archaeological, and historical findings, proving—at least to his satisfaction—that the temple had stood about a hundred yards north of the Dome of the Rock under a cupola that is known by the Moslems as the "Dome of the Spirit" and also by the title "The Dome of the Tablets." The tablets, of course, would remind us of the fact that the ark of the covenant sits in the Holy of Holies and inside the ark were the two tablets of the Law, the Ten Commandments given to Moses. Kaufman's ideas have been written

Professor Dr. Asher Kaufman, Hebrew University.

up extensively in prestigious publications. Perhaps the one that most of our readers would be best acquainted with would be the *Biblical Archeological Review* magazine, which carried a long and lavishly illustrated article on Dr. Kaufman's ideas.

We have gotten to know Dr. Kaufman as a personal friend throughout the last several years. He always speaks to our tour groups when we are in Jerusalem. We are very privileged to have him, because ours is the only tour group for which he takes time to speak and present a slide show.

The following words appeared in the *Jerusalem Post* and are worthy of inclusion at this point:

"Remains of a wall said to contain Herodian-style stones were found on the Temple Mount 12 years ago—almost precisely where a controversial researcher places the eastern wall of Herod's Temple.

"Knowledge of this wall—the first possible remains of the Jerusalem Temple ever uncovered—has been suppressed for the past decade because of its possible political implications. Although some scholars

Dome of the Tablets (Spirits): Possible location of the ancient Temple of Israel.

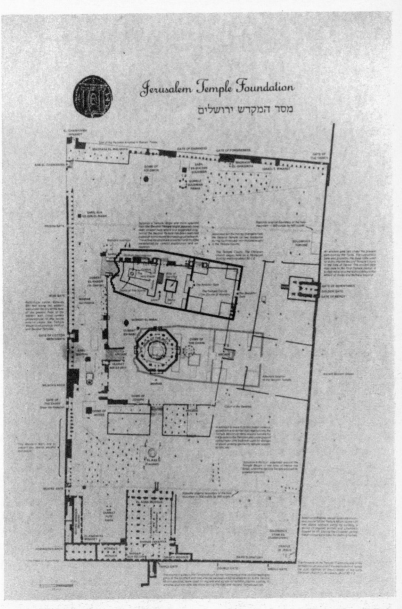

The Kaufman research places the temple one hundred yards north of the Dome of the Rock.

were aware of it, at least one of Israel's senior archaeologists heard about it for the first time in March, 1980 from a reporter.

"The Western Wall, the focus of Jewish prayer for centuries, is not a remnant of the temple but of the massive wall supporting the Temple Mount.

"The wall was uncovered in 1970 when the Supreme Moslem Council excavated a pit for water storage just off the northeast edge of the platform supporting the Dome of the Rock. A government archaeologist, who asked to remain anonymous, visited the site after being informed that ancient remains had been uncovered. He told *The Jerusalem Post* that he saw several courses of a massive wall, some of whose stones had the smooth margins typical of the Herodian stones seen in the Western Wall. By the time he returned with other archaeologists, however, the remains—five meters long, two meters thick and several courses high—had been knocked down. The archaeologist said he wrote a report on his find, including sketches of the stones, but did not publish it. 'I just felt the matter was too sensitive,' he said. The sensitivity lay in the proximity of the Jews' most holy site with the Islamic shrine.

"The water reservoir was being dug as a precautionary move against fire dictated by the arson at Al Aksa Mosque the previous year. That fire had been set by a crazed Australian Christian who wanted to destroy the mosque so that the temple could be rebuilt.

"Word of the report reached Dr. Asher Kaufman, a Hebrew University physicist of Scottish origin, who, for the past few years, has been devoting most of his time to research into the exact site of the First and Second Temples. Basing himself mainly on written sources, particularly the Mishna, his own archaeological observations and complicated scientific calculations, the orthodox scientist had already drawn up a detailed plan of the second temple. He contacted the archaeologist who let him read his report.

"They saw that the wall, whose remains had been found, was parallel to and 2.6 meters from where Kaufman had placed the eastern wall of the temple complex. Kaufman deduced that the 2.6 meter difference was due to his having erred in the thickness of the wall between the temple's two main courts. 'This is the only wall to which there is no written reference and its thickness must be guessed,' he said. By readjusting its thickness to that of the outer walls of the temple—five cubits, or 2.18 meters, according to his calculation of a cubit—he could place the eastern wall of his plan within a few centimeters of the wall uncovered.

"A dissenting description of the uncovered wall was given by the only other archaeologist known to have seen it *in situ*. 'I don't remember it as monumental and I don't remember any stones with margins,' said the dissenter, who also requested anonymity. 'It was plainly part of a large complex but there was nothing to indicate it was from the Temple period.'

"The archaeologist who did the report, however, has a photograph of a stone with a margin taken after the wall was dismantled. His sketches also show stones with margins and he writes of one stone 2.5 meters long. His report refers to 'monumental stones reminiscent of Herodian stones.' He also raises the possibility that they are part of the temple, or as he puts it, 'Perhaps we have a portion of a Herodian building in the temple area.'

"Departing from the universally accepted notion that the Dome of the Rock was built on the ruins of the temple, Kaufman places the temple about 50 meters north of the Islamic landmark. He described a roughly rectangular complex 149 meters long, 43.7 meters wide (100 cubits) and containing a sanctuary 43.7 meters high, equivalent to a 15-story building. Kaufman's temple is oriented east-west with the Holy of Holies—the room entered only by the high priest and then only on Yom Kippur—near the western edge.

"In first temple days, the Holy of Holies contained the foundation stone and the two tablets of the law. In the second temple, only the foundation stone remained. There is no description of what this stone looked like or what purpose it served. Some have even assumed that it was a meteorite. A more general belief identifies the foundation stone as the bare rock around which the Dome of the Rock is built, As-Sakhra.

"Kaufman, however, is convinced that the foundation stone is a virtually unnoticed bedrock floor beneath a cupola at the northwestern end of the temple platform known as the 'Dome of the Spirits' or the 'Dome of the Tablets.' The Arabic names, he says, associate the site both with divine presence and tablets of the law. The stone fits precisely into the chamber designated on Kaufman's plan as the Holy of Holies."

Reaction among Israeli archaeologists to Kaufman's theory—familiar to them from extensive conversations he has had with them over the years—ranges from almost total scepticism to interest and encouragement. Of eight interviewed, almost none dismissed it out of hand.

" 'It's a very interesting theory,' said Ze'ev Yelven, deputy director of the Antiquities Department. 'But establishing it would require excavations in the area.'

"Prof. Nahman Avigad, who conducted the Jewish Quarter digs, was the most outspokenly sceptical. 'I don't understand his theory, therefore I don't believe it.' Avigad had not known of the wall remains discovered 16 years ago.

"Prof. Binyamin Mazar, who led nine years of excavations at the foot of the Temple Mount, declined to comment. 'It's none of my business,' he said.

"Dan Bahat challenged Kaufman's archaeological evidence, saying that there was no proof that the stone remains in the northern part of the Temple Mount, cited by the researcher as part of the temple compound, were actually from the Second Temple period.

"One of the country's outstanding archaeologists, who requested anonymity, praised Kaufman as 'a thorough man and straight—and that applies to his scientific approach.' However, he said, there were few facts to sustain the theory. 'It could be, but the evidence isn't strong enough.'

"Meir Ben-Dov, who had been Mazar's deputy, also said that Kaufman had not proven his case but he agreed with the researcher that the temple must have been north of the 'Dome of the Rock.' A similar opinion was expressed by another archaeologist although several others said they continued to believe in the 'Dome of the Rock' as the temple site.

"Kaufman professed not to be disturbed by the reservations of the archaeologists, noting that his approach differed from their methodology. 'They've been trained to dig and ascribe dates according to layers. On the Temple Mount, where you can't dig, you have to rely on every possible piece of information.'

"Kaufman mentioned the wall in an article he published in a government magazine, *Christian News from Israel.*

"The only remains associated with the temple ever found are two stone markers warning Gentiles, in Greek, against entering the sacred precinct" (Reprinted from *The Jerusalem Post*—Abraham Rabinovich).

Normally when an archaeologist offers the academic community a theory representing a radical departure from previously-held ideas, there is great resistance, and many of his peers begin to write articles contradicting the new theory. It is in this fashion that archaeological theories get adequately tested and examined before the eyes of not only the academics, but the general public as well. It is interesting to take note of the fact that although some archaeologists have expressed doubt over Kaufman's position, no one has written a serious paper refuting the massive evidence that Professor Kaufman has offered. We have assisted Professor Kaufman with his research and upon occasion have donated to the purchasing of rare manuscripts, which have helped him to find even more details proving his concept.

TWO TEMPLES IN ISRAEL'S FUTURE

The Jewish people themselves speak of the possibility of two future temples. Christian scholars who study both the Old and New Testaments see a third temple, built upon Mount Moriah, which will be desecrated by the man of great evil (Antichrist). A concept of the Antichrist is also found in traditional writings of Jewish scholars. He is called anti-messiah or "the golem." The third temple will be of short duration. The final temple, which will be built in the Millennium under the auspices of the Messiah Himself, is described in chapters 40 to 48 of Ezekiel. Depending upon whether one accepts the short or the long cubit measurement, that temple will be either 750 feet by 750 feet or a thousand by a thousand feet.

ARK OF THE COVENANT

The finding of the lost ark (if it still exists on this earth) would almost demand the building of the temple! It can simply be stated that the search for the ark continues in at least four locations that I know of.

There is no biblical record of the disposition or location of the holy ark after the destruction of the first temple by the Babylonians about 600 B.C. It may yet be found. I have my own theories as to its possible location.

How exciting to hear of the find of even a replica of the ark in Israel a few years ago. Hollywood jumped into the act with the production of the movie *Raiders of the Lost Ark,* which was shown throughout the U.S.A.

The first time that Mrs. Lewis and I met Rabbi Hacohen, the founder of the School of the Levites, it was on a cold, rainy February day. After Rabbi Hacohen had assembled a small model of the temple and explained his vision for the school and for the rebuilding of the temple, he began to talk to us about some of the excavations under the Temple Mountain. He told of how he was working late at night with Rabbi Getz, a group of archeologists, and rabbinical scholars. Let me explain at this point that when you stand at the Western or Wailing Wall in Jerusalem, you are actually standing approximately fifty-seven feet above the level of Christ's time (Herodian Period). Jerusalem has been destroyed and rebuilt about twenty times. Each time the city was destroyed, the rubble was pushed into the valley. Thus the level of the valley floors gradually built up over the centuries. Hacohen told of how they were excavating along the lower level of the Western Wall of the Temple Mountain. At one point during the night, they came to a doorway in the Western Wall. Passing through this doorway, the crew entered a fairly long tunnel. At the end of the tunnel, Rabbi Hacohen said, "I saw the golden ark that once stood in the Holy Place of the Temple of the Almighty."

It was covered over with old, dried animal skins of some kind. However one gold, gleaming end of the ark was visible. He could see the loops or rounds of gold through which the poles of acacia wood could be thrust so that the ark could be properly carried by four dedicated Levites. Hacohen and his friends rushed out to the home of Chief Rabbi Shlomo Goren. They awakened the rabbi and excitedly told him that they had discovered the holy ark of the covenant! Goren said, "We are ready for this event. We have already prepared the poles of acacia wood and have Levites who can be standing by in the morning to carry out the ark in triumph."

At the earliest dawning of the day Hacohen, Goren, and the others went to the tunnel. To their shocked amazement they found that during the night, the Moslems had erected a wooden form and poured a concrete wall, sealing off the tunnel that would give access to the ark of the covenant. I asked, "Why didn't you break through the concrete? It would have been so easy to do."

He replied, "I begged Goren to give us permission to break through the wall, but Rabbi Goren replied, 'Every time we do anything around the Temple Mountain, it creates big problems for Israel with the Arabs, the United Nations, and the United States. It seems to make everybody upset, so we will not break through. We know where the holy object is and when we receive the word from the Almighty, we will go in and recover it. Don't worry, the Moslems revere the ark as much as we do and they would be afraid to touch it.' "

In years following, I talked to Rabbi Hacohen on a number of occasions about this previous discussion and each time I talked to him, he was more and more reluctant to have the subject brought up. Finally, in the presence of several people, he simply refused to talk about it at all. I suppose he got in trouble with his colleagues for talking to me and my tour group about their sighting of the ark of the covenant. I would like to point out, however, that we have a tape recording of his original discussion with our tour group on the very first occasion that he talked about the ark. It is our custom on our tours to record everything that every guide and every speaker has to say about any subject. So we have good records of everything that has been said. In addition to that, I have a colored slide showing Rabbi Hacohen holding a map and pointing to the tunnel as he is saying, "This is where I saw the golden ark of the Lord." Only time will tell what he and his friends actually saw. Did they really see the ark, or was it a replica? Until it is actually taken out and verified, we will have to keep the whole question on hold.

My good friend Grant Jeffrey, author of the bestselling book, *Armageddon, Appointment with Destiny,* firmly believes that the ark of the covenant is in Ethiopia. Tom Crotser from Winfield, Kansas, believes that he has seen the ark under Mount Nebo in the country of Jordan. Mister Blaser from Colorado is convinced that the ark is hidden in a cave in Ein Gedi on the shores of the Dead Sea. There is a group of American Christian archeologists who believe that the ark is hidden between Gordon's Calvary and the Garden Tomb. A digging project was in progress while we were there a few years ago. We joined in the search. I took some artifacts that we dug out from near Calvary to an archeological expert for evaluation and dating. We found coins and pottery shards all the way back to the Roman period and the time of Christ. Thus there are many theories as to where the ark might be located. The last biblical reference that we have for the ark is just before the first Temple of Solomon was destroyed by the Babylonians about 576 B.C. Whatever happened to the ark is not a matter of sure record. The Apocrypha does speak of Jeremiah and his friend, Baruch the scribe, hiding the ark. There is further speculation that Jeremiah and Baruch probably hid a replica or two to fool those enemies of God who would try to find the ark and destroy it.

There are several projects going on right now in Israel and other places making attempts to find the ark of the covenant. In Revelation 11, John says that he saw the holy ark in heaven. Some have concluded that the ark is no longer on earth. However, this would not be true inasmuch as the earthly tabernacle and temple and the articles of furniture therein were manufactured after a heavenly pattern. A heavenly temple and a heavenly ark exist, according to the writings of the book of Hebrews. What John saw in Revelation 11:19 was the heavenly ark, not any ark that had ever been on earth. That is my opinion.

We cannot prove to you that the ark of God is still in existence, but I will offer you my opinion that it is in existence and that it will be found. The Bible says in Jeremiah that the day will come when the children of Israel will no longer inquire after the ark of the covenant. That day has not yet arrived, for the inquiry after the ark of the covenant is intense and interest in its recovery is increasing. Many Jewish leaders, especially those who are religiously conservative, believe that finding the ark would be the one thing above all else that would literally force Israel to start rebuilding the temple. Rabbi Hacohen said, "If we find the ark, it will force us to build the temple. After all the first temple was built to house the ark of the covenant. If we find the ark, what would we do with it? We couldn't store it in the prime minister's basement. It would demand the rebuilding of the temple. However, if we find the ark or not, we are going to build the temple of Almighty God on the Har Habayit, the Temple Mountain."

A GREAT MYSTERY

I hardly know how to tell you what I am about to say. When I am in Jerusalem, some people come and visit me very quietly by night. They share secrets that are so bizarre that they are hard to believe. We stumbled upon something of this nature recently. First of all, I was talking one day to one of the gentlemen who heads up one of the temple organizations, and as you know, there are several of them. He said that there is a group of people who are sinking a shaft, a bore hole, down in the valley betwen the Abu Tor Observatory and the Temple Mountain. If you look at a map of Jerusalem, you will see that it is in the valley of Gehenna. My informant said that there is a belief that the Temple of Ezekiel was built long ago and buried under massive amounts of dirt and rubble.

I frankly admit that I find that very hard to believe. I am only sharing it with you because the information came independently from three different sources while I was recently in Israel. It is offered here only as a curiosity. We will watch and wait to see if there is any substance to the claims that have been made.

One night, a gentleman who came to me very quietly and secretly, was talking to me about matters concerning the temple. I related to him that the gentleman previously mentioned and yet another person had come to me with this idea, that the Temple of Ezekiel, the Millennial Temple, was already in existence and buried in the valley between Abu Tor and the Temple Mountain. This scholarly gentleman had previously said that he believed that the "spirit" of the Roman Caesar was alive in the world today. From his Jewish point of view, there would be a revival of the Roman Empire, which would bring a lot of trouble to Israel. He spoke of a man like the Roman Emperor Hadrian, one of the most evil of the Roman Caesars, who would rule this Revived Roman Empire. I told him that we Christians have a similar point of view.

Here is part of the discussion that took place between the two of us from a tape recording:

Lewis: There is an idea that has been presented to me since I came to Israel this time. There are some people who theorize that a temple is buried between the Abu Tor Observatory and the Temple Mountain, a temple constructed after the model in Ezekiel 40-48. It was built and then buried there. There is a theory that there will be two temples in the future: one will be constructed on the Temple Mountain and will be defiled like the second temple was profaned by Antiochus Epiphanes during the Maccabean period, 165 years before Christ, when Antiochus defiled the temple of the Jews.

During a time of great trouble for the whole world, a man of great evil, the man who will rule the new Roman Empire will, like a Caesar, declare himself to be God. Then the defiled temple will be replaced by the true fourth and final (Ezekiel) temple. So there will be two temples in the future. I hear the rabbis arguing about whether to build a temple now or whether to wait for the Messiah to come and build the temple.

Jacob: Ah, yes, there are two theories. Yes, but what we are looking for is the one that has already been there.

Lewis: These people I am talking about, they have dug a shaft...

Jacob: That's what we did. That's what we did... (Jacob is a fictitious name, used for security reasons, but the person and events are real.)

Lewis: And, they work at night...

Jacob: That's what we did, because it's very dangerous.

Lewis: Jacob, they believe there is a building underground.

Jacob: And I believe it too, and the place we are going we are not looking for a hidden cellar. It is not a cellar. It's a marvelous building and we have the proofs there.

Lewis: So maybe you are looking for the same thing?

Jacob: Yes. Now the entrance we are entering, you see, Ezekiel mentions a wheel within a wheel. So what do we have there, what did we find there as we dig our tunnel? Against the wall, a wheel within a wheel.

Lewis: You mean where you started digging?

Jacob: Yes. The stone is carved, wheel within the wheel. Wheel within the wheel. It goes like this [here he draws a "picture" with his hands, in the air]. What else could you want?

Lewis: You mean when you started digging it was like a design?

Jacob: Yes, there was a shaft [filled in with reconstituted rock]. There was a design [wheel in the wheel]. It is still there, on both sides—the wheel within a wheel. Then there is a lion. There is a large lion that faces the entrance, not us. It is beautifully carved. We got where we got, but that's it. So there must be something there. And it fits with the measurements.

Lewis: These designs don't happen by accident...

Jacob: No, no, it cannot. It cannot. And they are painted also—in red. And we found many things.

For many hours we discussed things pertinent to the discoveries of great treasures in the Holy Land. This secret informant whom we call Jacob has been coming to me for years with information that up until now has always proven to be accurate. I will admit that the idea of an underground temple is one of the strangest things that I have ever heard.

Ezekiel's description of the temple of the Messianic Era and the City of Jerusalem of that time describes great topographical changes. Jerusalem itself will become a great plain. Is it possible that the Ezekiel Temple, the Messianic Temple, is already in existence? I cannot say for sure, but I do know that the people who came to me before I talked to Jacob said that bore hole had been dug (not Jacob's project) and that some massive underground structure had been detected. What shall we say of these mysteries? Only time will tell.

This we know for sure: there is great interest in Israel in the rebuilding of the temple, the finding of the lost ark of the covenant, and the restoration of the priesthood. The high level of interest—in spite of contradictory stories and searches in places that look almost like rivalry between archaeological groups—should not discourage us from believing that the temple will be rebuilt. Indeed, the temple will be rebuilt, not because of all these activities, but because it has been so prophesied in the Word of God. These activities are simply an indication that we are living very near the close of this age and the fulfillment of incredible prophecies.

Mosque of the Dome on Mount Moriah (thought by some to be the location of the temple).

11

Levitical Priesthood
Being Restored

The news of an actual revival of Israel's priesthood was broken by the weekly *Jewish Press* published in Brooklyn, New York.

The *Jewish Press* speaks for large segments of Orthodox Judaism in the English-speaking world. It claims the largest readership of any Orthodox Jewish English-language publication in the world. Rabbi Michael Landy wrote the special article for the *Jewish Press*.

In my estimation this is the most significant news of recent times relating to this major prophetic development. To both Jews and Christians the rebuilding of the temple is a herald of the coming of the Messianic Era. Christian perception is that the next (the third) temple will be recognized by God as a holy temple but will be defiled by the Antichrist, the worst anti-Semite of all time. A fourth temple will be built by Messiah in the Millennium.

Years ago, Dr. David Flusser of Hebrew University, a New Testament scholar, brought this up in a conversation I had with him in his home in Jerusalem: "Your apostle Paul," he said, "spoke of a man of great evil who would defile our new and future temple." Dr. Flusser was one of few Jewish scholars who, at that time, would even talk to me about the possibility of the rebuilding of the bet hamikdash (house of the sanctuary—the temple).

Rabbi Landy stated: "Concerned Jews in Israel are continuing to focus attention on Har Habayit (*mount of the house—meaning Mount Moriah, the Temple Mount*) in their efforts to establish a Jewish presence there and regain rightful possession over our most holy of sites."

A LAMENTATION

The article laments the sad situation whereby Jews are not even allowed development of the holy place. Landy wrote:

"Religious and national sentiments are beginning to come to the surface and have manifested themselves in the formation of various movements, all designed to highlight the absurdity of a situation whereby Jews, in their own capital and back in their homeland after thousands of years of wandering, cannot participate in the Torah development of Yerushalayim Ir Hakodesh. (Torah—Biblical; Yerushalayim Ir Hakodesh—Jerusalem the holy city.)

"Many have expressed interest in prayer on the Har Habayit (although Halachically forbidden) and the reinstitution of sacrifices in Jerusalem" (Halachically—legal according to Jewish religious law).

The latter statement that Jews are Halachically or legally forbidden according to religious law to go on the Temple Mountain seems to be due to the fact that the mount is unsanctified at the present time. This can only be rectified by the re-establishment of the priesthood and a cleansing of the mountain by proper ceremonial action. You must realize that all of this is being debated by Jewish scholars and the final terms by which all of this is accomplished seems rather vague at the moment. The big news is that action and planning are taking place right now.

This sign is posted at the entrance of the Temple Mountain.

184

Medal struck by the Jeruaslem Temple Foundation—it portrays
Jewish longing for the temple.

Stanley Goldfoot (left) with Avigdor Rosenberg (our Israeli guide).
Mr. Goldfoot is the executive director of the Jerusalem Temple
Foundation.

TEMPLE TIMES

Some of the actions include the establishing of the Temple Foundation by Eduardo Recanate, Stanley Goldfoot, and others. I have personally met these people. I have spent hours talking to them about the rebuilding of the temple. These are serious people who do not perceive themselves as pursuing mere fantasies. They should be taken seriously, even if their views are controversial. It is of great importance that pastors and religious leaders who take groups to Israel for Holy Land tours meet these men and others, such as Dr. Asher Kaufman and Matteteau Hacohen (Yeshiva Aterit Cohanim). It is very interesting and beneficial to have one or more of these men speak to the tour groups. In this way Christians do a little more than just look at ancient ruins. It is indeed important to "walk where Jesus walked," and perhaps this is the most important objective. However, there needs also to be exposure to the living nation of Israel. Viewing prophecy in the actual process of being fulfilled has a most beneficial effect in people's hearts and minds.

CORNERSTONE OF THE THIRD TEMPLE

Imagine my surprise to pick up *The Calgary Sun* in Calgary, Alberta, Canada, Tuesday, October 17, 1989, and find this headline: "Riot Over Temple Stone!" This is what the UPI release, dateline Jerusalem, had to say about Gershon Solomon's group, the Temple Mountain Faithful, as they attempted to take a three-ton cornerstone of the next Temple of Israel to the top of Mount Moriah.

"Israelis sparked a riot yesterday when they tried to lay a cornerstone for a new Jewish Temple at the site of Islam's two holiest shrines in Jerusalem's Old City.

"Police barred the Jewish group from bringing the three-ton cornerstone within the ancient city's walls, foiling an effort by the Temple Mount Faithful movement to take a first step toward rebuilding the temple destroyed in A.D. 70 by the Romans."

THE CHRISTIAN CONNECTION

The *Jerusalem Post* published an article titled "The Christian Connection" in relation to aspirations of Jews to the rebuilding of the temple. Only a few of the people involved were actually mentioned. I personally know Christians who have made contributions to Jewish groups that hope for the rebuilding of the temple and have programs to further that aim. This is not to be taken as a recommendation, nor do we express disapproval of those who wish to contribute to the rebuilding of the temple.

It is rumored that American Christians in Texas and California have helped fund the Temple Foundation. We say "rumored" because those involved would not want to admit it for security reasons. As a matter of fact, I do know the identity of many of the people involved, but cannot refer to them by name for the reason mentioned. Journalistic attacks on these Christians have been mounted in some rather strange political publications and we do not wish to add to the problems these people face by giving them further exposure. The publications making these attacks also take a stand against Israel in general. Reporters for some of these publications have contacted us, but we have refused to talk to their representatives.

Other things of interest include a feasibility study done by SRI International, a "think tank" in Menlo Park, California, formerly known as Stanford Research Institute. This study, executed by Lambert Dolphin, senior research physicist at SRI, is in our files. Dolphin is an Evangelical Christian and has an intense interest in the temple. We have talked to and interviewed Mr. Dolphin on numerous occasions and are in constant touch with him. (Dolphin has recently left SRI and has launched a private consultancy.)

Lambert Dolphin at SRI International.

187

ORGANIZATION AND COOPERATION NEEDED

In the *Jewish Press* article, Rabbi Landy points out that in the past, all efforts to move in this direction have been frustrated by a lack of organization, the formulation of a workable plan and a lack of unity of the parties involved. He calls for a worldwide registration of the Jews who are qualified for the priesthood, and for organization of efforts to move toward the fulfillment of several goals which he spells out in the article.

Landy calls for cooperation among Jewish people of all degrees of religious observance, irrespective of political affiliation. The hope is to involve masses of people in pursuits that only a few have paid attention to (mostly secretly) in the past, to wit, the rebuilding of the temple and all that attends that action and concept.

TEMPLE ARTICLES IN SECULAR PRESS

It would seem that the rabbi's hopes of getting mass exposure is to some degree being realized. Barbara Ledeen, a Jewish author in Washington, D.C., has written extensively on the subject, hopefully to get an article published in the *New York Times* or the *Washington Post*. Barbara was formerly on the editorial staff of the prestigious *Biblical Archaeological Review Magazine*. She is now, among other things, a free-lance journalist. In addition, another important newspaper has given space to temple-oriented articles.

THE *JERUSALEM POST*

Some time ago, while in Jerusalem, Avigdor Rosenberg called to my attention that the weekend magazine section of the *Jerusalem Post,* the most widely circulated, English-language, secular Jewish publication in the world, was almost entirely devoted to the matter of the rebuilding of the temple. It briefly called attention to the functions of the priesthood. So the subject is now out in the open! "Everybody" is talking about it.

Suddenly what formerly was the domain of interest for a few Evangelical "prophecy buffs" is news even for the secular press.

SOCIETY OF FAITHFUL MEN

Unknown to most of the world, in 1979 an organization, Agudat Anshei Eimun (*Society of Faithful Men*), came into existence. Rabbi Landy comments: "It was with this reality that Agudat Anshei Eimun Organization, established in 1979, decided to try to establish a World

International Shmirat Hamikdash Society. Its main purpose was to organize and maintain a computerized list of qualified 'shomrim' for the Har Habayit in our time. It would be composed of all kohanim and leviim throughout the world who would be registered for their position of 'shmira' at halachically approved sites at the Har Habayit complex."

I am sure that it is necessary to define some of the above terms. Shmira and its derivations—shmirat, shomrim (plural), etc.—indicates "keepers" or "guardians"; Shmirat Hamikdash—guardians of the sanctuary. In the framework of the article it implies the Jewish priesthood. It will be necessary to define various Hebrew words as we proceed. Once defined, if a term appears a second time, it may be necessary for you to refer back for the definition.

A BOOK OF MAJOR IMPORTANCE

Agra Layasharim (Guide of the Upright Ones) by Gaon Reb Chaim Zimmerman deals with religious-legal aspects regarding the temple and concerning today's "status of the Kohen and the Levi." It was Reb Zimmerman who recently outlined a full program for the new society in his regular column "Torah and Existence" which appears in the *Jewish Press*.

A NECESSITY FOR OUR TIMES

Rabbi Landy strongly urges Jews to recognize the necessity of reorganizing the priesthood (shmirat hamikdash).

"In a new Sefer, entitled *Agra Layasharim,* by the Gaon Reb Chaim Zimmerman, the halachot concerning the Bet Hamikdash and what status the kohen and levi have today, are explained halachically.

"Recently, the Gaon outlined a full program for the 'Shmirat Hamikdash Society' to follow in his 'Torah and Existence' column in the *Jewish Press*.

"Accordingly, the Gaon proves that Shmirat Hamikdash is a chiyuv mitzvah (requirement) for all leviim in our time who are halachically prepared, and a kiyum haMitzvah (elective performance) for all kohanim. He maintains therefore that it is absolutely incumbent for klall (*klall: all, entire*) Yisrael today to actively embark upon and try to establish a full Shmirat Hamikdash program in Jerusalem as soon as possible. The greatest honor one can achieve is the honor of being a 'Shomer' at the Bet Hamikdash. Said Shmira is to be maintained by only kohanim and leviim whose job it would be to warn people against going up to the Har Habayit in a state of tumah (ritual uncleanliness)."

SANCTIFY THE MOUNTAIN

Emphasis is made on the present uncleanness of the Temple Mountain and the necessity of sanctifying it before the temple can be built. To this purpose a center will be constructed near the Har Habayit (Temple Mountain). Its functions will be multiple. It will be a headquarters for the priests.

The Orthodox Jews consider it a serious transgression to go on the Temple Mountain at the present time (with certain exceptions, although this is debated). The Shmirat Hamikdash Society hopes to gain full, religious-legal (halachic) and political authority to prevent all Jews from going on the Temple Mountain until the exact location of the temple is found. (Here Asher Kaufman may be of great help.) You can see that a very complex situation exists!

Landy's comments on *Agra Layasharim* by Reb Zimmerman indicated that: "Shmirat Hamikdash must be maintained each day, even now, at the minimum of four positions on the west side of the present Har Habayit parameters."

If I understand this statement correctly, since Israel has free access to the Western (Wailing) Wall, this should not be an impossibility as the Gaon says, "even now."

NEEDED: MORE PRIESTS

The *Jewish Press* article continues: "Since it is impossible to begin Shmira (priestly function) unless there will be someone to relieve the shomer (priest-keeper), there must be sufficient members in the society in order to guarantee the normal functioning of a person's life who will be involved in Shmira. He estimated that when properly developed, each Levi would have a minimum amount of Shmira every two to three years."

To facilitate these ends, Gaon Reb Chaim Zimmerman has asked Yehuda Schwartz, executive director of the Agudat Anshei Eimun, to undertake a program of both publicity and development of the new Shmirat Hamikdash Society. Apparently, no time is being wasted, for in the same issue of the *Jewish News,* in which the article appeared there is also a large advertisement calling on Levites and Cohens to register with the society. A handy coupon for reply was provided!

Rosenne To Be Guest Speaker

: on music's
lism will be
v Feitman,
ng Israel of
io, and Rabbi
versky, spiri-
The Talmu-
h Institute,
ado.

'Torah'' airs
at 9 p.m. on
1. For a free
this season's
il (212) 376-
of the day or

A leading figure in
Israel's diplomatic service,
Meir Rosenne, Israel's
Ambassador to the United
States, will be the guest
speaker, Saturday evening,
October 15th, at the fifth
annual dinner in support of
cancer research at the Lau-
tenberg Center for General
and Tumor Immunology at
the Hebrew University in
Jerusalem. The dinner will
be held at the Parsippany
Hilton Hotel.

ber 15th at 8

eier, spiritual
e Avenue N
r, president of
New York
he Religious
America, and
n Rabbinic
orator, will
e New Reality
Glance at Life
State.'
rier recently
n a compre-
y mission to
he met with
government,
academic life,
al section, in
e religious life
nity.
epresentation
lopments in
l; life is eag-
by the many

friends of the Yiddish
Forum.

Shragai Cohen, interna-
tional leader of Mizrachi,
chairman of the board of
the American Zionist Fed-
eration, who is the president of the Center, will
extend remarks on this
opening evening. Mr.
Cohen has been instrumen-
tal in giving leadership to
the effort to establish the
Yiddish Forum as a per-
manent feature of the Synagogue program, and he
has brought prominent
scholars and writers to
address the Yiddish
Forum.

The community is
invited to attend this and
all other programs of the
Yiddish Forum.

בס"ד

Many Sugyos in Shass!

לשמחת ב
זה עכשו נדפס:

אגרא ל
חידושים ו
משא ומתן בס
מאת הגא
אהרון חיים ד

dash

Relation To Our Time

יצא לאור ע"י אגודת
ת.ד. 675, ברו
בברוקלין:

—Price $14.95
Hard-cover — Indexed

Agudat Anshei Eimun
א.א.א. — אגודת

Box 7575, Jerusalem 91074, Israel
Box 675, Brunt Station
New York 11215

יהודת אנשי וימו

A New World International Organization is being established to endeavor to "Be Mekayem" the Mitzvah of

SHMIRAT HAMIKDASH

The "Mitzvah" is related to Leviim as a "Chiyuv Hamitzvah"
(absolute requirement) and to Kohanim as a "Kiyum
Hamitzvah" according to a new Sefer by Hagaon Reb
Chaim Zimmerman entitled "Agra Layasharim."
Every Kohen and Levi who wishes to try to fulfill this
Mitzvah is invited to join the now-in-formation

SHMIRAT HAMIKDASH SOCIETY

In due time, we hope to establish a computerized Registration of all Kohanim and Leviim and the time and date
for their individual Shmira.

Agudat Anshei Eimun
Jerusalem * New York * Chicago

For further information write
Yehuda Schwartz, P.O.B. 675
Brunt Street Station, Brooklyn, N.Y. 11215

All those interested in having their names added to the
Central computerized Registration of Kohanim and
Leviim are asked to send in the following coupon.

Name ....
Address ....
City .... State .... Zip ....
Hebrew Name .... Age ......
Father's Hebrew Name ....
Mother's Hebrew Name ....
Country of Origin ....

GOALS OF THE NEW SOCIETY STATED

Rabbi Landy clearly outlined goals for the new organization:

1. Publishing and distributing literature. Both technical literature for scholars and religious leaders, as well as materials in pamphlet form for the general public, will be produced and disseminated by the society.

2. The second goal is a bit more complicated so I will give you the exact quotation (with definition of some Hebrew terms) from the article: "The Shmirat Hamikdash Society will undertake to restore the Halachic and national dignity to the Jewish people by explaining the importance of the performance of Shmirat Hamikdash. The Leviim and Kohanim who will come from all over the world to do their particular 'Shmira' will comprise one big Shmirah Society which will join them into one unified purpose and destiny. This Shmira will enhance the corporate kedusha [kedusha: sanctifying, cleansing] stock of Klall Yisrael and will hasten the establishment of the Bet Hamikdash [the temple] itself and the Malchut Bet David [kingdom of the house of David] as described in the Gemara. Accordingly, each Ben Yisrael [Ben: son of] of Klall Yisrael will individually and collectively receive a kedusha benefit."

Please note well the words, "hasten the establishment of the Bet Hamikdash" (the temple). No longer can critics claim that the whole idea of the rebuilding of the temple of Israel is a fantasy in the minds of biblical literalists. No longer can it be said that only Fundamentalists, Evangelicals, and Pentecostals have an interest in the temple. No critic can say again that the Jewish people themselves have no interest in the matter! It is too late in the day and the evidence too strong for such criticism to be given much attention. The *Jewish Press* article makes this clear:

"It will establish a Board of Directors who will coordinate and be responsible for all activities and determine further actions to be taken as things progress politically, religiously and physically."

Note that last phrase. Remember it. Things are in motion. It is happening!

3. The third goal of the society is to call for an annual conference for all the priesthood—the Levites and Cohanim.

4. The organization will work worldwide to set up branch offices which will help collate information and verify the identity of the priesthood.

5. A center will be built in Jerusalem for the priesthood (as mentioned before). Mikvaot will be provided. (*Mikvaot—ceremonial baths—by immersion*. It is believed the Christian custom of baptism came from

192

the Jewish Mikvah tradition, as was being practiced by John the Baptist as he immersed Jesus in the Jordan River.) Rabbi Landy said, "The Shmirat Hamikdash Society will eventually undertake the establishment and maintenance of a building near the Har Habayit to house members on Shmira. It will also contain Mikvaot required for Shmira as well as mikvah facilities for all others who wish to pray at the Western Wall in spiritual purity, as required by halacha."

ISRAEL—AMERICA—WORLDWIDE

The importance of Jewish Community participation in the U.S.A. and in Israel (of course) is sharply defined by the statement:

"Prominent governmental, civic and lay leaders in Israel, America, and throughout the world will be invited to participate and sponsor this great undertaking. This will also encourage all Jews, interested in seeing the full restoration of the 'Kohanim la-avodatom uLeviim leshirom ulezimrom,' to particpate in this program."

The Hebrew phrase above is roughly to be translated, "priesthood of holy, joyful, and song-filled service." I discussed the phrase with a local rabbi who is a Hebrew scholar. He said it was difficult to translate into English, but that what we have given you is a satisfactory interpretation. Most interesting!

MEMBERSHIP AND ACTION

Members (Levites and Cohens) of the society will be issued a lifetime membership card. Private rather than Israeli government support will be sought and encouraged. This is to avoid any political influences on the program.

The membership list will be computerized and all registered Leviim will be given assignments and time of service for the "Har Habayit" center in Jerusalem.

When he accepted the call to involvement, Yehuda Schwartz said, "Et Laasot La-Hashem," meaning, "It is time to act in the name of the Almighty One." Schwartz claims that it is not only a duty but a privilege to serve. He stated that the movement will give spiritual direction to Israel, which he says is sadly lacking to this day. He believes that the hope of rebuilding the temple can be the greatest unifying force for the Jewish people of the entire world. It is hoped that this will be the thing that will draw the Jewish people of the world to make aliyah (return) to the land of Israel. It will act as a magnet to draw Jews of the diaspora (dispersion) back to the land of their fathers.

193

We Christians see this as another evidence of the fulfillment of the absolutely reliable, prophetic Word of God.

AGE OF REDEMPTION—MESSIANIC HOPE

One of the most powerful statements in the *Jewish Press* article was the closing line: "The Shmirat Hamikdash Society will earn an additional and important individual and corporate benefit for all Jewish people in this 'Atchalta de-Guela,' he concluded."

Atchalta de-Guela means "the age of redemption." This implies the coming of the Messiah! Even so, come!

HOLY LINEN

We have received very interesting information from our Israeli correspondent, Avigdor Rosenberg of Tel Aviv. It consists of an article that appeared in *Maariv,* a Hebrew language newspaper. Here is a translation of the article:

GARMENT OF THE PRIEST
Translation by Avigdor Rosenberg

"Former Chief Rabbi Shlomo Goren publicized his research about the Temple Mount. He had been working on it since the Six Day War.

"His conclusion is that Jewish people may enter and step in many parts of the Temple Mount.

"Note: There is a sign at the entrance of the Temple Mount forbidding Jews to enter. The fear is that someone might step on the location of the Holy of Holies and be guilty of defiling it.

"Rabbi Goren emphasized the need of erecting a synagogue and a place of worship on the Temple Mount! This he said in the gathering of the national meeting of the Temple Mountain Faithful Association.

"The chairman of this association, Mr. Gershon Solomon, announced that immediately after the Passover Holiday, he is going to present a plan to the Jerusalem authorities. The plan will be of a synagogue to be built on Mount Moriah."

Sceptics sneer at the idea that prophecy is being fulfilled. All of this activity, even the very existence of Israel, are mere coincidences of history. You who are wise, biblical students know better. You know that in His time there will be a new temple in Israel. You know that the eternal kingdom of God which today is "within you" and thus hidden will be manifested in glorious power and demonstration in the age of the Theocracy, the Millennium.

KEY TO PROPHECY

Remember, the key to prophecy is Israel. The key to Israel is the temple. "Look up for your redemption draweth nigh."

Accompanying the article that appeared in *Maariv,* there was a picture of David Eldbaum, a cohen who is weaving the linen cloth for the garments of the high priest and all the priests of the temple. There was a special dye for these garments, described partially in the Torah (Old Testament).

We do not wish to indicate in any way that Israeli President Chaim Herzog is connected with the temple movement, because he is not, to our knowledge. However, when I met with him at the Israeli Embassy I did ask him, "Mr. President, is it true that your late father of blessed memory, the Grand Rabbi Isaac Halevi Herzog, was the person who wrote the definitive dissertation on the subject 'The Source of the Dye of the Garments of the High Priest of Israel?' "

In a secluded workshop, far removed from the Temple Institute, an elderly rabbi, David Eldbaum, works day after day at his loom weaving linen for the garment of the high priest.

He avoided my question by answering with a question: "What do you know about my family, about my father?" He seemed amazed at my query.

I told him I knew that his father had been appointed successor to Chief Rabbi Kook in the era of the British Mandate over Palestine, before there was a State of Israel. The British hated Kook because they could not control him. They thought if they found a British subject, a resident of the British Isles, and appointed him, they could control him. They chose the president's father. However Herzog turned out to be as much his own man as Kook had been. I pressed my question about the dye upon him again.

President Herzog exclaimed, "I am amazed that you even know of my father's work. You would have to be conversant with at least twelve languages to even comprehend his research!"

I replied that I was interested in the Talmudic argument over whether the dye came from snails or the ink-fish. Then I asked, "Is it true, sir, that you are a member of a committee of about thirty scholars who are re-examining your father's work? And, is it further true that a new consideration has developed, that being the question, 'If the dye could be analyzed chemically and reproduced in the laboratory without the use of snails or fish would it be halachic' (legal in a religious sense)?"

After some further conversation I again asked about his involvement in such a committee. President Herzog admitted that such a committee did exist and that he was a participant. He did not elaborate further. It must be stated again that Chaim Herzog would not want to be connected to the temple movement, and his participation in the committee does not imply anything beyond a scholarly pursuit and participation in research honoring his father.

We find it interesting that exploration of these ideas is taking place. Even the most minute details are being examined and brought to light.

Discover magazine, November, 1984, had an article titled "The Die Is Recast." It speaks of the banded dye-murex, a snail with religious significance. This particular snail is found in the Mediterranean Sea. *Discover* magazine reveals the work of an Israeli scientist, Irving Ziderman, of the Israel Fibre Institute of Jerusalem and his research into this subject. The article does not mention the garments of the priests. Rather, it speaks of the use of the dye for the tassels of the prayer shawls used by male Jewish worshippers. We will try and find out if there is a connection. Probably it is the same dye as would be used for the tunic of the High Priest of the New Temple.

TEMPLE FACTS

Scoffers continue to scorn the idea that the temple of the nation of Israel will be rebuilt as the Bible predicts. Actually there will be two temples built in the future. Both are designated as holy temples of God and approved by God himself. The next temple is referred to in such passages as Daniel 9:24-27; Matthew 24:15-22; 2 Thessalonians 2:4; Revelation 11:1,2. The fourth and final temple will be built by Messiah himself in the millennial age. It is referred to in passages such as Zechariah 6:12-14 and Ezekiel chapters 40-48.

NO COOPERATION WITH TERRORISTS

Some try to identify all who are interested in the temple with extremists who are dedicated to using violence to bring their hopes to pass. The Australian Rohan tried to burn down the El Aqsa Mosque on Mount Moriah to hasten the building of the temple. A tiny minority of Jewish extremists tried to forcibly enter the area with explosives. They were jailed by the Israeli officials. None of the people we know in Israel, who are active in promoting the building of the temple, has any sympathy with these extremists. We have inquired diligently. Let me say again that we believe that only peaceful means should be used to study and promote the concept of the temple.

YESHIVA ATERIT COHANIM

Once again we took our group of Christian pilgrims to the School of the Levites where the Levites and Cohens are being taught in temple matters. Menecham Bar Shalom, the director of the school, met us, lectured, showed us the model of the temple at the school premises, gave us a walking lecture tour of the area, and in general gave us an update on the whole subject. While in the school I saw a large Hebrew language poster. It was an announcement of a forthcoming convention to be held in Jerusalem. The subject of all the lectures was the temple and various concepts of its rebuilding and dedication of the temple. The process of the restoration of the temple priesthood was another topic of discussion announced on the poster.

CHANGE OF ATTITUDE

A few years ago no one in Israel would even talk to you about the subject. The temple concept was too explosive. In April, 1972, *The Jerusalem Post* carried an article stating that official registration of an

This 1972 article from the *Jerusalem Post* illustrates the negative attitude of the Israelis towards building of the temple at that time.

This recent *Jerusalem Post* article is one of a series showing Israelis' changing attitude toward building a new temple.

organization for the promotion of the temple was denied by the Israeli government. Today there are a number of such organizations operating openly including the Jerusalem Temple Foundation (Stanley Goldfoot); the Temple Mountain Faithful (Eldbaum, *et al*); Institute of Research for the Temple of Jerusalem (Eduardo Recanate); Beit Elohenu (Rhoda Elovitz); Yeshiva Torath Hayim and Yeshiva Aterit Cohanim, etc. Pro or con everyone seems willing now to talk temple topics. The mayor of Jerusalem, Teddy Kolleck, expressed himself strongly the last time I talked to him. He is disturbed by the activity of the temple advocates. Concerned for the peace of Jerusalem Kolleck sees the whole thing as a potential time bomb.

It is interesting to note that Mayor Teddy Kolleck of Jerusalem has altered his view somewhat in the months that have gone by since his negative comments were made. Jan William van der Hoeven told me about Mayor Kolleck's comments at the Feast of Tabernacles celebration in Jerusalem sponsored by the International Christian Embassy. On the platform was a huge painting of a futuristic concept of Jerusalem with the temple in place. It was a part of the decor where the Christian celebration took place. As Mayor Kolleck was bringing greetings to the people, he turned to the picture of the restored temple and spoke of it in a complimentary fashion. I do not recall his exact words, but I saw a videotape of the mayor's speech to a Christian gathering of about four thousand people. He spoke of the hope that one day the temple would stand on the Temple Mountain as it was pictured in this work of art.

As for it being a potential time bomb, I certainly hope that this is not true.

Moslem opposition to the whole idea of the temple on Mount Moriah is understandable. Their buildings, the Dome of the Rock and the El Aqsa Mosque, are located on the Temple Mountain which they designate "Haram Es Sharif"—the most noble sanctuary. Asher Kaufman's scientific evidence locating the temple north of the Dome of the Rock at the site of the Dome of the Tablets (also called Dome of the Spirits) defuses the issue to some extent. His theory is not universally accepted. For a variety of reasons I believe he is correct. I have spent hours talking to Professor Kaufman and am satisfied that it is the most sound presentation of fact I have heard on the subject of the true location of the ancient temples.

We have printed several articles on this subject and *Biblical Archaeology Review* magazine devoted a large space in one issue to an examination of Dr. Asher Kaufman's concept. Barbara Ledeen is

Biblical Archaeology Review

MARCH-APRIL 1983
VOL. IX NO. 2
$3.50

Ark of Covenant Once
Stood on the Bedrock
Beneath this
Unimposing Cupola

BAR explored Kaufman's theory about the location of the temple.

probably the best informed person in North America on the temple subject and has shared a mass of data with us. She was an editor with *BAR* when the Kaufman articles were presented. In fact, she did extensive work on the articles. She feels that Kaufman's is the theory to be answered to by all who would have anything to say on the subject. I have been a proponent of this idea since 1968, when I proposed it without any concrete evidence at my disposal whatsoever.

An alternate point of view certainly seems possible. Whereas in the past the almost universal opinion was that the Dome of the Rock had to be destroyed by explosion, earthquake, or some other disaster, there is now the alternate concept that it is altogether possible that a temple could exist on the mountain beside the Dome. This is almost incomprehensible to many deeply religious Moslems and Jews, both of whom find the concept abhorrent. Never could a compromise of that magnitude be effected.

We note however that this "contrary scenario" fits well into the words of Revelation where John describes a temple being in existence in a time of great trouble and distress (tribulation): "And there was given me a reed like unto a rod: and the angel stood, saying, Rise, and measure the temple of God, and the altar, and them that worship therein. But the court which is without the temple leave out, and measure it not; for it is given unto the Gentiles: and the holy city shall they tread under foot forty and two months" (Rev. 11:1,2).

The picture we see is as follows: Israel has a temple. They do not control the area around the temple. It is given to the Gentiles. Right now, Israel does not have full control of the Temple Mountain (Moriah). Even though it was a part of East Jerusalem, captured in the Six Day War of 1967, the Israeli authorities turned control of the Temple Mountain back to the Moslems. Moslem police provide much of the security force on the Temple Mountain at this present time. One cannot be dogmatic about the next temple but it seems to me that this alternate solution lies within the realm of possibility.

THE POSSIBLE COMPROMISE

To those who think that a compromise between Jews and Moslems of this magnitude is not possible, I direct your attention to the first capital of united Israel. Remember, David was not crowned king of Israel in Jerusalem. It was not his first capital. David was crowned in Hebron, and later he conquered Jerusalem from the Jebusites. Then it became the capital of united Israel. A visit to Hebron today reveals some very interesting modern developments. Hebron is a few miles south of Jerusalem. It is the site of the cave of Machpelah, the burial place of the patriarchs Abraham, Isaac, Jacob, and their wives (except for Rachel who died on the road to Bethlehem, where her tomb is until this day).

Built over the cave of Machpelah is the great Mosque of Hebron, a Moslem place of worship. Adjacent to Hebron is the new Israeli settlement of Kiryat Arba, which was founded by the Orthodox Rabbi Levinger. Kiryat Arba is, of course, a Jewish settlement, while old Hebron is largely Arab. The Arabs slaughtered the Jewish community

The Mosque at Hebron. The author's mother stands in the foreground.

in the massacres of 1929 and 1936. Only in recent years have Jews in any significant number returned.

Let us visit the Mosque of Hebron over the Cave of Machpelah. How startling to discover that it is no longer exclusively a mosque. Indeed, it is partially used for a Jewish synagogue and partly as a Moslem mosque. Somehow the Jews and the Arabs are sharing the building and managing to coexist. The site is holy to both religions.

Similarly, the Temple Mountain is holy to both religions. Is compromise possible here? Only time will tell. We can only watch these developments with the greatest of interest.

COINCIDENCE, COINCIDENCE

Our friend, guide and charge d'affaires in Israel, Avigdor Rosenburg, rolled his eyes upward, smiled his enigmatic smile and said, "Well, Dr. Lewis, it looks like He has arranged another 'coincidental' meeting for you. Here comes M. K. Uzi Baram." We were standing in the entrance of the Great Synagogue of Jerusalem. Avigdor introduced me to Mr. Baram, member of Israel's Parliament (Knesset). Mr. Baram is highly active in promoting the release of the Russian Jews. Since my daughter Sandy Lewis Howell heads our Department of Concern for the Russian Jews, this meeting was most fortunate. We had an enlightening conversation and promise of further contact.

We had been running into so many "coincidental" situations of meeting with various people that one would strain his credibility to even believe in coincidence relating to the whole train of the week's events.

Standing in a little neighborhood restaurant one day, Avigdor said, "Well, here comes another one for you, Dr. Lewis." He called to the gentleman who had just entered. It was Israel Eldad, colorful character in modern Israeli history, eminent historian, a man for all seasons. As I was introduced, a memory stirred in my mind. "I am pleased to meet you, Mr. Eldad. I recall that you are the man who was quoted in *Time* magazine after the war in 1967 as saying, 'From the time that David captured Jerusalem until the building of the temple it was but one generation; so it shall be with us.' " He was surprised, to say the least, that I would quote his words of almost twenty years past. We just kept running into people connected with the whole temple concept and movement.

SEARCHER FOR THE LOST ARK

A couple of days later, sitting in another little local restaurant in Jerusalem, I noted a table of eight men next to our party. With me was the TV camera crew, Avigdor, Mr. Israel Ferri, my wife, and Yaakov Gallis. I studied the men at the other table. I said to myself, "That man at the head of the table looks like an archaeologist. Those two look like military people," and so on around the table. They were all wearing work clothes. The leader of the party leaned over and whispered a question in Avigdor's ear. Avigdor said, "Yes, this is Dr. Lewis from America; yes, you have probably seen him on TV."

The gentleman stood and said, "Dr. Lewis, I have been wanting to meet you for a long time; my name is Vendyl Jones."

Vendyl Jones searching in Israel for the ashes of the red heifer (necessary for the ceremonies of purification and rebuilding of the temple).

Standing to my feet, I responded, "Vendyl Jones! I have been wanting to meet you for a long time also. I have listened to many tape recordings of your lectures. You are the man who is searching for the ark of the covenant and the container with the ashes of the red heifer."

You can believe that we had a most fascinating conversation, and have had many more since. Vendyl recently spoke to one of our tour groups in Jerusalem. He is searching in a secret location near Qumran by the Dead Sea which we have visited recently. Vendyl is now an Israeli citizen. He has an incredible story to tell, you can be sure of that.

Vendyl Jones is not the only one who believes that he has the correct interpretation of the copper scroll. There is an alternate point of view that is embraced by Reverend O'Neil Carmen, who is digging for the ashes of the red heifer near the Qumran village about a half-mile from where Vendyl's location is found. When alternate projects and views are in contradiction to each other, all we can do is stand back and say that we will wait and see—after all, this is the nature of archaeological research. Many people dig in many places for various artifacts. Sometimes great treasures are found, and sometimes everyone comes up with empty hands. Once again, in this case, we will just have to wait and see.

One of our tour groups in Israel. In these caves, near the Dead Sea, Vendyl Jones believes he will find the second copper scroll which will lead to the ark of the covenant.

Vendyl Jones (left) with team of searchers.

Ramona Lewis climbing into the archaeological digs near the Dead
Sea.

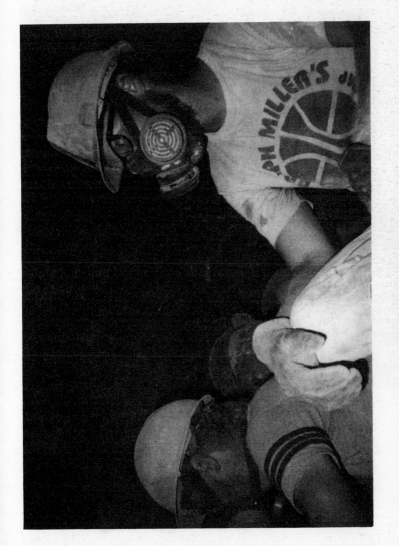

Workers in the digs searching for the ashes of the red heifer.

O'neil Carmen co-directs the archaeological team searching for the ashes of the red heifer near Qumran, Israel. This is near where Vendyl Jones is searching. It is a rival operation.

BACK TO THE GREAT SYNAGOGUE

I always like to take my tour groups to visit the Great Synagogue. There are things to see and learn there that can be found in no other place. The late Dr. Maurice Jaffe was the director and founder of both the Hechel Shlomo (Palace of Solomon) and the Great Synagogue. The Hechel Shlomo is the seat of the chief rabbinate and as such is the world headquarters of the Orthodox Jewish religion.

Some have fantasized that the Great Synagogue is the new temple of Israel, but it is not nor will it ever be. It is in the wrong location. Since the next temple is recognized by God as a *holy* temple, we are sure it will be in the only place God designated a temple could stand— right on Mount Moriah.

Dr. Jaffe has spoken to many of our tour groups at the Great Synagogue. We have all of his lectures on tape.

I asked Rabbi Jaffe if the Great Synagogue could possibly be the new temple of Israel. He laughed in his characteristic fashion and said, "Oh, no, no, no my dear man. That is totally impossible. When we build the temple it will be built right where it belongs, on Mount Moriah."

Believe me, no serious Jew who has anything to do with the building of the temple would tell you anything contrary to this. Only in the realm of fantasy would anyone imagine that the Great Synagogue is the temple.

It is with sorrow and regret that we report to you that Rabbi Doctor Jaffe has passed away. Recently, while standing in front of the Ben Zvi Institute, his son, an attorney in Jerusalem, walked up and greeted us. He said, "I remember how fondly my father spoke of you and how much he enjoyed speaking to the groups that you brought to the Great Synagogue. You know, you are one of the few Christian groups that he ever met with."

I said that we really missed him and his lectures, whereupon his son said, "I have to argue a case before the Supreme Court tomorrow morning, but if you can meet me at the Synagogue at 8:30, I'll be there and give you a special tour." I can assure you that it was a great delight. Until the temple is built, the Great Synagogue will stand as the most important edifice in all of Judaism.

12

Brutal War Against Bible Prophecy

As we approach the end of the age an incredible war against Bible prophecy is being waged on all fronts. We expected this. The New Testament warned of an onslaught against the message of our Lord's return: "There shall come in the last days scoffers, walking after their own lusts [desires], saying, Where is the promise of his coming?" Peter speaks of their willful ignorance! (See 2 Peter 3:1-18.)

Prophecy has always been important to our church. First of all, being biblically oriented, we respect the message because it comprises slightly over one-third of the contents of the Bible, including both prophecy fulfilled and prophecy anticipated.

Prophecy already fulfilled proves the veracity and authority of the Bible. Biblical prediction has been one hundred percent unerring in its accuracy thus far. Prophecy future will be consummated in the same literal way it has always been in the past.

FRONTAL ASSAULT

Who is making war against the prophetic Word of God? First of all there are the atheists, New Agers, and secular humanists. To them the prophetic message is a threat, and they never cease to attack it. The names of our Bible prophecy teachers frequently appear in the pages of atheistic and humanistic publications. We are viewed as the scum of the intellectual pond. Our views are ridiculed and we are described as being promoters of Armageddon. We are thought to be not only deluded, but dangerous.

A recently published book, written by a modernist, makes a broadside attack against Evangelicals who preach on end-time Bible prophecy. *Prophecy and Politics* by Grace Halsel takes a shot at almost every Evangelical who teaches on Bible prophecy, from Billy Graham to Hal Lindsey. This author would feel insulted if he had been left out of the book, but on page 118 Ms. Halsel makes her attempt at slandering this author, while in fact her statement has a reverse effect.

It is well documented that New Age thinkers (a host of them) teach the second coming of "a" christ, the Lord Maitreya, the Avitar, one of the great ascended masters of the universal hierarchy. Each of these writers specifically points out that the one coming is *not*, the historic Jesus Christ of the Gospels. One prominent New Age author has boldly outlined a detailed plan on how a *staged second coming of a new christ to the Mount of Olives* could be engineered.

While we are concerned with the frontal assault technique, actually it is not a major threat to most believers. It represents a far greater danger to unbelievers who will be turned away from the gospel without ever hearing what we really are saying.

THE FIFTH COLUMN

Of greater concern is the fact that some of the New Age message has infiltrated some of the historically older church denominations.

The fifth column concept was well developed during the Second World War. A fifth columnist was a person who infiltrated the ranks of the opposition, posed as one of them, and then worked for their destruction.

There are a multitude of fifth columnists in the churches today. Our own ranks have been somewhat, but hopefully not significantly, penetrated as yet. In our church we have consistently preached the second coming of our Lord Jesus Christ, primarily because of our commitment to the full gospel message of the Bible.

Additionally, our clergy have a strong commitment to a sixteen item Statement of Fundamental Truths. This statement must be signed annually for the minister's renewal of credentials. Significantly, four of the sixteen items in the statement deal with eschatology (end-time prophecy). By annually signing the renewal, each of our preachers commits himself to preaching a wide scope of Biblical doctrine as expressed in the statement.

Today we see people claiming to be prophets scorn normal interpretation of Bible prophecy, offering their own "inspired" utterances for the guidance of both the Church and individuals. Ezekiel speaks of prophets "that prophesy out of their own hearts...foolish prophets that follow their own spirit, and have seen nothing...They have seen vanity and lying divination, saying, The Lord saith: and the Lord hath not sent them...They have seduced my people" (Ezek. 13:2-10; read entire context). Peter warns the Church that there will be false teachers and prophets in our own midst (2 Pet. 2:1-2). Like Balaam, even when they are right they can be wrong! (2 Pet. 2:15-16; Num. 22).

FRIENDS, FANATICS

Far more serious in its potential for damage to the message is the fact that some of our friends, who love the message and proclaim it, venture into realms of fantasy and even fanaticism which rob Bible prophecy of its true nobility and purpose.

Irresponsibility, escapism, identifying the Antichrist, fables, doom saying, and sheer speculation are specters dreamed up by our fringe area fanatics. Unfortunately short-sighted persons might see this as characteristic of Bible prophecy. Nothing could be further from the truth.

How can one read the Book of Revelation and see more devil than God, more Antichrist than Jesus Christ? No! The Apocalypse is one grand, unified declaration of the ultimate victory of Jesus Christ over all the powers of darkness! Prophecy is a victory message, a message of hope, faith, blessing, and motivation. Our God is greater than Satan and all of his minions.

Here is a practical suggestion: When you want a doomsday message, watch the TV evening news or read your daily newspaper. The ancient Midianites were a source of trouble to the Israelites, alternately warring against them and tempting them to compromise with the pagan culture around them. Similarly we have our problems with the modern Media-nites. When you want a message of hope, turn to your Bible (Titus 2:11-14).

Other friends of the Bible have decided that, while it is the Word of God, it doesn't really mean what it says. They have accepted the allegorical (non literal) mode of interpretation for a general treatment of the Scripture. Certainly there is allegory and symbol in the Word, but in general, the Bible is literal. When an obvious symbol is used (Example: Rev. 12, the sun-clothed woman) we seek the literal meaning of the symbol. We never leave the pages of the Bible to interpret its symbols. The Bible is self-interpreting. Our scholars will recognize that this is a simplified overview, but this short chapter is not intended to be a course in hermeneutics.

Those who do not take the Bible literally now tell us that there will be no Rapture, other than a general feeling of being "caught up" in the excitement of the moment when (if) Jesus ever returns. There will be no literal thousand-year millennial reign of Christ on earth. We are in the Kingdom now. Satan is already bound. There will be no literal Antichrist.

THE KINGDOM IS NOW

Of course we are in the Kingdom now. When one is born again (John 3) he enters the Kingdom and the Kingdom enters him. This does not preclude that there will be a visible, manifested Millennium. This thousand year visible, earthly demonstration of the eternal Kingdom will be brought into being by the literal return of Jesus, not by the efforts of man. Some write that we are in the Millennium, but the Bible describes the Millennium as a time of blessing, peace, prosperity, law and order, and rejoicing. Look at the present climate of war, violence, hate, abuse, vile immorality, and then try to tell us this is the Millennium. If the binding of Satan described in Revelation has already taken place, all I can say is that the devil is on an awfully long chain.

FORSAKERS OF THE MESSAGE—THE GREATEST DANGER

The people most damaging to the end-time message are those who believe it, but choose to ignore it. The message is too controversial. Too many abuses have been promoted. It is too complicated. There are differences of opinion. It is divisive. So the field is abandoned to others, only too eager to take advantage of our shortcomings.

On the other hand, the doctrine of salvation is controversial. Every doctrine is abused. The gospel itself is both simple and complicated. There are differences of opinion on everything the Bible teaches. Truth is always divisive inasmuch as some receive and others reject it.

A pastor told me, "I am too busy to study and preach on prophecy." Having been a pastor I can sympathize with this problem. But the difficulty must be overcome. Pastor, no one expects you to be an eschatological expert. Preach simple, powerful biblical messages on the end-times. Don't concern yourself with fantasies, date setting, or naming the Antichrist. Stick to the basics. Any of us who specialize in prophecy stand ready to help you with recommendations for basic textbooks and other helps. We need to develop more outlines and tapes that we can pass around among ourselves. Nature abhors a vacuum. Ignore prophecy and undesirable ideas will flow with a hellish energy into the minds of our people.

Dr. James Brown has not made prophecy his primary emphasis. His career has been that of a seminary educator and pastor. When speaking to a group of clergy in the Indiana district, Dr. Brown made the following startling statement: "The greatest danger facing the Assemblies of God is the *abandonment of the preaching of eschatology.*" What do you think?

"Not forsaking the assembling of yourselves together, as the manner of some is...and so much the more, as ye see the day approaching" (Heb. 10:25). People, don't forsake attendance at your church. Don't forsake the message of the approaching day of our Lord, which makes our assembling, exhortation, and fellowship so rich and spiritually meaningful.

13

The Importance Of Prophecy

I will not bore you again with recitations of how much of the Bible is prophecy and how much Jesus talked about it. You have heard all that before. Let me get close to home.

The Church is now engaged in the greatest theological battle it has ever faced, and the bottom line is eschatology. You bemoan the sweeping advances of the Kingdom Now advocates, the Theonomists, the Reconstructionists, the Dominionists, The Manifest Sons, and the promoters of a host of other New Wave doctrines. We cry because our people are being deceived and churches are defecting. Yet we ignore the root cause and that is ignorance of the true prophetic meaning of the Word of God. I must assume (hopefully) that you understand what the issues are at this late date. However I am not unaware of the human capacity to ignore what is right in front of us. Numerous pastors have told me, "Oh, there is none of that in my congregation." How amazed they were when people from the church began coming to me either to argue from a Kingdom Now or Dominionist viewpoint or to express concern for the infiltration taking place locally.

I recently spent two hours talking to the man who headed up the Dominion Press—an Assembly of God Church member. I really liked the man and found him reasonable, entertaining, and easy to talk to. I also think he is one of the most dangerous men in the Church today.

IN THE LAST DAYS

Prophecy is a major subject in the Bible. Until I understand God's overall plan, how can I meaningfully relate my current activities to His ultimate realities?

The Dominionists and Kingdom Now teachers will agree with me that the key issue causing much of the disagreement in the Church today is prophecy. We all agree that we are living in prophetic times. How we interpret prophecy will determine our course of action from now until the Lord comes. This is no minor consideration.

The Kingdom Now teachers and the Dominionists blatantly accuse those of us who believe in literal interpretation, the Rapture, the thousand-year manifestation of the Kingdom (Millennium) and Israel's place in God's continuing plan for the nations of being rank heretics. As I understand the biblical concept, an heretic is a damned soul. I am not about to accuse the brethren who have thus slandered us of being heretics. I believe they are brethren who have strayed into a serious digression of a major truth of God's Word, but I do not question their salvation. That is between them and God.

TACTICS

Their tactics are simple and very clever. First of all they want to convert you to their point of view. If that fails, the second tactic is to silence you by saying, "Look, the major issue is unity in the Body. Eschatology and Israel are minor items on the Church's agenda. Ignore those subjects for the sake of peace." Third, if a person or ministry continues to be "troublesome," then the tactic is to try and destroy that person or ministry by accusing them of being troublemakers, thus distancing them from their uninformed friends and allies who fail to see how important the doctrinal issues are. Believe me the Kingdomists know the vital importance of these matters.

"Hardheaded" people who refuse to be silent on eschatological matters must be put down as dividers of the body of Christ. Major ministries that were once outspoken in agreement with our position on the second coming of Christ have become silent. When questioned privately, they protest that they have not changed their minds, but they have nevertheless been effectively silenced when warned that to speak out on these subjects brands one as being divisive. You could alienate yourself from all your friends by continuing to emphasize these areas of doctrines.

ISRAEL

Definitely any ministry that emphasizes Israel's role must be silenced. How many are there who once were strong advocates of Israel who have now fallen by the wayside? If they have not changed their minds, their mouths have been sealed. "Unity" is more important. Unity is important, but just think of how much the Bible talks about Israel and how much about unity and then decide where the priority lies. Unity based on compromise is a lie. It is not unity at all. It is deception of the subtlest kind.

SOLUTION

Our people must become Bible scholars. Our pastors and evangelists must take the time to study the prophetic word and to intelligently declare it. Sensationalism should be avoided like a plague. No longer should the flamboyant date-setters and antichrist-namers dominate the field of prophetic teaching. That has nothing to do with the real issues of the end-times at all.

Refuse to allow anyone to accuse us of being escapists because we believe in the Rapture. I want you to know that Rapture believers are at the forefront of social action, drug rehabilitation, missions, witnessing, and legitimate political action. The men who have launched the major Christian TV networks are all Rapture believers. Anyone can point to weakminded or theologically unsound people who are the escapists in our ranks. But don't tell me that believing in the Rapture makes one an escapist. When Paul writes to Titus of the blessed hope, he prefaces his remark with a call to responsible living in this present world and follows it with a call to good works.

Our book *Smashing the Gates of Hell in the Last Days* is an example of what we should be teaching in the light of these end-times. It is a call to present action in the kingdom of God while we await the potentially imminent coming of Christ.

SERIOUS CHOICE BEFORE US

Go ahead, believe that prophecy is not important, and you will suffer tragic consequences. On the other hand if this strong statement stirs you, then begin today to search the Scriptures and determine to know the Word of God and the issues of our times. The benefits will be beyond measure.

14

Setting the Date for Christ's Return Catastrophe of the 1990s

From the time of the early church until now there have been hundreds, if not thousands, of date-setting or date-suggesting or date-hinting schemes. All date-setting schemes historically have proven to be false prophecies.

Remember: Jesus could come today! Date-setting destroys the idea of the possible imminent return of Jesus. It is the unfaithful servant who says, "My Lord delayeth His coming." We must believe that Jesus could return today!

All date-setting and date-suggesting ideas have been wrong. This is not a new thing in the Church. It is an ancient, sick error that has always proven to be destructive. It has been recycled over and over with the same evil results.

This madness must be stopped now, or all credibility in prophecy will be dead. No one will listen any more to the true, noble, and reliable message of biblical prophecy.

THE DATING GAME

When is Jesus coming back? When is the world coming to an end? A lot of people think they have the answer and are setting dates. *Newsweek* magazine referred to the emphasis on the Apocalypse as the "Boom in doom."

I firmly believe Jesus is coming back. Over 300 Bible prophecies pointed to the first coming of Jesus. They were all fulfilled. The New Testament has 257 references to the future, literal return of Jesus to this planet. They, too, will be fulfilled!

No one can destroy the plan of God, but a lot is being done to erode people's confidence in Bible prophecy. In fact, more damage is done to the credibility of the message by the Bible's friends than by its enemies!

Our Saviour clearly warned: "But of that day and hour knoweth no man, no, not the angels of heaven, but my Father only" (Matt. 24:36). In spite of that plain statement, schemes for dating the Rapture, the beginning of the Millennium, or the end of the world are recycled over and over.

Let's take a brief look at the checkered history of the bewildering world of the date-setters.

Augustine suggested that the world would probably end in A.D. 1000. From about 950 to 1000, wealthy landowners all over Europe were encouraged to deed their holdings to the church in exchange for pardon for their sins.

Early in the last century, Dr. R. C. Shimeall wrote a book predicting that the Millennium would come in 1868. In that same century, a converted Jew, Joseph Worlf, began prophesying that Jesus would come to the Mount of Olives in 1847. Lady Hester Stanhope converted to his doctrine, moved to Palestine, and established residence on the Mount of Olives. She kept two beautiful white Arabian horses in stables there. One was for Jesus to ride through the Golden Gate. Presumably, the other was for her to accompany Him.

In 1918, H. C. Williams wrote a volume entitled *The Revelation of Jesus Christ*. In it he said, "A.D. 1914 is the time limit set in the Scriptures for the concurrence of the war: that the war broke out and continues in all details as described by the prophets is a complete fulfillment of the prophetic record."

In the same book, Williams predicted that 1934 would mark the downfall of the Gentile nations, and in 1972, the Millennium would begin.

In 1975, a widely circulated book proclaimed that probably the Rapture would take place on September 5 or 6, 1975.

Following the interpretations of this man, others began to preach the September 1975 date. One pastor even borrowed large sums of money, which he had no way of paying back, to invest in missions. In a sermon, he explained that he had nothing to worry about since Jesus was sure to come back on September 5, 1975.

This is the stuff that spiritual tragedies are made of, for on September 7 the bubble burst. Only eternity will reveal the tragedies created by those playing the dating game.

Date-setters claiming to be a part of the Church and citing biblical authority can potentially play havoc with the credibility of the Second Coming concept in the minds of millions. When people are disappointed with date-setting failures, they are tempted to "throw out the baby with the bath water." Their downfall is not being able to distinguish between the valid and solemn message of Christ's coming and the perversion of it as perpetrated by false shepherds, opportunists, and the deluded.

Date-setting is not just an historic phenomenon. Not long ago, numerous books and periodicals were predicting that the Rapture must take place in 1988. This was based on an interpretation of Jesus' words in Matthew 24:34: "Verily, I say unto you, This generation shall not pass away, till all these things be fulfilled."

They say a generation is forty years. Israel (the fig tree referred to in Matt. 24:32) became a nation in 1948. So 1948 + 40 = 1988.

There are several flaws in this superficial reasoning.

First, the generation concept is not that firmly fixed in Scripture. I am not sure that Exodus with the forty-year generation, or the Book of Job with the thirty-five-year generation, or the statement that the days of man are "three score and ten"—indicating a seventy-year generation—are to be taken as precisely describing a generation. The date-setters choose whichever one fits their scheme.

Secondly, why select 1948 for the year when the "fig tree" put forth its leaves? Why not the return of the Jews in the 1880s? Why not the founding of Zionism by Theodor Herzl in Basel, Switzerland, in 1897? Why not the founding of Tel Aviv, the first all-Jewish city in modern times, established in 1909?

Nineteen seventeen would be a likely year due to two major events: General Allenby's liberation of Jerusalem and Arthur James Balfour's famous declaration that "His Majesty's government view with favor the establishment in Palestine of a national home for the Jewish people, and will use their best endevors to facilitate the achievement of the object..."

The capture of old Jerusalem by the Israelis in 1967 is considered as a possibility by many.

May we suggest that is was not our Lord's intention in this passage to provide a means of fixing the time of His return since He immediately says this would be an impossibility (Matt. 24:36).

Thirdly, the word translated "generation" is *genea* and does not necessarily mean a literal generation. W. E. Vine's *Expository Dictionary of New Testament Words* gives one possible translation of *genea* as "A race of people."

Many outstanding scholars agree on that translation. If that is correct, then Jesus is simply declaring the indestructibility of the Jewish people. This would fit the context best.

I believe the coming of Jesus is imminent. He could come back today. But He may not.

I have believed that since I was ten years old. If you had asked me then if I thought I would grow to be a man of fifty years of age, I would have said that is was highly unlikely. After all, Jesus is coming soon.

I am still anticipating His coming. I will continue to proclaim His coming as imminent. But soon? I am not sure how you define that word *soon*, and the closer one gets to defining the word, the closer one is to being a date-setter.

It is better to live as if Jesus were coming today and yet prepare for the future as if He were not coming for a long time. Then you are ready for time and eternity.

A friend once asked the great evangelist Dwight L. Moody, "Mr. Moody, if you knew Jesus was coming back at six o'clock this evening, what would you do today?" I am sure the questioner was surprised at Moody's answer for he said, "If I knew Jesus was coming back this evening at six o'clock, this afternoon I would plant apple trees." That is a beautiful answer.

If you knew Jesus was coming back tonight, what would you do today? If there is something you would feel compelled to rush out and do, then you had better do it now, for Jesus might come back tonight! On the other hand, if you are daily living your life in His will, then you would not have to change one thing you are planning to do!

God designed His revelation to us so that we are always living on the edge of eternity, and yet always planning for our future here. Suppose He had revealed the very date of the rapture of the Church 1,900 years ago? I doubt if the Church would even be in existence now. It is good to live in anticipation, but to realize that we do not know when the trumpet will sound. Go ahead and make your five year and twenty-five year plans. If the Lord comes before you complete your venture, so be it. We won't mind the interruption in the least!

The moment you set a date for the coming, you upset this "divine balance," and you create havoc and distrust in the body of Christ. I tell you date-setting is a sin and should be denounced from every pulpit!

Pastors, if you ignore the subject of prophecy or accept some of the modern reinterpretations of prophecy, you have solved nothing. Only by diligent study of and declaration of the Word of God in this realm will you bring real hope and good works with stability to your flock. Ignore prophecy, and the fanatics and distorters will have a field day. Nature abhors a vacuum. If you create a spiritual vacuum by ignoring the prophetic Word, false teachers will supply something to fill that void.

Jesus said, "Watch therefore; for ye know not what hour your Lord doth come...Therefore be ye also ready: for in such an hour as ye think not the Son of man cometh. Who then is that faithful and wise servant, whom his lord hath made ruler over his household, to give them meat in due season? Blessed (happy) is that servant, whom his lord when he cometh shall find so doing" (Matt. 24:42-46).

We are not undertaking a mere intellectual exercise here. This dating game is dangerous.

In 1832 William Miller first preached, "And so, brethren, it has been revealed to me that the world is coming to an end. Repent, repent, I say, for you have but eleven years to be washed clean in the blood of the Lamb. In mighty fire and terror the world will end in 1843."

As 1843 approached, anticipation turned into a kind of madness. People abandoned homes, farms, material possessions, and even children to gather in homes, praying as they waited for the last trump.

In Westford, Massachusetts, about five hundred people gathered wearing white robes to wait for the Coming. When the midnight hour of December 31, 1842, arrived, an old town drunk, known as Crazy Amos, blew a trumpet outside the fine old mansion where the people were gathered. Pandemonium broke loose, and several were seriously injured in the stampede. Outside, they found not Jesus, but a bleary-eyed, laughing old drunkard.

Historians record a darker side of the debacle. Following disappointment upon disappointment and a continual readjusting of the dates, many lost their minds. The asylum at Worcester, Massachusetts, became so overcrowded that a large hall had to be appropriated to house the deranged.

In New Hampshire, New York, Vermont, Maine, and parts of Pennsylvania, the lunacy rate is said to have increased three hundred percent in 1843-1844 as a result of the date-setting.

People who were usually rational went everywhere in flowing white robes, ready for ascension. Suicides became common in the face of disappointment.

When it was all over, the disillusioned faithful went back to try to

LOUIS NAPOLEON
THE INFIDEL ANTICHRIST

PREDICTED IN PROPHECY TO CONFIRM A SEVEN YEARS

COVENANT WITH THE JEWS,

ABOUT THE YEAR 1861, AND NEARLY TO SUCCEED IN

GAINING A UNIVERSAL EMPIRE;

AND THEN TO BE DEIFIED, AND

IDOLATROUSLY WORSHIPPED,

AND ALSO TO INSTITUTE A 3½ YEARS

SANGUINARY PERSECUTION

AGAINST THE CHRISTIAN CHURCH, FROM 1864-65 TO 1868, DURING
WHICH TIME

WARS, FAMINES, PESTILENCES & EARTHQUAKES,

IF NOT RELIGIOUS PERSECUTION, WILL PREVAIL IN

ENGLAND AND AMERICA

......UNTIL THE......

SLAUGHTER OF THE WITNESSES,

ELIAS AND ANOTHER PROPHET; AFTER WHICH NAPOLEON, THEIR DESTROYER,
TOGETHER WITH THE POPE ARE FORESHOWN TO BE

CAST ALIVE INTO THE LAKE OF FIRE

......AT THE......

DESCENT OF CHRIST AT ARMAGEDDON

ABOUT THE YEAR

1868.

With an examination of the views of Sir E. Denny, Revs. E. Bickersteth, T. Birks, Dr. Tregelles,
C. Maitland, C. Molyneux, H. G. Guinness, W. Burgh, G. S Faber, H. Gauntlett, T. Jones,
B. W. Newton, J. Frere, M. Habershon, H. Kelshall, E. Taunton, etc:

BY THE REV. M. BAXTER,

OF THE CHURCH OF ENGLAND, LATE MISSIONARY AT ONONDAGA, CANADA WEST,
AUTHOR OF "THE COMING BATTLE."

SECOND EDITION OF 5000.

CANADA: M. SHEWAN, King Street, Toronto; G. BARNES, Hamilton; TAYLOR & WILSON, London.
UNITED STATES: SMITH & ENGLISH, Philadelphia; FRANKLIN KNIGHT, 846 Broadway, New
York; J. HIMES, 18 Washington Street, Boston.
ENGLAND: WERTHEIM & MACINTOSH, 24 Paternoster Row, London.

PRICE---SIX CENTS.

From Time Immemorial
this error of date setting
has haunted the Church.

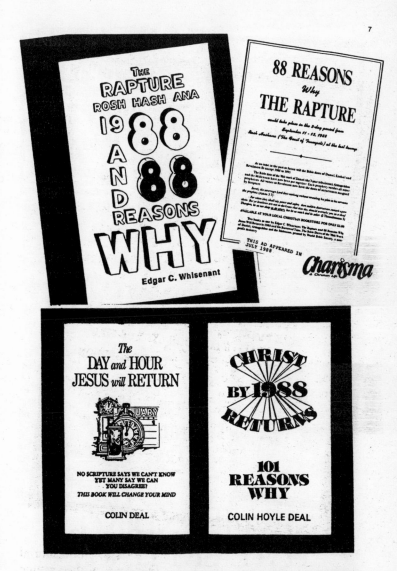

NEVER ENDING
DATE SETTING
DEBACLE

pick up the pieces of the lives they had abandoned. Many become atheists.

Modern date-setters are getting ready to rerun a tragedy of that magnitude—or worse. As world crises mount, people will find the date-setters' schemes alluring as a psychological escapism.

A book publisher recently told me, "If you want to write a best-seller in the field of prophecy, name the Antichrist and set a date." There is something sinister behind that suggestion!

Newsweek for September 16, 1974, carried an article entitled, "The Doomsday Effect." It said that in 1982, all nine planets or our solar system will be in conjunction—that is in a straight line in relation to the sun and all on one side of the sun. The combined gravitational pull may cause great storms on the sun. These storms could alter wind directions on earth, and this in turn could slow the speed of earth's rotation and trigger the worst earthquakes the world has ever known. I wrote several articles refuting the idea. I commented on it over TV and on our monthly cassette service, the Audio Prophecy Digest.

A number of nationally-known Bible teachers had used this as a basis for suggesting that the world would be in the Tribulation by 1982, but we could not accept it. Our conservative approach turned out to be right.

A periodical out of Florida calculated that the Rapture would take place soon and that the Millennium would begin by 1979. Other dates being set are 1992, 1993, and 2000.

Two thousand! It has an almost magical appeal! I recently heard a minister declare: "A day is as a thousand years and a thousand years as a day with the Lord. There were seven days of creation. It has now been six 'days' or six thousand years from creation (or will be about A.D. 2000, according to Usher's chronology). That leaves one day of a thousand years—the Millennium, so the end has to come by the year 2000."

Let us consider a possibility. If Jesus tarries in His coming, the date-setters will have a heyday as the year 2000 approaches. It will be like a fever. It will sell pamphlets and books by the millions, but if Jesus does not come back by the year 2000, it is hard to imagine any credibility being left for the Bible prophecy message unless we begin a strong program right now to offset the heresy of date-setting.

Ignoring it will not make it go away. Only by preaching the true and dignified message of the Lord's return and by strongly denouncing date-setting can we hope to maintain confidence in the Bible message of Jesus' return.

Pastors, evangelists, teachers—please do not ignore the prophecy message because it is too complicated, or because it has been abused by fanatics. Preach the Word. Only truth, strongly declared, overcomes terror and error.

I hope Jesus comes back before A.D. 2000. I am ready for Him to come right now, but if we are still here in A.D. 2001, the Bible prophecy message will be just as valid as it is today. The question is, will anyone be listening?

The following was written in July of 1988: "Jesus may come back today. He could come back on September 10. He could come back on September 14, or any other day, at any time. He definitely will not come back on September 11, 12, or 13, 1988, 'for in such an hour as you think not, the Son of Man cometh.' "

"Be patient. I am totally confident. Are you? Will you let the facts speak for themselves on September 14, 1988? Will you be so gullible as to wait for the next date-setting scheme? Or will you cast away your faith, incapable of discerning truth from error? It is not God, but man that fails. All date-setting systems fail and disappoint people.

"If we do not speak out now, here are results to watch for from now until Jesus comes:

1. People will ignore prophecy. Credibility will be lost.

2. Many will abandon the faith.

3. The New Kingdomists and Dominionists will use these failures to promote their errors in the Church.

4. The secular world will scoff and attack more and more.

5. The stage will be set for the New Age false christ.

6. People could commit suicide.

7. This may cause the government to step in and make preaching of premillennial prophecy and the Rapture illegal. It can happen here."

Since millions of Christians, unfortunately, accepted the date-setters' errors God definitely avoided those dates. While many had questions about what I wrote the answers were apparent on September 14.

ON AUGUST 12, 1988—WE SENT OUT
A SERIOUS CALL TO PRAYER AND FASTING

"We are in a real danger zone. We must be alert. There are many powerful enemies outside the Church and some enemy infiltrators, posing as spiritual leaders inside the Church. The last thing we need is craziness in our own ranks.

"We know the date-setters (hinters) think of themselves as friends of the prophetic message. We do not view them as enemies. We do not question that they are sincere brothers and sisters in the Lord."

230

On that basis, I appealed to them all: "Please, dear friends, if Jesus has not come by September 14, do not abandon your faith. Please do not commit suicide." This applies to all future date-setting schemes.

"Think now of how you can constructively help rehabilitate those who have been deceived. Date-setters should begin with public repentance and a public vow that they will never again have anything to do with date-setting (or suggesting). This is the least we expect of them. In this way only can any degree of credibility be maintained.

"Above all, don't tell us that your system just needs adjustment. Too many have tried that trick in the past. When the date fails they say, 'Oh, I made a slight miscalculation, the correct date is....'

"Dear Christians, we must fast and pray September 11-14. Especially the 13th and 14th. Most urgently, the 14th. This will be a dark day for many sincere people if the Lord has not come. Many could be tempted to commit suicide.

"A lot of people have quit their jobs to evangelize this false message. Many have given away their homes, money, and other possessions. They will feel abandoned by the Lord. They will feel like utter fools for being so gullible. Some will turn in anger on those who have misled them.

"Do not condemn these people, but fast and pray for their spiritual preservation. Satan will be attacking them with doubt and guilt as never before. The perpetrators will be tempted to sit around and concoct ideas to get themselves off the hook with their followers. Some will go into a cycle of identifying the Antichrist. Many will think they only do these things to make money by selling their sensational books and taking in huge donations. I will not judge this—it is in God's hands."

A MANIFESTO

The Scripture clearly says that no man can know the day or hour of the Lord's coming, thus indicating that date-setting serves no good purpose. And date-setting has historically always proven to be false prophecy which is damaging to the cause of Christ.

Then, too, we are living in the last days and nothing must be allowed to detract from the nobility and power of the message of end-time Bible prophecy.

Therefore we, the undersigned, hereby demand that all date-setting and date-suggesting cease immediately. Let abstinence from this type of speculation prevail until the Lord comes.

We absolutely must stop this type of activity or there will be few who will take the message of prophecy seriously.

If Jesus should tarry until the year 2000, we envision that by 2001 the message of Bible prophecy will be scorned, attacked, and possibly outlawed by legal means—thus giving the New Age movement a clear field for the introduction of their occult humanist messiah.

This manifesto has been signed by hundreds of church leaders, denominational officers, pastors, evangelists, seminary professors, teachers, etc. The list may be published in a later edition of *Prophecy 2000*. If you want your name added to the list please write David A. Lewis, P.O. Box 11115, Springfield, MO 65808.

15

Escapism

Are Pre-millennarians Socially Irresponsible?

It is hard for me to believe the harsh charges that are being hurled at those members of the body of Christ who believe in the rapture of the Church (the catching away as in 1 Thess. 4:17). We believe that following the rapture of the Church there will be a visible return of Christ (Zech. 14:4; Rev. 19) and then He will establish His reign of a thousand years of peace on earth—the Millennium.

Does that make us escapists? I say it does not. Pre-mils are some of the most active people in the kingdom of God here and now. Except in the case of a minority of extremists, most pre-mils are about as socially and politically active as any other sector of Evangelical Christianity regardless of eschatalogical views.

I see my pre-mil brothers and sisters at the vanguard of world evangelization, drug rehabilitation, political activism, protest against social evils, feeding and clothing the poor, etc.

A TESTIMONY

Let me approach this from a subjective point of view for a moment. I was brought up in a Methodist Sunday school in the small midwestern town of Britton, South Dakota. I don't remember that we were socially active except for sponsoring an occasional rummage sale or providing

Christmas gift boxes for the poor. When I was ten years old an Assembly of God minister came to Britton and started holding services in the I.O.O.F. Lodge Hall in the basement of Velta Carter's clothing store. My mother and I started attending the little mission and that is where we got saved.

Friends, we were poor folks. Back in those days almost everyone in the Pentecostal churches and the Evangelical churches was from the economically disadvantaged strata of society. Are we to be indicted for lack of social consciousness in those days? We were the folks others should have been socially conscious about. I lived in a one-room railroad "cook car" that had no indoor toilet facilities. Most of our neighbors were in the same fix. Times were tough. The dust storms and the depression had combined to just about wipe us out. My dad, my uncles, and my grandfather lost their farms to the banks. I remember my poor dad working from sunup to sundown, six days a week, as a farm laborer for twenty-two dollars a month. He had to walk ten miles south of town to get to work. He would come home after sundown Saturday and leave in the early hours of Monday morning to be there for work by Monday's sunrise. Later while working for Charlie Langenberg constructing metal buildings for farms, dad got a bonus of five dollars one Christmas. Charlie told him to get some whiskey and celebrate. Dad came home so happy, not with whiskey, but with the news that we could have a real Christmas, even with a turkey! Now sit in your dominion theology ivory tower and criticize the Evangelicals for being politically inactive from 1925 until recent times.

Were we, even then, totally irresponsible? Had we no social consciousness? How I recall the pastor taking special offerings for brothers and sisters who were suffering disasters. Was Mrs. Stadler sick? Let the ladies minister to her with gifts of prepared food and above all their loving presence in her home. Was one of the farmers in the church hurt and unable to harvest? Let the men of the church pitch in and bring the crops into the barns. Pastor himself would go out and work long hours in the fields to help an unfortunate brother. Tell me that Kingdom principles were not in operation until you came on the scene, Mr. Kingdom preacher!

SOME CHANGES

My father had one burning desire and that was that his son should have an education and better advantages than he had enjoyed. My frugal mother helped save the dimes and dollars for a college fund. When I was ready for college, there was enough saved to pay my way through school. God had called me to the ministry when I was just eleven years old. That is also when I "tried" to study the Book of Revelation for the first time. I had been inspired by a German preacher, Hans Bretschnieder, an evangelist who talked to us about prophecy and the idea that the Jewish people would return to Palestine and found a nation in fulfillment of God's Word. Somehow it burned in my eleven-year-old heart. When I was fifteen years old and listened to the news that the state of Israel was born in my day, I knew something about the validity of God's promises that no other generation has been privileged to witness.

When I was through school and going into itinerant evangelism, I discovered that "hard times" had not ended. They were days of greatest joy and fulfillment, but there were weeks when the income was ten or twelve dollars. I recall pawning a suit and some other things just to get gas money to get to my next meeting.

About to get married to Ramona Wellner, who was working for the Billy Graham Evangelistic Association in Minneapolis, I was informed by my mother that there was now money in the family coffers to purchase a new automobile for the newly-married couple. I rode to Detroit on the Greyhound bus to buy a car "wholesale" through the purchasing service of the National Association of Evangelicals. I drove back to South Dakota with a brand new 1954 Ford two-door, six-cylindar automobile with overdrive. No frills, no radio, just brand new transportation. It cost $1,612. No automobile I have ever driven brought me any more joy than that Mainline Ford. It was just in time. My old 1939 Nash was totally worn out and could be repaired no more. I sold it to a junk yard. They charged me the same amount to haul it away as they had promised to pay me for the old car!

In those early days of evangelistic ministry, I had an opportunity to see a lot of our churches. Mostly our members were from the less fortunate segment of society as far as economic condition is concerned. It was a marvel to hear of a professional man or factory owner having membership in one of our congregations. Mostly, these folks went to Episcopal or Presbyterian churches. But some quiet changes were going on.

Just like Joseph Arlington Lewis, who sent his boy through Central Bible College, countless Pentecostal families were sending their boys and girls to schools of "higher learning"—schools those moms and dads had never been able to attend. My dad had a third-grade education.

Those Pentecostal boys and girls pursued their educational goals and many became professionals—doctors, lawyers, highly successful businessmen. One is now the governor of Missouri, another is my family doctor. Today, when I minister in the Pentecostal churches, it is common to see a mixture of people of all professions and economic classes. This is the way the Church should be.

Along with education came wider horizons of perception of the ills that beset our world. Social consciousness was born in our midst. Before you charge pre-mils with social irresponsibility, ponder the fact that it was a pre-mil, David Wilkerson, who launched the Teen Challenge ministry, beyond doubt the most successful drug rehabilitation program ever known. Think of the late Mark Buntain, a pre-mil who built a magnificent hospital for the poor in Calcutta; whose on-going mission work daily feeds thousands of starving children at its doors.

A CHALLENGE TO MY COLLEAGUES

There are extremists in every camp. We pre-mils do have those (few) who use prophecy as an excuse for their escapism, irresponsibility, and general weirdness. If you ignore the noble message of Christ's coming because it is controversial, then don't be surprised if the extremists' voices are heard. I plead with Bible college presidents and boards to set up classes to deal with eschatology in a forthright, positive, and uncompromising manner. Don't let our young men and women enter the ministry ill equipped to face the confusion that is being dumped on us today.

16

The Rapture of the Church

Some Advanced Truths and Insights From the Scriptures

My book, *Smashing the Gates of Hell in the Last Days* (New Leaf Press) outlines an agenda for end-time victory. It is a positive affirmation of our eschatological position and it is a call to action for these end-times. This is what a lot of us have been preaching for many years. It was never written as an answer to all the doctrinal confusion prevalent in the field of prophecy, since it was originally written long before we had any awareness of all of these controversies.

I have always preached a pre-trib Rapture. I believe it. I also know that Jesus may not come for awhile. I am responsible to respond to the condition of life here and now. Activism has been in my blood as long as I can remember. Studying and preaching prophecy has been motivational for me. Does an escapist gather a hundred of his colleagues and stand in front of the White House in a prayer vigil, making certain statements to the heads of state? I have testified before the Senate Foreign Relations Committee, conferred with senators, congressmen, heads of state, functioning as an ambassador of the Church to Caesar's household—for the beneficence of the Church. Further, I am not alone. My pre-mil brethren have marched along with me and many have led their own way to the highest levels of conference with the leaders of our nations. It has been my privilege to organize groups of Canadian ministers to confer with their own leaders. Escapism? I don't know what it is. I am ready to go and I am ready to stay. We have plans for years to come. If Jesus comes today—hallelujah! But if not, then tomorrow we will be on the front lines working for our Lord in His kingdom here and now (God willing).

It is time to re-examine the subject of the rapture of the Church. In this essay I hope to bring you some overlooked factors relating to this blessed, though abused doctrine.

DEFINITION OF THE TERM

The word rapture appears in the Bible in the original Greek word *harpazo* which is translated "caught up" in 1 Thessalonians 4:17.

"For the Lord Himself shall descend from heaven with a shout, with the voice of the archangel, and with the trump of God: and the dead in Christ shall rise first: then we which are alive and remain shall be caught up (Greek: Harpazo - raptured) together with them in the clouds, to meet the Lord in the air; and so shall we ever be with the Lord" (1 Thess. 4:16,17).

You will find an abundance of information in *Things To Come* by J. Dwight Pentecost (Zondervan) and *The Rapture Question* by John Walvoord (Zondervan).

HISTORY OF THE DOCTRINE

The New Testament is the foundation upon which the Rapture concept rests. Refer to the following passages: 1 Corinthians 15:51-53; John 14:1-3; 2 Thessalonians 2:1, etc.

Critics point out that the doctrine was not strongly taught or declared until the early 1800s. That is simply not true. It was taught in the early Church as evidenced by many New Testament passages. In the Dark Ages almost every true biblical doctrine was distorted or totally lost to the corrupted church.

It is true that there was never a systematic theology in relation to eschatology until recent times. However, various of the early Church fathers wrote that they were looking for an imminent return of Christ, giving evidence to the fact that after the apostolic period the doctrine was not totally lost for a time.

Again, in the Dark Ages, almost every true doctrine of the Bible was either perverted or lost. The reformation, corrupt as it was, was a great advance over the errors of Rome and began a process of the restoration of biblical truth reminiscent of Isaiah's prophecy:

"Whom shall he teach knowledge? and whom shall he make to

understand knowledge? them that are weaned from the milk and drawn from the breasts. For precept must be upon precept; line upon line; here a little, and there a little; For with stammering lips and another tongue will he speak to this people. To whom he said, This is the rest wherewith ye may cause the weary to rest; and this is the refreshing..." (Isa. 28:9-12).

It is no wonder to us that as we approach the end of days that the Lord would revive interest in the important subject of prophecy. From the time of the reformation renewed interest in systematic Bible study can be traced, and an orderly statement of various Bible doctrines can be observed. Eschatology had its turn in the early 1800s.

It must be understood, however, that no doctrine rises or falls on the witness of history or of the testimony of church fathers. A valid doctrinal truth must find its authority in the words of Scripture alone.

ESCAPE OR ESCAPISM?

The Rapture will be an escape, but the doctrine is not for escapism.

The Rapture is an escape, at only one point of time for only a portion of the eternal body of Christ. What do these people escape from? What are they faced with that causes God to provide some special escape? Is it physical pain and suffering? Is it martyrdom? Is it deprivation?

No portion of the born again Church will have to undergo the specific seven years of God's wrath known as the "Tribulation"—the time of global sorrows and outpoured judgments. The Church will not live under the reign of the beast (Antichrist). But is this the principal reason for the Rapture? We think not.

NOT FOR ESCAPISM

Unfortunately a certain amount of misunderstanding has promoted an escapist mentality in some believers. We have witnessed this manifested in the recent date-setting debacle. Certain well-meaning but misguided people predicted that Jesus would rapture the Church on September 11, 12, or 13, 1988. One propagator of this error went so far as to say that if Jesus did not return by the thirteenth it was not because his calculations were wrong, but because the Bible is wrong. It must be noted that date-setting is forbidden in the Scripture (Matt. 24:36,44; 25:13; Mark 13:32,33). Especially note Mark 13:32,33:

"But of that day and hour knoweth no man; no not the angels which are in heaven, neither the son, but the Father. Take heed and watch and pray; for ye know not when the time is."

Time includes not only day and hour, but also week, month, year, etc.

All date-setting schemes have historically proven to be false prophecies which have damaged the credibility of the Bible prophecy message. We can no longer afford to be tolerant of further errors of this nature. There is just too much at stake.

NO RAPTURE FOR ROME'S MARTYRS

The early Church underwent horrible persecution and martyrdom at the hands of the cruel Roman Caesars. There was no rapture for them.

There have been persecutions of Christian believers in every century, somewhere in the world. Even today people are giving their lives for their faith. There has been no rapture for them. Belief in the Rapture should never promote an unhealthy escapist mentality. Escapists easily fold up under persecution, even thinking God has failed them.

If you and I are ever faced with martyrdom (it could happen), we must not allow our faith to be shaken because we do not escape the wrath of man.

ESCAPE FROM WHAT?

Jesus said, "Watch ye therefore, and pray always, that ye may be accounted worthy to escape all these things that shall come to pass, and to stand before the Son of Man" (Luke 21:36). This has to do with the living believers who are raptured before the specific seven years' Tribulation at the end of this age.

Experience shows us that some Christians do not escape all troubles and even martyrdom in this present age. You could suffer for your faith today or tomorrow. If you are not prepared for that, you have not matured in Christ as God has desired.

The promise of the Rapture is no absolute guarantee that you will escape mental or physical persecution, suffering or even martyrdom. Jesus said, "In this world you will have tribulation (trouble)." This refers to the general condition of tribulation which has fallen on Christians at various times and places throughout history. Belief in the Rapture is no guarantee that evil men will not persecute and even kill you. We despise the escapism that fanatics have attached to the Rapture doctrine. We denounce this escapist mentality at every opportunity. Our blessed hope of Christ's coming for the Church must not be tainted with a lifestyle of irresponsibility. We are to "occupy 'til He comes."

ON MOUNT OLIVET

In the Olivet discourse Jesus warns against deception in the end-times. The disciples asked Him, "What shall be the sign of thy coming and of the end of the world (aion-age)?" The Olivet sermon is the longest teaching on prophecy given by our Lord. It sweeps a wide panorama of last days' events and concepts.

But, before He talks about the signs of the times, the abominating of the temple, fleeing to the wilderness, the sign of the Son of Man in the heavens, the blossoming of the fig tree, the parable of the ten virgins, or of the judgment of the sheep and the goats, the first thing He talks about is deception:

"Take heed that no man deceive you. For many shall come in my name, saying, I am Christ: and shall deceive many" (Matt. 24:4,5).

Not only does Jesus preface His prophetic message with this warning, but He brings it up over and over in the discourse:

"And many false prophets shall rise, and shall deceive many...Then if any man shall say to you, Lo, here is Christ, or there; believe it not. For there shall arise false Christs, and false prophets, and shall shew great signs and wonders; insomuch that, if it were possible, they shall deceive the very elect...Wherefore if they shall say unto you, Behold he is in the desert; go not forth; behold, he is in the secret chambers; believe it not. For as the lightning cometh out of the east, and shineth even unto the west; so shall also the coming of the Son of man be" (Matt. 24:11, 23-27).

FAKE SECOND COMING A NEW AGE DECEPTION

Madame Helena Petrovna Blavatsky, a Russian noblewoman, founded the Theosophical Society in 1875. Most researchers think this was the beginning of the modern cultic New Age movement. *Encyclopedia Britannica*, under the entries on "Blavatsky" and "Theosophy," indicates that the Theosophical Society is the primary cause of the spread of eastern mystical cultism in the western world.

Blavatsky spoke of the coming of a new christ, a mystical avatar, and it would not be Jesus.

Alice Bailey, founder of the Lucifer Publishing Company (now Lucis Trust) was a disciple of Annie Besant who headed the Theosophical Society for a time. She wrote a book, *The Reappearance of The Christ*. Again, there will be an ascended master who will come to humanity bringing in the New Age, but it will not be Jesus.

The Bible says, "This *same* Jesus shall so come..." (Acts 1:11). "The

241

Lord *Himself* shall descend from heaven with a shout..." (1 Thess. 4:16). Jesus said, "I will come again, and receive you unto myself; that where I am, there ye may be also" (John 14:3).

A BOLD PLOT FOR DECEPTION

Peter Lemesurier's book *Armageddon Script* (St. Martin's Press, 1981, New York) outlines a New Age scheme to pull off a fake second coming. Why? The book says that because so many people are sitting around waiting for Christ to come, someone had better produce a "second coming event" through human effort and means. Then the New Agers can get on with ushering in the Age of Aquarius. By the way, the book is blatant. You do not have to read between the lines. On page 231 Lemesurier describes the New Age, humanistic "christ" standing on the Mount of Olives at Jerusalem, dressed in shining white robes, with robed followers. He enters Jerusalem via the Eastern Gate and is enthroned on the Temple Mount. His arrival is accompanied with lightning and supernatural actions. His arrival is followed by a time of struggle and wrath on earth. See 2 Thessalonians 2:3,4 and Revelation 13:13,14 for possible identity of such a figure. Since there are to be false christs (plural) and since there is infighting among the many New Age groups as to which "christ candidate" is to be the one, we could see multiple deceptions before the Rapture, the onset of the Tribulation, and manifestation of the ultimate and final false christ. In other words such a deception could be enacted even before the Rapture and subsequent Tribulation.

In 1983 one of the major candidates was announced in an advertising blitz costing over a half-million dollars. A full page advertisement announcing that "The Christ Is Now Here" appeared as a full page advertisement in the *New York Times*, the Stockholm *Daagens Nyheter*, Iceland's *Morgenbladid* National Newspaper, and in other major newspapers all over the U.S.A. and the rest of the free world. A similar announcement has since appeared in the national newspaper, *USA TODAY.*

THE BIG QUESTION

The question is, how could one tell the real Jesus from a false christ? Just suppose that someday a powerful psychic, a miracle worker (Matt. 24:24; Rev. 13:13,14) would appear on the Mount of Olives.

He is not in the desert or the secret chamber. He is not in New York, Dallas, or San Francisco. He is where Zechariah 14:4 says the Messiah will be one day, right on the Mount of Olives. But it is not the real Christ. How would one know the true from the false?

NAIL PRINTS IN HIS HANDS

A song says, "I shall know Him by the print of the nails in His hands." That may be a bit naive. I asked a plastic surgeon if he could make a set of nail prints in the palm and back of a persons hands, and how much it would cost. "Simple," he informed me, "It could be done as outpatient surgery in a short time. The cost would be about $1,000.00. Even a fake descent from the clouds could be technologically engineered."

I have heard certain well-known television evangelists say that they plan to televise the second coming of Christ at the Mount of Olives. They say that this is what is meant by "every eye shall behold Him." Impossible! Fifty percent of the world's population does not even have access to a television set. The Bible says that *every* eye shall behold Him. Furthermore television satellites are not the angels of God flying through the heavens with a message for mankind during the seven year Tribulation. Angels of God are living creatures of great dignity and purpose, not machines.

Imagine that one day someone on television says, "Tomorrow at eight o'clock in the morning (EST) the long awaited coming of 'the Christ' will take place at the Mount of Olives east of Jerusalem. Channel 13 will broadcast this epochal event live, via satellite. World leaders hail the appearance of 'the Christ' as the dawning of a New Age for mankind. No one should miss seeing this event!" Don't believe it! Don't even watch it! It is not Jesus! Dominionists and Kingdom Now adherents could be fooled by such an avatar, but believers in the Rapture are delivered from such deception even if it takes place before the Rapture!

I SHALL KNOW HIM

Listen, I don't care if he (it) looks like we think Jesus should look, works miracles, heals the sick, has nailprints in his hands, and a halo (aura) around his head, if it is not the real Jesus, *I will know it is a fake*. Why am I so sure of this?

RAPTURE MENTALITY SERVES A GOOD PURPOSE

If your feet are still flat on the ground, if you have not first risen to meet Jesus in the air, if you do not have your glorified, raptured, disease-free, fatigue proof, immortalized new body, *it is not Him—it is someone or something else over there on the Mount of Olives.* In other words if you have not experienced the Rapture first, you will know that any fake "christ" is false.

YOUR ESCAPE FROM DECEPTION

Understanding the Rapture teaching of the Bible does not insure you against all physical suffering or persecution, but it does insure that no false second coming of a "christ" that is not Jesus will ever fool you. There could be several such events, given the fact that the New Age leadership has a number of "christ candidates."

You must understand that before the real Jesus stands on the Mount of Olives, fulfilling the Zechariah prophecy, there is an event involving you personally. I refer to the "catching away" of the living believers, "our gathering together unto Him" (2 Thess. 2:1) when He "receives us unto Himself." In short I refer to the glorious rapture of the Church! You will hear His trumpet and victory shout. You will rise to meet Him in the air. Hello, Jesus! I know it is really You!

The pre-Tribulation Rapture is no guarantee that there will not be pre-Rapture Tribulation for some of us. The Rapture provides an escape from the seven years' Tribulation for only a portion of the Church—those who are alive at the time of the event.

The understanding of the Rapture concept makes you deception-proof in relation to the major end-time satanic delusion, the false second coming. First will come the rapture of the Church, the catching away. This is followed by the seven years of global trauma, the Tribulation. After the seven years the visible, manifest coming of Christ takes place. This is when He stands on the Mount of Olives. This marks the beginning, not of a humanistic New Age of Aquarius, but the glorious Millennium (thousand years), the reign of our Saviour, the real Jesus Christ our Eternal Lord. This Millennium is not an end, but a beginning, for it inaugurates the eternal kingdom of God which ultimately includes a new heaven and a new earth wherein righteousness eternally dwells.

WHO WILL GO IN THE RAPTURE?

All born again believers will go in the Rapture. When the trumpet sounds and Christ raptures the Church, not one saved person will be left behind. Every one will be taken to be with the Lord. This is our great comfort, it is our blessed hope.

Some believe that only a special class of "overcomers" will be taken and that most of the Church will be left to endure the Tribulation. I believe in a pre-Tribulation Rapture, but let me emphasize that *whenever* the Church is taken out, *we will all go at once.*

We are perfectly content to let God decide who is saved and who is not. We will not presume to make that judgment for brothers and sisters who make a confession of faith in our Lord Jesus. I may exhort believers to holy living, but I cannot judge their salvation, for that is done by the grace of God. I suspect that some are not truly saved who do not measure up to a biblical standard, but that I must leave to the Lord. Of this I am sure: that all who are saved will be in the Rapture. There is so much evidence for this that we would need to write a book to fully express it. In this chapter we will simply offer two powerful items of evidence that should convince anyone.

Why are we concerned with this matter? The devil would like to get you to live in fear and uncertainty. That is his best way to impede your growth and progress in the kingdom of God. If you are calm and confident of God's saving grace, you can get your eyes more fully on Jesus and "grow in the grace and knowledge of our Lord."

THE DEAD AND THE LIVING

One of the important passages teaching the rapture of the Church is found in 1 Thessalonians 4:13-18:

"But I would not have you to be ignorant, brethren, concerning them which are asleep, that ye sorrow not, even as others which have no hope. For if we believe that Jesus died and rose again, even so them also which sleep in Jesus will God bring with him. For this we say unto you by the word of the Lord, that we which are alive and remain unto the coming of the Lord shall not prevent them which are asleep. For the Lord himself shall descend from heaven with a shout, with the voice of the archangel, and with the trump of God: and the dead in Christ shall rise first: Then we which are alive and remain shall be caught up together with them in the clouds to meet the Lord in the air: and so shall we ever be with the Lord. Wherefore comfort one another with these words."

When the first resurrection and the rapture of the Church take place, "the dead in Christ shall rise." Not part of the dead in Christ, but all the saved people who have died in the faith will be resurrected. Jesus brings back their souls from heaven to receive resurrected bodies (verse 14). There is no division here of overcomers and a second class of saints (in the resurrection from the dead). Will God judge the living believers on a different basis? Truly God is no respecter of persons. "We which are alive and remain shall be caught up..." All the living believers, along with all the dead believers, will rise to meet the Lord in the air.

CHALLENGE TO LIVE VICTORIOUSLY

There is no doubt that some Christians have grown more than others. There is no question that some believers have not progressed as they should. Yes, there are saved people who are still babes in Christ. Of course this is undesirable. It cannot please the Lord. The greatest motive to living an overcoming life is not fear. That is the least and basest of motives. When the Bible says that the fear of the Lord is the beginning of wisdom it does not mean terror. It means reverential awe. The highest motive for a Christian is love for Christ, a love for His Word, and a desire to be more like Him. Most people who are motivated by fear on a continuous basis do not set much of an example of Christian growth and maturity.

IT JUST ISN'T FAIR!

Is there a lack of justice if carnal Christians "make it" in the same Rapture experience as mature Christians? Not at all. One problem is that the seriousness of the judgment seat of Christ has been overlooked by some. We will all appear before the bema judgment and give account of our performance as believers. It is at this time, after the Rapture, that our works will be evaluated and rewards given. This is not a matter to be taken lightly. All the seeming inequities will be settled there.

"(For we walk by faith, not by sight:) We are confident, I say, and willing rather to be absent from the body, and to be present with the Lord. Wherefore we labour, that, whether present or absent, we may be accepted of him. For we must all appear before the judgment seat of Christ; that every one may receive the things done in his body, according to that he hath done, whether it be good or bad" (2 Cor. 5:7-10).

JUDGMENT OF BELIEVERS—A SERIOUS MATTER

All born again believers will stand before the judgment seat of Christ and give account of the things done in this life. Some will receive great reward and others will receive nothing, but they are saved—they are there in the presence of our Lord to be judged. This is not a judgment to determine whether the individual is saved or lost. That is decided by the person himself, right here in this life. It is determined when one accepts or rejects salvation through Jesus. Paul had enlarged on this subject earlier in the third chapter of the first Corinthian epistle:

"And I, brethren, could not speak unto you as unto spiritual, but as unto carnal, even as unto babes in Christ. I have fed you with milk, and not with meat: for hitherto ye were not able to bear it, neither yet now are ye able. For ye are yet carnal: for whereas there is among you envying, and strife, and divisions, are ye not carnal, and walk as men?" (1 Cor. 3:1-3).

CARNAL BRETHREN

It comes as a shock to find that there are born again believers who are yet carnal, but here it is plainly stated in the Word of God. How can we deny it? Paul says that they are "brethren," a term he certainly would not use for unconverted Gentiles of Corinth! They are brethren, and they are carnal.

It is these same carnal Christians whom we see standing in the judgment seat of Christ, stripped of reward:

"Now he that planteth and he that watereth are one: and every man shall receive his own reward according to his own labour. For we are labourers together with God: ye are God's husbandry, ye are God's building. According to the grace of God which is given unto me, as a wise masterbuilder, I have laid the foundation, and another buildeth thereon. But let every man take heed how he buildeth thereupon. For other foundation can no man lay than that is laid, which is Jesus Christ. Now if any man build upon this foundation gold, silver, precious stones, wood, hay, stubble; Every man's work shall be made manifest: for the day shall declare it, because it shall be revealed by fire; and the fire shall try every man's work of what sort it is. If any man's work abide which he hath built thereupon, he shall receive a reward. If any man's work shall be burned, he shall suffer loss: but he himself shall be saved; yet so as by fire" (1 Cor. 3:8-14).

Some will receive great reward because of their works for Christ. Others will receive nothing, "but he himself shall be saved; yet so as by fire." Barely saved, but saved, raptured, and standing in the judgment seat of Christ. "I had rather be a doorkeeper in the house of my God, than to dwell in the tents of wickedness" (Ps. 84:10). It is better to be saved than lost.

THE BIG QUESTION

Why would anyone want to barely make it into the Kingdom? What is the best way to inspire people to strive for lofty goals, for "the prize of the high calling?"

Early in my ministry I spoke harshly to the congregation of the Lord. I tried to use fear tactics. I implied that people would miss the Rapture if they were saved but not living what we called "an overcoming life." My motives were good. I wanted people to live righteous lives, to abandon sin, and be good witnesses for Jesus. There was one big problem: It just did not work. It was so discouraging. The more I ranted and raved at people, the worse they lived. Those who frantically sought the Lord because of a sense of fear inspired by my preaching usually fell by the wayside. They just gave up even trying to live a Christian life. It seemed so impossible. My goals were right, but I could not get people to arrive at the destination.

Slowly I learned that people respond better to love than to scolding and condemnation. Most people in the Church really want to live good lives. They are painfully conscious of their faults and failures. The weak need help through good solid Bible preaching and pastoral counselling. They need a positive message of faith and hope. We know we are sinners. We need to learn of God's grace, and that we can become like Jesus. My ministry began to bear lasting fruit. Many people began to progress in God and the Lord helped me to become a more loving, compassionate servant of Jesus. He helped me to appeal to believers to make progress in the Spirit. I look with great joy on throngs that God has allowed us to lead into the Kingdom and on to higher dedication to the Lord. It is His perfect work of grace that brings salvation to our lives as we accept Him and what He has done for us. But works are important after we get saved. We are not saved by our works, but believers will be judged according to the works accomplished after they are saved.

"For by grace are you saved through faith; and that not of yourselves; It is the gift of God; Not of works, lest any man should boast. For we are his workmanship, created in Christ Jesus unto good works, which God has before ordained that we should walk in them" (Eph. 2:8-10).

I share the apostle Paul's concern lest you should be seduced from the simplicity of believing Christ for your salvation. Paul wrote to the Galatian church: "O foolish Galatians, who hath bewitched you, that ye should not obey the truth, before whose eyes Jesus Christ hath been evidently set forth, crucified among you? This only would I learn of you, Received ye the Spirit by the works of the law, or by the hearing of faith? Are ye so foolish? Having begun in the Spirit, are ye now made perfect by the flesh?" (Gal. 3:1-3).

DO WE ENCOURAGE CARNAL LIVING?

"Shall we continue in sin that grace may abound? God forbid" (Rom. 6:1, 2). Is our purpose to make people secure in their carnality? Of course not—the opposite is true. We want only to promote dedicated, holy living in the lives of believers.

Show me those who have been helped by fear and threats, and I will counter by showing you those who have been helped by balanced Bible preaching and true spiritual challenge. I desire no contest or comparison of results, for that in itself is carnal. But I tire of those who call others false prophets because they bring hope and comfort to the body of Christ through a declaration of His grace and mercy.

WHO ARE THE OVERCOMERS?

The overcomers are all the people who are born-again, who know Jesus as their personal Saviour. "For whatsoever is born of God overcometh the world: and this is the victory that overcometh the world, even our faith. Who is he that overcometh the world but he that believeth that Jesus is the Son of God?" (1 John 5:4, 5). Everyone who is saved has overcome the world by the grace of God. He is no longer in darkness but in the light. Of course there are strong challenges to believers to progress into greater relationship with Jesus, and to apply the power of the overcomer's position to all of life's situations.

While we use the word overcomer in various ways, it is interesting to note that the word overcomer never appears in the Bible. "Overcomer" is not an adjective describing a believer in Scripture. It better describes the believer's position in Christ, if the term is to be used at all. The concept is a powerful challenge for the saved one to grow in God.

People who describe themselves as overcomers in order to "lord it over" other believers ought to think deeply about this. The terms found in the Bible are overcome and overcometh but never overcomer. Overcome and overcometh are terms describing what believers are able to do in Christ, not a description of what believers are. Perhaps this is a bit too technical. I do not find it objectionable to use the term "overcomer" to describe a believer, provided it is used in a biblical context and sense. But strictly speaking it is not biblical terminology.

VIRGINS AND LAODICEANS

What about the five foolish virgins who were out of oil when the wedding feast was announced? They were barred entrance because of their carelessness. Is this an indication that Christians who do not have the baptism of the Holy Spirit will be left behind? No, it is not.

The parable of the ten virgins in the Olivet Discourse (Matt. 25) is one of the most misunderstood passages in the Bible. Supposedly the five wise are representative of the bride of Christ who will be prepared for the Rapture. Think of the following: First of all both the wise and the foolish were fast asleep at the midnight hour. If we must identify with anyone in the parable, it would be more likely that we should identify with the person who is wide awake and calling the slumberers to attention, shouting, "the bridegroom cometh." Secondly, Jesus does not have five or ten brides. The virgins do not represent the Church at all. The bride is not present at this scene. Thirdly, what we have here is a simply Oriental parable expressing one simple truth and that is that we should always be ready for the midnight hour. Usually the parables of Jesus are explained by the Lord in the context in which they are found. The meaning here is in the exhortation of Jesus, "Watch therefore, for ye know neither the day nor the hour wherein the Son of Man cometh" (Matt. 25:13). I suppose it is all right to use the parable for other illustrative purposes, but if you want to be accurate, do not try to identify the lamps, the oil, nor the virgins. Just let the explanation Jesus gives suffice.

The lukewarm of Laodicea (Rev. 3:14-18) receive this sobering word from the Lord: "...because thou art lukewarm, and neither cold nor hot, I will spue thee out of my mouth." Jesus does not cast away saved people. That treatment is reserved for the unsaved rebels and apostates. Those who are "hot" are those who are saved. The cold are unsaved and make no pretense at having a relationship with Christ. The lukewarm are religious hypocrites who infiltrate the Church and for one reason or another pretend to be saved but they are not.

SAINTS IN TRIBULATION

Some pre-tribulationists have correctly seen that there will be born again people on earth during the future seven-year Tribulation. If the Church is taken out before the Tribulation, who are these saints? Misunderstanding their identity has led to a "partial rapture" theory that has the overcomers or the Bride (as distinct from the Body) being taken out in a pre-Tribulation Rapture, and the lesser born-again-but-not-measuring-up Christians being left behind to pay for their salvation through refusal to take the mark of the beast and subsequent martyrdom.

This is not the case at all. All saved people will go up with Christ in the Rapture at the end of the Church Age. During the Tribulation 144,000 are saved and as a result of their work and witness, a multitude are saved out of every tribe and nation (see Rev. 7). There are born again people on earth during the Tribulation. They are saved after the rapture of the Church. Many will be killed, but martyrdom is not the price of salvation. Jesus paid the price for redemption on the Cross.

We do not have to add anything to what He did.

God does not have two different plans of salvation. He does not have a "salvation by grace" plan for the Church Age and a "pay for salvation with your own blood" plan for the Tribulation. No, salvation was bought and paid for by the atoning work of Jesus on the Cross.

Because some will receive Jesus by faith in the Tribulation, the Beast in fury will try to kill them and put out the light of their witness. They are martyred because they got saved, not saved by being martyred.

PRESS ON THE UPWARD WAY

Here we are in the age of grace. You are saved by faith in Jesus. Do not be content to live a minimal, carnal Christian life. Plan for your eternal future. Don't stand at the judgment seat of Christ with regrets. Now is the time to learn to know Jesus better and to grow in His truth and power.

Have you lived in failure? Jesus loves you. He wants to help you, not beat you down. "A bruised reed shall he not break and smoking flax he shall not quench, till he send forth judgment unto victory" (Matt. 12:20). The Living Bible expresses the sense of this passage very well: "He does not crush the weak, Or quench the smallest hope: He will end all conflict with his final victory."

I'm pressing on the upward way
New heights I'm gaining every day
Still praying as I'm onward bound
Lord plant my feet on higher ground.

17

The Work of the Holy Spirit in the Tribulation and the Millennium

The Lord Jesus taught us that one of the Holy Spirit's primary works was to reveal the future to the Church. We hold that the revelation of God to man—the entire Bible—is complete. However, our illumination of the revelation is progressive. This is how the Spirit helps us. "And when he is come, he will reprove the world of sin, and of righteousness, and of judgment...Howbeit when he, the Spirit of truth, is come, he will guide you into all truth: for he shall not speak of himself; but whatsoever he shall hear, that shall he speak: and he will show you things to come" (John 16:8, 13).

Perhaps the importance of prophecy is reflected by the fact that over one-third of the Bible was given in the form of prophecy, both in its aspect of foretelling and of forthtelling. Admittedly prophecy is a difficult and controversial subject. How we need the Holy Spirit's guidance as we undertake our eschatalogical explorations.

PRESENCE OF THE HOLY SPIRIT IN THE TRIBULATION

To some it might seem strange that we should expend energy proving that the Holy Spirit is present in the Tribulation, but nevertheless it is necessary. From my childhood I have heard people use the phrases, "When the Holy Spirit is taken out of the world...," "When the Holy

Spirit no longer works…," "When the Holy Spirit is not here to convict and save souls…"

Careful examination of biblical truth relative to the Spirit of God forbids such conclusions. Those who use such terminology are incorrectly interpreting certain passages in 2 Thessalonians 2 regarding the "restrainer."

IDENTITY OF THE RESTRAINER

The man of sin cannot be revealed as long as the withholder is in the way. "And now ye know what withholdeth that he [man of sin, Antichrist] might be revealed in his time. For the mystery of iniquity doth already work: only he who now letteth [holds it back, NIV] will let, until he be taken out of the way" (2 Thess. 2:6,7).

After considering many opinions on the withholding or restraining force or person's identity, I concluded that it is the Holy Spirit's work through the Church that restrains the Antichrist. It is the Church, not the Holy Spirit, that is removed. This is consistent with the fact that the Church is shown over and over to be the vehicle through which the Spirit of God restrains evil (James 4:7; Eph. 6:12; 2 Cor. 10:3-6; Matt. 16:19).

THE HOLY SPIRIT IS OMNIPRESENT

The Spirit cannot be removed, for He is God. There are certain immutable and nontransferable attributes that make God unique and above all creation. These include eternality, omnipotence, omniscience, and omnipresence. That He is omnipresent indicates that He is ever present in every state of reality at all times. How then could He be absent from the earth during the Tribulation?

MASCULINITY OF THE RESTRAINER

How can the Church be the restrainer since the pronoun *He* is used in 2 Thessalonians 2:7, and the Church is the bride of Christ? (2 Cor. 11:2; Rev. 19:7,8). Is it not unlikely that she should be described with a masculine pronoun? There is really no problem here. The Church is feminine in the love relationship that exists between the bride and the bridegroom (Eph. 5:22-32). On the other hand the Church's masculine nature is seen in the warrior relationship to God's enemy. Even our Lord Jesus is described by many diverse figures of speech denoting many aspects of His person and work: Lamb and Lion, bright and morning star, Rose of Sharon, Captain of our salvation, Bishop of our souls, our elder Brother, the everlasting Father, Prince of Peace, warrior of God. Similarly the Church is a star, a lampstand, an army terrible with banners, salt, light, restrainer, bride, the body of Christ.

We may conclude that the Holy Spirit is the restrainer in the day of grace. The means He uses to restrain is the Church; hence the Church in this secondary sense is the restrainer. It is the Church, not the Holy Spirit, that is removed.

THE HOLY SPIRIT AND SALVATION IN THE TRIBULATION

It is the Holy Spirit's work to effect salvation. Paul describes the working of the Spirit in salvation: "Not by works of righteousness which we have done, but according to his mercy he saved us, by the washing of regeneration, the renewing of the Holy Ghost" (Titus 3:5). Three times Jesus refers to salvation, the new birth, as being a process of being "born of the Spirit" (John 3).

In his monumental work, *Things To Come,* J. Dwight Pentecost writes of the Spirit's work in the Tribulation:

"It may be asserted with confidence, then, that the salvation offered through the blood of the Lamb, to be received by faith will be made effectual through the working of the Holy Spirit."

That people will be saved in the Tribulation is demonstrated in Revelation 7:3,4: "Saying, Hurt not the earth, neither the sea, nor the trees, till we have sealed the servants of our God in their foreheads. And I heard the number of them which were sealed: and there were sealed an hundred and forty and four thousand of all the tribes of the children of Israel."

Since these render service unto the Lord, it may be safely assumed that they are a witnessing company. Due to their influence a multitude are saved out of every nation on earth (Rev. 7:9-17). If I see the implication of 2 Thessalonians 2:10-13 correctly, those saved are people who have never heard the gospel with comprehension in the Church Age.

SALVATION OF THE NATION OF ISRAEL

At Christ's revelation the living nation of Israel will recognize Him as Messiah. A nation will be born in a day. This too is a work of the Holy Spirit effecting their redemption. Most premillennial writers affirm this truth. Even George Eldon Ladd, who denies that literal Israel has any part in the present working of God in prophecy, nevertheless admits in his book *The Meaning of the Millennium:* "...There are two passages in the New Testament which cannot be avoided. One is Romans 11:26: 'And so all Israel shall be saved.' It is difficult to escape the conclusion that this means literal Israel...the New Testament teaches the final salvation of Israel. Israel remains the elect people of God, a 'holy' people" (Rom. 11:16).

THE HOLY SPIRIT AND ARMAGEDDON

The battle of Armageddon is no mere wanton slaughter program. It is God's intervention to spare a remnant of humanity from the satanic Antichrist who would like to unleash super weapons that would potentially destroy all life on the planet (Matt. 24:22; Rev. 11:18).

Although the Antichrist and his armies will undoubtedly focus all the physical weapons at their command against Christ and the raptured returning Church, Jesus will use no physical weapon to destroy the beast. "And then shall that Wicked [Antichrist, man of sin] be revealed, whom the Lord shall consume with the spirit of his mouth, and shall destroy with the brightness of his coming" (2 Thess. 2:8). John speaks of a sword proceeding from the mouth of the Lord Jesus Christ (Rev. 19:15,21). It is the "sword of the Spirit, which is the Word of God" (Eph. 6:17).

THE MILLENNIUM

The kingdom of God is mentioned over four hundred times in the Bible. The Millennium is specifically mentioned only six times, all in Revelation 20. The words *thousand years* are the equivalent of the Latin *mille annum*. It is curiously interesting that a number of Jewish rabbinic scholars have come with the concept of a thousand-year reign of Messiah. Some of these are cited by the great Presbyterian scholar Nathaniel West in his book *The Thousand Years:*

"...Rabbi Eleasar said, 'Messiah's Days shall be 1000 years...' Elias, a Doctor of the Second Temple, and the School of Elias, both say Messiah's Kingdom is 1000 years...Rabbi Qatina and Rabbi Jose say the same, adding that 'Messiah's Days are the Days of Restitution for Israel, and are 1,000 years.' "

It should be pointed out that the Millennium is not the kingdom of God, but an aspect, or a part, of the kingdom of God. The kingdom of God is eternal. The Millennium is a physical, earthly demonstration of the kingdom of God.

The Millennium is an ideal age, not a perfect age. Perfection awaits the eternity that follows the Millennium. People will have children, and those children will have to choose to accept or reject Jesus Christ.

People will still rebel; there will be punishment, for Christ will rule with a rod of iron (Isa. 65:20; Zech. 14:16-19; Rev. 19:15; Ps. 2:9).

Because Jesus reigns, it will be a time of unprecedented blessing, prosperity, and peace. War and crime will not be tolerated. Satan will be bound.

Because people will be born and salvation will be a necessity, the Holy Spirit's work continues. There will be an outpouring of the Holy Spirit as the greater fulfillment of Joel 2:28 takes place. In *The Meaning of the Millennium,* Herman Hoyt speaks of the spiritual nature of the Millenium:

"Basically the kingdom will be spiritual in nature. This does not mean that it etherealizes. But it does mean that it belongs to and is governed by the Spirit of God. It possesses every tangible and material quality of a real kingdom, and these under the control and direction of the Holy Spirit. Forgiveness, direct knowledge of God (Jer. 31:34), righteousness (Jer. 23:5,6), spiritual cleansing (Ezek. 36:24-26), and regeneration (Ezek. 36:26-28) will all be present. The fruit of spiritual control will be manifest in ethical conduct...perfect social relations ...physical transformation...political changes...Religious purification ...and the Shekinah glory will again take up its rightful place in the temple (Ezek. 43:1-7). The original intention of God for Israel will be accomplished in this people becoming the leaders and teachers of religious truth (Isa. 61:6)."

CHRIST AND THE MILLENNIUM

The Antichrist is not the star of the end-time drama. "The testimony of Jesus is the spirit of prophecy" (Rev. 19:10). The central figure of the Millennium is the Lord Jesus Christ. He is heralded as King of kings and Lord of lords. L. Thomas Holdcroft writes in his book, *The Holy Spirit:*

"At the revelation of Jesus Christ, the divine Son of David;...will at last assume His place as King of kings. The Holy Spirit will suitably anoint and empower Him for His new role: 'There shall come forth a rod out of the stem of Jesse...And the Spirit of the Lord shall rest upon him...' (Isa. 11:1,2). It may be said that the governing skill of the divine Christ will be exercised in and through the Holy Spirit."

Of the Messiah Isaiah writes, "Behold my servant, whom I uphold; mine elect, in whom my soul delighteth; I have put my spirit upon him: he shall bring forth judgment to the Gentiles" (Isa. 42:1).

Jesus quoted the words of Isaiah 61:1,2 to announce His ministry and mission: "The Spirit of the Lord God is upon me; because the Lord hath anointed me to preach good tidings unto the meek; he hath sent me to bind up the brokenhearted, to proclaim liberty to the captive, and the opening of the prison to them that are bound; to proclaim the acceptable year of the Lord..." Jesus did not read on, for it was not yet time for the end-time and millennial accomplishments Isaiah spoke of in the remainder of the passage.

As the Spirit of the Lord anointed Jesus for His previous earthly ministry (Acts 10:38), so He will anoint Jesus for His future earthly ministry during the Millennium. The very title *Christ* "means anointed one," and bestowing the anointing is a ministry of the Holy Spirit.

THE HOLY SPIRIT AND ISRAEL IN THE MILLENNIUM

When the Holy Spirit was about to overshadow Mary, the angel Gabriel announced to her that the child Jesus would one day "be great, and shall be called the Son of the Highest: and the Lord God shall give unto him the throne of his father David: and he shall reign over the house of Jacob for ever; and of his kingdom there shall be no end" (Luke 1:31-33). Jesus told His apostles, "And I appoint unto you a kingdom...that ye may eat and drink at my table in my kingdom, and sit on thrones judging the twelve tribes of Israel" (Luke 22:29,30; Matt. 19:28).

Isaiah speaks of Israel's rebellion and scattering. Then in the end-time restoration, which comes to its fullness in the Millennium, he says: "And the Redeemer shall come to Zion...My spirit that is upon thee, and my words which I have put in thy mouth shall not depart out of thy mouth, nor out of the mouth of thy seed..." (Isa. 59:20,21).

The same pattern of prophecy is frequently found in Ezekiel. Israel is to be dispersed, regathered in unbelief; and then comes the Holy Spirit cleansing and outpouring (Ezek. 11:16-20; 36:19-28; 37:14-28; 39:23-29).

THE HOLY SPIRIT AND THE
GENTILES IN THE MILLENNIUM

J. Dwight Pentecost lists many passages proving that Gentiles play a role in the Millennium. Multiplied blessings of God's Holy Spirit are lavished upon all earth's residents. Especially magnified is the anointed teaching that will be extended to all. In this age of disinformation how refreshing to anticipate a time when "they shall not hurt nor destroy in all my holy mountain; for the earth shall be full of the knowledge of the Lord, as the waters cover the sea" (Isa. 11:9). Isaiah speaks of Messiah's reign in 11:1-16 and says, "To it shall the Gentiles seek and his rest shall be glorious" (Isa. 11:10; also see Hab. 2:14). We are reminded of Jesus' saying that the Spirit will lead us into all truth (John 16).

THE HOLY SPIRIT AND WORSHIP IN THE MILLENNIUM

"And it shall come to pass...shall all flesh come to worship before me saith the Lord" (Isa. 66:23). The center of this worship will be the fourth temple of Israel, the millennial temple. This temple is described in Ezekiel 40-46. James M. Gray wrote in the *Christian Workers Commentary:*

"We have here a prediction of the temple that shall be built in the millennial age. This appears a fitting and intelligent sequel to the preceding prophecies."

THERE WILL BE LITERAL SACRIFICES IN THE MILLENNIAL TEMPLE

The objection that the sacrifices in the millennial temple are unnecessary and redundant has always puzzled me. First of all, Ezekiel says there will be sacrifices. I know of no author who claims that the sacrifices have any redemptive value. Indeed, every author I know of who treats the subject from a literalist point of view states clearly that the sacrifices are commemorative of the Lord's death as the Communion commemorates His death. The sacrifices are necessary as a reminder of the awful price that was paid for the salvation of all who believe in Him.

The blessed Holy Spirit is ever the director of our worship to the Lord Jesus Christ. In *The Spirit Himself,* R. M. Riggs wrote:

"As our present baptism in the Spirit, walk in the Spirit, and knowledge of the Spirit are but a foretaste of the fullness which awaits us at the coming of our Lord and Saviour, so the whole work and ministry of the Spirit on the earth in this dispensation are but drops of blessing compared with the great, sweeping, universal work that is before Him during the Millennium. Christ in person and the Holy Spirit in immanent presence work hand in hand in the reclamation and transformation of the earth in this period...the Holy Spirit will then have full and free sway among the sons of men. Then shall Joel's prophecy find its full fulfillment.... This will be the grand climax of the work of the Holy Spirit. To pervade the earth with His presence, to teach men to glorify the Lord…to bring all things into subjection to Christ—these are His great objectives, and the thousand years of peace will witness His complete attainment of these great ends."

APPLIED ESCHATOLOGY

How shall we use these truths in the present season? Is prophecy only an intellectual exercise? Is it possible to be actually involved in the ongoing plan and purpose of God?

The fact that God chooses to reveal the future to us indicates we are not mere hirelings in the Kingdom. We are partners, "laborers together with the Lord" (1 Cor. 3:9). When you are a partner, you desire to know all the plans for the future growth of the firm, even if you are not directly involved in every phase of activity.

But it is more than this. Prophecy is not an excuse for passivism. It is a call to participation. Think of the Tribulation. Satan is unleashed to do his worst. But he is not sitting quietly by now. He wants to produce tribulation now. Remember tribulation simply means trouble. We are told to pray for an era of tranquility (1 Tim. 2:1-4). This is the will of God. What we see in the world today is not a manifestation of the will of God, but a manifestation of mankind's rebellions against the will of God. We are told to pray, "Thy will be done in earth…." Our prayers and good works can make a difference right now in our world. Satan would like to promote fatalism, negativism, and doomsday emphasis in order to rob us of correct participation in the end-time plan of God.

Prophecy should not promote defeatism, escapism, nor irresponsibility. Understanding prophecy should be a call to exercise the restraining power of the Holy Spirit, to a binding of Satan, to a loosing of men and nations.

18

Kingdom—Dominion—Millennium
What's Going On in the Church?

The kingdom of God is eternal, present, ongoing, and in its fullness anticipated. It will come to visible manifestation in our world. The big question is, "How will it come?" Will it be through the efforts of the Church, or will it be by a sovereign act of God—the second coming of Jesus Christ? What should men and women of the Kingdom be doing now? What should be our agenda and what is our list of priorities? Is world evangelization still the supreme task of the Church?

There is an almost unprecedented power struggle now taking place in the churches. It especially affects the Pentecostal, Evangelical, Charismatic, and Fundamentalist ranks. Most of the old-line churches are already sold down the river of error and apostasy.

Churchmen dream of political power and of ruling the planet in the name of God. It has been tried before, always with disastrous results, producing such things as the Dark Ages, the Inquisition, the tragic Crusades against the Holy Land, the burning of persons accused of being witches, and most recently, the Holocaust.

Unfortunately leadership in the churches is stunned by recent events and activities. We dream dreams of accomplishment but suffer setbacks as aggressive "prophets and apostles" of the Kingdom and Dominion movements hurl their accusations of escapism and lack of direction at us. Their accusations are not entirely without foundation. However,

"Wrong alternatives play a fundamental and disastrous role in the history of the human mind. Errors are often fought by means of an antithesis that implies a worse error than the one it claims to overcome" (Dietrich Von Hildebrand, *The New Tower of Babel*; p. 103; 1953; P. J. Kenedy and Sons; New York).

Pity the poor layman in our church pews. He pays all the bills and does much of the volunteer work, but is the last to be told what is going on in the church. One day he wakes up to find out that the church he has attended and served for so many years has changed into something he can hardly recognize or identify with.

In our books we hope to get information down to the grass roots level of the Church. Every pastor and each lay person deserves to know the major issues we are facing today. What you do with this information will be remarkable indeed. It has been said that "knowledge is power" and the Bible itself counsels that God's people can be "destroyed for a lack of knowledge." The day of "brother, it's better felt than telt" Christianity is all over. Only the informed and active will survive the coming changes we face.

If an informed clergy and laity in our ranks do not become active and overcome the devil of apathy, and if Jesus tarries, by the year 2010 you will not be able to recognize the church you belong to. So great are the winds of deceptive doctrines that are blowing, not as gentle zephyrs but as hurricane force gales. The Bible warns us not to be swept to and fro with every wind of doctrine. Unfortunately, many, while they feel the force of the winds about them, cannot recognize the root causes of changes going on in our ranks.

Premillennialists are being savagely attacked by brethren expressing concern for the "errors" they perceive us to be promoting. We are told to be quiet on subjects such as the Rapture, Israel, the Millennium, Antichrist, etc. They say that we must do this to promote unity in the body of Christ. They, on the other hand, vigorously publish and disseminate their variant theories. I question any call for unity that demands that I be silent on great biblical subjects. My spirit questions why discussion on matters of the greatest importance should cease. This is certainly not the way the early Church handled matters of controversy, and they provide the best pattern yet offered to us.

As a result of these and other factors most of your churches have abandoned the teaching of Bible prophecy. Dr. James Brown said of the church he belongs to, "The greatest danger facing the Assemblies of God today is the abandonment of preaching eschatology." It is a fact that almost no denominational Bible college today teaches adequate courses in eschatology (prophecy). Some pastors boast that they leave the subject alone since it is "too complicated" or "too controversial" or "I am too busy to study." Pity the poor church of the end-times if the shepherds are unwilling to spend time in the Word and the presence of God until they can declare the great truths of the Bible. How strange that the closer we get to the end-times, the less attention is paid to the subject of the end-times.

ETERNAL KINGDOM

Jesus Christ is King of kings and He shall reign forever and forever. No wonder we are inspired by the grand theme of Handel's *Messiah*, especially as we sing the magnificent "Hallelujah Chorus."

The kingdom of God! Could any theme or concept be more elevating or conducive to end-time encouragement? From the early pages of the Bible clear through to the Apocalypse, on the last pages of Holy Writ the glorious theme of God's kingdom is paraded before our wondering souls. Then to think, with wondering minds, of a thought so overwhelming—we are destined to reign with Him in His kingdom, and even now we reign in heavenly places with Him, as Paul taught the church at Ephesus.

Like all the truly important teachings of the Bible, the Kingdom concept has been terribly abused by its professed friends as well as its enemies. But the existence of false doctrines should not discourage us from seeking after the truth of God's revelation. To neglect this area of truth would be a tragedy, and an untold loss of richness to the body of Christ. When you find counterfeits, just remember that there are no counterfeit fifty-three dollar bills! There are counterfeit ten, twenty, fifty, and hundred dollar bills, but there are no phony eighty-seven dollar bills! Only real things with true value get counterfeited. That a counterfeit exists testifies that there is a true and real thing or concept in existence. But the counterfeit never really measures up—there is a flaw in it somewhere.

FIRST MENTION OF THE KINGDOM OF GOD

While there is previous usage of the word "king" and a couple of usages of the word "kingdom," the first reference to the *kingdom of God* is found in Exodus 19:6: "And ye shall be unto me a kingdom of priests, and an holy nation. These are the words which thou shalt speak unto the children of Israel." The children of Israel were deeply aware that while God uses human instrumentality the Kingdom belongs

263

to Him, and while there was a visible king on the earthly throne, Israel was a theocracy. God was the true King above all kings. King David extolled, "For the kingdom is the Lord's, and he is the governor among the nations" (Ps. 22:28). The prophet Obadiah declares "and the kingdom shall be the Lord's" (Obad. 21).

THE KINGDOM IN REVELATION

The last book of the Bible is a book of shining victory. The star of the end-time drama is not the Antichrist. The star of the grand finale of all history and prophecy is Jesus Christ, the Son of the Living God. How tragic that some teachers of prophecy see more defeat than victory, more devil than God, more Antichrist than Jesus Christ. The theme of the Book of Revelation is found in Revelation 1:1 and 19:10. It is "The Revelation of Jesus Christ..." not of the Antichrist, and "the testimony of Jesus is the spirit of prophecy." The last mention of God's kingdom is a shout of triumph! "The kingdoms of this world are become the kingdoms of our Lord, and of his Christ; and he shall reign forever and forever" (Rev. 12:15). Jesus is praised as "King of kings and Lord of lords" (Rev. 19:16).

THE THOUSAND-YEAR MILLENNIUM

There will be a thousand-year Millennium (Rev. 20), but this is *not* the totality of the Kingdom. The kingdom of God is eternal. It exists *now.* It will always exist. The thousand-year millennial reign of Christ on this planet is simply a physical demonstration of the Kingdom. It is not a perfect age, although it is an idealic age. Christ will rule with a rod of iron. He will hold rebellion in check. Satan will be bound.

Some have objected to the idea of a thousand-year Kingdom on earth on various grounds. One who has questions should read Paul Lee Tan's book *The Interpretation of Prophecy.* Also Dr. John Walvoord has well noted:

"The general features of modern premillennialism are highly significant and need to be outlined before assuming the larger task of the analysis and defense of premillennial doctrine. Even a casual observer of the premillennial movement in the twentieth century can see certain important tendencies.

"**Infallibility of Scripture.** Premillennialism is based on the thesis of the infallibility of Scripture. It stands or falls not only on the method of interpretation of Scripture, but also on the question of the infallibility of the Holy Scripture. For this reason, premillennialism is entirely confined to those who are conservative in their general theological position. Premillennialism has always been the foe of liberal theology and of unbelief in the Scripture. It has often been attacked for this very reason. Much of the modern zeal of its opponents has not arisen in love for doctrinal purity, but in hatred of conservative Biblical theology. To be a premillenarian exposes one at once to all who have departed from conservative theology. Premillennialism remains a bulwark against the inroads of modern theology" (*The Millennial Kingdom*; John Walvoord; 1959; Zondervan Publishing House; Grand Rapids, Michigan).

WHO WILL USHER IN THE KINGDOM?

This question could be a trap. One must define his terms and concepts before answering. First of all one cannot "usher in the Kingdom." The Kingdom is already here. It exists now. It has always existed.

There is a Kingdom Now doctrine abroad. It is growing in influence. It speaks of the Church's fulfilling certain tasks and thus ushering in the Kingdom. After this humanistic restitution Christ will return (maybe). But it is declared by these teachers, "Jesus *cannot* come now. His coming is in no way imminent." In fact, they say while the Church has an opportunity to fulfill its task (not world evangelization) in this present age, *it could fail.* On the basis of that, there is no assurance that the Church in any age will ever fulfill the task, and hence Christ may never return. I disagree with this concept entirely.

When a conservative scholar speaks of "ushering in the Kingdom," he is probably using the phrase in the restrictive sense, meaning the Millennium. We will not by any means usher in the Millennium. It will take the personal presence of Jesus to do that.

WHEN BRETHREN DISAGREE

I have no problem fellowshipping with those who disagree with me on these matters, provided they are truly born again believers who uphold the deity of Jesus, the true nature of the triune Godhead, the inspiration of the Scripture, etc. How can this be?

My brethren in the Church of God of Anderson, Indiana, believe in the doctrine of amillennialism. They say we are in the Millennium now. Satan is already bound. There will be no rapture of the Church. When the Church has completed its task Jesus will come. There will be no literal seven-year Tribulation. Since I disagree with this system of theology, how can I fellowship with these brethren?

First of all, these friends are Evangelical, and they preach a truly born again experience. (They are not part of the current Kingdom Now movement.) They are not compromisers in the area of the great truths of the Church. We disagree on the doctrines of the baptism of the Holy Spirit and in the field of prophecy. Nevertheless we are united in Christ.

Anyone who is a saved person is united with every other saved person by means of the real unity of the body of Christ (1 Cor. 12:12-27). How then do I deal with these areas of disagreement? I can do one of two things. I can say to my amillennial brother, "Look, we agree on so much more than we disagree on; let's fellowship on the basis of our mutuality and put aside those things we disagree on. The Lord will ultimately settle it." Or, I can enter into dialogue in the area of disagreement. My Church of God brethren believe the Bible is the Word of God as I do. We simply do not see eye-to-eye on how to interpret certain passages dealing with prophecy. As long as we are both gentlemen and can avoid heated arguments, we can discuss any subject. We can examine what the Word says on the subject, whether we come to final agreement or not.

DIVISION IN THE NAME OF UNITY

The proponents of the so-called Kingdom Now or New Wave theology do not allow such dialogue. Some of their leaders claim to be prophets. They claim divine revelation *equal to the Bible*. Some say that their statements are not to be judged or evaluated. We are told that the "new" understanding of Revelation and prophecy is direct from God by divine revelation, equal to what John experienced on the Isle of Patmos. Case closed. No room for discussion. Is this how we are to understand the Bible?

The teachers of the Kingdom Now theories are saying that their movement is a call to unity in the body of Christ. Actually it is a call for you to unite with them, on the basis of your agreeing with their doctrinal system. In the name of unity, division is being created. The Kingdom Now movement promises to be one of the most disruptive and divisive influences in the body of Christ in these last days. This is a tragedy, for many of the people in the Kingdom Now movement are good people doing a good work. But they have disfellowshipped masses of us because of their dogmatic doctrinal stance. Mark my words, what they are actually doing is starting another new denomination.

TRUE UNITY OF THE CHURCH

Frankly, I tire of hearing how disunited the Church is. The Church is divided, but it is not disunited. Our unity is spiritual, it is organic. If you are a born again Christian, then I am united with you. You may not like me. You might refuse to darken the door of the church where I worship. You may despise my teaching. But in spite of all your rejection of me, we are still united. We are one in the body of Christ.

You can destroy our unity only by leaving the body of Christ. "...the body is one...if the foot shall say, because I am not the hand, I am not of the body; is it therefore not of the body?...there should be no schism [division] in the body" (1 Cor. 12:12,15,25). Yes, the Church is united. There is division, but unity cannot be destroyed. What we need is to quit harping on the disunity of the Church. We need to recognize its essential unity and then begin to heal the divisions that exist, but this can never be until we recognize the unity that God has created and which no failure of man can destroy. God is not as feeble as some imagine. Jesus prayed that we might be one. We are.

INTERPRETATION AND ISRAEL

The Scripture is of "no private interpretation!" When the early Church (as recorded in the New Testament) had a dispute to settle, the brethren got together and had a council. They waited on God and looked to the Word. They discussed the matter. They believed, "...in the multitude of counsellors there is safety" (Prov. 11:14). Whatever happened to the humility manifested by the great apostle Paul who was not ashamed to admit that he did not have all the answers to the future?

"We see through a glass darkly; but then, [when Christ returns] face to face: now I know *in part,* but then I shall know even as also I am known" (1 Cor. 13:12).

A sobering note of caution is declared by Peter: "We have a more sure word of prophecy; whereunto ye do well to take heed, as unto a light that shineth in a dark place, until the day dawn, and the day star arise in your hearts: Knowing this first that no prophecy of the Scripture is of any private interpretation. For the prophecy came not in old time by the will of man; but holy men of God spake as they were moved by the Holy Ghost" (2 Pet. 1:19-21).

Here is a notable call to the study of prophecy: "Study to show thyself approved" (1 Tim. 2:15). It is a serious matter at hand, and these prophecies were given by God Himself, through the prophets. Further, no prophetic Scripture is to be privately interpreted. What more private interpretation could there be than for a modern man who calls himself a prophet to say, "God showed me this. It is equal to what John got on Patmos. I am not to be evaluated by any man. There is no room for discussion." This is in defiance of the teaching of the New Testament.

AGAINST ISRAEL

Another disturbing factor in the Kingdom Now teaching is the blatant theological anti-Semitism of the system. Israel, they say, no longer has a place in the plan of God. The Church, and only the Church, is Israel. There will be no restoration of natural Israel. This is a denial of the literal interpretation of the Bible. This they frankly admit to. They declare that the literal interpretation of the Bible is wrong. The Bible must be spiritualized or allegorized. It doesn't really mean what it says. One hundred forty-four thousand means something else—it means the Church, 1000 is not 1000.

This is a dangerous trend. Remember that Hitler could never have succeeded in persecuting the Jews in Germany and Europe if it had not been for these same anti-Semitic doctrines' having been taught by the Catholic and Protestant churches of Germany. Many of Hitler's henchmen quoted outstanding Christian theologians in justification for feeding the Jews to the gas furnaces. The Church in Germany had taught the "doctrine of contempt" for the Jews and it was grist for the satanic Nazi's mill. Beware of the Kingdom Now teachers for this reason, as well as all the other reasons.

PROBLEMS IN THE KINGDOM

I would not be writing this if it were not for the fact that the Kingdom Now, New Wave theology is spreading so rapidly. It is making deep penetration into the Evangelical, Charismatic, and Pentecostal ranks. Some of you that are reading this just don't know the proportions this thing is gaining. I hope you are prepared for what is coming your way. Churches are being split. Local churches are being swallowed up by this growing movement. A new denomination will be formed (is being formed). The cause of the unity of the body of Christ will not be served by this movement. Some of these people are indeed kingdom builders. The kingdom being built is their own.

A STRANGE TWIST

The Kingdom Now preachers and writers scurrilously attack people who believe like I do. I believe in a literal Rapture, a seven-year Tribulation, a literal thousand-year Millennium, that Israel will be restored and have a part in the end-time plan of God. They say that people like me are the greatest impediment to the advance of the kingdom of God. But here is a strange twist. One of the most prominent of the Kingdom Now teachers, a Charismatic who describes himself as a liberal Evangelical, castigates another TV minister who referred to a survey of beliefs held by old-line denominational preachers. The survey showed that most of them did not believe in the virgin birth, the inspiration of the Scriptures, or the resurrection of Jesus. The Kingdom Now preacher said that we should not separate ourselves from these "brethren."

I am sorry, but men who do not believe in the deity of and the resurrection of Jesus are not my brethren. I feel compassion for them. I long for their conversion. The Bible declares that those who believe that God raised Jesus from the dead and confess the same will be saved (Rom. 10:9,10). I will hold to the right of these modernists to preach whatever they want to. I will defend their freedom of speech, but *they are not my brethren.* The same Kingdom Now writer calls for unity among Evangelicals, Roman Catholics, Seventh Day Adventists, and Mormons. Let me zero in on the latter. Friend, Mormons have the right to believe whatever they want to, but they do not even serve the same God I serve. Their god is totally foreign to the Bible. Their added scriptures portray a god among many gods who left his other planetary home with one of his celestial wives, came to this planet as Adam, and founded the present branch of the human race inhabiting the earth. They say that God is evolving as I am evolving.

There is no basis of unity between a born again believer and those who promote a totally corrupt system of religion. I will speak out for their freedom to speak out, but we are not servants of the same God and there is no possibility of unity.

ISSUES NOT PERSONALITIES

Many of you have written to me asking, "Who are you talking about? Who are the leaders of the Kingdom Now movement?" Sorry, but I am dealing with issues, not personalities. First of all, many of the Kingdom Now men are true brothers in Christ, no matter how wrong their doctrine is in this area of Kingdom teaching. They may attack me, but I will not attack them. Anyway, you will know soon enough who they are. They are doing an adequate job of declaring themselves. They may call us "swine" (before whom they will not cast their pearls) but we will still love them and hope for a reconciliation.

THE DOMINIONISTS

On the other hand, brethren in the Dominion camp have invited discussion and do not mind having quotations of their works attributed to them.

I appeal to my Kingdom Now friends to achieve this same level of maturity. We should have a total "sunshine" policy. I do not mind being quoted (even critically) as long as it is done accurately and fairly. Why do the Kingdom teachers cry "martyrdom" when certain other authors do quote them?

WHAT'S NEW

The Kingdom Now people are always trying to impress us with how "new" is their teaching and understanding of the Bible: "This is a totally new revelation. No one ever understood this before." But I have searched through their writings. I do not find anything new at all. What we actually have here is a rehash of the tired, worn-out old doctrines of amillennialism and a smattering of postmillennialism in some instances.

For the first three hundred years of Church history the apostles and early Church fathers preached a literal millennial reign of Christ on this earth at a time designated in the future by the Father in heaven. Three things contributed to the rejection of literalism and the rise of allegorical interpretation, and hence the teaching of amillennialism (no Millennium). Actually amillennialism is a misnomer since most of them teach that we are in the Millennium (figuratively) now. Satan is bound now. The Church is reigning now. What is denied is that there will be a literal, future thousand-year reign of Jesus on earth.

The first factor contributing to the drift away from biblical premillennialism was the strong influence of Origin who taught at the Alexandrian School in Egypt. He introduced the system of nonliteral interpretation of the Bible. This was a seed beginning, and not at all accepted by the majority of the Church for quite some time. At the Council of Nicea in 325 it was still expressed that the Church believed in a literal thousand-year reign of Jesus on earth, to be inaugurated by His personal return.

The second thing that contributed to this ancient doctrine was the supposed, and highly suspect conversion of Emperor Constantine who passed the "edicts of toleration" and in effect made Christianity a state religion. He did not submit to Baptism himself until on his deathbed.

Most conservative scholars doubt his conversion. Christianity became popular. The idea of a future coming of Jesus was not so attractive anymore. The Kingdom is right here and now.

Finally, we note the influence of Saint Augustine who popularized the allegorical (not literal) method of interpretation and promoted the system of amillennialism. His book *The City of God* was a most powerful work used to spread this doctrine.

SOMETHING IS NEW

What is actually new is that the Kingdom Now doctrine is making such inroads into the ranks of the Charismatics and Pentecostals as well as some other Evangelicals. The Holy Spirit-filled teachers of the Pentecostal churches (Myer Pearlman, J. Narver Gortner, Frank M. Boyd, John Hall, etc.) have always held to a classic New Testament stance of literalism and premillennialism. How shocking to see some of the Pentecostal churches being swept off their feet by this movement. The blatant anti-Semitism of the Kingdom Now movement augurs no good for those who are sucked into its depths. The denial of literal interpretation will introduce an anarchy of interpretation until it is questionable if the Bible will mean anything at all to many who accept this teaching.

THE KINGDOM IS NOW

For over thirty years I have been preaching that, as men and women of the Millennium, we need to actualize millennial principles and works in the now season. Jesus said that the kingdom is now. He said, "The Kingdom is within you." Further, right now we reign in heavenly places with Christ (Eph. 1:3,20; 2:6). We shall reign with Him upon the earth (Rev. 5:19).

I do not believe that prophecy should be used to promote defeatism, doomsday, negativism, irresponsibility, or escapism. I believe prophecy is a faith message. It is a victory declaration. It is a call to arms against the spirit of Antichrist. God is looking for participants in the divine plan, not for spectators. We are not fatalists. We believe we can work with God to improve the quality of life right here and now. We anticipate the coming of Jesus, but in the meantime we "occupy 'til He comes." Please read my book *Smashing the Gates of Hell in the Last Days*. I believe that we have the power through the Spirit, by intercession and good works, to change the world today. I am not ready to give in to the devil.

The Kingdom is now. It is also eternal. It is forever. There will be a thousand-year Millennium, which is but the inauguration of the age of all ages and ultimate perfection of all things. Glory be to God.

A CALL FOR RECONCILIATION

I call to all my Kingdom Now brethren. Do not isolate yourselves from us. I cannot agree with your doctrine in the area of eschatology, but there is no need for an artificial division to exist between us. You have created this problem by your declarations of exclusivity and superiority. Leave the door open for discussion. Stop telling me that your words are equal to the Bible. Our only desire is to promote the true spiritual unity of the body of Christ. You have rendered this impossible. In the name of unity you have caused division. Let's leave all that behind and determine to emphasize the areas of our common agreement in Jesus Christ. The Kingdom is now; let's not destroy it.

WHAT'S GOING ON IN THE CHURCH?

We expect the world system to plot, scheme, and conspire for final conquest, but what if this same attitude comes into the Church? Time does not permit me to examine all possible answers to the question. We would have to deal with Modernistic Apostasy, Liberation Theology, Neo Evangelical Marxism, Radical Liberalism, new Roman Catholic trends (Tielhard de Chardin's New Age thinking, etc.), polluted Protestantism, and a host of other ill-fated Christian philosophies.

So, let's get right to the point, narrowing the spectrum of our question: "What is going on in the Evangelical, Pentecostal, Fundamentalist, and Charismatic wing of the Church?" What is going on is a monumental power struggle for control of the Church. Beyond this there are Christian leaders who envision a Christian dominated World Order, which they will bring to birth prior to the Second Coming.

Men proclaiming themselves to be apostles and prophets are vying for rulership. The reason for this is quite easy to understand. There are men in the Church today who plan to set up a New World Order—before the visible return of Jesus. Pluralism (people of different faiths coexisting in the same nation) and democracy will be abolished. Some even suggest capital punishment for all dissidents.

If the Church is the foundation upon which the New World Order (Theocracy) is to stand, then it is logical that the framers of the New World government must first conquer and dominate the Church. Since the Pentecostals, Fundamentalists, Charismatics, and Evangelicals are certainly the most vigorous and rapidly growing branch of the Church, they become a special target. The Pentecostals and Charismatics alone number 332,000,000 adherents worldwide. This is the largest Protestant group in Christendom. It could even be argued that these constitute the largest single community of the Church, even larger than the Roman Catholic church, though statistics would seem to discount this theory. But it is possible. The Evangelical says, "God has no grandsons." Everyone must be born into the Kingdom of God by his own decision, that is by a born again experience or conversion encounter with Jesus. Everyone on our Evangelical and Pentecostal church membership rolls is there because of personal choice. Not so with the Roman Catholic church, and some old-line Protestant churches. In many cases your family determines your religious identity. You have heard someone say, "I was born Roman Catholic" or "I was born a Methodist and I'll die a Methodist!" In some countries all people are registered, at birth, as members of the Roman Catholic or other state church. Only when individuals personally change their registration do the statistics change. Before we get too far from our topic, let's get back to the subject of eschatology.

THE MILLENNIUM—PRE OR POST?

Dominion teacher and publisher Gary North was right when he said that the Church is about to get into the shouting match of the century and that the key issue is eschatology (end-time prophecy). I wish every pastor and leader in my own denomination had this keen insight! North's advertising proclaims that the Dominion-Reconstructionists have consciously fired the first shots in this battle. Who needs another battle in the Church? But since we have been shot at, it is our obligation to give an answer. God does not allow us the luxury of silence when our faith is under attack. Jude writes that we should "earnestly contend for the faith once delivered unto the saints."

MILLENNIUM

A definition of terms is in order at this point: The Millennium is a thousand-year period of God's kingdom being manifested on this earth. The word Millennium comes from the Latin, *mille* meaning one thousand and *annum* meaning years. Hence Millennium means one thousand years.

The one thousand years is specifically referred to six times in Revelation 20. Hundreds of Old and New Testament passages describe a coming visible kingdom of God on earth. Both the Church and National Israel play a role in this coming Messianic Kingdom which will be personally governed by Jesus Christ and His resurrected ancestor, King David, who will act as co-regent with Christ. Jesus will rule the world from the reestablished throne of His father David. Jerusalem will be the capital of the New World government.

The present controversy revolves around the question of when Jesus will return to earth, in relationship to the Millennium. Will He come back before or after the Millennium? For the first two hundred years of the history of the Christian Church, the doctrine of Chiliasm, or a literal thousand-year Millennium was taught universally. The New Testament and the early Church taught that this thousand year reign would be preceded by and brought into being by the visible return of Christ. Jesus will come back and He will establish the visible Kingdom on earth.

AMILLENNIALISM

Largely due to the influence of Origin and Augustine, the concept of amillennialism (no literal thousand years) replaced the early Church doctrine of Chiliasm. (See the book *Dominion Theology, Blessing or Curse,* by H. Wayne House and Thomas Ice for an historical background on this subject.) Amillennialism is an old concept, but not as old as premillennialism. In its new, aggressive form it is described as the Kingdom Now or neo-Kingdom teaching. Kingdom Now teachers have charged that we premillennialists are heretics. According to Galatians a heretic is a damned soul. The neo-Kingdomist's judgment of us is very harsh. I believe that the Kingdom teachers are my brethren in Christ, but that they are teaching serious and potentially damaging error. But they are brethren and we do not question their salvation.

While we have peacefully coexisted with people with views on eschatology other than our own for over three decades of ministry, suddenly we find ourselves under attack along with all of you premillennialists. If you also believe in the Rapture (at any time before the Millennium), you are even more heavily condemned by the Kingdomists. Those who believe National Israel has a place in God's plan are the worst of all in their eyes. If we respond to their charges we are accused of being divisive.

POSTMILLENNIALISM—THE DOMINIONISTS

The concept of postmillennialism is a fairly new concept, having been first expressed clearly in the eighteenth century:

"Postmillennialism was in fact the last of the three major eschatological systems to be developed. It is true that postmillennialism maintained some features of the older amillennialism, but if postmillennialism is to be considered different from the amillennial view, which postmillennialists maintain, then it has to be recognized as just that—a distinct system. It did not originate as a system until the early 1700s...Daniel Whitby first put forth his views in a popular work entitled *Paraphrase and Commentary on the New Testament* (1703). It was at the end of this work that he first set forth what he calls in his own words 'A New Hypothesis' on the millennial reign of Christ. Thus, the system called postmillennialism was born in the early 1700s as a hypothesis. The three views of the Millennium did not appear at the same time in church history. Premillennialism was first held by the early church fathers who were the closest to the original apostles" (*Dominion Theology, Blessing or Curse,* H. Wayne House and Thomas Ice, Multnomah Press, 1988; pp. 208-211).

Postmillennialism is the idea that the Church will conquer and Christianize the world. When this is accomplished Christ will return and the Church will deliver the Kingdom into His hands. Postmillennialism is being revived by the Domionionists, who have come into prominence during the last twenty years. Our files contain documents listing many of their members and participants.

Those who read our articles, books, and publications know that we have been very deliberately selective when speaking of individuals involved in these various movements. The reason is simple. Some authors invite analysis and evaluation. On the other hand, some of the Kingdom Now, Restoration, and other brethren have expressed strong displeasure at being quoted with attributation to the source. It has been our policy to honor these sensitivities, as far as we know they exist. This is merely a personal policy and not a criticism of authors who do the opposite. Frankly, I think any man who puts his thoughts down on paper opens himself to examination by his audience and should be seasoned enough to endure examination and even constructive criticism. There are now scores of sources that will list involvees in the Kingdom Now and other movements. I confess that I find some of these lists flawed and some individuals being misinterpreted.

Furthermore, I have entered into discussion with some of the brethren teaching these alternate concepts, and further welcome dialogue with any responsible leader of these movements. Until now I have refused all public debate, but welcome private conversation and reasoned consideration. The courtesies we have extended the Kingdom Now teachers have not in general been returned, but that is in the hands of God. He will judge between us.

A GRAVE ERROR

The classic Pentecostals, early on in the Charismatic renewal, committed a serious error. Rather than move in and give the Charismatics teaching and fellowship, they tended to shun these neo-Pentecostals. They often used poor judgment by calling them "Charismaniacs," etc. On the other hand the Charismatics were rejectionists as well, saying that the denominational Pentecostals were dead and had lost the revival fire (the old wineskin syndrome). Of course to some extent both sides were expressing an element of truth. It is too bad that some of the Charismatics had to wait to get their eschatology from the Dominion crowd. We have yet to see the enormity of this tragic turn of events.

A DECLARATION OF WAR

How strange that Dennis Peacock prefaces his book *Winning the Battle for the Minds of Men* with a quotation from Karl Marx, father of the Communist Bolshevik Revolution: "The worker must one day seize power, in order to erect the new organization of labor; he must push to one side the old politics which uphold the old institutions, if he does not want to suffer the loss of heaven on earth, as did the old Christians who neglected and despised it" (Karl Marx. Address at the Hague Congress—1872).

Peacock envisions violent struggle as the Church marches on to world conquest: "You are involved in a battle to the death between two competing world systems over the control of this planet...This war is being fought both with ideas and raw power. In our lifetime...it will erupt into ultimate confrontation" (Peacock, *Winning the Battle,* p. XIII).

"God wants us to rule under Him over the world" (Ibid. p. 8). "The Church should exercise judgment over the nations" (Ibid. p. 68). "But we must 'pull the trigger' of judgment in order to release the cleansing flow" (Ibid. p. 74). All of this is to take place before the return of Jesus. A researcher, Mrs. May Eye, has produced a pamphlet with scores of radical quotations from various militant Dominionists. It will be available to the public shortly.

The terms Dominion, Theonomy, Reconstruction, and Restoration, are all interrelated. Proponents of all these views have a lot in common and regularly network and conference together. Some of these terms have a legitimate usage apart from the "movement" so be careful not to lump people into the Dominion camp if they don't really belong there.

IT WON'T WORK

The postmillennial hope will never be fulfilled. Instead, two undesirable things could happen. First of all, as the secular, humanistic, demonically-dominated world system becomes more and more aware that the Dominionists and Reconstructionists are a real political threat, they will sponsor more and more concerted efforts to destroy the Evangelical church. Unnecessary persecution can be stirred up. For the sake of the Gospel the Word of God commands us to live peaceably with all men as far as it lies within us.

This is not a call to compromise, nor is it a mandate against people's actively participating in the existing government for the betterment of the conditions of our society and well-being of the Church. Also we do not discourage those who wish to visibly protest injustice and immorality in our society. "Rendering unto Caesar that which is Caesar's" is, in our nation and time, a call to citizen participation in government affairs. This is a government "of the people, by the people and for the people." To be involved in our governmental process is desirable; however, it is quite another matter for the Church to strive to become Caesar.

SATAN'S WORLD SYSTEM—FOR NOW

This is Satan's world system for the present time. He is the ruler of this age. Thank God the day will come when Jesus will have "Abolished all rule and all authority and power" (1 Cor. 15:24). However, at this present time Satan has dominion over this world system by the allowance of God Himself, for the fulfillment of His eternal plan. No less than three times Jesus called the devil the "prince of this world" (John 12:31; 14:30; 16:11).

But what about the victory at Calvary? Did not Jesus put an end to Satan's reign? Years after the death, resurrection, and ascension of our Lord, Paul wrote that Satan is "the god (prince) of this world (age)" (2 Cor. 4:4). He is still the "prince of the power of the air," against whose "rulers of the darkness of this earth" we wrestle (Eph. 2:2; 6:12).

Jesus did win a total victory at Calvary. Satan is a defeated foe. The declaration has been made. However, it will be the actual second coming of Jesus that will finish the work. Jesus isn't done yet, or He would not come back to enforce His rule. We are to bind Satan continually by the authority of Jesus. We are to make war with him. God has a prophetic timetable in which that victory will be totally manifested on earth at the time of Christ's return. We do God no favors by trying to push the visible earthly Kingdom ahead of schedule. Dominionists slander God if they say that this is defeatism.

If Satan's activities are illegal, how is it that we must bind him and do battle against the powers of darkness?

We are God's ambassadors in this world. We are citizens of heaven. God has taken us out of the kingdom of darkness into His Kingdom of glorious light. We now represent God on earth, Satan's temporary domain. We will ultimately inherit final power over this world, when it is God's time and through the personal return of Jesus.

If Satan is already defeated, why do we war against him? The Mafia is also legally defeated. It has no legal authority to operate. However, they continue to operate illegally whenever law enforcement agencies fail to do their job efficiently. The Dominionists are right when they charge that the Church has not fulfilled her ultimate mission and must give account for failures. However, it is important to determine the actual mission of the Church.

SUPREME TASK OF THE CHURCH

The Word of God reveals that the supreme task of the Church is to evangelize the world. This is expressed in the Great Commission. Jesus speaks of preaching the gospel to every nation (Matt. 24:14). We are not to conquer the nations. That is something He is capable of doing at the time of His second coming. Dominion teaching prevents the Church from going about its real work, the evangelization of the world. It sets up false goals upon which we could expend our energies uselessly. Jesus said that, "One soul is worth more than the whole world." Most of the Dominionists believe in absolute predestination, so it is predetermined who will be saved anyway. No wonder they rail at those of us who believe in free will and in God's giving each person a choice whether to be saved or lost. This could indicate why the Dominionists have such a drive to conquer the world politically, paying less attention to evangelism. In all fairness I know of one Dominion teacher who is an aggressive soul winner, and I suppose there are others.

NO TIME TO WASTE

We are in the final era prior to the coming of Jesus and the establishing of the visible aspect of the Kingdom—the Millennium. We have no time to waste on wild experimentation with possible futures and postmillennial pipedreams. We premillennialists are not escapists. We are urged on by the nearness of the coming of the Lord. We must expend all our strength in obeying Him. We will do our utmost to fulfill His command to take the gospel to the whole world. That is still the supreme task of the Church.

VICTORIOUS CHURCH OF THE END-TIMES

Potentially the most powerful earthly body is the true Church of our Lord Jesus Christ. This is true because we are commissioned to be God's ambassadors. We are His representatives on earth. When the Church aligns with the purposes of God, our task can be accomplished. We must find out from the Word of God what is the true task and calling of the Church. It will never do for us to dream up a scenario we would like to see fulfilled and then ask God to rubber stamp His approval on our plan. It is His will and plan we seek to implement.

We are here to transform lives and prepare people for eternity. Each person is a lost soul. Only as political involvement aids in carrying out the supreme task, do we interest ourselves in the political realm. We never lose sight of the goal. We are here to win souls for the kingdom of God, which is eternal, invisible, within us now, but shortly to become visible when Jesus comes back. Time enough, then, under His command to witness His dominion over the nations.

SURE HOPE FOR OUR FUTURE

If man has to establish a world government which will rule with justice and equity for all, alas, it will never be done. If the promises of the Bible are literal, if there is to be a peaceable Kingdom on earth, established by Jesus in person, then we have real hope.

This does not mean that heads of nations should not work for the best peace that can be attained. Treaties should be signed and honest agreements entered into. Peace by negotiation (not surrender) is preferable to war. Christians should work and hope for tranquility in our time. Believing in Bible prophecy should not make one bloodthirsty. We are not called to be promoters of Armageddon. That will come in due season, not from our efforts, but from the hand of God as He cleanses the earth. We are followers of the Prince of Peace.

That does not mean that we flow with everything that calls itself a "peace movement." We will not be taken in by phony peace movements that mask ulterior motives. We fully support our nation's efforts to attain peace with other nations through sensible and legitimate means.

"The easiest way to make peace is to surrender to your enemy. All you have to do is agree to live by his rules. But that is called slavery. The other way to keep peace is to be so strong that no one would dare attack you. That is called peace through strength. Throughout history, weakness has always led to war. Aggressive powers take advantage of weakness, but they respect superior strength...Disarmament has never led to true peace. It always leads to surrender. Is that the kind of peace we want?" (*The Selling of Gorbachev,* Marlin Maddoux; p. 66).

Our privilege as Christians, even greater than the privileges we enjoy as citizens of this free nation, is to seek the "peace of God which passeth all understanding." Of lasting, true peace, the Scripture says, "There is no peace to the wicked, saith my God." The greatest promotion of peace on earth comes through a gospel witness that leads men and women to a saving knowledge of Christ. Bringing men to formal religion or church membership will not do, for we have seen many horrible wars spawned in the name of God and religion. People whose lives have been transformed and who are properly taught in the Word of God will be peacemakers in their generation.

Since the Bible tells us that "the world lies in the lap of the wicked one," we know that lasting world peace will not come until the Prince of Peace makes His personal appearance. But, thank God, He will come and establish His kingdom.

In the Millennium there will be no poverty or war. Even wild animal nature is tamed. A child will play with the lion and not be harmed. The miraculous will be the everyday occurrence. As the old gospel song declares, "There will be peace in the valley for me someday."

Many times I have stood in upper Israel at the town of Metullah looking into war torn Lebanon to the north. This is where the good neighbor gate is located. This is the place where Southern Lebanese people are allowed to enter Israel without passports or visas for medical care, food, and assistance. At the fence near the gate, there are three stone tablets written in Hebrew, Arabic, and English, proclaiming, "They shall beat their swords into plowshares and their spears into pruning hooks." Here is an expression of the longing desire of all mankind. Yes, peace will come, when Shiloh comes.

How is it that our Dominionist brethren can believe that the efforts of man will finally bring about a World Order, but find it impossible to believe the Bible's literal declaration that God Himself will bring it to pass? Since they are brethren and do believe the Bible is God's Word, they are forced to reinterpret the plain teaching of the Word. They reject literal interpretation and impose allegory. The evidence, both biblical and extra-biblical, strongly favors the former, and noting the sad performance of sinful mankind, indicates the unlikelihood that man will bring it to pass through his own efforts.

The visible, manifested Kingdom of the Millennium is only the beginning. It is not the Kingdom but a part of the Kingdom. The Kingdom is eternal. Of course the Kingdom is now. It is invisible, within us now, according to the words of Jesus. But there will be a visible one-thousand-year demonstration of the Kingdom on this earth during the Millennium.

Following the thousand years we enter into eternity, the age of all ages. Jesus will take up residence on the new planet earth for there will be a new heaven and earth wherein dwelleth righteousness forever. We will always have access to both heaven and earth. Earth will always be home base, and Jesus will make His residence there. What a marvel of the grace of God for all to behold throughout eternity. (For an excellent study of the Millennium see *Things to Come* by Dr. J. Dwight Pentecost. Zondervan.)

Premillennialists have a real message of victory both for the present and for eternity. We have confidence that God will bring His purposes to pass. We want to pass through time traveling the high road of cooperation with His divine will. Show us, Lord, Your will for today, we pray. Daily we cry in the midst of our tasks, "Even so come, Lord Jesus." That has to be a legitimate prayer, a holy cry. It is in the Bible. Look it up. It is easy to find. It is in the last paragraph of the last page of the Book.

STRUGGLE FOR CONTROL OVER THE CHURCH

A power struggle is going on to determine who will ultimately control the Evangelical, Pentecostal, Fundamentalist, and Charismatic sectors of the Church [E.P.F.C.]. Dominionists, Theonomists, and Reconstructionists (all very similar) are aggressive, bright, and on the move. They are publishing some of the sharpest-looking books on the Christian market. They tackle topics that a lot of publishers won't touch. They boast that the theologically weak Charismatic movement will be easy to take over. They network and conference with Kingdom Now leaders on an ongoing basis. Their goals are similar.

These people believe in postmillennialism. That is they believe the

Church will conquer and rule the world in an established kingdom age before Christ returns. When they have established the visible Kingdom, Christ will return.

We, on the other hand, believe in a premillennial concept. We see the Bible teaching that Jesus will return at the end of this present age and He will establish the visible Kingdom or Millennium of a thousand years of peace prior to the final judgment. We will be involved in spiritual warfare right up until Christ raptures the Church. We are not, as accused, escapists. We present the only real hope for humanity both on the short term and long term. We believe that the evangelization of lost mankind is the supreme task of the Church, not a political takeover. On the other hand, we encourage Christians to get involved, on an individual basis, in all realms of society, including the political arena. This is partly to insure that Christians are in place in every strata of society for the purpose of sharing the gospel message. Our vision is to obey and fulfill the command of the Great Commission.

Since Dominionists believe that the Church must politically conquer the world, it is easy to see why they feel that they must first conquer the Church. The Church, under their dominion, will be the platform for world conquest. They have had little use for Pentecostals in the past. Now they admit that Pentecostals and Charismatics have the best control of the Christian media. They recognize that it is necessary for them to make an alliance for the sake of having access to the best means of communicating their ideas and goals. Actually they are still scornful of the Pentecostals and only want to manipulate them for their own purposes. Common cause makes strange bedfellows.

I spent a couple of hours at Dominion Press in Texas talking to their publication manager about these matters (tape recorded). He was very clear and forthright in describing the Dominion position on various topics. In addition the Dominionists have been much more open than the Kingdom Now advocates in letting it be known what they hope to accomplish. You won't hear the Dominionists back down from what they have written. You will not hear them say, "That is not what I really meant...My secretary wrote that...That wasn't meant for general distribution." The Dominionists, on the other hand, actually invite discussion and response.

Years ago people found it hard to believe my reporting on the Kingdom Now movement and its aspirations. For a long time the only piece of literature being circulated on that subject was our tabloid paper published a few years ago and reprinted over and over to supply the demand. Now many of our allies are writing on the subject. Dr. House and Rev.

Ice (former reconstructionist) have written a book titled, *Dominion Theology, Blessing or Curse?* David Hunt's new book *What Ever Happened to Heaven?* also deals with the subject. Hal Lindsey's book *Road to Holocaust* is also available.

Please don't make the mistake of thinking that because you have heard little about Dominion that it is not significant. I must inform you that this is a major error besetting the Church today.

They won't like this and will deny it, but I will tell you anyway that like the Kingdom Now, some Dominionists are theological anti-Semites (against the Jews) and I can prove that to anyone from their own writings. You don't even have to read between the lines—it is there in plain English for anyone who wants to take the time and check this out.

WHY THE CHARISMATICS AND PENTECOSTALS?

Why would postmillennialist promoters of Dominion and Theonomy want to ally with the Pentecostals and Charismatics, whom they have historically despised? We have given you the "media reason" but there is another reason which we must not overlook.

The Pentecostals are the largest body of Protestant Christians in the world according to statistical studies done by *Encyclopedia Britannica* and by the *International Bulletin of Missionary Research.* The *I.B.M.R.* claims that fifty-four thousand new members are being added to the Pentecostal ranks daily. That comes to nineteen million per year. The Pentecostals and Charismatics have three hundred thirty-two million affiliated church members worldwide. They have sixty-six percent of the Christian membership of the third world nations. They have the vast majority of the world's megachurches (superchurches). Pentecostals and Charismatics give thirty-four billion dollars annually to Christian causes. Of all the plans presently known for fulfilling the Great Commission (world evangelization) two-thirds of them are in the hands of the Pentecostals and Charismatics. The Assemblies of God currently plans to launch five thousand new churches in the United States alone in the next ten years. In statistical studies done by Burgess, McGee, and Alexander we are told that the classical Pentecostal denominations (Assemblies of God, Church of God, Open Bible Standard, Foursquare Gospel, etc.) have one hundred seventy-six million members, worldwide.

Charismatics have one hundred twenty-three million adherents in the world. Add thirty-three million third wave Charismatics and you have three hundred thirty-two million Pentecostals and Charismatics. There are eleven thousand Pentecostal and three thousand Charismatic denominations. In 1988 the Pentecostals and Charismatics comprised twenty-one percent of all the Christians in the world.

The statisticians suggest that there are forty-one million "underground" Pentecostal believers in China. While Mrs. Lewis and I were ministering in Hong Kong and the free territories, we were told that the figure is closer to seventy-five million. While we were in Mainland China we providentially met some of these believers of the underground church. It is my understanding that these Chinese believers were not included in the statistics of the previous paragraph. Also it is known that there are millions of Pentecostals behind the Iron Curtain (not included here).

If you are a Dominionist and you dream of using the existing church to take over and rule the world by a Theocratic government, it is easy to understand why you have targeted the Pentecostals and Charismatics.

The Dominionists feel that they can easily take over and supply the intellectual and theological muscle for the Charismatics, but they have a harder time with the classical Pentecostals. The reason is very simple. Pentecostals have some stable convictions concerning what they believe. That is why they are constantly ridiculed for having doctrinal statements of faith to which their clergy are required to adhere. At present strong efforts are being made to persuade the Pentecostal clergy that their statements of faith are divisive and unnecessary. Well, we will see about that.

NEW APOSTLES AND PROPHETS

There have always been men in the Church who have fulfilled the role of apostles and prophets. I have known and recognized some of them. However, I never heard them making any claims and no one felt it necessary to give them a title.

Our clergymen are now being told that if they do not allow the prophets to walk in and speak out in the local churches, God will remove His anointing from the Church. Your pastor has been, or will be, told that if he does not bow to the apostle for his area there is some question as to whether God will even recognize his fellowship as a part of the Church any longer.

We were told that the shepherding movement had withered away. The fact is that it has been reborn on a grand scale. Now it is the shepherding of the shepherds that is at stake. You need to talk to your pastor about these things both to alert him to what is coming and to let him know that you stand with him in maintaining the biblical standards of your church. Please try to get your pastor to read this book.

It's not really about apostles and prophets at all. It is about political control of the church. Any local minister who accepts the apostle of his region opens the door for an outside authority to bypass the authority of his fellowship or denomination. We then have a super ecclesiastical authority which exercises authority beyond the pastor's fellowship of affiliation and ordination. It looks like the big question might turn out to be "Who will be the pope of the Pentecostals?"

ANTICHRIST?

It makes you wonder if the Antichrist might not turn out to be a renegade Pentecostal or Charismatic miracle worker (Rev. 13). Sounds unlikely? Just remember that Gregori Efimovitch Rasputin, one of the most notorious antichrists of all time, was a renegade Charismatic monk. A Pentecostal revival fell in Russia about the middle of the last century and hundreds of thousands of Russian Christians were filled with the Spirit, spoke in tongues, and prayed for the sick. (See Demos Shakarian's book *The Happiest People On Earth* for documentation.) Rasputin was a Charismatic, miracle-working monk who became morally corrupted but retained some kind of ability to prophesy and heal the sick! He was the greatest single influence in the life of the czar in preparing the way for the fall of the czar and the success of the Communist revolution.

Since I am an ordained clergyman in the Assemblies of God, no one can put this down as the ranting of a rabid anti-Pentecostal Fundamentalist. I speak as one who has been in the movement since childhood and seen the best and the worst it has to offer.

WILL JESUS FIND FAITH ON THE EARTH?

In the Gospel Jesus asks the question, "Will the Son of Man find faith upon the earth when he returns?" We can be thankful that it is a question and not a prophecy. There are alternate courses we can follow. May God help the Church today as she stands in the valley of decision!

A few years ago the National Christian Leadership Conference for Israel held its quarterly meeting in Albany, New York. One evening we had a social gathering for local Christian and Jewish leadership. During the evening a highly respected minister of the United Methodist Church approached me and asked for private conversation. He had been gripped by some things I had said in my remarks to the group. This minister had been honored in the gathering for his long years of service to the Church and college. He was in his late 80s.

As we went aside from the group he asked me quietly, "Tell me, Brother Lewis, are there any of the brethren left who still believe in the second coming of our Lord Jesus Christ?" I had a long conversation with him and assured him that there are many of us who still believe in and preach the second coming of Jesus. He was thrilled to hear this good news.

A few years have gone by and a lot of things have changed in the Church. As we approach the day of the Lord, fewer and fewer really fervently believe in the second coming of Jesus. Very few pastors ever preach a message on the subject. I have asked many of them. Other than a slight passing reference to the doctrine, little is said and less taught to the churches. It grieves me when I go to a church and get introduced this way: "Well, folks, as you know I never deal with prophecy. I leave that to the experts. That is why we have Brother Lewis here." How can the people take prophecy seriously? Why should they pay any attention to the prophecy teacher? After all, pastor has Brother Lewis here to satisfy the prophecy buffs in our congregation. I am not complaining about the attendance or the offerings in our meetings, for God has been good and the people, kind and generous. On the other hand, I know I get invited to churches where the pastor at least has respect for the message, or I would not be there. I cannot help thinking of the churches where no one ever speaks on the second coming of Christ any more. Seldom if ever do some pastors deal with contemporary issues like Israel, the New Age, and other vitally important topics.

LAY PEOPLE WANT TO KNOW

Pastors, you do your people a disservice if you do not preach the whole counsel of God to them. A genuine interest in prophecy is latent and can be fully awakened in the churches.

While I was in the hospital for surgery in January, one of the nurses heard me talking about prophecy to a local pastor who was visiting me. She walked in the room to say, "I could not help but hear what you were saying. I left the church I belonged to because they never talked about prophecy. I asked the pastor why he never preached on the signs of the times and he said that it was too complicated." The sad side of the story is that after leaving the church, the only literature this ill-informed lay person came upon was cultic in nature. I do thank God that He gave me the opportunity to talk further to her and give her some of our literature. Nature abhors a vacuum. If you do not fill your people with truth on a given subject, many will find teaching from other sources, not always healthy sources.

Our Bible colleges do not teach adequate courses in eschatology. I asked a faculty member in one of our fine denominational colleges why prophecy was mostly ignored in our schools. He said, "I think it is because we are afraid if we ever really looked closely at our church creed on the subject we would have to make some changes, that it could not stand up to a critical examination, for example the Rapture..." I do not know about "critical examination," but the concept can stand up to a biblical examination.

I further asked the gentleman how clergymen teaching in our colleges could sign their annual renewal papers for ordination, which includes a required reaffirmation of our sixteen-point creed (four of which statements have to do with prophecy, including a part that indicates our belief that God has an ongoing plan for National Israel). He replied that he imagined it was done with a certain amount of "mental reservation." In plain English that is called lying. Any clergyman who cannot truthfully sign affirmation to the Statement of Fundamental Truths ought to be graceful and honest enough to withdraw from the fellowship and find a more liberal church in which to minister.

AWAKENING INTEREST

The good news is that many of our Bible college professors, denomination leaders (various), Charismatic leaders, and others are looking to us for resources and information. We are prompt to respond to all requests of this nature. The doctrinal warfare which we never asked for, but which has been thrust upon us by the Dominionists and others, is now spreading worldwide. We get phone calls and letters from overseas with inquiries into these matters on a regular basis. We thank God that we can function as a resource center and information bureau for the leadership of the Church.

PROPHESY AGAINST THE PROPHETS

"There were *false prophets* also among the people, even as there shall be false teachers *among you*" (2 Pet. 2:1). "Many will say to me in that day, Lord, Lord *have we not prophesied in thy name?* and in thy name have cast out devils? and in thy name done many wonderful works? And then will I profess to them, I never knew you; depart from me"—Jesus (Matt. 7:22, 23).

"Son of man, *prophesy against the prophets*...that prophesy out of their own hearts, Hear ye the word of the Lord...Woe unto the foolish prophets that follow their own spirit and have seen nothing...Mine hand shall be upon the prophets that see vanity, and that divine lies; they shall not be in the assembly of my people...Set thy face against the daughters of thy people, which prophesy out of their own heart; and prophesy thou against them...Therefore ye shall see no more vanity, nor divine divinations; for I will deliver my people out of your hand; and ye shall know that I am the Lord." Selections are from Ezekiel 13, KJV.

"For such are *false prophets,* deceitful workers, transforming themselves into the apostles of Christ. And no marvel; for Satan himself is transformed into an angel of light. Therefore it is no great thing if his ministers also be transformed as the ministers of righteousness" (2 Cor. 11:14).

"Unto the church at Ephesus write:...thou hast tried them that *say they are apostles* and are not, and hast found them liars" (Rev. 2:2).

There are those in the Church who have true apostolic and prophetic ministry and office. This has always been recognized, although seldom have they been credentialed as such.

When a person claims to be a prophet: 1. If they ignore or are ignorant of Bible prophecy, I am concerned. 2. If they say Bible prophecy is unimportant and substitute their own revelations for guidance in the churches, I am suspicious. 3. If they reject prophetic concepts of the Bible (ridicule the Rapture, Millennium, etc.) then it would seem possible that the individual is a false prophet.

GLOSSARY OF TERMS:

ALLEGORY: System of interpretation which denies literal meaning of the text. Allows one to make the Bible mean almost anything one desires it to mean.

AMILLENNIAL: The theory that there will be no literal Millennium, or that we are in the Millennium now (see Millennium). The prophetic passages of the Bible are spiritualized. There is a wide variety of interpretation among the amillennialists.

ANTICHRIST: A literal person. A human satan, who will rule over ten nations (Revived Roman Empire) for three and a half years, then over a loose world coalition of nations for another three and a half years. To deny that there will be a literal Antichrist could be very deceptive for many people. How can they recognize one who cannot exist?

DOMINION: A modern form of postmillennialism with a strong program for conquest, first of the churches, then the world.

EISEGESIS: Reading meaning into the text, depending on your own preconceived ideas. To insert meaning into the text from outside sources. Webster defines: "improper method of exposition by which the expounder introduces his own ideas into the interpretation of a text: [as] opposed to exegesis." Method used by all but premillennialists in the general interpretation of prophecy.

ESCHATOLOGY: Greek: *Escha* - the end; *ology* - knowledge of. Hence, the study of end-time prophecy.

EXEGESIS: Seeking the meaning that is inherent in the text. To take out from the text the meaning that is actually there.

KINGDOM NOW: Covers a wide variety of teachings. In general, it embraces a denial of the literal Rapture, Antichrist, Tribulation, thousand-year millennial reign of Jesus. Strong emphasis on social action, much of which is commendable. However, while preaching unity they strive to discredit and silence those who disagree with them. They offer little or no room for meaningful dialogue or discussion. Some traditional Pentecostalists have tried to accommodate the doctrine of their church to the Kingdom Now social action program, while still giving a nodding acquiescence to the premillennial mode of prophetic interpretation. Their association and networking with the divisive Dominionist and Kingdom Now groups opens questions regarding ultimate motivation.

LITERAL INTERPRETATION: Taking the plain meaning of the text, with consideration of the culture, background, and understanding of both the writer and the original recipient.

MILLENNIUM: A literal one thousand year period in which Jesus Christ will rule on earth after His literal return at the end of this age.

POSTMILLENNIAL: The Church will conquer and dominate the world, thus ushering in the visible Kingdom before the return of Christ. When the Church has fulfilled this task, then Jesus will return.

PREMILLENNIAL: The idea that Jesus returns before the thousand-year reign on earth. It is His coming that ushers in the visible aspect of the Kingdom.

RAPTURE: Prior to the Millennium Christ will remove the believing Church from the earth. Some place this event before the seven years of trouble, some during, some after. It is important to know that before the Lord Jesus places

His feet on the Mount of Olives, He will gather the Church unto Himself. The Church returns with Him in victory for the establishment of the visible Kingdom.

RECONSTRUCTION: Similar to Dominionism. This form of postmillennialism is attributed to John Rousas Rushdoony, founder of the Chalcedon Foundation.

RESTORATION: A loose term, usually describing the ideas and efforts of some who align with the Kingdom Now faction.

SYMBOLISM: The Bible does contain symbols. Occasionally the context demands symbolism (example): "learn a parable of the fig tree" Matthew 24:32). When one encounters a symbol, the literal meaning conveyed by the symbol should be sought. One should never bring data from outside the Bible to interpret its symbols. We should allow the Bible to be self-interpreting. By comparing all the Scripture says on a given symbol, we can usually arrive at a satisfactory definition of the symbol. See Amos Millard's *Literal Interpretation of the Christian and Jewish Scriptures* and *The Literal Interpretation of Prophecy* by Paul Lee Tan.

THEONOMY: The law of God, especially as the Dominionists and Reconstructionists plan to re-establish Old Testament law over the nations, with themselves as the governors and judges administering these laws.

TRIBULATION: Seven years of trouble on earth. Antichrist reigns. Pre-tribulationists believe the Church will be removed before the onset of the seven years.

19

New Age—Ancient Error
Who's Messing With Your Mind?

On December 31, 1986, one of the strangest and most significant occurrences of modern times took place. Fifty million people went to prayer simultaneously. Normally one would think of this as a very positive occurrence. This, however, is not the case. The "World Instant of Cooperation" was promoted by New Agers who believe that man is his own deity. This may be hard for conservative Christians to believe. You may wonder how anyone could be so gullible or spiritually blind, but millions got involved in this worldwide effort to begin the new phase of the establishment of the Age of Aquarius, another term for the New Age movement. The December 31 prayer meeting was actually started in 1975 by anthropologist Margaret Meade and Robert Muller, former assistant secretary general of the United Nations. It went public in 1986 and has continued annually until now. Called the Tri Millennial Count Down it is to continue until the year 2000 when allegedly the New Age is to dawn upon the earth.

IT'S NOT NEW

I first became aware of the New Age movement when I was just seventeen years of age. At that time I was going to Central High School in Aberdeen, South Dakota.

291

A Baptist evangelist spoke in the church I attended. Rev. Silas J. Rexroat was my pastor. I clearly recall the evangelist teaching about the New Age which he also called the Network of Light and Illuminism. At that time I began to research esoteric literature furnished to me by an adult who wished to enlist me in the occult. I also obtained limited materials at the public library. This research brought a certain degree of bondage into my life and caused many struggles. It was through the prayers and counselling of Rev. Rexroat that I got firmly established in Jesus Christ, and I have never deviated since in my service to Christ and in my search for His truth as revealed in the written Word of God, consisting solely of the sixty-six books of the Old and New Testaments, commonly known as the Bible. I do believe God still speaks to man by the gifts of the Spirit. But all revelation gifts must be judged by the elders of the church and they must measure up to the Bible. Never do we interpret the Bible by the revelation gifts. We interpret the revelation gifts by the Bible. Never is a revelation put on the same level of authority as the written Word of God, the Bible.

When Ramona and I were married in December of 1954, we continued in the evangelistic-teaching ministry that God had called us to. I had started in ministry as an evangelist in June 1954, having graduated from Central Bible College in May of that year. From the very beginning I taught extensively in the area of Bible prophecy, making some emphasis on the things I had learned in the time of my dark journey as a teenager. It was my urgent desire to warn the Church of the dangers that beset us. Frankly, this emphasis did little to establish my credentials or to promote a demand for my ministry. Fortunately, we were able to stay busy. Many young people found Christ and many were called to the ministry of the gospel. Many of those people are in full-time ministry today. Many were equipped by our teaching for the conditions they would later be facing and are facing today.

CREDIBILITY

Some of the experiences of those days can now be looked upon with a bit of wry humor, although at the time they were a source of distress and frustration to me. I recall speaking in the little Assembly of God Church in Gaylord, Michigan, where Herbert David Kolenda was the pastor. Herbert himself was a daring soul and never "cramped my style," allowing me to preach whatever the Lord laid upon my heart. This caused some small troubles for both of us. On one occasion I was bringing an exposition of several verses of Scripture in the Book of Revelation which indicated to me (as I interpreted them literally) that the day would come when Satan worship would be practiced openly, boldly, widely. Following that service, the elders asked to talk to me privately. You must understand that these were loving, well-intentioned men. They meant only to do me good. In essence they said, "David, you are a young man. You have great promise in the ministry, but we must caution you not to preach such things as you did tonight. God never intended that Revelation be taken literally. People will never worship Satan."

The watchman on the wall always has a problem with credibility. From his vantage point he can clearly see conditions beyond the walls of the city that are not apparent to the inhabitants. Sometimes the dwellers inside the walls find it hard to believe or heed his warnings. The watchman is always ahead of his times.

Today there is no problem persuading people that satanism and witchcraft are real and commonly practiced. Were I to devote a message to the subject now, no one would find it so strange, although even today some are shocked to find out how close to home it is. In many communities where I have ministered we have made some discreet inquiries in advance. Standing in the pulpit I may ask, "How many of you are aware of the existence of a house of Satan worship here in your community?" About forty percent of the people (sometimes more if there have been bizarre occurrences) will raise their hands. How shocked are some of the dwellers inside the walls, especially in smaller communities.

HOW SHALL WE PERSUADE YOU?

But to persuade the Church that there really is a pervasive New Age movement—that is another problem. However, we are patient and full of confidence that our words will not fall on deaf ears altogether. We also know that Gideon only needs three hundred to win the battle. The prophets of Baal can pray their heathen prayers all day long to no avail. Elijah prays for twenty seconds and the fire falls. (I have a feeling Elijah was spending some hours in prayer before he undertook the brief public prayer that brought dramatic results when the fire fell on the sacrifice.) So it is my hope that we shall be able to persuade a few of you of the validity of our claims. There really are antichrist forces out there. There really is a New Age Globalist movement and they do have a plan to eliminate all who disagree with their vision of a new One World Society. Yes, their numbers are growing.

In this ministry there is plenty of opportunity to say, "I told you so," but that really doesn't accomplish anything. However, just to set the record straight, the New Age movement is not a fantasy invented in 1983 by a lawyer, Constance Cumbey and a CPA, David Hunt. A lot of us have been talking about it for a long time. But maybe it took the shock tactics of the lawyer and the CPA to get the Church talking about the subject, even if it is surrounded with controversy.

In 1966 I wrote an article which appeared in the *Pentecostal Evangel* in which I referred to the New Age Cult. In 1970, I entered into correspondence with a Lutheran minister in St. Louis, Missouri, with whom I still share research. At that time, both of us were talking about the New Age and the Network of Light.

THE DECEMBER 31 EVENT

Suddenly there is a much higher visibility of the New Age movement. A new boldness accompanies the words of those involved in the new metaphysics. There seems to be no reticence in proclaiming that the year 2000 is the year for the "takeover" by the New Age movement and for ushering in the Age of Aquarius. Boldly they proclaim that those who refuse to cooperate will be eliminated. Since murder is justifiable—no problem! Just get the dissidents (born again Christians) out of the way so the New Agers can get on with the business of ushering in world government, world religion (metaphysical humanism), and a new world economic system for a more equitable distribution of the planet's wealth. Do you think I am speaking fantasies? If you do, it is you who needs to wake up to the reality of our times. It seems that there is a conspiracy of silence designed to keep our churches in ignorance and darkness. I do recognize that this may be more of apathy than of design on the part of some. A failure to assign priorities correctly is also a besetting sin of the Church. We may wake up to find that we have overlooked the major issues while spending most of our time and energy on minors.

One of the purposes of this "watchman on the wall" ministry is to sound a trumpet of alarm to the churches. We must stir our brothers and sisters out of their slumber. The pastor of a large Charismatic church in the East told me that when he tries to teach his congregation solid biblical doctrine they rebel. Attendance goes down. I asked him what they wanted to hear. He said, "They want to know how to get something from God. They are not interested in becoming active in the Kingdom." I am pleased to report that this condition is not universal. There are Gideon bands who are determined to press the spiritual battle against the forces of darkness to gain end-time victories beyond anything we have experienced before. May God grant it!

On December 31, 1986, fifty million people, orchestrated by the New Age movement, entered into a form of meditation that for the most part was a hypnotic trance state designed to bring about a paradigm shift of perception. That is to say there was to be a radical change in the way humanity understands reality. It sounds like an attempt to brainwash the whole human race. Since New Agers believe that reality is what you imagine or desire it to be, it is easy to see that the real purpose of the movement is to transfer their brand of "reality" or belief system on the rest of us.

Billed as "The World Instant of Cooperation," the aim of the organizers was to get the consent of five hundred million people for the "healing" of the planet earth and for fifty million people to enter into the meditative "prayer" state at 7:00 a.m. eastern standard time (noon Greenwich mean time). Participants were to meditate for one hour or longer.

DECEPTION RAMPANT

The owner of a well-known book publishing house sat in my home recently telling of his distress when he discovered that certain evangelicals in his area were going about to churches, prayer fellowships, and Full Gospel Business Men's meetings signing up participants for the December New Age event. Of course, it was not described in these circles as a New Age event. Probably these folks did not know the true nature of the December 31 moment of "prayer." However, when these born again Christian "leaders" were shown by my friend that the nature of the pact was satanic and deceptive, he met with hostility. These naive subversives continued their activities.

THE ORGANIZERS REVEALED

The principal promoters of the "World Instant of Cooperation" were Barbara Marx Hubbard and John Randolph Price. Both of these people have written books which reveal their beliefs and purposes. For example, I have Price's book *Planetary Commission* before me at this moment. Price is the president, founder, and executive director of "Quartus Foundation for Spiritual Research," located near Austin, Texas. It is in *Planetary Commission* that Price calls for the enlistment of fifty million people for the December 31 event. Price claims that he is being directed by ascended masters or illumined ones from a higher plane. His book *Superbeings* is probably available at your public library. I found our local library able to order these books in from the state depository for my examination. In addition, I was able to purchase some of the books at the local New Age bookstore here in our quiet Bible Belt town of Springfield, Missouri. In *Planetary Commission* Price indicates that the World Instant of Cooperation could bring about a "second coming of Christ," which would satisfy the longing of everyone from fundamentalists to astrologers, seers, science fiction fans, and occultists (see pp. 29, 30 *Planetary Commission*). Price says that while the fundamentalists expect one thing, what very well could happen is "the return of Christ as a new ENERGY FIELD" (emphasis his). He concludes the chapter with the words, "The salvation of the world does depend on you."

CRITICAL MASS

Price and his followers saw 1987 as the year to achieve "critical mass." The theory is that if one percent of the world's population can be brought to a state of meditation simultaneously (as on December 31), the whole perception of reality could be altered. Some of the organizations that have worked for or have given approval to the World Instant of Cooperation include The Association of Unity Ministers, Findhorn, the Elizabeth Kubler-Ross Center, Association of Independent Ministers, the Passionist Nuns, and networks among many metaphysical groups, New Age and occult bookstores. Actually there are many more who are involved. Probably most of the New Age movement has a hand in the 1987 "plan." Only today a friend of this ministry handed me a mailing from Lucis Trust (formerly Lucifer Publishing) indicating that they give approval to the program. Price writes that the light-bearers from around the world are gathering for the fulfilling of the mission.

Please do not think that because December 31, 1986, is past that this is irrelevant. December 31 was only the beginning. Nineteen eighty-seven was marked for the beginning of the "takeover." They think it will be finished around the year 2000. If we stop them through intercessory prayer and by informing the body of Christ, hopefully rousing the Church to action, the New Agers will simply project their plans into the future. The struggle will continue until the real Jesus Christ returns and puts all of His enemies under His feet. We must never cease our vigilance and we must never give up. If you are a serious Christian who wants to see the Church in victory as we approach the end of the age, I urge you to obtain a copy of my book, *Smashing the Gates of Hell in the Last Days* (New Leaf Press).

While ministering in seminars in December 1986, I warned the people about the coming attempt of the New Agers to increase the level of their power. While driving through Charlotte one day, I noticed a large sign in front of the public coliseum announcing the world day of prayer (December 31). My inquiries led me to an awareness that not only old-line churches and cults were involved but that many local Evangelicals had put their seal of approval on the event. I am sure that many of those poor souls acted out of ignorance of the true nature of this spiritual debacle. The organization of the event was worldwide. It is estimated that in India alone there were about fifty to one hundred million participants.

IS MAN GOD?

The "god-man" theme is repeated over and over in the writings of Price and most New Agers. In the chapter "Your Role as the Christ" Price says, "Christhood is—right now! I am the Christ of God. You are the Christ of God" (p. 143, *Planetary Commission*). Price denies the fall of man, hence denies the need for redemption in the biblical sense (p. 144). "You became aware of your God-Self as never before...You are the Omnipotent Christ" (p. 145). In a chapter titled "The Christ Connection" he writes, "The identity of God is individualized as me now. I am the Self-Expression of God. I am the presence of God where I am. I am the Christ, Son of the Living God."

To claim that man is Christ or that any person or group of human beings (including the Church) is the "ongoing incarnation of Christ" is to deny Jesus of His unique divinity. A born again Christian rightfully says, "Christ dwells within me." He knows that became true when as a lost sinner he repented and found Jesus as Saviour. While I can say Jesus has come into my heart, I can never say that I am Christ in the flesh. Of only one man it was spoken, "The Word was made flesh and dwelt among us" (John 1:14). Only one man, Jesus, could say, "I am God in the flesh." This is what we mean by the incarnation of Christ, and it was unique in the one person, our Lord Jesus Christ. I can never say, "I am Christ in the flesh." This does not deny that Christ dwells in the heart of every saved person, but it preserves the unique nature and identity of Jesus.

BARBARA MARX HUBBARD

Barbara Marx Hubbard, author of *Revelation: The Book of Co-Creation* joins Price in the god-man concept, that man is his own deity. Hubbard indicates that the chief sources of her inspiration were Teilhard De Chardin, Abraham Maslow, John Glen, Karl Marx, Sigmund Freud, and Albert Einstein. According to her, Jesus and Satan are brothers. She says that Jesus revealed this to her and that Satan will one day return to God (*Revelation: The Book of Co-Creation*, pp. 114-118).

ELIMINATION OF THOSE WHO DO NOT COOPERATE

One of Price's spirit guides, Asher, speaks through the pages of the book *Practical Spirituality*: "Nature will soon enter her cleansing cycle. Those who reject the earth changes with an attitude of 'it can't happen here' will experience the greatest emotion of fear and panic, followed by rage and violent action. These individuals, with their lower vibratory rates, will be removed during the next two decades." John Price then observes, "I know that one of the most serious problems we have today is overpopulation, but wiping more than two billion people off the face of the earth is a little drastic, don't you think?" John says that what Asher calls for is both "horrible and hopeful." (See *Practical Spirituality*, pp. 15-20.)

If Price is reticent to speak clearly about the elimination of those who disagree (leaving Asher to speak for him?), Barbara Marx Hubbard leaves no room for doubt as to her views of the matter. In her book *Revelation: The Book of Co-Creation* she says, "As you have learned to abort a genetically defective child who will inevitably be a monstrous human, so we have learned to abort a monstrous planetary civilization which gains its evolutionary technologies for transcendence and misuses them for self-annihilation" (p. 29). "Evolution is good, but it is not nice. Only the good can evolve. Only the God-centered will survive to inherit the powers of a universal species" (p. 56). "Now, as we approach the quantum shift from creature-human to co-creative human—the destructive one-fourth must be eliminated from the social body..." (p. 60). "We come to bring death to those who are unable to know God" (p. 61). "We will use whatever means we must to make this act of destruction as quick and as painless as possible to the one-half of the world who are capable of evolving" (p. 62).

You may recall my previous writing about the Georgia Guidestones (fashioned after the Stonehenge in England). The ten statements on the huge granite monument near Elberton, Georgia, have been called "the Antichrist's ten commandments" with their call for global rule. The first of the statements falls strangely in place with Hubbard's reference to the future elimination of a great deal of the human race. The first of the statements on the Georgia Guidestones is "Maintain humanity under five hundred million in perpetual balance with nature." This envisions the elimination of four-and-a-half billion people off the face of the earth.

Hubbard claims that her commentary on Revelation was given to her by her "spirit guides." Their message is explicit when they speak of the elimination of masses of people who fail to go along with the program. The spirit elders are ready to "take action to cut out this corrupted and corrupting element in the body of humanity." Further, Hubbard seems to take comfort in the words of her spirit guide who says, "Fortunately; you, dearly beloveds, are not responsible for this act. We are. We are in charge of God's selection process for planet Earth. He selects, we destroy. We are the riders of the pale horse, Death. We are come to bring death to those who are unable to know God. We do this for the sake of the world..." Try guessing whose death list you born again Christians are on.

Barbara Marx Hubbard, an executive director of the World Future Society, a former Democratic Party nominee for the vice-presidency of the United States, claims that what was done on December 31, 1986, could bring about a "planetary pentecost" that would bring mass transfiguration and empowerment of millions at once. It would be a "second coming" whereby men would transform themselves into "Christ."

John Randolph Price reveals that while "peace" will be the rallying cry for the New Age, it will not be the true motive behind the World Instant of Cooperation. He wrote, "The Commission is not like the Peace Movement...December 31...will release so much Love, Light, and Spiritual Energy into the race mind that the hypnotic spell for the majority of mankind will break up like a thawing of a frozen lake in springtime. And that will be the true beginning of the New Age... Yes, we have entered the New Age, but now we have the responsibility, the obligation, to create the civilization of the Aquarian Age. That's our purpose."

Why am I suddenly recalling the words of a true prophet of God who had the seal of approval of none other than the Lord Jesus Christ? It was Daniel who prophesied of a coming ruler (Antichrist) who would come with a peace program but "by peace would destroy many."

RAMTHA, THE 35,000 YEAR OLD MAN

On January 22, 1987, the commentators on ABC Television's *20/20* program discussed one of the fast growing New Age groups. It is called the Ramtha manifestation. Allegedly Ramtha is a 35,000-year-old spirit who channels his messages through a trance medium, J. Z. Knight. Ramtha claims to be divine. That comes as no surprise since the basic teaching of the New Age movement is that all humans are divine. While this may be expressed in varying ways, it is nevertheless at the heart of all New Age philosophy.

Barbara Walters correctly identified the Ramtha teaching as a part of the New Age movement which she said involves the teaching of reincarnation, human potential groups, and psychic healing.

Since the New Age movement so boldly proclaims its own existence, its aims and its beliefs, it seems very strange that so many church leaders are ignoring its existence, or in some cases actually stating that it does not exist at all. Here is ABC television speaking openly about the New Age movement, even while I am hearing some Christians say that if the New Age does exist, it is of little consequence.

If we believe the Bible predictions of an end-time warfare in the spiritual realm, how can we ignore the manifestation of it in our times, especially when it is so blatantly promoted in so many and in such diverse ways?

People, we had better wake up. It is to our shame that ABC television called attention to the fact that Ramtha is being called the Antichrist while we are blithely ignoring this and a host of other New Age manifestations. I personally do not believe Ramtha is the final Antichrist, but one of the many forerunners spoken of by the apostle John (1 John 2:18).

J. Z. Knight lives near Yelm, Washington, south of Seattle. A breeder of expensive Arabian horses, she is building a huge mansion for her personal dwelling. To support her lifestyle, she travels to various parts of the country allowing Ramtha to speak through her and bring the message of New Age to audiences who are eager to pay four hundred dollars per person to attend a session, or $1,500.00 for a weekend. The Ramtha organization often earns up to $200,000.00 for a single appearance. Knight claims that she changes into the 35,000-year-old man named Ramtha. Indeed, her appearance changes and she speaks with a voice much deeper than her normal voice, as was shown on ABC television.

ABC news correspondent Judd Rose, who went to investigate J. Z. Knight, correctly noted that while she calls herself a channel she is what was formerly called a medium. Rose stated that while there are hundreds of channelers, J. Z. Knight is the most popular of them. Knight has had a powerful influence in the life of Shirley MacLaine.

When she transforms into Ramtha, she preaches and answers questions for hours. *20/20* produced on the TV screen several Hollywood celebrities and others who gave their testimony of what

Ramtha means to them and what he has done in their lives.

Rose said that Knight's presentation of Eastern mysticism, Western pos-philosophy and some theatrics has a message. That message is that man is divine and the master of his own destiny. Ramtha spoke through J. Z. saying, "Who needs to be worshipped? Indeed, you do. And who needs to save your hide? You do. And indeed, who can answer your prayers? You do."

ABC television's Rose said that what has done the most to promote the Ramtha message is Shirley MacLaine's film, *Out On A Limb*. The book with the same title is on sale in our local Wal-Mart store as well as in bookstores and department stores in general. The TV film mini-series showed on ABC for a total of four hours. I have both read the book and viewed the film. The most impressive scene in the film is where David and Shirley stand on the seashore shouting, "I am god. I am god. I am god." Rose stated that one of the actress's best selling books identified Ramtha as her spiritual guide. Having read some of her works, I would say that Ramtha is only one of her spiritual guides, although certainly one of the most important to her. MacLaine is only one of many celebrities who are involved with Ms. J. Z. Knight and her Ramtha spirit.

Can you guess what I think Ramtha is? Oh yes, I believe Ramtha is real. It is nothing more or less than a deceptive demonic spirit against which we have been repeatedly warned in the Bible. We have many statements in Scripture telling us that this type of demonic delusion, "doctrines of devils," would be on the increase in the last days.

The *20/20* program listed only a few of the prominent people who have been involved with Ramtha: Philip Michael Thomas, Christy Jenkins, Athena Pettingil, Mike Farrell, Richard Chamberlain, and *Dynasty's* Linda Evans. Evans told *20/20* that her experience with Ramtha had been profound. She appeared on *20/20* to say, "Ramtha is an enlightened master, like Christ was, like the Buddha was, like Mohammed—they're enlightened masters, and thank goodness we have had them on the planet." *20/20* noted that Ramtha followers appeared to be affluent, successful, and well-educated. They seem to have it all, but according to one analyst on *20/20*, they feel they are lacking a spiritual dimension in life. They like to hear the Ramtha message that they are god, that they are divine. There is no call to a changed lifestyle, as there is for the born again Christian. Nothing is wrong, for evil does not exist.

Not everyone on the *20/20* show spoke well of Ramtha. A lady from Colorado was shown saying that the Ramtha tapes put her into a state of hypnosis and caused a radical personality change. She said that after some time of listening to the Ramtha tapes, her nerves were shot and her marriage coming apart. She was in danger of losing her job. Having never seen J. Z. Knight (Ramtha) in person, she went against the advice of her husband and went to a Ramtha retreat in California. She said on *20/20*, "I was obsessed. I couldn't stop. I don't know how to explain it except that when I tell you I was on a roll, and you are going down hill, you can't stop. I really needed help at that point." She got help, according to *20/20*, upon her return home where her husband had her "deprogrammed."

Ramtha has predicted that volcanoes, earthquakes, plagues, droughts, tidal waves, and other natural disasters will destroy much of America. Ramtha is advising people to leave their homes in many areas and go elsewhere. Ramtha says that the Pacific Northwest will be safe from those disasters. ABC television indicated that upwards of fifteen hundred people have left families, businesses, and homes behind to move to Northern California, Oregon, and Washington State. One Ramtha devotee divorced her husband, left her home in Hawaii, and moved to Yelm, Washington, with her new boyfriend. ABC referred to many tragic situations where Ramtha teaching has torn families apart.

20/20 called attention to the bible of the movement, the *Ramtha White Book*. I have had a copy of this book along with several Ramtha tapes in my possession for some time. Believe me, it is a very strange document. Rose pointed out that the Ramtha philosophy states that reality is whatever you want it to be. There is no right or wrong. There is neither good nor evil. "Even murder is not wrong or evil," said Rose in describing the teaching of Ramtha. Knight says it helps to believe in reincarnation. She said, "If you only believe that you are born and you die—there is no afterlife—murder is definitely wrong. If you believe in the continuation of life, that's a different story. In a divinity, if we are immortal and we are going to live again, then how could murder be a wrong? The person who commits a murder, for instance, doesn't need to be punished by being put into prison. He is going to be punished because he is going to hate himself for eons of years, and he is going to live with that guilt and it will set his process of evolvement back for ages and ages." Knight says that Ramtha told her that in a previous life she was one of his daughters.

Rose decided to explore J. Z. Knight's more recent past. One of her closest friends from school days, Sandy Fallis, came on the *20/20* show to tell of a strange incident. Both were attending a prayer meeting in Artesia, New Mexico, where she grew up as Judy Hampton. At the prayer meeting Judy began to speak in a strange male voice and identified herself as a demon named Demias. Fallis said a voice spoke through her saying, "I have possessed this body and you cannot have it. I have possessed it for many years." Knight, when questioned about this incident, denied that it ever happened. Regardless of this denial that it ever happened, Rose continues by saying, "But if it did, it would seem to support a theory that Knight has and may have had another personality that comes out that she can't entirely control."

THE NEW AGE NETWORK SYSTEM

Networking, a large book by Lipnak and Stamps, lists 1,526 organizations that requested to be included in the directory. We find information on diverse groups dealing with such things as holistic health, environmental concern, parapsychology, cultic religion, peace activism, anti-nuclear action, natural childbirth, etc. in this volume.

What links all of these groups together is that they are part of a movement. They are not an organization, with a central office, but part of a vast network of individuals and organizations that have a philosophy in common. That philosophy has been described as the teaching of the New Age movement.

After the December 31 event, several things happened. Tara Center placed a full-page advertisement in *USA Today*, the nation's largest newspaper. The ad announced that "the christ" is now in the world, as did the previous Tara Center advertisement, which appeared in the *New York Times* and a host of other major newspapers throughout the free world. It is estimated that the 1982 ad campaign cost Tara about one million dollars.

One might ask if New Age analyzers are not stretching their imagination a bit when they see a linkage between the Tara Center advertisement, Planetary Commission (Dec. 31 event), Lucis Trust, and other New Age groups.

I think the significance of these groups and the fact that they are linked together will be seen only by the "watchers on the wall" and those who are fortunate enough to hear and heed the watcher's message. You will never see what the New Age is or what it is doing unless you watch its manifestations and activities, or unless you heed what God's watchman is saying to you. Not everyone is called to be a watcher, but everyone must be careful to find a reliable "watchman on the wall" who is worthy of confidence. Then you must listen very carefully to what the messenger of God has to say. Ignore the watchman and as God warns that His people "will be destroyed for a lack of knowledge."

I do not take my calling as a "watchman on the wall" lightly. I deeply feel my responsibility to you as members of the body of Christ who have been called to be partakers of this ministry.

LINKAGE OF NEW AGE GROUPS DEMONSTRATED

As we have documented, December 31, 1986, marked the day when the New Age movement shifted into high gear and began its major thrust for world domination and the elimination of all who refuse to "evolve" with them into the new race of super beings.

In January, Lucis Trust (formerly Lucifer Publishing) sent out a mailing which is in our possession. It heralds the December 31 event and identifies with its intent and purpose. This demonstrates a linkage between John Randolph Price's Quartus Foundation (Planetary Commission) and the Lucis Trust.

On January 12 the Tara Center advertisement appeared in *USA Today* newspaper, heralding the coming of the new "christ."

The principal spokesman of the Tara Center is Benjamin Creme who wrote the book *The Reappearance of the Christ and the Masters of Wisdom*. This book firmly establishes the New Age belief that the man is divine. Creme says in response to the question, "Who is God?" that God does not exist and yet that everything is God. Creme says, "You are God, I am God, everything is God." Creme presents himself as the forerunner of the New Age "christ." The "christ" is currently living in London waiting for his world manifestation. A more recent book published by Tara is titled *Messages from Maitreya the Christ*. In it Maitreya says, "My army moves, my lieutenants know the result of the battle and know the plan of action. That action involves you all, for through you, My friends and brothers, must the New World be made... May this manifestation lead you into the battle, and, with your brothers to victory" (pp. 98, 99). "I am the prince of Peace. I am the Sword Bearer...I am the lawgiver...I awaken the New Spirit in man...The New Day beckons...My Army shall triumph...My name is Oneness...My Law creates...My Masters stand ready. The Day is at hand. The Prophecies of old are being fulfilled...May this manifestation lead you quickly to see yourselves as Units of God" (pp. 208-209).

Now let me demonstrate the linkage between Tara Center and Lucis Trust. Lucis Trust published a prayer as a full-page advertisement in the *Reader's Digest* magazine called "The Great Invocation." The Invocation is printed and distributed in many forms by Lucis Trust which has its headquarters in New York. A high-ranking UN official is part of the Lucis Trust and has spoken to their Arkane school on occasions.

The Great Invocation "prayer" says, "From the point of Love within the Heart of God Let love stream forth into the hearts of men. MAY CHRIST RETURN TO EARTH" (emphasis ours). The literature of Lucis Trust clearly demonstrates that the christ that is called for is not Jesus, but a new christ, an Avatar who is also known as Buddha, Maitreya, the Avatar, the Bodhisattva, etc.

The linkage? The Great Invocation of Lucis Trust is printed on the back cover of Tara Center's book *Messages from Maitreya the Christ*.

It is hard for a person not involved in this research to fathom the vast reach of the New Age movement. In our own personal files we can document the existence of over five thousand organizations that are part of the New Age movement and that is only the proverbial tip of the iceberg. There are probably twelve to fifteen thousand groups in the U.S.A. alone which identify with the New Age.

SHIRLEY MacLAINE
Mediums, Movies, and UFOs

In 1955 I was ministering as an evangelist in the Dakotas, Minnesota, Wisconsin, and Michigan. Pastor Harley Hansel graciously invited Ramona and I to hold several series of meetings at the assembly in Saint Ignace, Michigan.

It was during one of those meetings that I predicted what later came to be known as the "Von Daniken theory" although none of us had heard of Erich von Daniken at that time. Von Daniken is the author of the internationally famous book *Chariots of the Gods* and several other books expanding on his theories. I met von Daniken at Southern Missouri State University where he was lecturing a few years ago. I asked him some questions and got strange responses. I still have the tape recording of that conversation, and someday I will write concerning my own theories on the UFO mystery. In brief, Von Daniken has looked at ancient monuments such as the pyramids and other mysterious phenomena, such as the markings of the Nazka Plains in the Andes Mountains of Peru, concluding that early, primitive man was not capable of constructing these marvels. Therefore, they must have had outside help. That help was nothing less than the assistance of astronauts from other planetary systems with civilizations far more advanced than ours. The planet earth has had alien visitations from ancient times until now. When asked why he had formulated the theory, von Daniken admitted that his prejudice against religion in general was the motivation and that this bias pre-dated the formulation of any part of his theory.

Von Daniken and scores of other authors explain away the Bible as early man's crude attempt to account for the space visitors and their seemingly miraculous activities which were simply marvels of advanced technology. From this misinterpretation of the UFOnauts, early man invented stories about God, gods, demons, angels, and miracles. Thus the Bible came into being as a perverted record of these visitations. Christian authors such as Dr. Cliff Wilson, Dr. Emil Gaverluck, and others have written powerful refutations of von Daniken's theories.

For some time I have been predicting that there would be a revival of interest in the UFO phenomena, but everything has been fairly quiet for the past few years. Now all of that is going to change. You will hear more and more of extraterrestrial visitations here on planet earth. One of the major reasons why there will be a renewed emphasis on flying saucers is because of a book and a movie, both titled *Out On A Limb*, by Hollywood actress Shirley MacLaine. We are going to make another reference to the outer space connection later in this chapter because it is so important to the MacLaine story. This trend is not to be taken lightly by the Church.

OUT ON A LIMB

The two-night mini-series recently aired on ABC television and was viewed by millions of people across America. Major magazine articles have commented on the production. Two books tell the story of Ms. MacLaine's spiritual search. They are *Out On A Limb* and *Dancing in the Light*. The January 26, 1987, issue of *People* magazine reviews MacLaine's TV movie and comments on her spiritist activities. *People* tells about her contacting spirits beyond the grave, that she has discovered spiritism in her "New Age soul-searching." *People* observes that Shirley MacLaine has done more than anyone to focus attention on this "suddenly chic phenomenon" through her four-hour mini-series *Out On A Limb* (*People*, see pp. 28-35).

MacLaine claims to communicate with a variety of ancient people who come to her in spirit form through trance mediums with whom she works, including J. Z. Knight (Ramtha). Another medium, Kevin, "channels" the personality of "John" who predicted that *Out On A Limb* would be an outstanding success in its ratings, that "it will get the highest share of anything on TV this year." That seems to have turned out to be incorrect, for while millions did see the movie, the initial reports are that the public response reflected in the ratings was a disappointment to the producers and Ms. MacLaine.

WHO IS GOD? WHO IS MAN?

According to MacLaine and many of her New Age associates, God and man are one and the same. Not one to merely hint at her meaning, Shirley MacLaine bluntly proclaims, "We are part of God" (*Dancing in the Light*, p. 104; also see pp. 247, 251). Shirley says, "Therefore if one says audibly 'I am god,' the sound vibrations literally align the energies of the body to a higher atunement. You can use 'I am god' or 'I am that I am,' as Christ often did, or you can extend the affirmations to fit your own needs" (*Dancing*, p. 112). Even more explicitly she proclaims, "You are god," and "Each soul is its own god...You must never worship anyone or anything other than self. For you are god. To love self is to love god...we are our own creators...everyone is god..." (*Dancing*, pp. 340, 343, 344, 398). In the book *Out on a Limb*, the actress frequently repeats this theme. In the TV movie mini-series by the same title, one scene depicts Shirley and David (one of the mediums) standing on the seashore, shouting over and over, "I am god. I am god."

METAPHYSICAL INVOLVEMENT

It didn't all come together at once for MacLaine. Her search has been a long and arduous one. She tells of her early involvement in Oriental approaches to karate, judo, and aikido. Meditation played a big part in her progress into the realm of the paranormal (*Dancing*, p. 93). Much later she is so finely tuned to the spirit realm that beings materialize and show themselves to her. One particularly disturbing scene is described. A being comes to her as an overpowering person over seven feet tall. When she asks the entity who it is, it replies that it is her "higher unlimited self...I am you...I am your unlimited soul...I am the unlimited you that guides and teaches you through each incarnation" (*Dancing*, p. 335). In the course of her journeys, MacLaine witnessed a Bhutanese lama (demon priest) levitate; that is, he floated above the ground by supernatural power (*Out On A Limb*, p. 87).

It occurs to me that it is possible that spiritually uninformed persons might find these phenomena attractive. It would defeat my purpose if my writing drew you to the New Age. As one author notes, there is a "beautiful side to evil." The Scripture warns that Satan and his servants appear, not as monsters but as angels of light. Attractive or not, they are demonic. (For more information, see my book, *Dark Angels of Light*. New Leaf Press.)

MORALITY AND THE NEW AGE PHILOSOPHY

Evil simply does not exist, according to the New Agers. It is impossible to do wrong. Murder is not altogether wrong and murderers should not be punished. The process of reincarnation will settle all the problems of what appears to be evil.

Shirley MacLaine's account includes the story of her adulterous relationship with a married member of the British Parliament (*Dancing*, p. 33). Her use of coarse obscenities, using the Lord's name in vain and explicit references to her immoral escapades with both the British M.P. and her Russian lover Vassily is a reflection of the New Ager's acceptance of the "New Morality." (See *Dancing*, pp. 180, 199, 202, 203, 265; and *Out On A Limb*, p. 127, etc.) Although there is a general appeal throughout these books to the Bible, (supposedly it teaches reincarnation, etc.), there is little regard for the moral code of the Bible. This is understandable when you realize that the New Ager does not believe in the reality of evil. Guru Kevin says, "I don't believe that there is any such thing as evil" (*Dancing*, p. 246). The spirit identified as "John" speaks through Kevin: "You must not resist what you call evil" (*Dancing*, p. 256).

THE NEW AGE CONNECTION

Some sheltered persons might still wonder if there is a New Age movement, but the adherents of the movement have no doubt of its existence. MacLaine makes liberal use of the term New Age. "I found...reincarnation had become a part of new age thought systems..." (*Out On A Limb*, p. 350).

The *People* magazine article quotes one of MacLaine's gurus: "Combining Eastern mysticism and New Age self-reliance, Ramtha/Knight proclaims: 'Love what you are. Love the god that you are'...Ramtha, who predicts a New Age of the superconsciousness in the year 2000" (*People*, January 26, 1987, pp. 20-31).

The same *People* magazine article describes another medium/spiritist, Ruth Norman, as "the grande dame of the New Age spiritists." Norman believes that she is the reincarnation of Mary Magdalene of New Testament times and that her late husband was a reincarnation of Jesus Christ. This seems to be strangely similar to the theme of the book *Holy Blood, Holy Grail* by Lincoln, Leigh, and Baigant who document the existence of a mystical European organization, the Priory de Sion, that teaches that Jesus never died on the Cross, but was revived by the disciples. Jesus then married Mary

Magdaline. They had several children. After the natural death of Jesus many years later, Mary, some of their children and a couple of the original apostles moved to France. The Priory de Sion is an ancient organization which has kept track of the blood descendants of Jesus, according to their claims. A picture of the head of the organization is included in the book. It is the belief of the Priory de Sion that they are destined to revive the Holy Roman Empire and rule the world by the 1990s. Here is yet another mystery for the New Age.

REINCARNATION

Two themes predominate in MacLaine's teachings, as they also dominate the thinking of the New Age movement in general. One is the deity of man and the other is the concept of reincarnation.

One may believe in reincarnation if he wishes, but never fool yourself into thinking that the teaching of reincarnation is compatible with the teaching of the Bible. MacLaine and her friends would like to persuade us that not only is the concept of reincarnation compatible with the Bible but that it is a major teaching of the Bible. Strange that the Bible never uses the word. The Bible does use a word which describes what happens after this life is over. That word is "resurrection." Resurrection implies, not a recycling of souls, but rather that if I die, this spirit will live again in this very body brought forth from the grave. When Jesus came out of the grave He did not come as someone else, but as Himself, glorified and resurrected. The biblical doctrine of resurrection and the New Age teaching of reincarnation are totally incompatible.

MacLaine claims that the "spirit" John told her that all the ancient psychics including Moses and Jesus taught reincarnation. Friends, there is absolutely no biblical evidence for this at all. It is a fantasy. She notes that John said, "Well, not all of them used that word" (reincarnation). The fact is the word is not used in the Bible at all. John says, "They didn't always use the words karma or reincarnation, but the meaning was the same." Let's be honest. The Bible never uses those words. Further, the meaning is not there either. (See *Out On A Limb*, pp. 105-106.)

A totally unsubstantiated claim is made several times in MacLaine's writings that the Church removed the doctrine of reincarnation from the Bible. "I read that Christ's teachings about reincarnation were struck from the Bible during the Fifth Ecumenical Council meeting in Constantinople in the year 553 A.D." (*Out On A Limb*, p. 246). The fact is that the Nicean Church Council condemned the totally nonscriptural doctrine of reincarnation and the preexistence of all souls which certain heretics had begun to teach in the churches. Nothing was removed from the Bible. An endeavor was made to remove heresy from the Church. (See *Out On A Limb,* pp. 105, 181, 235, 246.)

CHRIST IN INDIA

Jesus is just one of the boys according the New Agers. He is one member of the hierarchy of ascended masters. He is a member of the gang of gurus. MacLaine believes that Jesus spent eighteen years in India studying with the Hindu masters before returning to Israel to launch His own ministry. This is a blanket denial of all that the Bible actually teaches about Jesus, His unique divinity, His atoning death, and provision of redemption for fallen mankind.

EXTRATERRESTRIALS AND FLYING SAUCERS— THE KEY TO MACLAINE'S CALLING

Just like most pastors sense a calling to their ministry, Shirley MacLaine also has had a definite calling to her "ministry."

A big part of her story deals with her spiritual pilgrimage to Peru with her guru, David. There she was told of Mayan, an alien visitor from the star system Pliades, who came to earth in a space craft to effect certain things vital to the spiritual evolution of humanity. In Peru, David revealed to Shirley that an alien female named Mayan had told him that he was to convey a message to Shirley. She was to become the spokesman for the New Age message that was imparted to her. She was to write a book and reach the masses with the gospel of man's divinity, of reincarnation, and of the New Age now dawning upon the human race.

When MacLaine expressed concern that she might be ridiculed if she consented to be the bearer of this message, she was reassured that the way has been prepared in the minds of the masses. Movies like *2001, Star Wars,* and others have prepared people to accept the new supernaturalism. She wanted to know, "Well, were people relating to the metaphysical aspects of *Star Wars* or were they mostly drawn to it because it was an adventurous space opera?" (*Dancing,* p. 261). She was assured that while people went to movies like the *Star Wars* series for entertainment, it made them receptive to the metaphysical concept of the force. They would accept the force concept as the power of God (*Dancing,* p. 262). I would like to note that *Star Wars, Close Encounters, 2001,* and similar movies are totally occultic in their philosophy. They emphasize things like spiritism (communication with the dead) and the deity of man. The background music for *2001* included Strauss' *Ulso Sprak Zarathustra* (Thus Spoke Zarathustra). This idea came from the mad philosopher Fredrich Nietzsche who proclaimed the death of God and the deity of man. Zarathustra was allegedly a forerunner and spokesman of "antichrist" of whom Nietzsche spoke in glowing terms.

I have researched the UFO concept for over thirty years. I have interviewed and corresponded with many alleged contactees (those who claim that they communicated with the space people). There may be exceptions, but as far as my research and experience goes, I observe that every so-called contactee had previously been involved in Eastern mysticism, demonism, satanism, witchcraft, or some form of occultism. When I have interviewed born again Christians who had such experiences prior to their conversion to Christ, I found that every one of them attributed their contact experiences to demonic materializations or demonic delusion or trance hypnosis.

MacLaine had a mystical experience involving astral projection there in Peru with David. While in a hot tub together she stared into the light of a candle until her spirit left her body and soared out into the universe. This vivid experience conditioned her to believe in the validity of the "calling" that David brought her from the extraterrestrial, Mayan.

TIME TO PRAY

As you pray for Shirley MacLaine, please claim her for the kingdom of God. I believe she can find the real peace of salvation in Jesus Christ. What a powerful testimony she will have to the whole New Age crowd as she reinterprets her past experiences in the light of the true gospel of Jesus Christ. It is a sure thing that Shirley and many of her friends are searching for a reality greater than the secular world and the realms of materialistic science can offer. Their quest will finally be satisfied when they find Jesus Christ as their personal Saviour and Lord.

It is easier to win a New Ager to Christ than it is to win an atheist. Keep that in mind as you talk to your friends who are caught up in these strange metaphysical ideas. We do not threaten to take supernaturalism away from them but to lead them into supernatural deliverance in Christ and into the gifts of the Holy Spirit which always glorify Jesus, His deity, and majesty.

NEW AGE LEADERS CONFERENCE WITH EVANGELICALS

We are all aware by now that some strange things are going on in the body of Christ, relating to the radical anti-prophecy teaching. Some modernistic Charismatics and Evangelicals are denying the Rapture, the Millennium, and the prophetic significance of Israel.

A whole new wave of anti-Semitism is sweeping the ranks of the Evangelical and Charismatic churches! I am not sure how strong it is yet—but it is enough that I am deeply concerned. But of these things we are all aware. Now comes a development that is truly even more shocking! A liaison has been formed between New Age leadership and some Evangelical leadership!

David Spangler (New Age leader, Findhorn Foundation) held a meeting at the Gold Lake Convention Center in Boulder, Colorado, a short time ago. The meeting involved New Age leaders, as well as Evangelical, Pentecostal, and Charismatic leaders. The purpose was to *explore ways the Evangelicals and the New Agers could join hands to cooperate in bringing their mutual goals to pass.*

We know this meeting took place because Spangler spoke of it at a church in Boulder, identifying only one of the Evangelical groups involved—but that one *really shocked me.*

Spangler indicated that by joining hands with these Evangelicals the New Age movement has overcome a final barrier which could prevent the realization of New Age goals. We know this is authentic information because we have the two cassette tapes of Spangler's speaking at the Boulder, Colorado, Episcopal Church. He clearly states these and many other things. Subscribers to our Monthly Audio Prophecy Digest tape service heard his actual voice speaking on this subject.

I am currently trying to obtain more information about the Gold Lake meeting and a list of participants. It is important to know if any significant Evangelical leaders were there, and if so, who. This is a very serious matter, as you can well discern. If by any chance you hear anything of this meeting, or a similar one, please inform us.

A NEW AGE PRAYER MEETING

Regarding the New Age—I went to one of their prayer meetings last December 31 in Kansas City. God really intervened to shield and protect me. Over one hundred intercessors were on their knees here in Springfield from five a.m. onward to surround me with God's shield.

I saw and heard prayers offered to "Mother Goddess Earth" and witnessed visualization meditation. I heard it stated that the planet is now a living intelligent being which is in communication with the heirarchy of ascended masters of the universe. We were told that human beings are simply sensory extensions of the living planet. Since the New Agers believe in reincarnation, the death of an individual is insignificant. They think the dead souls will be recycled and come back as another sensory extension of the living earth.

SPECIAL FIFTEENTH ANNIVERSARY RETROSPECTIVE

January/February 1990 $2.95
Foreign $3.50
Display through February 28

NewAge

RETHINKING THE WAY WE LIVE   *Journal*

15

FROM
ABBIE & JERRY
TO
Ben
& Jerry…

FROM
TURNING ON
TO
Booting up…

FROM
BROWN RICE
TO
Green politics…

SNAPSHOTS
FROM AN
Ongoing
Journey

SOLAR
ENERGY
NewAge

20

Is Satan Our Brother?
New Age Luciferian Deception

Those who elect to comment on the Book of Revelation undertake an awesome task. Indeed the book carries this sobering warning:

"And I testify unto every man that heareth the words of the prophecy of this book, If any man shall add unto these things, God shall add unto him the plagues that are written in this book: And if any man shall take away from the words of the book of this prophecy, God shall take away his part out of the book of life, and out of the holy city, and from the things which are written in this book" (Rev. 22:18,19).

Barbara Marx Hubbard is a New Age teacher of reknown. She is one of the principal promoters of the annual December 31 New Age prayer meeting, The World Instant of Cooperation.

As far as we have been able to ascertain, her complete commentary on the Book of Revelation has not been printed in bound form as yet. However, portions have been prepublished and distributed in manuscript form. Here are quotations from her *Revelation: The Book of Co-Creation, Volume 3*.

These quotations will vividly show that the New Age movement, while it speaks the words peace, love, harmony, and brotherhood, actually envisions vast numbers of human beings being "eliminated" in order to bring in the New Age, the Age of Aquarius, the Age of Flowers.

Hubbard's radical views calling for the elimination of masses of humanity to prepare for the New Age World Order are shared by many New Age leaders.

It might be countered that Fundamentalists and Evangelicals also see a time of great destruction before the Millennium. That is true, but we will do nothing to promote it. We leave it in the hands of God to bring His purposes to pass. We are committed to "occupying 'til He comes," busy with the task of preaching the good news that all men can be saved by the grace of God.

It is interesting to note that both New Agers and Bible-believing Christians foresee a coming time of trouble, then a time of peace on earth. We believe the New Age is a counterfeit of Christianity. The fatal flaw is that they substitute man or "the force" for Jehovah, the God of the Bible. It will be interesting to see who wins in the forthcoming confrontation, Jehovah or Lucifer, whom many New Agers such as Spangler, Hubbard, and others glorify.

As for me, I am putting my trust in the God of the Bible, Father, Son, and Holy Spirit. The Lord Jesus Christ shall reign forever and forever. I tell you, we are on the winning side. We urge all New Age-connected people to reconsider the claims of Jesus Christ (not some "new" christ) and find Him as their Lord and Saviour—then they will truly survive the coming days of tribulation.

HUBBARD'S NEW AGE COMMENTARY ON REVELATION 6:4—RED HORSE

"The great reaper must reap before we can take the quantum leap to the next phase of evolution (p. 55).

"No worldly peace can prevail until the self-centered members of the planetary body either *change or die*...The red horse is the destruction...of those who refuse to be born into God-centered universal life...They must surely die, or change" (p. 56).

Here Hubbard declares that those who resist the New Age must die!

"Evolution is good but it is not nice...Only the God-centered will survive to inherit the powers of a universal species" (p. 56).

By the "God-centered" Hubbard means those who accept their own godhood. This does not mean centered in Jesus Christ, or Jehovah, the God of the Bible. Also note the constant emphasis on evolution—as opposed to the biblical concept of creation.

"Evolution empowers the horseman upon the red horse to kill that which cannot love God above all else and his neighbor as himself and himself as the son of God (p. 56).

"Be prepared for the selection process which is now beginning (p. 56).

"[This] book is the guide to the new Jerusalem. It is the code for the next stage of evolution, the building plan for a universal species...it tells you how to get through the evolutionary straits from Homo Sapiens to Homo Universalis... (p. 56).

"It is written for the 'elect,' the *self-selected* people throughout the globe who are acting to discover and implement God's plan now—that the end is here and the new day is dawning (p. 57).

"It [Book of Revelation] is written for us by those who have gone before and know the way (p. 57).

"...process which shall rip apart the old order and destroy those who choose to remain self-centered, womb-centered remnants of the past (p. 57).

"Affirms the capacity of the individual...and the future of *humanity as a God-like species* (p. 58).

"The period of co-creative revolution has already begun (p. 58).

"We are co-creative with the energy that creates the universal. We are new alchemists, conscious evolvers..." (p. 58).

HUBBARD COMMENTS ON THE FOURTH SEAL, THE PALE HORSE

"They cannot be reached...one-fourth [of humanity] is destructive...they are defective seeds. In the past they were permitted to die a 'natural death.' Their bodies were recycled to new life, and their souls reincarnated...the 'evil personality is one who suffers the defects of a disconnection between the higher self and the ego' (p. 59).

"This defect plagues one-fourth of humanity (p. 60).

"We the elders, have been patiently waiting until the very last moment before the quantum transformation, to take action to cut this corrupted and corrupting element in the body of humanity. It is like watching a cancer grow; something must be done before the whole body is destroyed" (p. 60).

Note the phrase above, "We the elders..." Barbara Marx Hubbard is the author of the manuscript from which these quotations are taken. However, "we" indicates that she received the thoughts from an entity or entities who "channelled" the information through her. This explains the "We the elders" phrase.

"In the past...the effect of the one-fourth was painful, but not deadly to the whole planetary system. Mother Earth is forgiving. You can get away with murder while still in the womb. Your power was not sufficient to destroy the world. Now, as we approach the quantum shift from creature-human to co-creative human—the human who is an inheritor of *God-like powers—the destructive one-fourth must be eliminated from the social body* (p. 60).

"We have no choice, dearly beloveds. It is a case of the destruction of the whole planet, or the elimination of the ego-driven, godless one-fourth who, at this time of planetary birth, can, if allowed to live on to reproduce their *defective disconnection,* destroy forever the opportunity of Homo Sapiens to become Homo Universalis, heirs of God (p. 60).

"We come to bring death to those who are unable to know God. We do this for the sake of the world" (p. 61).

"Those who are unable to know God" are the Evangelical Christians and others who do not accept the New Age idea that man is God.

"The riders of the pale horse are about to pass among you. Grim reapers, they will separate the wheat from the chaff. This is the most painful period in the history of humanity" (p. 61).

HUBBARD'S NEW AGE COMMENTARY ON REVELATION 6:9-11—FIFTH SEAL SOULS UNDER THE ALTAR

"Once the tribulations are over, and the *devil of separation* is destroyed forever, *no more self-centered humans will incarnate on earth*" (p. 63).

Note the continual emphasis on reincarnation. This is totally opposed to the biblical doctrine of resurrection. One cannot believe in both concepts.

"If this is to occur, one of your women will be taken up into space. I will conceive in her my child the child of Christ. This child will be a *natural Christ.* He will be born outside the contamination of Earth by a woman who is to be called Eve. She is the second Eve, and is to give birth to the second Adam through union with me. The second Adam is the natural Christ, the future human...Then shall be re-enacted the events of Sodom and Gomorrah" (p. 114).

Could this be a prophecy of the coming Antichrist?

HUBBARD'S NEW AGE COMMENTARY ON REVELATION 12:7-9—DRAGON CAST DOWN

"It is a conflict between suprahuman good and suprahuman evil. Who is that devil...That devil is my brother, the *brother of Christ, the other son of God, who went astray*" (p. 114).

The devil may be the brother of the New Ager, but he is not my brother—he is our enemy! Satan is not the "other son of God."

"Nothing is guaranteed for an individual" (p. 115).

By contrast Jesus guarantees the ultimate victory of the Church (Matt. 16), and salvation is guaranteed to the believer through the redemption that Jesus Christ provides through His atonement.

"Therefore your mission, dearly beloveds, must be to overcome all fear within yourselves...God loves humanity as the Son of God ...Know that, and *the devil shall wither away* (p. 115).

"There are two defects from which you suffer, *carniverous behavior* [eating meat] and the *illusion* of separation from God. Neither are of human origin. The animals made the first mistake. *Satan, my brother,* made the second mistake" (p. 117).

The Bible warns against those who forbid the eating of meat (see 1 Tim. 4:3). Furthermore, separation from God is not an illusion. It is a reality and only the new birth brings us into fellowship with God. The New Age, on the other hand, teaches that we are God and all we have to do is come to this self-realization. This is totally contrary to the Bible.

"You are innocent, O humanity. The *forces* of God are on your side. My brother, the pathetic self-rejected Son of God, must die. We can have pity for him too, even though he would destroy us. Have pity on the devil, dearly beloveds. He is the fallen Son of God...Have pity on yourselves who inherited these mistakes and correct them. You are empowered to correct the twin defects that have plagued humanity, carniverous behavior and the illusion of separation from God (p. 117).

"This awareness of your innocence is essential for your salvation" (p. 117).

On the contrary one must recognize his sinful nature and repent of it to be saved!

"Do not feel guilty, humanity. *You are innocent...*Forgive the animals for eating flesh. Forgive Satan for fearing God. Love the animal in the world and in yourself, and do not kill him any more" (p. 117).

Love the animal in yourself? More evolutionary nonsense.

"Love Satan, my fallen brother, and do not let him make you reject God any more" (p. 118).

HUBBARD'S NEW AGE COMMENTS ON REVELATION 12:11

"This means that it is the life force of the risen Son of God that defeats the death force of the fallen Son of God...The fallen Son is that part of your being which urges you to believe only what your animal senses tell you; that you are separate from God and you will surely die" (p. 118).

Note how this New Age writer not only sees man as God, but also

319

Satan as part of our nature. Note how the final phrase of the above statement contradicts the first chapter of Genesis.

"The risen Son of God is that part of your being which urges you to believe that which your higher self, your suprahuman aspect, tells you; *that you are one with God...* (p. 118).

"You are here to help everyone who can personally be attracted to a personal future as the Son of God, *to do so en masse at once*" (p. 118).

This illustrates the purpose behind the annual December 31 World Instant of Cooperation and the August Harmonic Convergence: the New Agers' hope to release psychic energy and effect a paradigm shift in the way humanity perceives reality. They believe this is essential to the establishment of the New Age.

"The Book of Revelation reveals the violent scenario to salvation, wherein the good are killed to get rid of the bad, as in Sodom and Gomorrah. The book of Co-Creation reveals the gentle scenario to salvation, wherein the good create a field of empathetic force [*the 100th monkey concept*] so powerful that the fallen son of god himself revives and returns willingly to God" (p. 118).

The fallen son of god here is Satan. Hubbard now speaks of Satan's returning to God—this seems to contradict the earlier statement that the devil will wither away.

"This scenario has never been written before. It has come into being because there has grown up in the world a generation of lovers of the future who believe in me, and *their capacity to become me [God]*. They are you, dearly beloveds" (p. 118).

CONCLUSION

The most disturbing element in this New Age commentary is the anticipated elimination of those that Hubbard identifies as the "bad seed," incapable of evolving into "godhood." Since the New Agers believe themselves to be God, or part of God, who is to say they will not take matters into their own hands and start eliminating those of us they see as resistant to their vision of a New Age of Aquarius? If they ever get political supremacy (which they are trying to do), they will certainly contemplate and perhaps endeavor to implement such a plan.

Hubbard's glorification of Satan-Lucifer is particularly disturbing. This commentary is, in my opinion, inspired, not by Jehovah but by Lucifer, the devil himself. There is no regard for the actual (that is to say, literal) meaning of the Scripture. Other errors in this commentary will not be difficult for our calibre of readers to locate and analyze.

This is written to alert you to thinking that is common to New Agers, of whom, we are told, there are approximately one billion in the world today. In the U.S.A. alone there are over ten thousand New Age organizations. While there is infighting amongst their own leadership, nevertheless they have a common ground. They declare the godhood of humanity. They share a vision for a world government and a new one-world religion (psychic humanism). Most New Agers desire a new economic system which would provide for a "more equitable distribution of the world's goods and wealth." The latter augers the advent of the "mark of the beast" (Rev. 13:16-18).

We protest the New Agers' using the Christian Scriptures (such as the Book of Revelation) to promote anti-Christian concepts and doctrines.

"Woe unto them that call evil good, and good evil; that put darkness for light and light for darkness...Woe unto them that are wise in their own eyes ...Which justify the wicked..." (Isa. 5:20-23). *Woe unto those who call Bible-believing Christians the bad seed. Woe unto you who say the "New Age" is the hope of humanity.*

The New Age movement is worldwide and knows no boundaries. It wears many masks and identities in various nations and sectors of society.

In my recent trip to Iceland, I found the Filadelfia churches very concerned about the New Age movement. They took me to see the impressive Icelandic headquarters of the Theosophical Society (Blavatsky's movement, the grandmother of the current New Age movement). We also noted the facilities of the Sri Chemoy cult. I was told that the temple of the god Thor is being rebuilt in Northern Iceland. A brother who works for the television industry furnished me with a tape of the Harmonic Convergence (August 16, 1987) held at Snaefensjokul glacier, which allegedly marks an opening to the nether world, the center of the planet earth. This inspired the novel by Jules Verne, *Journey to the Center of the Earth.* A large idol of Thor is prominent in this location and was shown several times on the TV special. Extensive coverage of the Harmonic Convergence was aired both on state television and on private television.

Idols of Thor, as figurines, jewelry, etc., are for sale in stores all over Iceland. Thor's hammer is a popular design often worn as a pendant, a necklace, as earrings, or on a keychain.

The New Age movement considers Iceland very important to its plans.

The Evangelical Icelanders tell me that the real aim of Greenpeace Organization is not so much to save the whales and seals as it is to upset the natural balance of things, ruin the fishing industry (which will happen if no whales are harvested), and enforce vegetarianism on the people. If this is accurate it would not be surprising considering the Theosophic Hindu background of many New Agers. Most reincarnationists promote vegetarianism. We are exploring this theory.

The Icelanders say that what Greenpeace has done to the native people of Greenland is horrible and unimaginable. Forced to stop living on seals the natives are poverty-stricken, forced to move into undesirable urban areas, and are now victimized by alcoholism, poverty, unemployment, and a general malaise. When Greenpeace leaders were shown these conditions, resulting from their agitation, they are said to have shrugged their shoulders, commenting, "Too bad." Evidently animals are more important than humans. Further I was informed that when seals are not harvested, they overpopulate and turn to cannibalism, eating their young. So one way or another, the herd is thinned.

The Icelanders tell me that Greenpeace is a part of and a tool of the New Age movement. I wonder if anyone involved in Greenpeace could respond to the Icelandic claim? Would they be willing to meet with some more of the people they are affecting by their agitation? Are they open to dialogue? We would like to know.

Other nations the New Age believes very important to the fulfillment of their goals are the United States of America, Mexico, South Africa, Canada, Israel, Brazil, India, China, Russia, France, Sweden, England, Scotland, Ireland, Wales, Peru, Sweden, Norway, Egypt, and Belgium. This is not to say that they do not have plans for each and every other nation of the world, for they certainly do.

Let Gideon's three hundred be alert. Let the men of Issachar go about their task of declaring their understanding of the issues of our times. Let men and women of God be keen to hear the word from the men of Issachar. Let the Jericho trumpeters prepare to sound. Let all the people of God intercede for the world and the salvation of mankind.

Let the army of God prepare to march. "The weapons of our warfare are not carnal after the flesh, but *mighty through God* to the pulling down of strongholds." No one needs fear this Bible-believing army of God for we will harm no one. We will draw no sword. Our "weapons" are spiritual. They are prayer, witnessing, persuasion, and love. All the judgment aspect will come direct from God without our help. It is Jehovah you should fear (with circumspect and reverential awe) and not His peaceful servants who desire only your present and eternal salvation and your ultimate well-being.

21

End-Time Spiritual Warfare And Victory

Early in the 1980s, and certainly in every period before that, we found it very difficult to persuade even Christians that there was such a thing as demonic activity or that there were people who would go the extreme of worshiping Satan as the devil. However, only the most obtuse individual has such tunnel vision that he cannot see that Satan worship, demonic activity, and spiritual warfare are increasingly significant features of our times.

As previously mentioned, in 1955 I preached a revival meeting and Bible conference in a small church in Gaylord, Michigan, where Herbert David Kolenda was the pastor. Herbert was very sensitive to spiritual issues and open to every aspect of the Word of God. This emboldened me to say things to his congregation from the pulpit that I might have been hesitant to talk about in other churches where I could not be sure of having a sympathetic ear, at least from the senior pastor. I read to the people the passage in Revelation 9 about the demonic hordes that would be loosed upon the earth during the time of the Tribulation. Then I zeroed in on verses 20 and 21: "And the rest of the men, which were not killed by these plagues yet repented not of the works of their hands that they should not worship devils...neither repented they of their murders, of their sorceries, nor their fornications, nor of their thefts."

I coupled these verses with several other passages in the Book of Revelation and other parts of the Bible, indicating that as a fulfillment of prophecy, degenerate man would actually worship Satan (in the last days). To illustrate my point, I referred to a group in California known as the Legion of Lucifer and to a group in Washington, D.C. who were merely known as Satanists or Devil Worshipers.

I was too much ahead of the times. The elders of the church were kindly men and it was not their purpose to be mean or harsh in talking to me as they did after the service. They took me aside to a little room and said, "David, you are a fine young evangelist and you have a great future before you. However, you must stop fantasizing some of the things you said tonight. If you don't stop taking the Book of Revelation literally, you are going to ruin your credibility and your ministry will come to an end."

I want to say again that these elders were not being in any way mean-spirited. They only had my best interests at heart. Of course, they were wrong. Another one of the elders said to me, "David, God never intended that we should take the Book of Revelation literally. Why, common sense would tell us that people are not going to be so stupid or naive as to worship the devil as the devil! What these passages actually refer to is the general struggle between good and evil throughout the ages of time."

I confess that I was somewhat intimidated by this encounter, and I backed off from preaching on this subject at that time. However, as the months went by and as I prayed and sought the Lord, I came to the conclusion that I should preach the Word exactly as it is. To this day regardless of the consequences, that is exactly what I have done in thirty-five years of ministering the prophetical Word of God.

Life does have some small ironies. A few years ago—long after the Gaylord, Michigan, incident—I was preaching at Trinity Bible Institute in Ellendale, North Dakota. We were having morning and night services for a week's time for the entire student body and such local individuals as were interested in our teaching. Reverend Roy Wead was the president of the college at that time. One day he came to me and said, "David, we have a young lady student here at the college who used to be a priestess in a satanist cult. She would like to talk to you about some of her experiences and perhaps get some counseling from you."

In the course of our conversation, I asked her, "By the way, where are you from?"

She said, "I'm from the state of Michigan." (She named the town where she was from.)

"Oh," I exclaimed, "I spoke to a youth rally at a church in that town."

She asked me if I had had ministry in other churches throughout that area. I said that we had traveled around in Michigan for quite some time and preached revival meetings in Petosky, Boyne City, St. Ignace, Grayling, Gaylord…At that moment she exclaimed, "Gaylord! Did you say you held meetings in Gaylord?"

I affirmed that we had been with Rev. Herbert Kolenda, the pastor in Gaylord, for services on quite a number of occasions. "Why did you react so strongly when I mentioned Gaylord?" I asked.

"Dr. Lewis, I don't know if you are aware of it or not, but Gaylord, Michigan, is one of the headquarters for the Satanist movement for the five-state area surrounding Michigan," she responded.

I sat there silent for a moment, stunned by the strange turn of events. In the same town where the elders had cautioned me not to speak of devil worship as a literal prophetic reality, the satanists had come in force and—according to this young lady—were even performing human sacrifices there. I have no documentation for this; nevertheless, that is what she said.

Friends, the Bible says that we are involved in a spiritual warfare. It is going to intensify as we get closer to the second coming of our Lord and Saviour, Jesus Christ. The devil is making a last ditch stand against the Church. Not only satanism, but cultism of every variety, the New Age movement, Eastern mysticism, and a host of other spiritual ill winds are blowing throughout the land. Unfortunately, even some Evangelical Christians who are not well-grounded in the Word are getting swept up into some of these organizations (especially those that appear to be benevolent), through ignorance—and quite innocently. Regardless of their innocence, at the point of entry, however, the devastation of people's lives is a tragic reality.

Paul wrote powerful words concerning spiritual warfare to the Corinthian church: "For though we walk in the flesh, we do not war after the flesh: (For the weapons of our warfare are not carnal, but mighty through God to the pulling down of strong holds;) Casting down imaginations, and every high thing that exalteth itself against the knowledge of God, and bringing into captivity every thought to the obedience of Christ…" (2 Cor. 3:3-5).

WAR DECLARED AGAINST THE CHURCH

In 1975, anthropologist Margaret Mead and United Nations official Robert Mueller launched a New Age prayer movement, and several unsuspecting Evangelicals got sucked into these spiritual dark forces.

They thought they were simply joining in a prayer for peace on earth, and that is how "the World Instant of Cooperation" was promoted. Throughout 1986, I and a small handful of my colleagues, did our best through every means available to us to communicate to the Church that it would be necessary for us to set up a counter-attack against these spiritual forces on December 31. Look back once again and reread the above Scripture passage to see if we were not justified in calling for this kind of spiritual encounter. My friends and I sent information concerning the 1986, December 31 New Age prayer event to every major television evangelist and ministry throughout the nation. We asked them to alert the Church to this great danger that was facing us. As far as we know, only one responded, Marlin Maddox, who has a nation-wide radio ministry. He mentioned the event on one of his programs.

In the meantime, some really weird and strange events were taking place. For example, in the fall of 1986, two covens of witches marched around the International Headquarters of the Assemblies of God (a Pentecostal denomination) located in Springfield, Missouri. They called down curses on the Assemblies of God and swore to destroy this Pentecostal fellowship through the demoralization and discrediting of the ministry. I do not know if the officials of the Assemblies of God were even aware of this. To my knowledge the only people in Springfield who paid any attention to the threat was a Charismatic church which held a prayer meeting on one occasion to intercede for the Assemblies of God.

Personally, I think that all of our warnings to the Evangelical churches about the December 31 event were in vain. I know it sounded bizarre. It seemed like it was straight off the wall, but we told the Church that if the believers did not respond with a counter-reaction against this December 31 New Age release of psychic, demonic force, terrible consequences, and tragedies would touch the Church in 1987 and years following. Of course we now know of the tragedy that touched a major television ministry in March, 1987, and all of the horrible consequences that have followed. Just a short time later, another major television ministry went into a downward spiral of scandal. During the summer of 1987, possibly because of the state of shock that the Church was in after the tragedy of March, 1987, we were able to get a little more attention as we started to warn our friends of the coming Harmonic Convergence New Age event that would transpire August 16 and 17, 1987. The Harmonic Convergence was the brain-child of New Ager Jose Arguelles. He called for 144,000 Shamanic priests and practitioners to join in a time of psychic prayer to affect a major push of the entire world toward or into the New Age.

New Agers of every stripe gathered in various "power points" of the earth, such as the pyramids in Egypt; Central Park in New York; Mount Fuji in Japan; Chaco Canyon in New Mexico; Sedonia, Arizona; Boulder, Colorado; Mount Shasta, California; Serpent Mount near Cincinnati, Ohio; the Enchanted Rock in Texas; the Stone Faces of the Easter Islands; Stonehenge in England; the Georgia Guidestones in Elberton, Georgia; and the list goes on and on. In addition to the 144,000 Shamans, witches, and warlocks, there were to be millions of other ordinary people who would gather together in this convergence of New Age psychic force. Many publications, both secular and New Age, observed after the Harmonic Convergence was over that the whole thing had been a failure, or as the Gastonia, North Carolina, paper headlined it: "The Occult Convergence Fizzles."

Magical Blend, a major New Age magazine, printed an interview with Jose Arguelles. He was asked if the Harmonic Convergence fulfilled his expectations. Arguelles replied, "No, it did not" and indicated that as the New Agers projected out in the realm of the paranormal, it was like they were hitting a brick wall. Something was out there waiting for them and stopped them dead in their tracks. Arguelles philosophically commented, "When the Light hits, the Dark gets tough."

Arguelles continued to comment that there were probably going to be tough times ahead and said that there was a distinct possibility of a major economic collapse and a depression that will mark the end of history as we know it.

When Arguelles characterizes the force that ran into him as the "darkness" and his efforts as the "light," I can only quote the words of Isaiah 5:20, 21, and 24: "Woe unto them that call evil good, and good evil; and that put darkness for light and light for darkness; that put bitter for sweet and sweet for bitter! Woe unto them that are wise in their own eyes and prudent in their own sight!...Therefore as the fire devoureth the stubble, and the flame consumeth the chaff, so their root shall be as rottenness, and the blossom shall go up as dust: because they have cast away the law of the Lord of hosts, and despised the word of the Holy One of Israel."

Let me recapitulate: We had warned many Christians throughout the summer of 1987 to be in a state of readiness and spiritual warfare on August 16 and 17. We went to the Assemblies of God General Council and distributed thousands of papers to the delegates of that Pentecostal convention. I think that many people were in a state of shock over previous events and were beginning to take spiritual warfare seriously for the first time. I believe that we were able to raise up, through our publications, an army of a few thousand prayer warriors who stood against the powers of the occult on August 16 and 17. I also believe that is why the New Agers themselves felt that their efforts were a failure.

Now will we sink back into apathy and think that the war is over? Believe me, it has only just begun! It is very difficult to get Christians to see the reality of spiritual warfare, but unless we recognize the reality of it, we are never going to be effective in combatting the powers of darkness. Satan is going to make more of an effort to corrupt the Church and destroy our credibility. The easy path is to sit around and criticize the brethren who have gone through failures of a moral (or other) nature. What we must do is work for their restoration and gather around them to provide them with a way back into the full fellowship of the body of Jesus Christ. Furthermore, if we do not take the spiritual warfare seriously, there are going to be more and more ministries that are going to fall into a state of chaos and loss of credibility. This credibility loss is going to affect not just these few brethren, but the entire Church.

Over twenty years ago, I met an ex-witch who had gone out of witchcraft into satanism and had risen to the status of priestess. I asked her to tell me the prime objective of the Satanists and the witch covens. She said that the main task of the Satanists and witches was to morally corrupt the clergy of the Evangelical and Pentecostal churches. Those who were physically attractive were instructed to infiltrate churches, fake a born-again experience, and work for the physical seduction of the clergy, their wives, and other prominent people in the church. This would create confusion in the flock as the leadership fell into moral failure. Both those engaged in this type of wicked and abominable activities and those who were not so physically attractive were to engage themselves in spiritual warfare and intercession to the devil. They were to ask him to undergird their efforts in the demoralization of the Bible-preaching churches. During the last two decades I have talked to a number of people who have come out of the New Age and the occult, and they have confirmed what Sharon Harrington told me about twenty years ago.

Recently, I was talking to Reverend James Graziano, pastor of the Church of God in Babylon, New York. Babylon is a small town on Long Island, east of New York City. James got on an airplane one day and sat down in his assigned seat. The gentleman next to him bowed his head in prayer, his hands folded in an attitude of prayer. When he was through praying, James put out his right hand to shake hands and said, "Praise the Lord, brother, nice to see a fellow believer!" The man would not touch James' hand. He looked at him strangely and said, "I don't know your name, but I know what you are. Before you shake my hand, you had better know that my god is not the same as your God."

James was startled at this and asked, "What is the name of the god that you serve?"

"I serve the one that you call Lucifer. He is the one to whom I address my prayers," he answered.

Curiosity burning in his mind, James asked the man, "What were you praying about?"

The man replied, "I was praying for your moral destruction. We satanists pray for the moral corruption of all Evangelical leaders so that their credibility with their congregations will be destroyed. We are making war on the Bible churches."

Paul wrote to the Ephesian church as follows: "Finally, my brethren, be strong in the Lord, and in the power of his might. Put on the whole armour of God, that ye may be able to stand against the wiles of the devil. For we wrestle not against flesh and blood, but against principalities, against powers, against the rulers of the darkness of this world, against spiritual wickedness in high places. Wherefore take unto you the whole armour of God, that ye may be able to withstand in the evil day, and having done all, to stand. Stand therefore, having your loins girt about with truth, and having on the breastplate of righteousness: and your feet shod with the preparation of the gospel of peace; above all, taking the shield of faith, wherewith ye shall be able to quench all the fiery darts of the wicked. And take the helmet of salvation, and the sword of the Spirit, which is the word of God: Praying always with all prayer and supplication in the spirit, and watching thereunto with all perseverance and supplication for all saints: And for me that utterance may be given unto me, that I may open my mouth boldly, to make known the mystery of the gospel" (Eph. 6:10-19).

NOTED COMMENTATOR SPEAKS OUT

"Good morning, Americans. I'm Paul Harvey. What the devil is this all about? In Chicago, the respected Department of Psychiatry at Rush Presbyterian St. Luke's Hospital held a conference early this month in Chicago. The fourth international conference on multiple personality dissociative states. Several of the seminars dealing with dissociative disorders focused on satanic cults." Harvey went on to tell the story of a man who belongs to a coven of devil-worshipers accused of raping a fifteen-year-old girl. "The accused man claimed that his satanic order directed him to kill the girl and bury her and he would thus earn a death star to wear around his neck, which would give him special powers." After accounting this, Harvey said, "What in the devil is this all about?" Harvey tells of ritual abuse by satanic cults that is coming to light everywhere around the nation. He said, and this is shocking, "One out of every five young people that disappears or is apparently a runaway ends up being a ritual sacrifice, and some victims of cannibalism."

I live in Springfield, Missouri. This area is called the Bible Belt of America, because the Bible Baptist Church has its college and headquarters here, and the Assemblies of God, the world's largest Pentecostal denomination also has its headquarters here. Someone has quipped, "If there is a Bible Belt in America, surely Springfield, Missouri, is the buckle."

Springfield prides itself on being the Queen City of the Ozarks. In a book titled *What They Do Not Want You to Know About Satanism in America,* the statement is made that there are certain geographical centers of satanist activity. "The center down geographical for occult activity in America is in the Ozark Mountain Range. This does not mean that there are no other centers, but the Ozarks give natural wooded cover and unpopulated spaces necessary in order that the horror that occurs in some rituals can go unnoticed."

I have communicated with police officials in this area and they are literally horrified at some of the ritual sacrifices and cannibalism that are going on in this Bible Belt area. This is by no means unique. Every area of America now has its outreach of witchcraft and Satanism. I wonder when the Church is going to wake up to its own message, the message of the Bible that has long warned us that this kind of warfare would be taking place in the last days?

GOD GIVES VISIONS

God has spoken to mankind in various ways. He has spoken personally, by visions, by sending Christ to earth, by angelic visitation, by the prophets, by dreams, and by His written Word, the Bible.

Nothing takes precedence over the written Word. Every revelation and word of knowledge must be measured by the Bible. According to Paul's teachings all prophecies are to be "judged" by the elders of the church. On the other hand we know God sometimes does give direct guidance by dreams and visions, even today. Some fundamentalists who reject current supernatural workings other than for salvation have a problem with that. Because the New Age cultists enter into unbiblical, antichrist visionary techniques there are those on "our side" who want to throw out all supernatural visitation in the Church today. Nothing would delight the devil more than to be able to manifest his supernatural power while persuading us to reject the supernatural provision God has made for the Church.

"If there be a prophet among you, I the Lord will make myself known to him in a vision, and will speak unto him in a dream" (Num. 12:6).

The concept of "vision" is first met in the Book of Genesis 2000 years before Christ. In Genesis 15:1 we are told that God appeared to Abram in a vision. The first communication by means of a dream is also in Genesis. In this case God warns a king: "But God came to Abimelech in a dream by night and said to him, Behold, thou art but a dead man..." (Gen. 20:3).

Many books of prophecy, almost in their entirety, came by means of visions, as in the case of Jeremiah, Isaiah, and Ezekiel. This visionary quality also characterizes the Book of Revelation. Remove all the things in the Bible revealed by dreams and visions and the volume would be much slimmer indeed.

"And it shall come to pass afterward that I will pour out my spirit upon all flesh; and your sons and your daughters shall prophecy, your old men shall dream dreams, your young men shall see visions" (Joel 2:28).

The Bible gives certain warnings about dreams and visions. Not every dream or vision is from God. Some are merely from our own minds. Some people have gotten them from Satan. As with all things spiritual, we need understanding of the Word of God and a keen discerning of spirits. "For a dream cometh through the multitude of business; and a fool's voice is known by multitude of words...For in the multitude of dreams and many words there are also divers vanities: but fear thou God" (Eccles. 5:3,7).

As a general rule, if you don't understand a dream or vision, if you have to ask someone else what it means—you probably should forget it, and certainly you should be quiet about it. I am quite confident that if God reveals a thing to you, He is capable of imparting understanding with the revelation. The exception to this would be in a case of clear satanic harassment (nightmares, fearful and tormenting dreams, evil apparitions, and the like). In this type of situation you would certainly be justified in approaching another Christian for prayer in getting rid of the manifestation.

VISION OF THE BEAR

Earlier in this chapter, I shared with you Scriptures and biblical principles concerning spiritual warfare. I also shared with you the personal testimonies of various people who speak from a position of experience and authority.

In September, 1973, God gave me a vision of the potential for end-time victory in the Church. This is described in chapter nine of our book *Smashing the Gates of Hell in the Last Days*.

In February, 1976, I was holding meetings in the First Assembly of God Church in Chula Vista, California. Once again the Lord spoke to me in a visionary experience. I immediately sat down and typed out a description of the vision. I have made it a practice of writing down a vision or dream at once. As time passes by, one's perception of the dream or vision fades and may not be accurately recalled. I have carried that rough, hastily typed piece of copy with me since 1976.

As far as I can remember I have shared it publicly with only one congregation. We printed it once in our prophecy newspaper.

I believe most dreams and visions are for the recipient's personal edification, and are not to be shared with the body of Christ in general. A lot of confusion could be avoided if this rule were followed. The prophets of old normally showed a reluctance to speak out even though they knew the message was from God. Only when extremely urged by the Spirit of God did they speak to the congregation of the Lord concerning their revelations. We should never easily or lightly say, "The Lord told me...."

NOW IS THE TIME

After years of hiding this vision in my heart, I now feel absolutely compelled to share it with you. Any reluctance I have in giving you this information arises from the fact that I have tried to emphasize the positive side of prophecy. I believe our message is one of end-time victory. This vision, on the other hand, is the most somber of warnings. However, we have long said that victory is available, not inevitable. Therefore this message is not inconsistent with our overall emphasis. Even more important is the fact that I know God gave me the vision for a purpose. Sometimes these things are given to a servant of the Lord for his own personal motivation, but now I perceive that this is intended for the Church for this immediate season of danger. Had the Lord not revealed this to me years ago—had I just now had such a vision, perhaps my own heart would suspect that it was merely arising from pressures that are now upon us. In 1976 the vision came at a period of time when we were feeling relatively tranquil in the Church. Perceptive Christians are feeling anything but tranquil at this moment when the wolves of hell are howling for our own blood.

Here is a description of the warning God gave me for the Church and is now compelling me to reveal to you. It is a severe warning and it must be heeded or the most dire of consequences will befall us. We are in the most dangerous period of modern church history. It is not a time for fatalism, but for intercession, fasting, holy living, and sanctified action.

ACCOUNT OF THE VISION AS I WROTE IT DOWN

"February, 1976, Chula Vista, California. This morning I had a dream of graphic, visionary quality. I was on the platform of a church in Washington, D.C. I stood in the pulpit trying to minister to the congregation. I was speaking to them about the power of prayer and fasting. I was warning the people that the world desires to rob us of our freedom to worship God and spread the gospel.

"The people were not hostile toward what I was saying, but they were not paying attention. They were distracted with inconsequential things. Some looked apathetic and bored. Some were yawning. I thought, 'What is wrong? I can't get their attention.' I started to make a stronger emphasis. I raised my voice. Nothing helped. I was so frustrated. The people were looking at their watches and ignoring me. They just wanted to get out of church and go home.

"The pastor started making little comments that had no connection at all with what I was saying, or anything else for that matter. He addressed some irrelevant question to me, interrupting my train of thought. My level of frustration was increasing. I couldn't make any sense out of what was going on. 'What in the world am I doing here?' The pastor kept talking about inane things. The people were not paying attention to him either.

"Finally I just quit preaching and stepped back to try and figure out what was going on. It was then that I looked out a side door that led to a room off the platform area. I was horrified to see a huge sleeping grizzly bear. I knew he could easily wake up and come out where the people were.

"I slipped over to the side of the platform and quietly closed the door. It did not seem like a very strong door. I was terrified. There was no latch or lock on the door. I stood holding it shut but knew my strength would not be enough if the sleeping bear woke up. I called to the men of the church to come and help me hold it shut. No one, not even one person, paid me any attention. I kept warning the people. I said, 'If you won't help me hold the door, at least get out and save yourselves.' Most of the people didn't even look my way. The few who did chuckled tolerantly. These people were not hostile. They were just blind to the danger we faced. They were apathetic.

"I was fully aware of the implication of this vision as it unfolded before me. I knew it was a warning from God that evil forces could awaken and damage the Church as never before. The help I needed was not for actual physical restraint against a physical threat. The need was for intercessors to bind the powers of darkness and destruction.

"I heard the bear stirring, awakening. He started to push the door. I could not hold it. Suddenly I was swept back as the door came crashing open. I was slammed against the wall. The bear lumbered out past me onto the platform and with one sweep of his powerful paw, he killed the pastor. The animal then began savagely to ravage the people as he moved among them. No one could resist. The people screamed in terror. Their cries were so awful I cannot even describe it. The beast attacked one after another of the people. I heard a young girl crying for help as the bear tore off her leg and then chewed on her body. People were crying pitifully. Another girl screamed, 'Mama, mama, help me; it's biting my head.' There was a horrible crunch as her voice was silenced."

THE THREAT IS REAL

Right now the bear has awakened. He knows we are there. He is at the door of the Church.

Awaken people of God. There is still time and there is still hope. Will you help hold the door?

Of course I am not so foolish as to think I am the only watchman on the wall. I do not have such a grand evaluation of my own role in spreading the end-time message of warning. No one in this ministry feels that we have an exclusive on declaring both the message of warning and of potential victory. But this is the voice God is allowing you to hear right now. This is the watchman God has led to warn you at this moment. There are others crying out too. There is a point to all of this. The beast is stirring, awakening. He has the scent of blood in his nostrils. He is hungry. He is the devourer. But he is not invincible.

"Awake thou that sleepest, and arise from the dead, and Christ shall give thee light...Redeeming the time, because the days are evil" (Eph. 5:14, 16). Evil days call for extraordinary spiritual response from believers in Jesus Christ. Awake! Let us begin.

22

The
Supercannon

"**A**nd there went out another horse that was red: and power was given to him that sat thereon to take peace from the earth, and that they should kill one another: and there was given unto him a great sword" (Rev. 6:4). There was given unto him a superior weapon! The events portrayed in the sixth chapter of Revelation yet lie in the future. But if ever there was a time in the history of mankind when we could hear the hoofbeats of the red horse of the Apocalypse it is today as he rides out of Babylon with the challenge by Saddam Hussein, filling a self-appropriated dual role of both the new Nebuchadnezzar and the new Saladin. He hopes to rule the Arab world and banish Jews, Christians, and Westerners from the land of Israel and the Middle East.

GERALD BULL, INVENTOR OF THE SUPERGUN

The fate of the supplier of "superior weapons" was sealed the day he first negotiated with the dictator of Baghdad. Gerald Bull was described in *Der Spiegel* (April 23, 1990) as "the most prominent Artillery-genius of this generation, said U.S. arms expert John E. Pike." "Bull war kein gewöhnlicher Geschäftsmann, sondern, 'das größte Artillerie-Genie dieser Generation,' wie der angesehene US-

335

BARBADOS — Courtesy of *Nation*, daily newspaper. The Barbados government was embarrassed after the assassination of Gerald Bull in Brussels, Belgium. The connection to South Africa and the fact that Iraq had received the weapon caused discomfort to the Bajun prime minister. As a consequence, the project was partially dismantled. Actually the project is viable as a non-weapons system, and should be revived. Certain satellites can be placed into orbit at 1/10th the cost of the usual rocket launches.

Rüstungsexperte, John E. Pike findet."

The Canadian inventor, scientist, and international arms dealer was assassinated in Brussels, Belgium on March 22, 1990. The world press took note of the assassination, but since arms merchants are frequently embroiled in precarious circumstances, the event did not create any immediate international commotion.

The Iranians said that the Israelis did the deed and, in turn, the Israelis pointed a finger of blame at the Iranians. Only when a connection between Bull and Saddam Hussein of Iraq was detected did the media begin to pay particular attention to the past activities of Gerald Bull.

The Iranians had reason to fear and hate Saddam Hussein after eight long years of the Gulf War between Iran and Iraq. The Israelis have been constantly threatened by the Iraqi dictator. Both would have reason to seek the elimination of someone promising to deliver a superior weapons system to Saddam.

REPORT FROM GERMANY

Months after the death of Bull we began to hear rumors of a supercannon which he had invented, designed, and was in the process of delivering to Iraq. I picked up a copy of *Der Spiegel*, a German language magazine, when I noted a cover article "Die Wahrheit über Tschernobyl." The cover photos portrayed horrible birth defects that were a result of genetic damage caused by the nuclear disaster in the USSR at Chernobyl. As I scanned the inner contents of the German language publication I came to an article titled, "Irak: Gigantisches Geschütz...(Iraq's Giant Cannon)." It was about the supercannon. The pictures that accompanied the article were startling. There before my eyes was an actual photograph of a slightly smaller prototype model of the cannon, fully set up and operational. The gun has been tested on weapons ranges in the U.S.A., Canada, Barbados, and Iraq.

I do not read German, but with a background of Latin studies, and a natural interest in languages, I am able to laboriously wrestle the primary meaning out of the text. This endeavor is assisted occasionally by the use of a dual language dictionary. The article seized my attention, for if it was accurate it would indicate either that Iraq possesses a superior weapons system or that they narrowly missed getting it. Obviously I needed more information. Where could I possibly find it?

CANADIAN INFORMATION SOURCES

As I was contemplating this my phone rang and a colleague, Grant Jeffrey of Toronto, Ontario, Canada, began to tell me about a monstrous cannon capable of delivering a projectile weighing three thousand pounds, with incredible accuracy over a distance of six hundred kilometers (372 miles). Various articles and reports vary on the specifications of the weapon. This could be due to the fact that various models of the supercannon have been tested. The weapons system was allegedly perfected, delivered, and set up at four locations in Iraq. Grant claimed to have diagrams and specifications on the supercannon. When I called back for more information he had left

This incredible picture of the cannon with a 112-foot barrel is just a prototype of the one(s) made for Iraq. It was tested many times here in Barbados.

GERALD BULL SUPERCANNON. The Bull cannon was not originated as a weapon! It was made to put satellites into space cheaply. Only after Bull was disappointed with Canada and the USA did he seek help from Iraq. It became a weapons system. Originally it was called HARP — High Altitude Research Project.

on a trip to Africa.

The following week Ramona and I flew to Buffalo, New York, rented a car, and drove to Collingwood, Ontario. A gentleman in the village church told me that he had seen information on the weapon in an August, 1990 issue of the *Toronto Star*. The helpful local librarian was most congenial, and assisted me in searching the files of the *Toronto Star*. Eureka! We found it. In the August 18, 1990 edition there is an article, "Saddam and the Canadian Connection." There before our eyes was the Gerald Bull story, along with a diagram and specifications of the supergun.

AMAZING CAPABILITIES OF THE SUPERCANNON

The *Toronto Star* article describes a cannon with a barrel 487 feet long, capable of firing a missile weighing one and a half tons (three thousand pounds) a distance of six hundred kilometers (372 miles). It could deliver, with extreme accuracy, either nuclear warheads, conventional explosives, poison gas, nerve gas, biological weapons, etc.... As I write this I am sitting in the home of my daughter and son-in-law, Neil and Sandy Howell. CNN-TV "Headline News" has just announced (October 5, 1990) that Iraq has yet another "superior weapon." It is a non-nuclear superbomb, which has the destructive force of a small atomic bomb, such as was dropped on Hiroshima and Nagasaki, Japan at the end of World War II. CNN stated that our military experts said that we have no way at present to counteract this device. If the supercannon exists in Iraq it would give them an ideal way to deliver their new superbomb, rapidly and with great accuracy.

ADVANTAGES OF THE SUPERCANNON

The supercannon shoots its missiles at a rate of two or three per minute. Compared with the missile system Iraq presently possesses, the performance of the supercannon is truly awesome. The best missile Iraq has in its arsenal is the Russian Scud-B, notoriously inaccurate and difficult to work with. It takes twenty-four hours to fuel the Scud-B with its required liquid propellant. Our satellites can easily observe the fueling activity and take steps to eliminate the missiles. Once the fuel has been loaded into the Scuds the missile has to be fired almost immediately as the fuel is unstable. If not fired, the fuel is removed and the whole process must be repeated at any future time that they want to use the missile.

On the other hand, the supercannon is ready to fire at a moment's

Gerald Bull's "supergun"

Less than one month after Gerald Bull was murdered, he was linked to hundreds of tonnes of seized equipment believed to be part of a so-called "supergun" destined for Iraq. Below is a look at the trail of seizures and the gun itself.

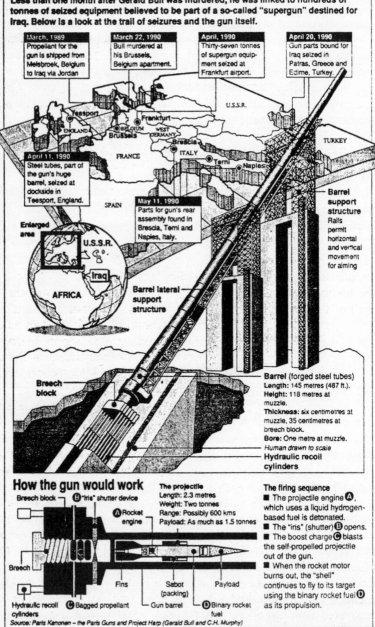

March, 1989
Propellant for the gun is shipped from Melsbroek, Belgium to Iraq via Jordan

March 22, 1990
Bull murdered at his Brussels, Belgium apartment.

April, 1990
Thirty-seven tonnes of supergun equipment seized at Frankfurt airport.

April 20, 1990
Gun parts bound for Iraq seized in Patras, Greece and Edirne, Turkey.

April 11, 1990
Steel tubes, part of the gun's huge barrel, seized at dockside in Teesport, England.

May 11, 1990
Parts for gun's rear assembly found in Brescia, Terni and Naples, Italy.

Enlarged area

U.S.S.R.
Iraq
AFRICA

U.S.S.R.
ENGLAND
Teesport
Frankfurt
BELGIUM
Brussels
WEST GERMANY
FRANCE
Brescia
ITALY
Terni
Naples
SPAIN
TURKEY

Barrel support structure Rails permit horizontal and vertical movement for aiming

Barrel lateral support structure

Breech block

Barrel (forged steel tubes)
Length: 145 metres (487 ft.).
Height: 118 metres at muzzle.
Thickness: six centimetres at muzzle, 35 centimetres at breech block.
Bore: One metre at muzzle.
Human drawn to scale
Hydraulic recoil cylinders

How the gun would work

Breech block
Ⓑ "iris" shutter device
Ⓐ Rocket engine
Breech
Fins
Sabot (packing)
Gun barrel
Payload
Ⓓ Binary rocket fuel
Hydraulic recoil cylinders
Ⓒ Bagged propellant

The projectile
Length: 2.3 metres
Weight: Two tonnes
Range: Possibly 600 kms
Payload: As much as 1.5 tonnes

The firing sequence
■ The projectile engine Ⓐ, which uses a liquid hydrogen-based fuel is detonated.
■ The "iris" (shutter) Ⓑ opens.
■ The boost charge Ⓒ blasts the self-propelled projectile out of the gun.
■ When the rocket motor burns out, the "shell" continues to fly to its target using the binary rocket fuel Ⓓ as its propulsion.

Source: Paris Kanonen – the Paris Guns and Project Harp (Gerald Bull and C.H. Murphy)

TREVOR JOHNSTON/Southam News Graphics

340

notice. The cost factor of firing off a multi-million dollar missile as opposed to firing off a projectile and retaining the means of delivery at your ground base (as with the supercannon) demonstrates further the desirability of the new weapon.

Gerald Bull has long been regarded as one of the world's most brilliant weapons developers. He is the inventor of the 155mm cannon, a heavy-duty weapon that is almost universally used by the armed forces of the world. This is only one of his many accomplishments. After a number of disappointing experiences in negotiating with the military leaders of the U.S.A. and Canada, Bull moved his home and base of operations to Brussels, Belgium. Was it there he got involved in international arms deals? What chain of events led to his tragic assassination on March 22, 1990?

DID THEY GET IT ALL?

The *Toronto Star* said, "Less than one month after Gerald Bull was murdered, he was linked to hundreds of tons of seized equipment believed to be part of a so-called 'supergun' destined for Iraq." The *Toronto Star* outlined the facts as follows: "In March, 1989 propellant for the gun was shipped from Meisbroek, Belgium to Iraq. In April of 1990 thirty-seven tons of supercannon equipment was seized at the airport of Frankfurt, Germany. On April 11, 1990 steel tubes, part of the gun's huge barrel were seized at dockside in Teasport, England. April 20 saw gun parts bound for Iraq seized in Patras, Greece and Edima, Turkey. On May 11, 1990 parts for the gun's rear assembly were found in Brescia, Temi and Naples, Italy."

The *Toronto Star* gave the following specifications on the supercannon. The barrel of forged steel tubes measures 145 meters (487 feet). The height at the muzzle is 118 meters. Thickness of the barrel measures six centimeters at the muzzle, thirty-five centimeters at the breach block. The bore is one meter (about thirty-nine inches). Therefore the cannon shoots a "bullet" over three feet in diameter! The *Toronto Star* diagram of the cannon indicated that it would fire a payload of 1.5 tons (three thousand pounds) a distance of six hundred kilometers (372 miles). However, information we have recently read, after getting a full translation of the *Der Spiegel* article done by two ladies in St. Catherines, Ontario, Canada, shows that by a modification of the system the payload is vastly increased and the range extended to one thousand kilometers (620 miles). Publications we discovered later even say that the gun could launch a missile that would travel three thousand miles. The missile-projectile would have its own source of power to attain such distances. It does seem a bit fantastic and perhaps is an exaggeration. This cannon could also put small satellites in orbit around the earth.

FRENCH OPINION: SADDAM A MEGALOMANIAC!

The French magazine *L'Express* in its cover article for September 14, 1990, described Saddam Hussein as a megalomaniac. The supercannon was described as something out of science fiction, like the writings of Jules Verne! But it is real! "Emporté par sa boulimie mégalomaniaque, Saddam est prêt à acheter tout et n'importe quoi. Jusqu' à un projet, digne de Jules Verne, de canon géant de 120 mètres de longueur, capable, selon son concepteur, l'ingénieur canadien Gerald Bull, de satelliser de petites charges en orbite basse. Une invention extravagante, que l'armée améericaine avait rejetée dans les années 60, après expérimentation. Seule la mort mystérieuse de Bull, en mars dernier, mettra un point final à l'entreprise" (*L'Express,* 14 September, 1990, p. 15).

Grant Jeffrey got back from Africa. I talked to him about the Bull cannon again. I pressed him for details on his claim that four of the weapons were in place and operational in Iraq. He said that his Canadian intelligence sources are impeccable and that he stands by his assertion. He is satisfied with the accuracy of these reports, but I confess that I am still desirous of getting closer to primary sources of information. I must hold that the existence of operational supercannons in Iraq is still speculative.

INFORMATION FROM DALLAS

Today Neal Howell, a television producer in Dallas, told me that he recently saw a CNN report on the supercannon. He recalls that CNN indicated that the weapon system was fully constructed and in place in Iraq. That is as much as I can tell you. After I get back from my next trip to the Middle East I may have more information for you. (Read all late updates on information in this book in our quarterly publication *Prophecy 2000 Digest*—sent free upon request. See the coupon in the back of this book.)

Here is another late report. I saw on today's news that Iraq has announced that they have the means of delivering a missile "hundreds of miles" with accuracy. They could be talking about the supercannon.

Iraq's sources of high-tech material for the weapon may be cut off in some places in Europe, but with such countries as Brazil helping Iraq develop a wide range of weapon systems, it is conceivable that they may have gotten parts needed to complete the cannons from alternate sources.

THE THREAT TO AMERICA

The Pentagon is taking this threat seriously. The reason we have not attacked Iraq at this juncture is probably because our experts think that we cannot quickly win the war, if indeed it could be won at all. I do not mean that we could not damage Saddam Hussein badly, but short of using nuclear weapons, which I think we will not do, we will be engaging in an exercise of war that will bog us down in the region for years to come.

The Muhajadin guerrilla forces in Afghanistan wore down the Soviets and became a prime cause of the breakup of the Red Empire. After years of war the Russians had to withdraw in defeat and disgrace (like Vietnam for us). The Iraqis showed their determination in their lost cause war against Iran. They held out for eight long, grinding years of savagery, which cost the lives of over a million victims.

Iraq could become our Afghanistan. After our losses in the no win wars in Korea and Vietnam we probably could not stand a ten-year war in the Gulf region. Already crippled economically, our government bankrupt and in uncontrolled debt, with radicals waiting to march again in the streets protesting Washington's foreign involvement, it is not hard to see an Iraq war as a time of humiliation and ultimate defeat for the United States of America.

POSTSCRIPT

Here is a final postscript on the supercannon. Last week Neil Howell did a computer search of fifteen hundred publications for Gerald Bull information. Also Neil and I spent a day in the Dallas Public Library where we were assisted in a computer data search for this information. From these two searches we located nine more articles in *The Los Angeles Times, The Wall Street Journal, U. S. News and World Report, The New York Times, The Akron Beacon Journal* (AP dateline, London), *The Philadelphia Inquirer,* and the *Canadian MacLeans Magazine.* We also discovered that a book, *The Paris Guns* is in existence, although we do not have a copy as yet. We are having a search conducted for a copy of the book co-authored by Bull and Gerald Murphy, a U.S. ballistics expert who now works at the army's laboratory at Aberdeen, Maryland.

At first we wondered at the diverse descriptions of Bull's guns. Then we realized that a number of different experimental models have been put together and tested in various places, all of them having different specs and capabilities. At a later time we may give you a further update on this matter, especially if our research indicates that Iraq has the supercannon system operational. One of these guns was used to put a projectile into space, 112 miles above the earth. This experiment is reported to have been conducted on the island nation of Barbados in the Caribbean. We recall that *Der Spiegel* magazine (Germany) included a photograph of the supergun taken in Barbados. Some think that South Africa may have the weapon system, for at any rate Gerald Bull's company sold multi-millions of dollars' worth of weapons and ammunition to South Africa.

BARBADOS — Many bunkers and storage rooms inside the mountain behind the supercannon are filled with incredibly expensive high-tech equipment and instruments, all a part of the HARP supercannon project. It is now useless junk. We wonder which nation will pick up the technology and build the next generation of supercannons.

23

Israel's Temple Mount, The Dead Sea, and Intefida

The Intefida, the Palestinian Arab uprising against the State of Israel has been troubling the region for over two years.

What does Israel's Dead Sea have to do with her current troubles? If a certain man is right about certain things, then the answer is, "Far more than you would ever expect!"

Early in November of 1987 we sat entranced as Shlomo Drori, a man of vision and great dreams for Israel's future, told of a most amazing international scheme to bring peace to Israel and her neighbors.

Mr. Drori is the head of the information department of the Dead Sea Works, and is probably the best informed man in the world relative to the Dead Sea, its needs, its potential, and its wealth. Many times in the past we have visited with this great teacher and have profited from it each time. On several occasions we did television programs with him for our program on the PTL satellite network.

Long ago Drori called our attention to the fact that the water of the Dead Sea is getting dangerously low. This has to be corrected to protect the balance, evaporation rate, chemical content, and beneficence of the salt sea of Israel. The Dead Sea contains minerals vital for industry and agriculture. There is enough of eleven vital minerals to supply the needs of the world for thousands of years to come.

Also, solar pond technology for the harnessing of the sun's rays to produce electrical energy is being developed in a joint project linked to a similar U.S. operation at California's Salton Sea. There is nothing exactly like this development at any other place in the world. The harnessing of solar power to produce cheap energy further opens the door to inexpensive methods of desalinating sea water to be used for agricultural irrigation purposes. Link together the production of bromines and potash (for fertilizer) with cheap water supply and you have solved the famine problems of vast areas of desert land that can now be transformed into a bountiful paradise, just as Israel has converted vast areas of her deserts to productive land.

When we first met Shlomo Drori he was telling us about the plan to build a canal from the Mediterranean to the Dead Sea. A flow of water controlled by a series of locks would provide hydroelectric power as it makes its descent from sea level to the lowest spot on earth. It would, by the year 2005, bring the Dead Sea level back to normal without disturbing its chemical balance.

SECRET TALKS

In November, 1987, however, Drori was literally enthused about a new prospect. Israel had sacrificed the plan for the Dead-Med Canal because the money was needed for defense. But a new, secret plan had been developed. Instead of a canal from the Mediterranean Sea there would be a canal built from the Red Sea to the Dead Sea with the same results. This canal would lie along the border between Jordan and Israel. The World Bank had already secretly agreed to supply the funds for it, with one provision. The canal must be a joint project between Jordan and Israel, and this would necessitate a peace treaty between the two nations. Drori said that undeclared talks were taking place between Jordanian and Israeli leaders to this end. The harnessing of the Dead Sea in such a joint project would bless both nations and the whole region beyond imagination.

SHATTERED DREAMS

These hopeful visions were dashed to the earth when the Palestinian Intefida (uprising) started shortly after we met with Drori in the late Fall of 1987. How can this be linked to the Dead Sea Canal plan? Very simply: Learning of the plan, the leaders of the PLO realized that if there was a treaty between Israel and Jordan they would effectively be put out of business. This could not be tolerated. The

Intefida was the answer. Very little happens in the Middle East that is not carefully plotted and programmed in advance.

RECENT TROUBLE ON THE TEMPLE MOUNTAIN, JERUSALEM

During the Feast of Tabernacles (Succoth) hundreds of worshipers, Jewish and Christian, had gathered for prayers at the Western Wall of the Temple Mount in Old Jerusalem. Suddenly, a hail of lethal rocks poured down from the top of the wall about a hundred feet above them. The security police (about forty-five were in the area when it began) responded. At first, the security police used only rubber bullets (shooting in the air) and tear gas. As the lethal rocks continued to rain down on them they then began firing real bullets. Twenty-one Arabs were killed and more injured. This is what the news media reported. What is wrong with this picture? It is a classic example of media dissembling. The secular media is great at selective reporting, just telling part of the story, picking out the parts that suit their manipulative self importance. The media will not simply report the news, they will create it! They will shape the flow of history! Delusions of messianic grandeur!

Now that the United Nations Security Council has condemned Israel again, and now that the United States administration has further distanced itself from our Israeli allies the true picture may slowly leak out and come together.

A CORNERSTONE FOR THE TEMPLE

It is true that a small group of Orthodox Jewish people wanted to carry a cornerstone somewhere into the temple area, but they were not allowed to place it on Mount Moriah and lay a claim for a future temple to be built there. We accept, according to the Bible, that this inevitably will be done. These people were not representative of ninety-eight percent of the worshipers gathered there, many of whom would say that the act of laying a cornerstone now was bad timing.

Gershon Solomon's Temple Mountain Faithful group tries to get the stone in place every year during the Feast of Tabernacles (Succoth). The Israeli police always turn them back as soon as they get inside the dung gate and they drag the stone back to the pool of Siloam. That is what happened again this year. They never got near the mountain. Only about thirty or forty people participated. Few of the thousands of worshippers in the Wailing Wall plaza even knew of the action. The Palestinian organizers of the demonstration very well knew of these circumstances from the past years performances. They knew that the stone would never make it to the mountain. To blame the incident on the bearers of the stone is ludicrous.

The stone throwing was no spontaneous, spur-of-the-moment act. It was a carefully planned act of war against Israel. Hamas, a Palestinian terrorist organization, has boldly claimed credit for planning and carrying out the operation. The purpose was to get attention back from the Gulf Crisis to the Palestinian Homeland question.

THE TEMPLE MOUNT—TAKE A GOOD LOOK AT WHERE YOU STAND

Let's go to the top of the Temple Mountain. The rectangular platform is thirty-five acres in area. The Dome of the Rock and the El Aqsa Mosque are prominent features of the Haram Es Sharif, or "most noble sanctuary" as the Moslems call Mount Moriah, the Temple Mountain. (The Dome is a shrine not a mosque, and it is not "the Mosque of Omar," as ill-informed television reporters so frequently mislabel it.)

Now that we are on top of the Temple Mountain (Moriah) look about you carefully. Look at the beautiful, firmly set paving stones that cover the area. How many loose stones do you see? None, or almost none. Now, since it was from here at the top of the mountain that the demonstrators stood to hurl their stones on the worshipers below, we wonder, WHERE DID ALL THOSE ROCKS COME FROM? They were previously prepositioned!

Having just received an overseas telephone report from Tom Brimmer, a Christian minister who lives in Meveserit, suburb to Jerusalem, we can share some interesting information with you. Tom has interviewed a number of eye witnesses who were at the Wailing Wall at the time of the incident. The demonstrators had huge piles of thousands of rocks to hurl. They had been busy for some time carrying them up in sacks, wheelbarrows (looking like construction materials), boxes, and knapsacks. The signal was given and the terror began for the unsuspecting people at prayer below. Many were severely injured.

LIVE BULLETS—DEADLY FIRE

Eye witnesses, in speaking to Reverend Brimmer, claim that the security police initially responded with great restraint. They at-

---

348

tempted to negotiate with the rioters. Then they used loudspeakers to plead with them to cease their violent attack. Nothing was achieved. Next, they fired into the air and used tear gas. This did not stop the frenzied furor of the attackers. Finally, with his men in peril of their own lives and the worshipers being brutalized, the leader of the Israel police gave orders to use live ammunition. Twenty-one Palestinians died. Had it been wanton slaughter on the part of the Israelis hundreds would have been killed. We remember when a political demonstration in Hama, Syria was broken up by the armed forces. Twenty thousand Syrians were killed by their own brothers in two days time.

A rock can be as deadly as a bullet. I know, for as an eleven-year-old boy living in Britton, South Dakota, my friends and I got into a fight with a lot of other boys. Rocks were thrown and I got hit in the head. I was carried to the local hospital bleeding profusely. The doctor said that I was fortunate not to be blind or dead. I would have been if the rock had hit me from a slightly different angle.

Throughout early history more people were killed by rocks than almost any other weapon. The lethal quality of hurled stones is well attested from the dawn of history until the invention of modern weapons.

RELIABLE LOCAL EYE WITNESS

Mr. Jack Cole is a local resident here who is both a dear personal friend and a charter member of our Springfield Regional Eschatology Club. Jack is a highly-respected local business man, member of the Springfield Symphony Orchestra, active in religious and political community affairs. His witness to the recent events is valuable because he too was at the Western Wall by the Temple Mountain when the incident occurred.

Mr. Cole told us that the police negotiated, pleaded, and used non-lethal force to persuade the rioters to stop. It is a fact that this went on for two hours before they finally used live ammunition. Bob and Ramona Dicks from Branson, Missouri, were in Jerusalem at the time of the incident. They add the interesting note that among the forty-five police who killed the Arab rioters were uniformed Arab policemen who are authorized to provide security on the Temple Mountain. It appears that the police were responsible people doing their job of providing security for all the people who were under attack.

SIX DISTRESSING RESULTS OF THE INCIDENT

Israel's enemies, with whom she has been at war since 1948, achieved six things in the recent Temple Mountain incident.

1. The Intefida, eclipsed by the Gulf Crisis, is again on front burner of world attention.
2. Israel has again been condemned by the Gentile nations in the U.N..
3. Worse, the United States joined in the condemnation.
4. Still worse, Christian support of Israel is eroded. Christians sometimes foolishly take the lying media's words at face value.
5. It is easier now to be openly anti-Semitic.
6. It is easier for Iraq's withdrawal from Kuwait to be linked with a demand that Israel withdraw from the West Bank (biblical Judea and Samaria), the Golan Heights, and the Gaza Strip.

U.N. OBSERVERS FOR ISRAEL AND THE U.S.A.

I wish to further address the matter of point six, above. There is a hypocritical double standard manifested when the United States condemns Israel for her internal security control. When the riots in the Watts district of Los Angeles took place we hurled the local police and the National Guard into the area. Many black Americans were killed in that action. The mayor of Philadelphia ordered the bombing of a residence suspected of drug activity. Force is constantly used to control rioters and those who disturb the peace. If the hooligans come into your neighborhood and start stoning you and your family you would want the police to stop them, and if necessary shoot them dead.

We should allow a United Nations team of observers and peace keepers to enter California to keep the peace. A U. N. team should be rushed to the war zones of North Philadelphia and New York where violence and racism are rampant.

Israel should give up the West Bank when Texas is returned to Mexico and when all who are not of native American ancestry retreat to the area of the original thirteen colonies, behind an internationally recognized "green line." Jerusalem should be taken away from Israel when Washington, DC (murder capitol of America) becomes an internationalized city under United Nations control and supervision.

Foreigners of European and African descent will be allowed to remain in the area of the thirteen original colonies, but even that will have to be negotiated in the future.

OH, CANADA!

Canada must immediately accept a U.N. peacekeeping team of observers at Oka, Quebec because of their harassment and mistreatment of the native North Americans who only want to repossess the land that belonged to their ancestors and is rightfully theirs. Today Quebec, tomorrow all of Canada. (Not very likely.) All foreign Canadians must return to England, France, Yugoslavia, Pakistan, Africa, Arabia, and India. The Dukabors should return to Russia.

When these things have been accomplished the United States and Canada will have some authority to advise Israel on the West Bank and Jerusalem. Not before.

Crowd of worshippers at the wailing wall taken just before the rocks began to fall. Cement blocks and chunks of iron were also hurled down on the people. (Photo by Steven Schnipper)

Is this the cornerstone of the temple? Gershon Solomon and the Temple Mountain Faithful believe that it is or could be.

Gershon Solomon (center). The press crowds in around Gershon. One person shouted, "Would you use violence to get your cornerstone on the mountain?" Solomon replied, "Never. When it is God's time I will be ready and in place if He wants my stone. My job is to be ready. But not with violence." This answer displeased the reporter who had hoped to trip Solomon up.

24

Baghdad, Bush & Babylon—Between Iraq and a Hard Place

And he cried mightily with a strong voice saying, Babylon the great is fallen, is fallen and is become the habitation of devils. (Rev 18:2).

Iraqi President Saddam Hussein's nation occupies the territory of the ancient Chaldean empire of Babylon. This modern Belshazzar of Baghdad has demonstrated his disregard for human life by his callous use of poison gas against Iranians and against his own Kurdistani population. Whole villages of Iraqis have been murdered in cold blood by the use of these dreaded chemical weapons.

Hussein's forces started the Persian Gulf War by invading Iran, and waging a grinding eight-year-long offensive which cost the lives of over a million victims. Now the bully of Baghdad has further manifested his Hitler-like designs by invading his defenseless neighbor, tiny, oil-rich, Kuwait. Kuwait is awash with oil and has, until now, enjoyed the resultant affluence. But now that small Arab nation is in shambles, her Emir in exile, her people trembling in fear and virtual slavery.

JIHAD — "HOLY" WAR

The *Dallas Times Herald* reported that Saddam Hussein has declared that his military action against Kuwait is actually a "Holy war on the United States." He has proclaimed it to be a Moslem Jihad against the West. But his incredible and cruel actions are anything but holy in any sense of the word. Saddam has hurled scurrilous accusations against United States President George Bush, repeatedly calling him a liar. His invectives include such graphic verbal attacks as, "We will pluck out the eyes of those who attack the Arab nation."

DREAMS OF EMPIRE

Reference to the "Arab nation" means more than might meet the eye. Hussein dreams of not only controlling the oil riches of the Middle East, but of ruling over a new Pan-Arab nation comprised of all Arab countries. His recent actions are interpreted as being a first step toward the realization of that fantastic dream.

It does not seem fantastic at all to a man who believes that he is a direct descendant of the prophet Mohammed, founder of the Islamic faith of all Moslem believers. Indeed, he may envision himself as being a fulfillment of the Moslem hope for the Imam Mahdi. This refers to the Moslem version of the Messiah.

"Husseins face appears on Baghdad billboards as both Saladin and King Nebuchadnezzar" (*National Review*, p. 8, September 3, 1990). Please take careful note of the fact that Babylonian King Nebuchadnezzar was the conqueror of Israel and removed the Jews from the Holy Land about six centuries before Christ. Saladin was the Arab conqueror who battled the Christian Crusaders who had established a kingdom in the Holy Land during the Middle Ages. Saladin was the one who defeated and largely drove the Christians out of Israel. Hussein reveals himself as the enemy of both Christians and Jews. He would like to defeat Israel and her allies in the "Christian" West. It is Hussein himself who chose the images of Saladin and Nebuchadnezzar as powerful symbols to characterize himself and his plans.

IF THE U.S.A. ATTACKS IRAQ

If the United States enters into direct military confrontation against Iraq there is little doubt that the U.S.A. could smash Iraq into submission, depose Saddam Hussein and, then—what? Strange as it may seem, many analysts think that President Bush may also be scheming the formation of a Pan-Arab Republic, headed up by Hosni Mubarak, President of Egypt, Hafez Assad of Syria, or less likely, King Hussein of Jordan. The exclusion of Israel from the current U.S. action in the Middle East might be a strong indication that the Bush administration would like to do away with the popular idea that "Israel is our one reliable democratic ally" in the region. President Bush may envision himself as a sort of modern diplomatic Lawrence of Arabia.

AMAZING PROPHECY

No Pan-Arab union is likely to hold together for long. The Arabs have a history of fighting among themselves from time immemorial. That sad scenario is not going to change until the Lord Jesus reigns on earth and Isaiah's prophecy of Israeli-Arab unity is fulfilled. It must have taken an incredible faith for Isaiah to pen the words:

> In that day shall there be a highway out of Egypt to Assyria [Iraq], and the Assyrian [Iraqi] shall come into Egypt, and the Egyptian into Assyria [Iraq], and the Egyptians shall serve with the Assyrians [Iraqis]. In that day shall Israel be the third [in partnership] with Egypt and with Assyria [Iraq], even a blessing in the midst of the land: Whom the LORD of hosts shall bless, saying, Blessed be Egypt my people, and Assyria [Iraq] the work of my hands, and Israel mine inheritance (Isa. 19:23-25).

It takes faith today to believe that a partnership will ultimately be formed between Egypt, Iraq, and Israel. But we nevertheless do believe that the Lord Jesus will effect just such blessed beneficence upon all mankind in the millennial reign.

BELSHAZZAR'S BARBARIANS

Saddam Hussein's battle-hardened troops have manifested a barbarity that has shocked the world. They have, by all reports, behaved more like a band of hoodlums than an invading army. *Time Magazine* reported widespread raping of women and children. Various newspapers and news magazines have portrayed greed driven soldiers breaking into homes, ransacking valuables, and abusing families. Stores are looted everywhere. Jewelry stores were a favorite target, although nothing has been spared. All medical and most food supplies were appropriated for the foreign invaders. Patients in hospital beds were thrown out to make room for Iraqi soldiers. Auto dealerships were looted and the stolen cars driven back to Iraq. Mercedes Benz dealerships were among the favorite targets. Horror stories of the brutal beating, torture, rape, and murder of innocent civilians flow out to us in a steady stream. Women and children not involved in any military action have been raped, beaten, and brutalized beyond belief.

How calloused is Saddam Hussein who gathered British and other foreign hostages about him for a television propaganda ploy, manifesting a hypocritical friendliness and concern for children and their mothers who were plainly terrified? Hussein used these tactics to broadcast fear to the families of these prisoners of his cruelty. It was a not-so-subtle threat as to what would happen to these innocents if the West did not back off in its resistance against him. His placing of foreign civilians around strategic military installations and power plants was plainly to use them as a defense shield against Western military attack. If America attacks the defense positions she would have to kill her own citizens to do so.

All eyes are on the Middle East today. Here is the cockpit of the world. Here destinies are being shaped that will impact the entire planet. Step by step we are moving toward Armageddon. Nothing that happens in this area of the world is without significance. However, there are a lot of things which will transpire before the Armageddon battle. Here is an outline of some end-time prophetic events.

OUTLINE OF THINGS TO COME

1. Wars and rumors of wars will continue. Worldwide peace efforts will be offset by continued disturbance and unrest.
2. Continued movement toward European Unity and a revived Roman Empire.
3. The rapture of the Church.
4. Antichrist manifested as ruler of a ten-nation federation, probably mostly in Europe, although this is not completely clear.
5. Antichrist, having deluded the Gentiles, now forces Israel into an ill-advised covenant of seven years. Signing of this covenant marks the beginning of the seven years tribulation. This is the only event that fixes the time parameters of the tribulation. See Daniel 9:24-27 (70 Weeks Vision).

6. Antichrist rules over a part of the world for three and a half years.

7. The Battle of Gog and Magog (Ezekiel 38,39). Russia invades Israel, accompanied by selected (some Arab) allies. Some Arab nations along with western nations represented by Tarshish protest the Russian action. Russia is defeated by God's direct intervention.

8. Emboldened by the final collapse of the Soviet Empire the Antichrist extends his reign worldwide. It is a shaky coalition put together with the consent of the nations. Antichrist rules worldwide, but his power is never as absolute as some have pictured it to be. There are sporadic uprisings against the Antichrist.

9. Finally with the Antichrist's troops, and representative armies from all nations, gathered in the Middle East, and with a massive army moving in from Asia the battle lines for Armageddon (Revelation 16, etc.) are drawn.

10. Jesus Christ comes back with the raptured Church in His entourage (Rev. 19). Jesus defeats the Antichrist. Israel is restored. The nations are judged. The thousand-year millennium begins.

For an exhaustive and reliable study of these events please read *Things To Come* by Dr. J. Dwight Pentecost.

A NO-WIN SITUATION FOR THE U.S.A.

The intervention of the U.S.A. will brand our nation as the neighborhood bully, all because we came to the aid of Kuwait and Saudi Arabia. Saddam Hussein is already being pictured as the victim. We are accused of being guilty of "overreaction." Iraq's ambassador appeared on American television and brazenly condemned our nation's leadership, saying that all Iraq ever wanted was peace. What a farce! If all Hussein wanted was peace, why did he invade Iran and conduct an eight-year war? Why did he invade Kuwait and threaten Saudi Arabia? Why does he continually threaten tiny Israel? Why does he support the PLO and other terrorists?

Even those Arab nations currently standing with us may turn against us if the U.S. presence in the region is prolonged. They will simply get tired of us, and after all "Saddam is still our cousin. Maybe we misunderstood him. After all, Arab unity is more important than ties to the decadent West. Anyway, look how America befriends our enemy the Zionist State of Israel!" How easily perspectives can change. Let me give you a recent illustration of this.

In 1982 Israel invaded South Lebanon to save the Christian community which was threatened with extinction. Do you remember how the Arab people greeted the Israeli army as liberators? There was dancing in the streets. Lebanese Arab people pressed gifts of flowers, rice, and candy on the Israeli's. However, when the U.S. State Department pressured Israeli General Ariel Sharon to stop driving the PLO out of Beruit the fortunes of the war reversed. Lebanon could have been set free at that time and reestablished her sovereignty, but bad judgment on this side of the Atlantic killed that possibility. I testified to this upon request of the U.S. Senate, before the Senate Committee on Foreign Affairs. We saw the further destruction of Lebanon, the PLO momentarily fighting within it own ranks, and the horrible debacle of the blowing up of our Marine base in Lebanon, with the tragic death of over two hundred American Marines. The hopes the Israeli invasion as a liberating force had brought to Lebanon turned to ashes.

Now there is little sympathy for the U.S.A. or Israel in Lebanon, with the exception of the extreme south of the country, where Israel still protects the Christian population.

In like fashion, as most of the Lebanese turned against the Israelis, if we are forced to maintain our armies in the Persian Gulf area for a long time, sentiment could turn against us.

ARABIAN AFGHANISTAN?

As we examine several possible scenarios please also consider that the Arabian Peninsula could be the United States' Afghanistan, especially if it does come to open conflict and fighting. Add to this the problems we will face if our forces have to stay in the region for a long period of time. It would resemble a tragic rerun of Vietnam.

Watch for the American radicals to march in the streets, throw blood on the door of the Pentagon, and burn the American flag just like they did during the Vietnam debacle.

Just like Afghanistan was the first domino to fall for the Soviets, in the chain of events that crumbled the Soviet Empire, even so events in the Arabian Peninsula could mark the death knell of the United States as a major world power.

With Europe flexing its muscles, with the upcoming 1992 European Economic treaty, with Europe's hope of central political authority being persued fervently, we behold the specter of the Roman Empire coming back to life again. Europe will eventually become the major power factor in the world of nations in the end times.

WORLD GOVERNMENT—WHO WILL ESTABLISH IT?

At some future point a global government will seem to most politicians to be the only hope left for world peace. Then a cunning man of incredible evil, the Antichrist, the son of perdition will emerge on the world stage. He will look like the answer to the dilemma of the ages. His new peace proposals will look attractive to this war weary world. Daniel, by Divine inspiration sees beyond the Antichrist's facade and proclaims, "And through his policy also he shall cause craft to prosper in his hand; and he [Antichrist] shall magnify himself in his heart, and by peace shall destroy many: he shall also stand up against the Prince of princes; but he shall be broken without hand" (Dan. 8:25). Antichrist will bring an era of false peace and prosperity, but it will not last!

Fortunately the reign of the beast is of short duration. Mankind's extremity will demand the intervention of the Almighty. Jesus Christ will return to earth again and when His marvelous work is undertaken there will dawn a visible manifestation of the eternal kingdom of God on this planet earth. The Millennium will begin. Many Bible passages extol the glories of the manifested kingdom of God on earth but none more exquisitely than the prophet Isaiah:

"For thou hast broken the yoke of his [Antichrist] burden, and the staff of his shoulder, the rod of his oppressor, as in the day of Midian. For every battle of the warrior is with confused noise, and garments rolled in blood; but this shall be with burning and fuel of fire [Armageddon]. For unto us a child is born, unto us a son is given: and the government shall be upon his shoulder: and his name shall be called Wonderful, Counsellor, The mighty God, The everlasting Father, The Prince of Peace. [Messianic prophecy concerning Jesus Christ]. Of the increase of his government and peace [there shall be no end,] upon the throne of David, and upon his kingdom, to order it, and to establish it with judgment and with justice from henceforth even forever. The zeal of the LORD of hosts will perform this" (Isa. 9:4-8). Note: The thousand-year Millennium is only one manifestation of the Eternal kingdom of God.

Jesus will preside over the only workable world government this world will ever see. God haste the day of His coming!

WILL THERE BE A WAR?

Will Saddam Hussein risk confrontation with the forces being rallied against him? Given the man's delusions of grandeur, that is certainly a possibility. Many military analysts believe that either he will invade the land of Saudi King Faud or some other scenario will draw U.S. forces into conflict with Iraq. If this happens we may be in the region for a long time to come. Other military experts doubt if he will be so foolhardy as to risk total loss by going to war against the U.S.A. They believe he will back down and withdraw from Kuwait, hoping that we will then remove ourselves from Saudi Arabia.

Suppose Hussein decides to retreat for the time being. Will he submit to our dominance of the region? Not likely. Unless he loses such credibility that his own people overthrow him, he will simply bide his time, work on the production of nuclear weapons, missile delivery systems, and poison gas production. Above all his diabolically demented, though brilliant mind will weave a pattern for his next move toward the fulfilling of his destiny.

SUPERCOMPUTERS—THE BRAZIL/IRAQ CONNECTION

The New York Times (July 29, 1990) reported that U.S. technology may help arm Iraq with nuclear weapons. Senior officials in the Commerce Department and the U.S. State Department have been working to clear the way for I.B.M. Corporation to sell highly sophisticated supercomputers to Brazil. The deal has been opposed by the Arms Control and Disarmament Agency and by the Energy Department. Brazil has direct military ties to Iraq and shares technology with Hussein's community of scientists. Remember, Iraq was so close to having the bomb that Israel felt forced to bomb the Iraqi atomic reactor at Osirak, near Baghdad a few years ago (1981).

A Brazilian newspaper report confirmed by U.S. officials reveals that a Brazilian team has been training Iraqis in rocket aerodynamics, and other high-tech military matters. The Brazilian team headed up by General Hugo Piva has been in Iraq at least since the Spring of 1989. This explains how Iraq was able to launch a space rocket big enough to orbit satellites in December, 1989. General Piva has been in charge of another project in Iraq designed to secretly make nuclear weapons material by a special process of uranium enrichment.

The I.B.M. supercomputer would be just what they would need to finish production of atomic bombs, perfect a guidance system for the normally unreliable Russian Scud missiles, and to perfect a surveillance system which would allow the Iraqis to detect incoming aircraft or missiles. A German magazine, *Der Spiegel* reported that Iraq has purchased a machine for making gas centrifuges from a German firm. These gas centrifuges are necessary for the process they hope to perfect for the enriching of uranium and making nuclear weapons material. *Der Spiegel* reports a "dense network of relations between nuclear bomb builders in Iraq and Brazil, on one hand, and German contractors on the other."

REBUILDING OF BABYLON

The name Babylon appears 286 times in the Bible, thirteen of those occurrences being in the New Testament. Careful examination of both the Old and New Testament indicate that there will most likely be a rebuilding of the ancient city of Babylon in the end days. The Old Testament prophetic warnings of judgment on wicked Babylon would then find their final fulfillment in a time that yet lies ahead of us.

There was an interesting comment on the rebuilding of the city of Babylon in the August 25, 1990 international edition of the *Jerusalem Post*.

According to [their] ideology...the purported descent of Iraqis from the peoples of ancient Mesopotamia makes them superior to other Arabs. In this context, Israel and the Jews have on occasion offered Saddam a useful link between the Babylonian past and that most salient of Pan-Arab issues, the Palestinian question.

Thus Saddam declared after the 1978 Camp David Accords that Egypt's agreement with Israel was proof that Iraqis had been "chosen yet another time as were their forefathers, the Babylonians and Assyrians to defend the honor of the nation and of usurped Palestine."

The reference to an ancient usurped Palestine drew upon a myth crafted by the regime that Nebuchadnezzar and other forefathers' of present-day Iraqis had exiled the Jews from

361

Palestine and that modern-day Iraqis are chosen for the same mission....

Simon Henderson a journalist for the *Financial Times* who is writing a biography of the Iraqi leader, believes that Saddam's efforts to rebuild Babylon and hark back to the ancient Mesopotamian civilizations demonstrate that he does in fact accord importance to his place in history. "Saddam wants to be more than just the man of the year for 1990," Henderson said. [The *Jerusalem Post* referred to the views of Amatzia Bar Am, Haifa University Historian indicating that]:

He [Bar Am] strongly doubted whether even a desperate Saddam would use chemical weapons aginst Israel: That would be inviting doomsday and his idea, if desperate, would not be to destroy Iraq....He cares about his place in history, but he cares more about his place among the living.

Of the thirteen "Babylon" references in the New Testament six are in the Book of Revelation. These especially reflect the possibility that literal Babylon on the Euphrates may be rebuilt.

Further research could be done on "Assyria and The Assyrian" in the Bible inasmuch as the Assyrian Empire preceded and was conquered by the Babylonians. Therefore both ancient Assyria and Babylon link to modern day Iraq!

We are not in agreement with the new and novel theory that Saddam Hussein is the beast of Revelation. Some of our over-zealous colleagues are quick to brand any malevolent personality with a high profile as the very Antichrist of the end days. That Saddam Hussein is an antichrist there is not a doubt, but we do not believe that he is the prophesied "man of sin, son of perdition."

The Bible plainly declares that there will be many forerunners of the final Antichrist: "Little children, it is the last time [final era]: and as ye have heard that antichrist [the beast, the final one] shall come, even now are there many antichrists; whereby we know that it is the last time [final era]" (1 John 2:18).

NOTE: Chapter 24 was written before the Gulf War. Chapter 25 was written during the war, and the following chapters were written after the war.

25

WAR!
Desert Storm

A fateful day it was, when on the second of August, 1990 the blood red beast of war came forth from his ancient Babylonian lair and thrust again the horror of armed conflict upon our already battered world.

Iraq's cruel attack on Kuwait was clearly a case of premeditated aggression and was in violation of all standards of conduct known to man. Behind the Iraqi action we see the cause — the unbridled violence and greed of one person, Saddam Hussein.

SADDAM'S AMBITIOUS GOALS

Saddam's goals reached far beyond Kuwait. As long as he survives they will continue to burn deep within his heart. Were it not for the bold intervention of U.S. President George Bush, Iraq would have quickly conquered Saudi Arabia. The ultimate goal of Iraq's modern Belshazzar was to forge a united Arab empire with himself at the head of it. He has not changed his utmost intention, although if U.S. leaders have their way his days are numbered.

But Saddam is simply waiting, rebuilding, dreaming for another tomorrow, another lunge into his ill conceived destiny. As long as he lives Saddam will liken himself to Nebuchadnezzar, ruler of ancient

Babylon. I prefer to liken him to Belshazzar, for like Belshazzar, successor to Nebuchadnezzar, he is doomed. The handwriting is on the wall: "Mene, Mene, Tekel, Upharsin . . . God hath numbered thy kingdom and finished it . . . Thou are weighed in the balances, and art found wanting . . . Your kingdom is divided . . ." (Dan. 5:25-28).

A TEMPTING TARGET

A short while before Saddam's move against Kuwait the Saudi Arabians had discovered five new oil fields. We are told that they are the largest deposits of petroleum ever found. The oil of those new wells comes out of the ground looking as clear as water. You could pump it right out of the earth into a truck or car, and drive away. The only reason this so called "honey" or "sweet" oil will need refining is to satisfy the regulations of environmental protection agencies by putting in proper additives for the protection of the atmosphere. Are you also aware that Saudi Arabia has some of the largest gold deposits in the world? Did you know that an American consortium is working with the Saudis, providing new techniques for mining out huge quantities of gold? A tempting target, indeed!

WORLD SHAKEN BY INVASION OF KUWAIT

Ken Breck, researcher for Info Media Information Services, astutely observed, "In the first weeks following Kuwait's invasion more than 1.5 million foreign workers fled to their homes [home countries]. Refugees from seventy nations were affected.

"World investment markets have been shaken. In the first three weeks of August shares on the New York Stock Exchange lost $350 billion of their market value. Price declines on the European and Asian stock markets have been precipitous. Japan's Nikkei stock average lost one-third of its value during the initial crisis. These blows rained down on an economy more fragile than at any time in recent memory. The United States and other developed nations are sliding into recession with major corporations carrying high debt loads at staggering rates of interest. The sudden rise in energy prices is seriously damaging the economy of poor and developing nations least able to absorb the impact.

"After forty years of conflict with the Soviet Union, with the fall of communism in Eastern Europe and the rise of the new democracies, while the world celebrated new freedoms from fear . . . one more dictator thrown onto the stage of mankind's theater threatened to plunge the

Mideast and a thoughtless dependent world into chaos." The event of a war, and the ending of it, nevertheless leaves the world markets on a dizzying rollercoaster course.

WAR, AGAIN

The skies roared. The atmosphere thundered with a loud noise not of nature's making. Hundreds of U.S. F15 and F16 fighter bombers lifted off the sands of Saudi Arabia, plunging through the black night toward an awesome target: Baghdad! It was 6 p.m. (EST) Wednesday night when they released their deadly load upon the capital of Iraq. Death and destruction rained down from the rent skies. The world's biggest war in more than twenty years was in progress. Saddam was taken by surprise. The advance stealth bombers had done their job well.

On January 20, 1991 we read in the *London Sunday Express* that at that time more than 4,000 Allied sorties had been hurled at the Iraqi forces. Following that early announcement wave after wave of aerial attacks were completed. What followed was one of the most devastating air assaults in history. It was estimated that eighty percent of Iraqi military installations had been hit. Later it was reported that some of the early "stealth bomber" sorties took out the super cannons which we had reported about earlier.

It is distressful to find that those figures are now considered to have been overly optimistic. We note with caution that U.S. Army General Robert Johnston warns that about thirty permanent scud missile sites are still in operation. Others think even that is a low figure. We know that Saddam has actually retained a large amount of his artillery and forces. Saddam has the capability of manufacturing his own scuds, and is no longer dependent on an outside source of supply. Hussein still has horrendous weapons in reserve, waiting for another go around. He is actually not far from attaining nuclear capabilities, although the U.N. is supposed to be monitoring that situation. It is questionable whether the U.S.A. and our coalition would respond so quickly the next time. An important question is, "How long, with our country in virtual bankruptcy, can we keep on financing such adventures?"

ISRAEL UNDER ATTACK

For the first time in her history Israel did not respond to an attack upon her sovereign territory and upon her people. Just as he warned,

Saddam made Israel the target of both his Russian and Iraqi made scud missiles. The *Miami Herald* for January 23 was bannered "THE WAR: DAY 7." The first headline reads, "Scud Slams Tel Aviv."

Michael Huler, an Israel radio reporter gave a startling eyewitness account of the scud attack. "From the east I heard a tremendous whistle out of the sky. I turned and looked and saw a huge object descending toward me, a kind of large shadow in the sky.

"And it emitted a frightening sound. I saw no tail of fire behind it. It kept falling and falling at a dizzying speed. I laid down in the mud leaving my microphone open pointed toward the sky. A huge explosion, a tremendous impact, so big an impact that the microphone broke in my hand and did not record the final explosion. The missile fell several dozen yards away from me. Afterwards, moments of stillness, a terrible silence followed the noise. A mushroom of dust and smoke was around me. I checked myself. I wasn't hurt. Only sprayed by pieces of glass and other objects that flew from all around. After the stillness, there were shouts, screams, children crying, people are running."

LIVE REPORT FROM ISRAEL

My son-in-law and daughter, Thomas and Rebecca Brimmer, reside and work in Israel. Here is their on-location report:

"We arrived back in Israel during the heat of the war. Fear, a palpable terror was in the air everywhere. Yet in the midst of tribulation there were rays of hope and whispered words of miraculous deliverance.

"When we surveyed the ruins of scud-bombed homes and apartments, we wondered how much more the poor Israeli people could be asked to endure. Almost five hundred homes were totally demolished and about eleven hundred others suffered damage. It is a wonder that only seventeen people lost their lives. Most of them were not directly from the scud hits, but from heart attacks, brought on by the catastrophic fear that only one who has lived through a bombing raid could imagine.

"One orthodox Jewish couple never left their home on a Friday evening except to attend the synagogue. The wife in this family told her husband, "We must leave the house tonight." He felt the urgency with which she spoke and reluctantly agreed. While they were in the home of nearby friends their house took a direct scud hit and was absolutely destroyed. Another man was in his home when the bomb hit, and it was devastated. The next day this orthodox Jewish man was seen standing beside the ruins, wearing his prayer shawl and thanking God for a miracle of deliverance.

"Though buried up to his chin in the rubble, the man was without a scratch or bruise! His neighbors dug him out and were amazed that he was unhurt. He attributed it to God's protective care. We heard so many stories like this that we left Tel Aviv to go back to our apartment in Jerusalem with hearts full of praise to God for His watchful care. Consider the beautiful and assuring words of the psalmist David:

Behold, he that keepeth Israel shall neither slumber nor sleep The LORD is thy keeper: the LORD is thy shade upon thy right hand.

The LORD shall preserve thee from all evil: he shall preserve thy soul. The LORD shall preserve thy going out and thy coming in from this time forth, and even for evermore.

Our feet shall stand within thy gates, O Jerusalem. Jerusalem is builded as a city that is compact together: Pray for the peace of Jerusalem: they shall prosper that love thee. Peace be within thy walls, and prosperity within thy palaces. For my brethren and companions' sakes, I will now say, Peace be within thee. (Selections from Psalm 121, 122.)

GULF WAR I IS OVER
What Next?

Now the war is over . . . but the *Wall Street Journal* for March 3, 1991 editorialized, "After Saddam, another Saddam?" We all wonder who will supply the power and leadership for Babylon (Iraq) in time to come. So far Saddam is surviving very nicely. The oil fields are burning in Kuwait. The atmosphere is thick with filthy pollution, filling the lungs and eyes of the people. Amnesty International is horrified at the abuse of human beings by Kuwait, now that we have given them back their country. The Kurds were and are pursued and tortured. The war in the Gulf is not over.

I wrote the original draft of this chapter for our *Prophecy Digest* newspaper on Friday the 25th of January, 1991. Mrs. Lewis and I were in the island nation of Barbados. It was dictated to our publisher over the telephone, for immediate release. (This revised and expanded version is being completed on May 5, 1991, and slightly annotated Feb. 23, 1992). On the evening of January 25th I spoke at the Sabbath service of the National Jewish Synagogue in Bridgeton. On Sunday we began services at the People's Cathedral with Pastor Holmes Williams. We have assisted with the distribution of 40,000 copies of a special Barbados edition of our *PROPHECY 2000* Newspapers. The witness teams report hundreds of souls coming to Christ as a result.

In the meantime we were assisted by a local Barbadian, who prefers to remain anonymous, in researching the site where the Gerald Bull Supercannon prototype or "Baby Babylon" was tested. It has a barrel 112 feet long. I was able to get to the cannon and photograph it. Bunkers line the cliffs behind the cannon site. In these bunkers we photographed hundreds of thousands of dollars' worth of high tech electronic devices which are best described as being in a "junked" condition. Also, we extend thanks to newspaper reporter Ms. Cheryl Harewood of the *NATION* daily newspaper for her assistance in supercannon research.

AFTERMATH OF GULF WAR I

We are waiting for the other shoe to fall. The U.S.A. got what it wanted in the war. We prevented Saddam from taking over the oil fields of Saudi Arabia and having the power to shut off the energy tap to most of the world. But in our victorious wake we left behind a scene of human misery, abuse and terror, desolation, and pollution so vile as to defy imagination."

In Israel hundreds were injured in the scud attacks. Apartment houses were reduced to rubble. Miraculously the loss of life was very low, and in most cases it was due to fear-aggravating heart attacks and an improper use of gas masks causing suffocation in a very few cases.

Saddam's goal was to draw Israel into the war, hoping that the Arabs in the Allied coalition would turn against the U.S.A. If Israel had responded, Radio Baghdad would have broadcast to the Syrians and other Arabs in the coalition to turn their weapons on the Americans, British and French. Oh, dread treachery! Oh, day of infamy! It could have happened if the Israeli's had not practiced an admirable restraint. The next time around Saddam or his successor may have to be dealt with directly by the Israelis.

Israel's apprehension was heightened because of the fear of Saddam's using poison gas, nerve and chemical gasses, and finally germ warfare. Each Israeli had been issued a gas mask and each home had a sealed room to retreat into in case of gas attacks.

President George Bush asked the Israeli's to refrain from responding. They complied with that request. However, Israeli Brigadier

General Nachman Shai said, "We are at war here . . . We are not going to tolerate such things. We have a lot of patience. We'll figure out the time and place, and what to do."

Pulitzer prize winning journalist A. M. Rosenthal declares that it is absolutely imperative that Israel retaliate sooner or later. He wrote for the Miami Herald, "As long as his life lasts, Saddam Hussein can count on two inevitabilities. Each day the sun will rise and set — that is one. The second is that on one of those days, Israel will present him with its bill of reckoning . . . The open questions are when — and what way would bring Saddam most grief and Israel and the United States most benefit. In spite of these opinions Israel has not retaliated against Saddam in any way. The U.S. owes Israel a lot for taking the scuds without responding.

WHAT DOES SADDAM HAVE UP HIS SLEEVE?

Right now many are asking, "What is Saddam planning?" A worst case scenario has been suggested. Saddam still does not believe at this moment that he is defeated. He is probably planning another move. He knows he can count on irresponsible demonstrators in the U.S.A. who are ready to start marching in our streets again, if we get involved in another military action anywhere near the magnitude of Desert Storm. Thus Saddam is encouraged to think that he can wear us out. He wants a repeat of our Vietnam defeat. We have been defeated by an inferior power in the past. Could it happen again?

WILL SADDAM ADMIT DEFEAT?

Actually Hussein does not admit that he has been defeated. In his mind he has only suffered a temporary setback. If the day comes that Saddam knows he is truly is beaten, what will he do? Quiet surrender is not in his blood. Horrified military analysts and political psychologists think that if he cannot reorient his efforts for conquest and dominion, he can make a final lunge for ultimate revenge on the whole world. He would predictably try to set the oil fields on fire in Saudi Arabia as he had already done in Kuwait.

Does he have the means to do it? It could be accomplished by infiltrated terrorists on location in Saudi Arabia. Some think he has weapons systems held in reserve. Here are some possibilities.

The Gerald Bull supercannon may be one weapon held in reserve, if any survived, or if he has the means to build new ones. Since writing

Chapter 22 of this book, we have found many more references to the Bull weapon. The JTA news service reported that Israel's Mossad (secret service) informed Greece of *another* Iraq bound super gun. The item was then confiscated by the Greeks. It was described as part of a gun barrel. It was 67 feet long, with a diameter of 5.28 feet and interior rifling. The piece of the gun barrel weighed 29.5 tons. How many super guns of how many sizes actually were in place in Iraq? History and research will reveal the full magnitude of this story which we have been reporting for some time. Now in 1992 all the TV networks are now bringing out more information weekly. Yet many thought our reporting of it was speculative, sensationalist and unlikely. But we were right, weren't we?

An interesting observation just slipped past in an interview granted to *U.S. News and World Report* by CIA Director William Webster. He was quoted as saying, "So, we get the combination of proliferation of weapons and proliferation of missiles. The long cannon that he called a throwing pipe is just one way to deliver weapons of mass destruction at a distance." *U.S. News and World Report,* September 10, 1990.

U.S. News also reported in the June 4, 1990 edition that *most* of the parts of the supercannon had been delivered to Iraq. Only parts of it were confiscated. Saddam has manufacturing capabilities, and along with the help he could get from other countries friendly to his cause, the task could well have been completed, or in the process right now. Time will tell.

Grant Jeffry, a Canadian writer, also declared that his sources indicated the existence of at least four operational supercannons in Iraq. Grant reported accurately, if somewhat conservatively.

We know that Saddam has the Air Fuel Explosive bomb. This bomb carries a load of conventional plastic explosives and also a payload of gasoline in high pressure beryllium chambers. As the target area is approached the bomb ejects the gasoline as a vapor or fog. It blankets a huge area. When the conventional explosives detonate upon impact at the target area this in turn explodes the gas fog creating a monster fire storm over a large area. The resultant burning of the oxygen and the blast of the gas fog produces a destructive force equal to the A-bombs that were dropped on Hiroshima and Nagasaki at the end of the second world war.

Less likely, but still possible is the opinion of a few analysts that Saddam has an A-bomb or two at his disposal. In a future act of desperation, should Saddam Hussein's awful plans be realized, if

Saddam manages to set the Saudi oil fields to blazing, not a hundred Red Adairs could put out the fires that would burn for hundreds of years, creating a black pallor of smoke in the atmosphere of the whole earth. A calamity as bad or worse than a feared nuclear winter would fall upon planet earth. The skies of earth turn wretchedly black. Crops refuse to grow. The gloomy vision of Isaiah becomes a harsh reality. "The earth is drooping withering . . . and the sky wanes with the earth, for earth has been polluted by the dwellers on its face. Therefore a curse is crushing the earth, alighting on its guilty folk; mortals are dying off, til few are left" (Isa. 24:4-6). Recent translation.

THE NEW WORLD ORDER

One product of the Gulf Crisis is the emergence of a globalist mentality unequaled for intensity in all of earth's history. President Bush refers constantly to the need for a New World Order. He speaks of this new international coalition of nations as if it were already an accomplished fact. We will not fail to warn our president of the dangers inherent in this concept. Forthcoming editions of our newspaper *Prophecy 2000* will expand on this theme. We will also be dealing with the pressures that will be brought upon Israel for an international peace conference to solve the Palestinian problem. [Written before the Madrid conference, this is now a reality.]

Israel will be asked to give up the Golan Heights, the Gaza and the areas of biblical Judea and Samaria, described as the "West Bank" in the secular media. Giving up Judea and Samaria would narrow Israel down to a country only 10 miles wide between the Mediterranean and the enemy line.

Remember, only Egypt, of all the Arab neighbors is not officially at war with Israel, a condition prevailing since 1948. It should be plain to see that the scud missiles carrying a limited payload due to the over 400 miles they had to travel did great damage. But suppose they only had to travel five miles to get to the heart of Tel Aviv? The bomb load they could carry that distance would level the most populous area of Israel to rubble in a matter of minutes. Tel Aviv would be awash with blood and piled with bodies. That is, unfortunately, exactly what her enemies have boldly declared to be their desire for the hated Zionist state.

DISTURBING REPORTS OUT OF KUWAIT

Newsweek, May 6, 1991 printed a scathing denunciation of Kuwait.

The article on page 42 is titled "With Friends Like These — The Trouble with Kuwait."

While noting that Emir Jabir Al-Ahmad al-Sabah, back from exile, has "grudgingly entertained the idea of a new Kuwait . . . the old Kuwait is only now emerging from ruins — thanks largely to the U.S. Army Corps of Engineers — and the new is yet to be born." *Newsweek* cites the distress of Secretary of State James Baker as he spoke of the Emir's reluctance to reform his system. The Bush administration was shaken by a recent Amnesty International report that called on the Emir "to intervene personally to end the wave of arbitrary arrests, torture and killings in the country since the withdrawal of Iraqi forces." The reports speaks of Palestinians and others being beaten, subjected to electric shock and burning with cigarettes and acid. Reference was made to sexual assault and executions.

The ruling Al-Sabah family was further criticized by *Newsweek* as it described the entourage of the Emir as being a display of licentious behavior, gambling, excessive drinking, sexual assaults. *Newsweek* noted that White House aides had joked about sending U.S. troops to Kuwait to keep the world safe for feudalism. Today, however the laughter has a nervous edge.

Newsweek further commented that a senior White House administrator, while noting embarrassment with the situation, "We must grit our teeth and wait." *Newsweek* added, "Kuwait is still a rich country . . ." Well, there is the bottom line, friends. Money. Mammon reigns. Morality comes second. "The *love* of money is the root of all evil."

NOW WATCH QADAFFI
Libya Marches on Stage — Again

Dictators may be deterred by half measures, but when they survive they can make a comeback. *New Dimension* magazine for June 1991 brings a strong warning. "While the world has been transfixed by events in the Persian Gulf and the Soviet Union, the terrorist godfather, Libya's Mohammar Qadaffi, has made a major and ominous comeback. Last December in a bloody coup the African nation of Chad fell under his influence, and that seems only the tip of the iceberg. Like Saddam Hussein, Qadaffi has lots of oil money." Chad has rich uranium deposits, necessary for making atomic weapons.

When Reagan sent our planes to bomb Libya he sent a strong

message that terrorism does not pay . . . for a while anyway. After a long silence from Libya now a strident voice is again being heard. *New Dimension* comments that "Qadaffi is attempting to build an Islamic alliance throughout the Third World . . . Some Third World leaders, such as Sudan's Lt. General Omar Hassan Ahmed el Bashir, seek Qadaffi's backing at least in part because they support his pan-Islamic and pan-Arabic political agenda, which Qadaffi contends, is a 'third way' between communism and capitalism."

Qadaffi's dream of a Moslem world empire reaches beyond the Middle East. In the Caribbean he recently supported a Moslem uprising in the island nation of Trinidad, where a failed coup was attempted in June, 1990. He supports the terrorist Polisaro movement in the Western Sahara. In Kenya Qadaffi is endeavoring to destabilize the pro American regime of Daniel Moi by backing the savage Kenyan terrorist group Mwakenya. Repeat the same story for the moderately pro-Western African nations of Mali and Niger.

REPEAT OF LEBANON, 1982

In 1982 our book *Magog 1982 Canceled,* the story of the Lebanon War, shocked the world with the revelation that under the surface of Lebanon the Soviets had assisted the PLO in digging miles of underground bunkers and tunnels stocked with billions of dollars of pre-positioned, sophisticated Russian armaments. We revealed the plot the Soviets had for an August 4, 1982 invasion of Israel. Israel's military incursion into Lebanon in June, 1982 preempted the Soviet, Syrian and PLO plans.

Subsequently, while I was testifying before the United States Senate Foreign Relations Committee, I was questioned about this. My documentation was and is firm.

I had been led to this startling information by a report sent to me from Monte Carlo by an old time intelligence agent, Hillare du Berrier. From the same source we recently were informed that the fantastic digging machines of the same type used in Lebanon to dig the underground facilities are in use in Libya where 1026 miles of tunnels and bunkers have been dug. In them are stored, according to du Berrier, fifteen billion dollars' worth of pre-positioned Soviet supplied armaments. What is Qadaffi planning? Three guesses . . .

New Dimensions, June 1991 also cites "reports . . . that Qadaffi was digging new bunkers and tunnels, which are likely designed to shield chemical weapons components. Libya is believed to be engaged in large-scale productions of such weapons at its Rabta complex, some 25 miles outside of Tripoli . . . Right now he [Qadaffi] is among the world's most dangerous geopolitical forces . . . The coup in Chad should be our wakeup call — the tyrant of Tripoli is back." Watch Libya, pilgrims. Libya, slated to be one of the allies of Magog in the future invasion of Israel! (Ezek. 38:5,6).

A FINAL WORD

The late Dr. Albert Einstein was a Deist. He was of Jewish ancestry. Only as an illustration of the desperate nature of the times we live in did he make the following statement: "If the Christ of the Christians ever plans to come back to earth He had better do it soon or He won't have a world to come back to."

"Even so, come, Lord Jesus." We are ready and waiting for Your return.

26

Four Spectres Over the Gulf

Consequences of the First Gulf War

A horrified world watched the callous brutality of Saddam as he slaughtered innocent civilians, women, and children, and set Kuwait's Kuwait's oil fields on fire. Four major trends emerged while the dust still hovered over the arena of the first Gulf War. Those four trends have advanced like specters of doom; their faces are not friendly.

1. PRESSURE ON ISRAEL

Having assured Israel that if they stayed out of the Gulf War the linkage of the Palestinian question would not be brought into play, nevertheless President Bush and Secretary of State Baker are working day and night to put pressure on Israel to cede "land for peace." Israel has already given land for peace — the entire Sinai Peninsula was given to Egypt for a peace treaty. The Sinai represents 91 percent of the land that fell into Israel's hands as a result of a war her neighbors brought upon her. Now the demand is for Israel to give away the Gaza, the Golan and the regions of the biblical Promised Land, Judea, and Samaria (West Bank).

On January 22, 1992 Jeanne Kirkpatrick, former U.S. ambassador to the United Nations observed, "Quietly, without discussion, the Bush administration has reversed long-standing American policies toward

Israel and the PLO." We remember that in a 1988 campaign speech, candidate George Bush said, "No land for peace, no Palestinian state on Israel's borders."

Israel offered a peace proposal quite a while ago. It consisted of a plan for local elections among the Palestinians living in Judea and Samaria (the West Bank). Israel must be recognized as a legitimate country. The Arabs are to have self-rule for a period of a few years and then negotiations for land settlement will take place. This plan has not been given adequate nor fair consideration by the Bush administration, nor the leaders of the much vaunted "New World Order." Further, no Arab nation, except Egypt, has recognized Israel's right to exist. Recently, while the peace process initiated in Madrid continued, Yassir Arafat, Fatah/PLO terrorist leader again called for Jihad (holy war) against Israel!

HE SPOKE AS A PROPHET!

In 1969 the late Zeev Koffsman, pastor of the Messianic Assembly of Jerusalem, told me, "David, today Israel is the darling of the Western World. We can seemingly do no wrong in their eyes. But this will all change before long. Even America will ultimately turn against us and sell us out. As we experience military battles and preemptive strikes, uprisings and wars of attrition our allies will finally get tired of us. New leadership will arise in the Western World. Sympathy will turn toward the Arabs." How unlikely that seemed in 1969.

Now, as I write in early 1992 it is being fulfilled! While blessing accrues in the Divine account books for those who bless Israel, God is explicit in warning the world that he will curse those who curse Israel. Jesus taught that while offenses will come in this world, those who offend the Divine sense of rightness will be judged: "Woe unto the world because of offenses! for it must needs be that offenses come; but woe to that man by whom the offense cometh!" (Matt. 18:7). Even while recognizing that evils will be done in our time, believers are mandated to resist evil with all that is within us.

In 1969 Pastor Koffsman had said, "At last the leader of a Western Coalition of nations will come to us with harsh demands." This seemed almost impossible for me to believe in 1969. Koffsman said that the demand would be, "All right you Jews! We have had it with you. War after war, constant trouble; it has to end now. Here is a seven year agreement for you and your neighbors. We will ensure your safety. You must give up land for peace. If you refuse we will simply back off from you and you will be destroyed."

Kaufman continued, "The day will come when we will be forced into an ill advised covenant that will not work. It will not stand. At some time the West will be willing to sell us out to form alliances with the Arabs and keep the oil flowing, insuring a more stable economy in the West. Israel just does not have oil with which to buy friends."

Although Israel now is being assured that this will not happen, we know how quickly politicians change their position — without apology. No one really expects most politicians to keep their word. Will Rogers

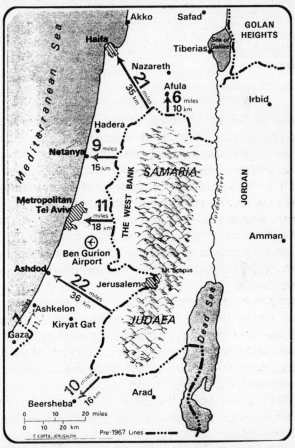

Israel's vulnerability within its pre-1967 boundaries. If Israel gives up biblical Judea and Samaria (the West Bank), she is only 11 miles wide from the enemy line to the sea, in her most populous area.

said, "It's 95 percent of the politicians that give the remaining 5 percent a bad name." (Thank God for the 5 percent.)

A year after the "end" of the first Gulf War former U.N. Ambassador Jeanne Kirkpatrick wrote, "Although they have not said so outright, administration officials have already pressured Israel into negotiations with the PLO. By linking US loan guarantees to Israel's participation in the peace process, Bush and US Secretary of State James Baker forced Israel into talks with a Palestinian delegation that operates under the instruction of the PLO . . . The PLO meanwhile has made no concessions or modifications in its implacable hostility toward 'the Zionist entity.'

"Defending against the Jihad was made increasingly difficult by Bush administration policies in the U.N. last week. The U.S. joined a resolution 'strongly condemning' the decision of the Israeli government to deport to Jordan twelve Palestinian extremists [convicted terrorists] in retaliation for the murder of four Israeli civilians in the last ten weeks. [No word of condemnation for Kuwait, Saudi Arabia and Jordan deporting 450,000 hopeless Palestinians.]

"Moreover, last week's resolution went further than any previous action of the Security Council in characterizing the West Bank, Gaza, and Jerusalem as 'occupied Palestinian territories.'

"Last week the U.S. voted yes on a resolution with an operative paragraph describing Jerusalem as 'occupied Palestinian territories . . .' The fact that the U.S. would join in a resolution that condemned Israel's response to violence, without ever mentioning that violence, is also significant. It is a new departure by the Bush-Baker team — one which creates severe problems for Israelis who are still the target of the deliberate, organized violence of the Palestinian uprising, or intifada . . .

"Asked if Palestinians would suspend their war if Israel suspends the creation of new settlements, Palestinian spokeswoman, Hanan Ashrawi indicated the violence would continue. The intifada, she said, was a 'natural and normal reaction' to occupation. By its U.N. votes the Bush administration signals that it sees Palestinian violence against Israelis as more acceptable somehow than Israel's legal retaliation against Palestinians. This is a new American policy."

In December, 1991, while Ashrawi was charming Americans through our own television and news media, Arafat was in Dakar, Senegal when he called for holy war against the Jews (December 10, 1991). On December 12, during an interview on ABC's "Prime Time Live" with Chris Wallace, Hanan Ashrawi excused herself on camera to take a direct call from Yassir Arafat. When she returned, Wallace asked her if she considers Arafat to be her leader. She said, "Oh yes," without hesitation. We wonder why Chris Wallace didn't ask her how she could reconcile this allegiance with her alleged commitment to making peace with Israel and Arafat's continual and abusive threats to destroy the Zionist state. Al Fatah, Arafat's organization carried out 320 acts of violence in 1991, including shootings, bombings, grenade attacks and stabbings. We wonder why the media in the U.S.A. said almost nothing about the Jihad speech in Dakar. The *Boston Herald* was probably the only newspaper to comment editorially on the implications of Arafat's remarks (January 19, 1992). The national TV networks ignored the story.

ALL NATIONS AGAINST ISRAEL AT ARMAGEDDON

Zechariah declared:

Behold, I will make Jerusalem a cup of trembling unto all the people round about, when they shall be in the siege both against Judah and against Jerusalem.

And in that day will I make Jerusalem a burdensome stone for all people: all that burden themselves with it shall be cut in pieces, though all the people of the earth be gathered together against it.

A DIVINE RESCUE

In that day shall the LORD defend the inhabitants of Jerusalem.

And it shall come to pass in that day, that I will seek to destroy all the nations that come against Jerusalem.

And I will pour upon the house of David, and upon the inhabitants of Jerusalem, the spirit of grace and of supplications: and they shall look upon me whom they have pierced, and they shall mourn for him, as one mourneth for his only son, and shall be in bitterness for him, as one that is in bitterness for his firstborn.

In that day shall there be a great mourning in Jerusalem, as the mourning of Hadadrimmon in the valley of Megiddon.

In that day there shall be a fountain opened to the house of David and to the inhabitants of Jerusalem for sin and for uncleanness.

And one shall say unto him, What are these wounds in thine hands? Then he shall answer, Those with which I was wounded in the house of my friends.

Behold, the day of the LORD cometh [the tribulation], and thy spoil shall be divided in the midst of thee.

For I will gather all nations against Jerusalem to battle; and the city shall be taken, and the houses rifled, and the women ravished; and half of the city shall go forth into captivity, and the residue of the people shall not be cut off from the city.

Then shall the LORD go forth, and fight against those nations, as when he fought in the day of battle.

And his feet shall stand in that day upon the mount of Olives, which is before Jerusalem on the east, and the mount of Olives shall cleave in the midst thereof toward the east and toward the west, and there shall be a very great valley; and half of the mountain shall remove toward the north, and half of it toward the south.

THE MESSIANIC AGE OF PEACE

And the LORD shall be king over all the earth: in that day shall there be one LORD, and his name one.

And men shall dwell in it, and there shall be no more utter destruction; but Jerusalem shall be safely inhabited.

ARMAGEDDON — ATOMIC WAR?

And this shall be the plague wherewith the LORD will smite all the people that have fought against Jerusalem; Their flesh shall consume away while they stand upon their feet, and their eyes shall consume away in their holes, and their tongue shall consume away in their mouth.

And it shall come to pass in that day, that a great tumult from the LORD shall be among them; and they shall lay hold every one on the hand of his neighbour, and his hand shall rise up against the hand of his neighbour.

ISRAEL DEFENSE FORCES

And Judah also shall fight at Jerusalem; and the wealth of all the heathen round about shall be gathered together, gold, and silver, and apparel, in great abundance.

THE GLORIOUS MILLENNIUM

And it shall come to pass, that every one that is left of all the nations which came against Jerusalem shall even go up from year to year to worship the King, the LORD of hosts, and to keep the feast of tabernacles.

And it shall be, that whoso will not come up of all the families of the earth unto Jerusalem to worship the King, the LORD of hosts, even upon them shall be no rain." (Selections from Zech. 12, 13.)

2. THE NEW WORLD ORDER

The final human effort at New World Order is described in Revelation 13. It is the beast (Antichrist) kingdom and is doomed from the start. Proclaiming world peace it actually creates havoc. It never succeeds. Daniel, whom Jesus called a prophet (Matt. 24), spoke of a coming "king of fierce countenance" whom we understand to be the very Antichrist: "And through his policy also he shall cause craft to prosper in his hand; and he shall magnify himself in his heart, and by pe**ace shall destroy many**: he shall also stand up against the Prince of princes; but he shall be broken without hand" (Dan. 8:25).

All the major world leaders are talking about the New World Order. President Bush speaks of it in almost every public address. Here are a few documented quotations:

Out of these troubled times, our fifth objective — a New **World Order** — can emerge . . . We are now in sight of a United Nations that performs as envisioned by its founders (September 11, 1990, TV address to the people of the USA).

The United Nations can help bring about a new day . . . a New **World Order** and a long era of peace (October 1, 1990).

Regarding the U.N. sanctions Bush said, ". . . when we succeed . . . We will have invigorated a U.N. that contributes as its founders dreamed. We have established principles for acceptable international conduct and the means to enforce them." (October 26, 1990).

Two days after the air offensive was launched against Iraq he spoke to the Arab nations that were not part of the coalition: "Look, you're part of this New **World Order** . . . You can play an important part in seeing

381

that the world can live at peace in the Middle East and elsewhere" (January 18, 1991).

When President George Bush spoke to the U.S. Reserve Officers Association he said, "From the day Saddam's forces first crossed into Kuwait, it was clear that this aggression required a swift response from our nation and the [world community]. What was, and is at stake is not simply our energy or economic security, and the stability of a vital region, but the prospects for peace in the post-Cold War era — the promise of a **New World Order** based on the rule of law" (January 23, 1991).

In his address on the State of the Union, January 29, 1991 Bush said, "What is at stake is more than one small country; **it is a big idea: a New World Order,** where diverse nations are drawn together in security, freedom and the rule of law."

"There is no room for lawless aggression in the Persian Gulf for this **New World Order** we are trying to create, and Saddam Hussein will know this" (January 1, 1991).

We hear our president talking about "our friends and fellow members of the coalition." Some of these friends are the most dangerous cutthroats of modern history. They are the creators and supporters of world terrorism. Blood flows from their hands. They rank with Hitler, Antiochus Epiphanes, and Nero. Allied intelligence reports that our Soviet "allies" continually helped launch the scudswhich they had furnished to Saddam in the first place. The Soviets refused to recall their advisors who were doing this. The U.S.S.R. kept right on shipping materials to Iraq. Up to the time of the actual attack, the U.S.S.R. was flying twelve AN-124 and AN-22 transports into Baghdad daily. Gorbachev admitted to President Bush that this was happening and said, "The Soviets need cash."

While George Bush rightly portrayed Saddam Hussein as a Hitler-type monster, he nevertheless gave a friendly embrace to President Hafez al-Assad of Syria, one of our most reliable enemies in the Middle East. He was welcomed into our coalition in the Gulf War. It is now apparent that he joined the coalition so he could fill the power vacuum when his old enemy Saddam Hussein was toppled. Assad has a standing army of 600,000 men, well equipped with state-of-the-art weapons supplied by the former U.S.S.R. Now he is negotiating with Boris Yeltsin's Russia for another two billion dollars' worth of arms — including sophisticated MIG-29 and Sukhoi 24 jets, and SAM-10 and SAM-11 missiles. The deal is supposed to be secret, but information was leaked to the U.S.A. and Israel. (Reported in *New American*, Feb. 24, 1992; page 31.) The U. S. State Department still lists Syria as a nation aiding and abetting international terrorism. Syria is one of the biggest suppliers of narcotics to the U.S.A.

Our president is evidently unaware (even though he is a Christian) of the biblical implication of the New World Order concept. It leads to the Antichrist regime! From his lips drop the phrases, "global community," "world community," "brotherhood of nations," "merger into the family of nations," etc.

Just today we were informed that Bush has read Pat Robertson's book on the New World Order. It is rumored that Robertson was summoned to the White House to meet with the president because of the book. If that rumor is true, then time will tell if President Bush wakes up to biblical reality, or if he merely scolded Pat Robertson for what he had written.

3. THE TWO COALITIONS

During the first Gulf War we heard a lot about the allied "coalition." For forty years I have been teaching that there would be two major end time coalitions. One is an alliance of the western (Tarshish) nations and certain Arab allies represented by "Sheba and Dedan."

Sheba, and Dedan, and the merchants of Tarshish, with all the young lions thereof, shall say unto thee, Art thou come to take a spoil? hast thou gathered thy company to take a prey? to carry away silver and gold, to take away cattle and goods, to take a great spoil? (Ezek. 38:13).

In Chapter 7 of this book "The Young Lions of Tarshish," we established the identity of the United States of America in this amazing Old Testament prophecy. The research of Dr. Barry Fell, professor of Harvard University, is cited. Please refer back to that chapter. Sheba and Dedan are Arabic nations seen here in a coalition with Tarshish (Great Britain) and her young lions, including America, and maybe other Western powers. Sheba and Dedan are probably Jordan and Saudi Arabia, and possibly Yemen. If so, watch for Jordan to join Egypt to make a peace treaty with Israel. Could Saudi Arabia also join in?

POLISHING BRASS

While the Antichrist will make a seven year treaty with Israel and her neighbors, it must be emphasized that not all peace treaties are evil. Any peace treaty that works is beneficial for all concerned. We must not study prophecy and get freaky or bloodthirsty. Armageddon will come in God's time. In the meantime we have to do the best to keep things working in the world. The carrying out of the Great Commission is best realized in a tranquil climate. The fundamentalists of the 1920s had a slogan, "There's no use polishing brass on a sinking ship." But thank God someone kept on polishing brass for the past seventy years. We just don't know how long it will be before the ship goes down! So we have to make the best of things in the present season, working hard for the good of all, all the while looking for the coming of our Lord and the ultimate rescue of our world from the forces of destruction.

Finally the two coalitions will oppose each other at the battle of Magog (Ezek. 38). The Tarshish, Dedan, Sheba group of nations are set in array against the Northern Power — Magog and her coalition, Persia (Iran), Ethiopia, Libya, Gomer, and Togarmah. This is the Magog (Russian) coalition. See the chapter on Magog in this book.

4. THE BABYLON FACTOR

Babylon (Iraq) is yet to be reckoned with. Saddam has survived and become an even greater hero in the eyes of many of his friends. If as Secretary of Defense Dick Cheney speculated last week Saddam Hussein is about to be overthrown by his own people we are left with major questions: Who will take his place? Who will rule the region? When will be the final fall of Babylon? Will the work on the rebuilding of the ancient city of Babylon on the Euphrates continue? The Allied Coalition refrained from bombing the archaeological site of Babylon, and the extensive new buildings were also spared. Surely, we have not seen the end of Babylon (Iraq) as an end-time prophetic factor. We will be watching the situation very closely.

REPORT FROM JERUSALEM

Dateline: Jerusalem. February 1992. The newsletter of the International Christian Embassy reports that a new Gulf War is possible.

"The Director of the Institute for Strategic Research at Tel Aviv University suggests this grim possibility when he warns that Saddam

Hussein was beaten and humiliated in the Gulf War, but not defeated. He won't rest until he possesses atomic weapons.

"He will make superhuman efforts to obtain the atomic bomb. Saddam believes that money can buy everything from everyone. The arms race also concerns the other Gulf states, who buy from anyone willing to sell.

"U.N. experts estimate that some 18,000 people are employed by Iraq in its atomic bomb program and that its completion was much closer than is generally believed. Western secret services, including that of Israel, were, it seems taken by surprise at their findings."

The Christian Embassy Newsletter also commented, "An interesting footnote was added by the religious community of Jerusalem's Mea Shearim quarter. Hearing Mr. bush's boast that America had finished the war in 100 hours the cry was heard: 'It should have been 101 hours.' The reason? All Hebrew names have a numerical number, and that of the Archangel Gabriel, a protector of Israel, is 101."

THE SUPERCANNON WEAPON SYSTEM

Both in our *Prophecy Intelligence Digest* newspaper and in Chapter 22 of this book we wrote about the Gerald Bull super cannon. There you will find a diagram of a cannon with a barrel 487 feet long. When this chapter was first written we suggested that Saddam had this weapon completed along with the 112-foot "Baby Babylon cannon." We noted that both of these cannons could fire a projectile nearly a thousand miles. The "Big Babylon" with its 487-foot barrel could fire a shell weighing 3,000 pounds a distance of 620 miles, and with a rocket booster in the projectile its range increased to over 1,000 miles. We also queried, "Why didn't Saddam use it? Was it destroyed by the stealth bombers in the first strikes? Is it still intact and usable for a yet-to-come assault on Saudi Arabia or Israel? These are questions yet to be answered." Now, in January, 1992 we have the answers!

Since my last writing on the subject I have been in Barbados, in the Caribbean, where I personally saw and photographed the prototype "Baby Babylon." It took some doing to get onto the military base where the HARP (High Altitude Research Project) gun invented by Gerald Bull was located. This gun was also tested in Canada, Vermont, Arizona, South Africa, Iraq and possibly other places. South Africa and the Soviet Union may have a version of it.

The Gerald Bull gun was not devised by the inventor to be a weapon, strange as this may seem. It was produced to provide a way to launch satellites into orbit at one-tenth the cost of conventional rockets. The big gun on the island nation of Barbados launched an experimental satellite into sub-orbital space, 112 miles above the earth! Rebuffed by Canada and the U.S.A., Bull turned to Saddam Hussein as a sponsor. Saddam, of course, wanted it for a powerful weapon system!

We now know that the early stealth bomber strikes took the giant cannons out. Some were not yet operational. Every major news magazine has written about it. Recently a television show, "Frontline" visually documented the super cannon story. Numerous pictures of the weapons in Iraq were shown. Now that we know this incredible technology exists, we wonder, who has it? Is it in the hands of the Europeans? The Commonwealth of Independent States (former U.S.S.R.)?

The C.I.S. is almost sure to have Gerald Bull's plans, for Iraq was a client state of the Soviet Union. Some of our intelligence people believe that there is evidence that New Russia is building the super cannons. They have the heavy steel industrial factories and the engineering skills to do so. Our American engineers had better look into this, for whoever develops the weapon will have a tremendous advantage in the next go-around. Remember, our best field artillery only fires a shell about 45 miles.

For your information, please note that Chapter 25 of *PROPHECY 2000* is completely revised and expanded in this fifth edition.

27

Is Russia
Off the Hook?
Magog Is Still Magog

A bored gentleman at the opera asked his wife, "Is this thing about over?" She testily answered, "It's not over 'til the fat lady sings!"

In other words, it's not over until it's over. Prophecy confuses some people because they lack patience. They want it all right now. They don't like to adjust to God's time table. Some have a sense of urgency which is good in a way, but which needs to be tempered with disciplined endurance.

Gorbachev's doctrine of perestrioka (restructuring/rebuilding) caught the imagination of his nation and of the world. It seemed like a tidal wave of inevitable change swept the U.S.S.R. Then came the collapse of the Gorbachev regime. Communism is dead! The cold war is over! Euphoria settled like a cloud over the West. The accelerated rate by which these things happened was nothing less than startling.

NOT ARMAGEDDON

Some of our hasty friends had been quick to declare that the Gulf War was the beginning of Armageddon. That just was not so. Now, willy nilly, these sometime prophets begin to question, "Maybe we misunderstood the Ezekiel 38 prophecy. Maybe Russia is not indicated in this passage at all." The occasional prophets will quietly lay their sensational prophecy sermons to rest until the next world crisis comes along. Then the eschatology lectures are brought out of the closet for another short run of sensationalism.

It is hard for some to have patience when dealing with prophecy. Nevertheless we must wait for God's timetable, not for the fulfillment of our own speculative prognostications. As we said, early on, the Gulf War is not the Armageddon battle. Before the battle of Armageddon there will be a Russian invasion of Israel. The Ezekiel 38 Magog battle is the beginning of forty-two or more months of world wide unrest which culminates in the Armageddon campaign.

FALL OF THE U.S.S.R. — LONG LIVE THE C.I.S.

On August 19, 1991 a military coup attempt was launched against the Gorbachev political machine in the failing U.S.S.R. Perestroika had gotten out of hand. A cry for true freedom arose among the masses. Blundering military leaders thought they could cease power for themselves. The coup failed, Gorbachev survived, but for such a short time.

On August 24, 1991 Mikhail Gorbachev resigned as head of the Communist Party. Then just 13 days later, on September 5, 1991 at 11:40 AM, Moscow time, the Union Of Soviet Socialist Republics ceased to exist. *Maclean's,* the weekly newsmagazine of Canada, reported, "The Soviet legislature voted to surrender power to a new republic-controlled government and to recognize the independence of the Baltic States." (*Maclean's*, Sept. 16, 1991, page 24.) After languishing under Lenin's shadow for seventy-five years the Communist dream of world conquest was over. Of course there are scheming, conspiring holdouts, but for now it looks like it's over for them.

THE NEW SHAPE OF MAGOG

Latvia, Estonia, Lithuania, the Baltic republics declared their independence. The remaining republics, Russia, Belorussia, the Ukraine, Moldava, Georgia, Armenia, Azerbijan, Kazakhstan, Kirghizia, Turkmenia, Tajikistan, and Uzbekistan joined hands to form an economic common market and military alliance known as the Commonwealth of Independent States (C.I.S.). The names of the republics are changing and the C.I.S. is recognized to be very unstable. A lot of further changes could take place!

Prophecy does not change because of the latest trends reported in the news media. The prophecies do not rise or fall with the fall of the

U.S.S.R. and the rise of the new C.I.S. The Commonwealth itself may not survive for long. But the same land mass, population, weaponry and perhaps leadership will still be there in some form or another. God's Word towers above all the ponderings and doings of man.

Friends, Magog is still Magog and Russia is still Russia and they are still the same thing. Magog was Magog before the rise of Russia as a superpower, long before the formation of the ill-fated U.S.S.R. The basis of the prophecy has not changed. Russia is still a military giant and her mighty military machine will be fielded at least one more time in the future. It's not over yet. But when it is time, the fat lady will sing.

Isn't it interesting that two coalitions of world powers are described in Ezekiel 38? One is headed by Russia and includes Iran, Iraq, Ethiopia, Libya, and some European powers. The other is headed by Western powers (Tarshish) who also have Arab allies (Sheba and Dedan). The struggle between the two coalitions leads to the collapse of one (Magog) and the establishment of a disappointing New World Order of short and miserable duration by the other, the Western Coalition.

IDENTITY OF MAGOG

There is a way of identifying Magog with Russia in the text, but first let me mention that this is not a modern idea, "cooked up" retrospectively by someone trying to make world events fit prophecy.

First of all Flavius Josephus, a Jewish historian who lived and wrote in the time of Christ, said that there were Scythian tribes who lived in the region of the Caucasus (part of Russia today) who were known as the tribes of Magog. In the early 1800s a brilliant Hebrew scholar and lexicographer, Willhelm Gesenius, made the same identity, declaring that Magog was Russia. Concerning the "Rosh" in the passage Gesenius says, ". . . name of a northern nation, mentioned with Tubal and Meshech; undoubtedly the Russians, who are mentioned by Byzantine writers of the tenth century, under the name of [Hebrew spelling given] dwelling to the north of Taurus, and Arab called [Arabic spelling given] described by Ibn Fossian, an Arabic writer of the same age, as dwelling on the river Rha (Wolga). C. Refs. given. Mentioned in Koran; Kor XV:31; 1:12."

I have read Gesenius and have examined his statements carefully. His predictions seemed exceedingly unlikely then since Russia was not a major world power. Russia was the hinterlands of Europe, the boondocks of the world. It was the only major European power by-passed by the Protestant Reformation, the Industrial Revolution, and the Renaissance. Other scholars through the ages have made similar assertions.

HISTORY OR PROPHECY?

Bear in mind that nothing at all in history comes anywhere near to fulfilling this ancient prophecy. So its fulfillment must lie in the future. The only alternative is to say that the whole thing is an allegory and only illustrates the general struggle between good and evil. But too many specific nations and events are described to make this even feasible. We are forced to see a future fulfillment of Ezekiel 38. Of course if you reject the full inspiration of the Bible you can accommodate to anything to explain its prophecies away. We refuse to accept these liberal, neo-modernistic trends, even in our own ranks.

Now, carefully read the text of Ezekiel 38. Words in square brackets are my added comments.

EZEKIEL 38

Gog is the ruler, Magog his domain. The entire Ezekiel 38 prophecy is addressed to Gog of the land of Magog, the chief prince of Rosh, Meshech and Tubal. This is not a prophecy against the people of Russia, many of whom are godly folk, our brothers and sisters in Christ. It is a prophecy against corrupt, power hungry leadership which mounts a misadventurous against Israel.

1. And the word of the LORD came unto me, saying,

2. Son of man, set thy face against Gog, the land of Magog, the chief prince of [Rosh — see Amplified Trans., the New King James Trans., Rotherham Emphasized Trans., and others], Meshech and Tubal, and prophesy against him,

3. And say, Thus saith the Lord GOD; Behold, I am against thee, O Gog, the chief prince of Meshech and Tubal [Moscow and Tobolsk]:

4. And I will turn thee back, and put hooks into thy jaws, and I will bring thee forth, and all thine army, horses and horsemen, all of them clothed with all sorts of armour, even a great company with bucklers and shields, all of them handling swords.

HORSES, TANKS OR SYMBOLS?

No message of prophecy is fully understood until it is fulfilled. When questioned whether there will be cavalry actually used in this battle, we simply and honestly must answer, "We do not know." I suppose that previous wars could so cripple the industrial capabilities of the nations that archaic methods could be used. Or, again, I suppose treaties against weapons and implementation of widespread disarmament could produce these conditions. I am not in the guessing business.

IDK and ANDY

I can see the broad parameters of the final outcome of all things, but all things are not clear at the present. "For we know in part, and we prophesy in part . . . For now we see through a glass, darkly . . ." (1 Cor. 13:9,12). It would be well for thoughtful prophecy teachers to invoke the IDK principle once in a while (IDK = I don't know). And don't forget the ANDY factor! (ANDY = And neither do you). Some things we know for sure — we exercise patience and wait on the rest. Remember the Bible is not a crystal ball nor a deck of tarot cards. When things happen, then the Bible helps us understand the events of our times.

If the horses and equipment here are symbolic of modern machines of warfare it could be explained in one of two ways. First of all, the prophet Ezekiel had to use terminology he and his people were familiar with, regardless of what he saw in the vision. Secondly, if it is purely symbolic this does not destroy the literal overall quality of the prophecy. A literal prophecy can embody figures of speech, just like in our every day conversations, we use metaphors, allegories and various other figures of speech, but with the intention of conveying literal facts and truths, even through the use of the figures of speech employed.

ALLIES OF MAGOG

5. Persia [Iran-Iraq] , Ethiopia, and Libya with them; all of them with shield and helmet:

6. Gomer [parts of E. Europe?], and all his bands; the house of Togarmah [Armenian Turkey?] of the north quarters, and all his bands: and many people with thee [many people *could* include Syria and other Arab nations].

38:7. Be thou prepared, and prepare for thyself, thou, and all thy company that are assembled unto thee, and be thou a guard unto them.

8. After many days thou [Magog] shalt be visited: in the latter years thou shalt come into the land that is brought back from the sword, and is gathered out of many people, against the mountains of Israel, which have been always waste: but it is brought forth out of the nations, and they shall dwell safely all of them.

Please note that it is in "the latter years," a phrase which meant to the Hebrew writer the period of time preceding the dawning of the Messianic era. The text shows Israel having been regathered from dispersion. They are back in the land of Israel. The fact that they are "dwelling safely" when it happens most likely indicates that the Magog invasion will take place during the first three-and-one-half years of the tribulation (see verse 11).

The Antichrist breaks the covenant and abominates the future temple half-way through the seven-year period and there is a time of "great tribulation on earth for three-and-a-half years (see Matt. 24:15-22).

We see that Israel will be invaded in a time of peace and security. Israel will be in an ill-advised seven-year treaty or covenant relationship with a coalition of western nations headed by the Roman Prince (Dan. 9:24-27), the Antichrist. Remember that the Antichrist has the gentiles deceived before he forces his agreement on the Israelis. The time of peace when Magog invades Israel seems likely to be during the first three-and-one-half years of the seven years of the peace covenant, hence Russia invades Israel in the first half of the seven years tribulation period. I think it could happen just before the midway point of the tribulation. The Antichrist breaks the covenant half way through the seven year period and it is hell on earth for Israel three and a half years.

The collapse of Russia emboldens the leader of the Western Coalition to spread his reign worldwide. A shaky coalition World Government is formed. It is never very successful. The "beast" has continual uprisings against him. The Magog war is the beginning of a three-and-a-half-year period of world unrest that culminates in the campaign of Armageddon. That battle is concluded by the reappearance of Jesus Christ on earth and His subsequent victory over all world powers. In Daniel, Chapter 2 we see the Rock (Christ) smiting the image of gentile world power and destroying it. It is replaced by the visible manifestation of the eternal kingdom of God.

MAGOG INVADES ISRAEL

Once again, remember that Gog is the ruler, Magog his domain. The entire Ezekiel 38 prophecy is addressed to Gog of the land of Magog, the chief prince of Rosh, Meshech, and Tubal.

Ezekiel 38:9. Thou [Gog] shalt ascend and come like a storm, thou shalt be like a cloud to cover the land, thou, and all thy bands, and many people with thee.

10. Thus saith the Lord GOD; It shall also come to pass, that at the same time shall things come into thy mind, and thou shalt think an evil thought:

11. And thou shalt say, I will go up to the land of unwalled villages; [Israel]; I will go to them that are at rest, that dwell safely, all of them dwelling without walls, and having neither bars nor gates,

12. To take a spoil, and to take a prey; to turn thine hand upon the desolate places that are now inhabited, and upon the people that are gathered out of the nations, which have gotten cattle and goods, that dwell in the midst of the land.

MAGOG'S MOTIVATION

Why will Russia Invade Israel? There are seven reasons, and there may be others.

1. The Bible declares that it will happen. This is the number one reason; everything else follows.

2. Since the time of Peter the Great, Russia has desired warm water ports on the Mediterranean.

3. The Dead Sea is the richest single mineral deposit on the face of the earth. According to Shlomo Drori, head of the Dead Sea Works Department of Information, there are enough quantities of eleven vital minerals to meet the needs of the entire world for hundreds of years to come, or possibly indefinitely. The Salt Sea could be captured and exploited.

4. Magog "thinks an evil thought:" If the USA can put together a coalition and punish Saddam Hussein for his criminal acts against Kuwait, then Russia has the right to put together a coalition and punish

Israel for their occupation of "Palestine." A good excuse for making an entrance into the region.

5. Oil is another reason. Israel is the primary target, but the ultimate target of the Magog invasion could be to take over the entire Middle East and control the oil supply. Shutting off the oil tap to the West could bring us to our knees. The following is a whisper from the intelligence community rumor mill: It was whispered in my ear in Houston, Texas that Saudi Arabia has discovered gold deposits more valuable than all her oil put together (2-19-92). Remember, this is only a rumor. Maybe it is true. We will wait and see.

6. There are from sixty to eighty million Moslems in the C.I.S. Their numbers are increasing. A Russian medical doctor appeared last night on American television lamenting the zero population increase of the "White Russian" population. He said the maternity wards in Moscow are practically empty. On the other hand the Moslems are experiencing an exponential population explosion. The C.I.S. could find great encouragement if not outright pressure from these Moslem citizens to invade Israel. Coupled with the rising tide of anti-Semitism in the C.I.S. this will likely be a major factor in promoting the invasion.

The headline in the *Jewish Press,* February 7-13, 1992 read, "With the demise of the U.S.S.R. — Moslem Republics Imperil Israel." The article stated, "With the breakup of the Soviet Union, the stability of Moscow's centralized command and control system is all but gone. Now there is a major threat that technologies and materials could be released that had previously been kept under control. With such weapons in the hands of Moslem republics in Russia [C.I.S.], there is a considerable concern in Israel. The central Asian republics with large Moslem populations — Azerbijan, Turkmenistan, Uzbekistan, Kirghizia, Kazakhstan — have both tactical and strategic nuclear weapons. It is believed they could become partisans in the Arab cause with very little urging. Israel, meanwhile, is attempting to establish diplomatic ties with two of these republics . . . If the Iranian fundamentalists can stir up the Moslem citizenry in those former Soviet republics, Israel may have a major problem on its hands." The article in the *Jewish Press* (The world's largest independent Anglo-Jewish weekly newspaper) notes the existence of 30,000 nuclear warheads in the C.I.S.

7. In a time of internal unrest in a nation, starting an outside war is a welcome diversion, and it employs manpower in the armed forces and in the infrastructure of the defense industrial complex. Russia and the whole C.I.S. is in deep trouble. After seventy-five years of Communist

economic failure there are deep economic woes, and we can not afford to bail them out any longer, due to our own nation's financial distress.

THE TARSHISH (WESTERN) COALITION PROTESTS THE RUSSIAN INVASION

Ezekiel 38:13. "Sheba, and Dedan, and the merchants of Tarshish, with all the young lions thereof, shall say unto thee, Art thou come to take a spoil? hast thou gathered thy company to take a prey? to carry away silver and gold, to take away cattle and goods, to take a great spoil?"

Sheba and Dedan are Arab nations, Saudi Arabia, Jordan, and Yemin could be included. Tarshish has long been thought to be Great Britain. The young lions are English speaking nations, including the U.S.A. (See Chapter 7, "The Young Lions of Tarshish.") See how the Gulf War brought together just such a coalition. Tarshish could also include any allies in the Western Block of nations.

OUT OF THE FAR NORTH

Ezekiel 38:14. Therefore, son of man, prophesy and say unto Gog, Thus saith the Lord GOD; In that day when my people of Israel dwelleth safely, shalt thou not know it?

15. And thou shalt come from thy place out of the north parts, thou, and many people with thee, all of them riding upon horses, a great company, and a mighty army.

The phrase "out of the north parts" is translated "uttermost parts of the north," in the Amplified; "out of the remote parts of the north," in the Rotherham Trans.; "from the far north," in the N.I.V. and so on in many other modern translations. **Just look at a map of the world! Look at your globe!** The only land mass that fits the description in relation to Israel is Russia, the new C.I.S. Also see Ezekiel 39:2: "And I will turn thee back, and leave but the sixth part of thee, and will cause thee to come up from the **north parts,** and will bring thee upon the mountains of Israel."

AGAINST ISRAEL

Ezekiel 38:16. And thou shalt come up against my people of Israel, as a cloud to cover the land; it shall be in the latter days, and I will bring thee against my land, that the heathen may know me, when I shall be sanctified in thee, O Gog, before their eyes.

17. Thus saith the Lord GOD; Art thou he of whom I have spoken in old time by my servants the prophets of Israel, which prophesied in those days many years that I would bring thee against them?

Let me reemphasize that it is Israel which is the primary object of attack by the great Northern power, Magog, and its coalition. Israel is referred to eighteen times specifically and alluded to many more times in Chapters 38 and 39 as being the target of Magog's invasion.

MAGOG'S ARMIES DEFEATED
God's Wrath Unleashed

Ezekiel 38:18 And it shall come to pass at the same time when Gog shall come against the land of Israel, saith the Lord GOD, that my fury shall come up in my face.

19. For in my jealousy and in the fire of my wrath have I spoken, Surely in that day there shall be a great shaking in the land of Israel;

20. So that the fishes of the sea, and the fowls of the heaven, and the beasts of the field, and all creeping things that creep upon the earth, and all the men that are upon the face of the earth, shall shake at my presence, and the mountains shall be thrown down, and the steep places shall fall, and every wall shall fall to the ground.

21. And I will call for a sword against him throughout all my mountains, saith the Lord GOD: every man's sword shall be against his brother.

22. And I will plead against him with pestilence and with blood; and I will rain upon him, and upon his bands, and upon the many people that are with him, an overflowing rain, and great hailstones, fire, and brimstone.

Earthquakes! Pestilence! Hailstones! Fire! Brimstone! By these supernaturally directed phenomenal weapons God will defeat Magog leaving only a sixth of his armies alive (Ezek. 39:2).

GOD'S POWER, PRESENCE, AND PERSON
— MANIFESTED TO THE NATIONS

Ezekiel 38:23 Thus will I magnify myself, and sanctify myself; and I will be known in the eyes of many nations, and they shall know that I am the LORD.

RECAPPING THE DAY'S NEWS

Selected verses from Chapter 39:

Ezekiel 39:1. Therefore, thou son of man, prophesy against Gog, and say, Thus saith the Lord GOD; Behold, I am against thee, O Gog, the chief prince of Meshech and Tubal:

2. And I will turn thee back, and leave but the sixth part of thee, and will cause thee to come up from the north parts, and will bring thee upon the mountains of Israel:

4. Thou shalt fall upon the mountains of Israel, thou, and all thy bands, and the people that is with thee.

5. Thou shalt fall upon the open field: for I have spoken it, saith the Lord GOD.

THE CONFLICT WIDENS
World War III (Or IV)

Ezekiel 39:6. And I will send a fire on Magog, and among them that dwell carelessly in the isles: and they shall know that I am the LORD.

In Revelation 6:4 the going forth of the red horse and his rider is described. It pictures a global conflict. This grows out of the Magog war of Ezekiel 38. It introduces the global trauma which finally ends in Armageddon at the visible second coming of Christ.

WITNESS TO ISRAEL

Ezekiel 39:7. So will I make my holy name known in the midst of my people Israel; and I will not let them pollute my holy name any more: and the heathen shall know that I am the LORD, the Holy One in Israel.

8. Behold, it is come, and it is done, saith the Lord GOD; this is the day whereof I have spoken.

9. And they that dwell in the cities of Israel shall go forth, and

shall set on fire and burn the weapons, both the shields and the bucklers, the bows and the arrows, and the handstaves, and the spears, and they shall burn them with fire seven years:

This activity could extend into the early part of the Millennium. There will be natural activity for the natural people allowed to enter the Millennial period. They will repopulate the earth. If you can find the secrets of Matthew 25:31-46 you will understand this.

Ezekiel 39:10. So that they shall take no wood out of the field, neither cut down any out of the forests; for they shall burn the weapons with fire: and they shall spoil those that spoiled them, and rob those that robbed them, saith the Lord GOD.

GRAVES FOR GOG BRINGS GLORY TO GOD

Ezekiel 39:11. And it shall come to pass in that day, that I will give unto Gog a place there of graves in Israel, the valley of the passengers on the east of the sea: and it shall stop the noses of the passengers: and there shall they bury Gog and all his multitude: and they shall call it The valley of Hamon-gog.

12. And seven months shall the house of Israel be burying of them, that they may cleanse the land.

21. And I will set my glory among the heathen, and all the heathen shall see my judgment that I have executed, and my hand that I have laid upon them.

22. So the house of Israel shall know that I am the LORD their God from that day and forward.

A WITNESS TO THE GENTILES

Ezekiel 39:23. And the heathen shall know that the house of Israel went into captivity for their iniquity: because they trespassed against me, therefore hid I my face from them, and gave them into the hand of their enemies: so fell they all by the sword.

24. According to their uncleanness and according to their transgressions have I done unto them, and hid my face from them.

ISRAEL'S FINAL AND FULL RETURN
A Millennial Forview

Ezekiel 39:25. Therefore thus saith the Lord GOD; Now will

I bring again the captivity of Jacob, and have mercy upon the whole house of Israel, and will be jealous for my holy name;

26. After that they have borne their shame, and all their trespasses whereby they have trespassed against me, when they dwelt safely in their land, and none made them afraid.

27. When I have brought them again from the people, and gathered them out of their enemies' lands, and am sanctified in them in the sight of many nations;

28. Then shall they know that I am the LORD their God, which caused them to be led into captivity among the heathen: but I have gathered them unto their own land, and have left none of them any more there.

29. Neither will I hide my face any more from them: for I have poured out my spirit upon the house of Israel, saith the Lord GOD.

Do not search for exact chronologies in the Old Testament prophecies. Frequently you find the writer speaking of things having to do with this age, then the Millennial reign of Messiah, then back to the Tribulation.

Sometimes I think God allowed the prophets to present this disorderly array of facts so the Bible would never be a book we had "mastered." It is a living epistle, and we are constantly searching its living pages for further illumination of the events affecting the world we live in today. Certainly we understand prophecy better than we did thirty or forty years ago. Many things have fallen into place. Still we "see through a glass darkly." It's not all over yet. Many fascinating days lie ahead. Be patient. God is in control!

Finally, let's thank God for the open window of opportunity the Church has in the C.I.S. at the present. Hands reach out for Bibles and Gospel literature. We are involved in this mass literature distribution, along with other members of our family, and other ministries. Pray for the salvation of the people of Russia. Pray for a mighty revival to sweep the Commonwealth. We do not know how long the door will be open. We must do all we can while we can.

28

Exodus — 1990 - 2000

The Miracle of the Soviet Jews

At last, as by prophets foretold, they come streaming from the land to the far north of Israel. The Jews from the Soviet Union are coming home to the land of promise. For decades we have foretold this latter day Exodus, as we saw it portrayed in the pages of the Bible. Many years before it began we penned and published essays about it.

In the early 1980s we joined the Mordachai Outcry in Jerusalem which saw the gathering of thousands of Christians demonstrating for the Russian "refusnik" Jews. Refusniks are those who had applied for visas to leave Russia but had been refused by the Soviet government.

When we printed an entire issue of our *Jerusalem Courier* in February, 1984 predicting this return of the Russian Jews, people cried out, "How can it happen? How can it be?" We could not answer, but simply affirmed, "It will be for our God has said it." We did not know about Michail Gorbachev, glastnost, or perestroika. We knew that ultimately Communism would collapse, but we had no idea that it would be so soon or that it would happen so fast. We did not envision how the gates would open for the Russian Jews to come to Israel. We just knew that God's Word prophesied it and so it had to happen.

These words are being written in 1992. The rest of this chapter is an annotated edition of the lead article we published in our *Jerusalem Courier* newspaper in 1984.

"I Say To The North--Give Up!"

LET MY PEOPLE GO!

This sketch was done under our direction in 1982, long before the breakup of the U.S.S.R. See the hand of the Almighty pulling at the Magen David, representing the Russian Jews in bondage. See the hammer and sickle of Communism—cracking under the pressure. This proved to be a prophetic work of art.

Elizabeth Howell, granddaughter of David and Ramona Lewis, wears a T-shirt depicting the struggle of the Soviet Jews.

AT A TIME MOST UNLIKELY

When we published our first full paper on the return of the Soviet Jews early in 1984 it should be noted that that was the period when Jewish immigration out of Russia was at its very lowest level! Thus, when it seemed most unlikely we were led of the Holy Spirit to publish these prophecies from the Bible.

We had written articles much earlier and had spoken of this miracle in churches in the early 1970s. Then it seemed a dream, almost a fantasy. Now the reality of fulfilled prophecy unfolds before our eyes. See how timely the 1984 article is today!

THE BIBLE PREDICTS

From the Jer*usalem Courier*, First Quarter Edition, 1984:

EXODUS! The very word conjures an image of Moses parting the waters of the Red Sea as the children of Israel "go out from" the Land of Egypt. The English word "exodus" is from the Greek "exodos", which in turn is from two Greek roots — ex, meaning "out" and "hodos," meaning "way." Hence exodus is "a way out." In the biblical sense it means "a going out from."

The word "exodus" never appears in the Old Testament even though it is the name of one of the Books of the Pentateuch written by Moses, hero of the Exodus adventure.

Exodus is a Greek word used in the New Testament, there translated "departing". The passage in Hebrews indeed refers to the Old Testament Exodus which was prophesied by Joseph son of Jacob: "By faith Joseph, when he died, made mention of the departing [Greek, Exodos] of the children of Israel; and gave commandment concerning his bones" (Heb. 11:22).

THE FOURTH EXODUS

The first Exodus witnesses Israel going out of Egyptian bondage. The second Exodus sees the children of Israel being delivered from Babylonian captivity via the decree of Cyrus the Persian. The third Exodus has been observed in modern history as the Jewish people have gone out of the many lands of Diaspora. It especially evokes a vision of the Jewish people fleeing from the European hell of the Holocaust in the 1940s and from many other inhospitable lands as the nation was forged in the furnace of war in 1948. Hundreds of thousands poured in from all over the globe.

The next Exodus [we wrote in 1984], the fourth in Israel's history, will be so great that the preceding ones will pale into insignificance when compared to it. Thus declares the Hebrew prophet Jeremiah. [Please bear in mind that all of this is from articles we published in February, 1984, unless otherwise indicated in the text.]

GOD'S COMMAND TO THE NORTH COUNTRY

Isaiah declares that God will gather the children of Israel from the four quarters of the earth. This was never the case at any time in previous history. It was for our day to behold as we approach the Messianic age of peace on earth. Note well, there was never, before modern times, a regathering from all over the world! This is a day of miracles. The existence of Israel is a miracle, but the greatest miracle is yet to come.

[Writing in 1992 we note that while the exodus has begun, there is much more to follow. There will be changes in Russia that will create difficult times for the Jews remaining there. Later there will be a final surging return of the rest of the Jews of the North. As of February, 1992 about 400,000 Jews have come from Russia to Israel in a very short time. The immigration continues, although the rate has slowed down at this point of time.]

GOD SPEAKS TO THE NORTH

We get one of our first clues by reading this prophecy from Isaiah:

Fear not: for I am with thee: I will bring thy seed from the east, and gather thee from the west; I will say to the north, Give up; and to the south, Keep not back: bring my sons from far, and my daughters from the ends of the earth (Isa. 43:5,6).

Notice the command to the North Country. It is a severe command shouted out by the Lord — "GIVE UP" — release them and let them go. "Amar tsaw-fone nathan teni!" Literally from the Hebrew this is translated: "I speak my shouted command, 'yield them to Me'."

BEFORE IT STARTED WE WROTE IN 1984:

It is noteworthy that the only country to the north of Israel with a significant Jewish population is the U.S.S.R. Can it be that we are living in the age that will soon see the release of the Soviet Jews? We believe that it is so. Certainly the release of the Soviets is a major concern of the Israelis and the world Jewish community, for to be a Jew (openly) in the Soviet Union is to be a second-class citizen. Anti-Semitism is rampant in that land. [I remind you, these words were written years before the current return of the Russian Jews began!]

Over 400,00 of the 3.5 million Jews in the Soviet Union have applied for exit visas and have been refused. Hence they are called "refusniks." [1992 note: Now 400,000 have arrived in Israel and two million more will come.]

DAVID SMITH, MAN OF GOD,
MEMBER OF CANADA'S PARLIAMENT
CANADA — 1983

Following the example of the prophet Daniel, many believers come to understand a prophecy and then get involved as implementers of the Divine plan. (See my book, *Smashing the Gates of Hell in the Last Days*. New Leaf Press, 1987).

Recently, with Al Lazert, director of the International Christian Embassy of Jerusalem, Canadian Branch, and Clyde Williamson, associate pastor at Queensway Cathedral, Toronto, I went to Parliament Hill in Ottawa, Ontario, Canada.

Earlier in the year I had introduced Bill Prankard, Canadian director of Christians United for Israel, to Israeli Ambassador Yeshayahu Anug.

Early in the day, before our visit at Parliament we had gone with all of these men to the Israeli Ambassador's home in Ottawa.

In the Canadian Parliament building we met with a member of Parliament, the Hon. David Smith. Smith is a devout Christian and is very concerned for the fate of Soviet Jewry. In fact he has personally gone to the Kremlin to argue for the cause of the Soviet Jews who wish to leave to emigrate to Israel. M.P. David Smith gave us valuable insights into the problems involved in the situation.

I asked David Smith, in a taped interview, "How many of the Jews of Russia would leave if freely allowed to do so?"

He said, "Nearly all of them, except for those who have become assimilated and have hidden their Jewish ancestry."

SHARANSKY - REFUSNIK

Having read the book by Avital Sharansky concerning the struggle that has, thus far [1984] unsuccessfully, been made to get her husband Anatoly [Nathan] Sharansky out of the U.S.S.R., I could appreciate all that David Smith shared with us relating to the difficulties a Jew experiences once he becomes a "refusnik."

[Now, in 1992, I can report Sharansky has been freed and is living in Israel where he plays an active role in the affairs of the Soviet Jews. I had the privilege of meeting Sharansky at a gala reception given in his honor at the Israeli Embassy in Washington, DC shortly after he gained his freedom. Later I chatted briefly with him from time to time in Jerusalem.

In January 1992 I introduced him to the Executive Council Meeting of the National Christian Leadership Conference for Israel in session in Jerusalem. Sharansky brought an inspired message, telling of his love for the Bible and the inspired words of the prophets. As the Chairman of the Board of NCLCI I was privileged to bring the response to his speech. We presented him with an award and assurance of our prayers for him and Avital, and also for all the Russian Jews still trying to get to Israel.]

COMMUNIST WEDDING PRESENT

Nathan (Anatoly) Sharansky had been arrested on the day of his wedding many years earlier and put into a Soviet prison. His new bride was given a visa and sent to Israel. This dear lady, Avital, roamed the world over for twelve long years writing, speaking, appearing on TV, crying out for the release of her beloved husband. Jews and Christians demonstrated on his behalf. He became a symbol of the refusniks (those who requested to leave Russia but were refused by the Soviets).

At last the Soviets relented. Anatoly Sharansky was to be released in East Germany. The KGB brought him to the gate in the infamous Berlin Wall for his imminent release. They said, "You can take nothing with you. What do you have in your pockets?" All he had was a Book of Psalms. They grabbed it from him saying, "You cannot have this. You must leave it here." Sharansky had been given the Book of Psalms by a Christian inmate of the Soviet prison. He has always testified that it was his source of strength and courage. They were never able to break his spirit or brainwash Sharansky.

When the KGB officer seized his little Book of Psalms, Sharansky's hand shot out and tore it away from the KGB bully. He clutched it to his chest and shouted, "Then take me back to prison, BUT YOU CAN'T HAVE MY BIBLE."

Sister Rose Thering, NCLCI executive director, asked Sharansky about the little book when he was answering questions for our group following his speech. His hand went into an inside coat pocket and brought it forth, as he said, "Here it is. I am never without it. It is still the source of my strength and hope."

OPERATION EZRA

Almost every one of our executive council members had brought an extra suitcase full of clothes and other things for Russian immigrants. We visited the Bridges for Peace Foodbank for the Soviet Jews and were thrilled to see the work being done, especially in providing groceries, clothing and kitchen utensils for the older Russian Jews who are unemployable. NCLCI made a financial contribution, knowing that this concerned Christian brother, Clarence Wagner, Jr., distributes about $30,000.00 worth of food every month! I also gave $1,000.00 from Christians United For Israel. Pray for the Russian Jews. Many have no jobs and housing is in demand. Yet they are glad to be in Israel — free at last. Israel has solved refugee problems in the past and will do so again. Now we continue with the text of the *Jerusalem Courier* from the first quarter of 1984:

A MIRACLE

It will take a miracle from God to get these people out of the nation whose leaders are the sworn enemies of God and the Divine purposes. But you may believe and know that a miracle is on the way!

While we can speak of some remarkable dreams and visions that God has granted many of His servants in recent times (regarding the fourth Exodus, or as Steve Lightle was later to label it, Exodus II), our basis of projecting the very thought of a miraculous release of the Jews from Russia is the prophetic Word of God.

JEREMIAH BEARS WITNESS

Jeremiah, the weeping prophet of Israel, saw visions of far tomorrows, reaching across the centuries to the very last days of this age! He too saw the return of the Jewish people from the land to the north.

Stephen Lightle (left), author of the visionary book *Exodus II*, stands with the captain of the ship which is bringing Russian Jews to Israel.

In those days the house of Judah shall walk with the house of Israel, and they shall come together out of the land of the north to the land that I have given for an inheritance unto your fathers (Jer. 3:18).

The passage that is most persuasive of our concept is also found in the book of the prophet Jeremiah:

Therefore, behold, the days come, saith the Lord, that is shall no more be said, The Lord liveth, that brought up the children of Israel out of the land of Egypt; But, The Lord liveth, that brought up the children of Israel from the land of the north, and from all the lands whither he had driven them: and I will bring them again into their land that I gave unto their fathers.

Behold, I will send for many fishers, saith the Lord, and they shall fish them; and after will I send for many hunters, and they shall hunt them from every mountain, and from every hill, and out of the holes of the rocks (Jer. 16: 14-16).

We note that as Isaiah speaks of a regathering in the last days from the four quarters of the earth, Jeremiah speaks of the Jews being brought back not just from Egypt or Babylon, but from "all the lands." But the emphasis here is on the regathering from the land of the north, the land of Russia, identified as Magog in Ezekiel 38, 39. The ingathering from the North is singled out and set apart from the general gathering from "all the lands."

[1992 — Now we have seen the results of Glastnost and Perestroika effecting the very thing we wrote of in 1984, those very things written by the prophets of Israel six hundred years before Christ.]

GREATER THAN THE FIRST EXODUS

(Written in 1984)

So marvelous will this regathering be in the eyes of latter-day Israel that when they wish to speak of the might and power of God, they will no longer refer to the Exodus from Egypt under the leadership of Moses. But they will speak of the Fourth Exodus, the deliverance from the land to the north.

There are many conjectures on how this miracle will be effected, but we will simply maintain a "wait and see" attitude. In other articles in this issue [*Jerusalem Courier,* First Quarter, 1984] you will read of supernatural revelations being given to some of God's servants related to these forthcoming events. Since evangelicals have various schemes of interpreting end-time prophecy (even though we agree on the major themes), there are various concepts of "when" this will fit into the end-time scenario.

Some see it as being simultaneous with the defeat of the Russian armies on the mountains of Israel (Battle of Magog, Ezek. 38, 39), when the northern power (U.S.S.R.) invades Israel and is defeated by God himself. Others offer various ideas, but no one knows for sure how it will happen. But it will happen! It is a wondrous thing to see how Christians are involved in this end-time stream of miraculous prophetic events.

1990 — THE YEAR OF MIRACLES

Since the above thoughts were penned and published in 1984, what wondrous developments have taken place. The great immigration actually began in 1990. Now the Jews of the North are coming home by the hundreds of thousands. The planes unload their human cargo at Lod Airport near Tel Aviv and great is the rejoicing in the land. In August, 1991 at 3:30 in the morning Ramona and I, along with our

409

מסע אודסה – חיפה

541 עולים היטלטלו ארבעה ימים על הקו
אודסה-חיפה, ביוזמתם ובסיועם של
מתנדבים נוצרים מארגון בלתי ברור
ותחת עיניהם המשגיחות של אנשי הרב
פרץ. צוות "חדשות" הצטרף למסע

Steven Lightle gave me this article taken from a 1992 Israeli Hebrew
language newspaper. The headline on the left side reads "Greater Than
the Exodus out of Egypt." Pictured is a Russian Jew about to board the
Exodus II ship in Odessa, Russia. On his way to the promised land!

410

daughter Becky and son-in-law, Tom Brimmer, stood at the foot of the stairway of one of the big 747 airplanes as hundreds of Soviet Jews came down, eyes moist with tears, to touch the land of Israel for the first time. Home at last!

PRIME MINISTER SHAMIR

I sat in the office of Prime Minister Itzhak Shamir in December, 1991 with my wife Ramona, my daughter Rebecca, and her husband Tom Brimmer. (Tom and Becky reside in Jerusalem and along with Jay and Meridel Rawlings are very active in the affairs of the returning Russian Jews.) We discussed the Iraq-Gulf crisis, but most of all Shamir was delighted to speak of the return from the North, reminding me that in our

Prime Minister Yitzmak Shamir welcomes Russian Jews at Lod Airport.

Recent meeting with Israel's prime minister. Right to left, Prime Minister Yitzhak Shamir, Dr. David Lewis, Ramona Lewis, Rebecca Brimmer, Thomas Brimmer. We spent forty-five minutes in profitable discussion of current affairs and the Bible, including the Russian Jews.

previous conversations we had discussed the prophecies mentioned in this very article. I had delivered a copy of the 1984 *Jerusalem Courier* to him much earlier. This was our fourth meeting with Prime Minister Shamir. He spoke of the return as a modern day miracle.

I asked him about the problems of housing and employment. He said that Israel's greatest joy is also a source of problems and difficulty, but that with the help of the Almighty, Israel will survive the problems and pain and come forth to the joys of the Return.

In August 1991 we met with Harry Hurvitz, one of Shamir's top advisors. We had first met Mr. Hurvitz in 1977, shortly after he came from South Africa to be a part of the Begin administration in Israel. We were discussing plans for the January 1992 meeting of the Executive Council of the National Leadership Conference for Israel in Jerusalem, at which time we were to have a meeting with Prime Minister Shamir. As usual the conversation got around to the aliyah (immigration, lit. "going up") of the Russian Jews. It is a prime topic with everyone in Israel.

A VISIT WITH SOVIET JEWS

Tom Brimmer, Avigdor Rosenberg, and I had the privilege of

spending an evening in the home of Avraham Shifrin, meeting some of his newly arrived friends from the USSR. Shifrin had been imprisoned in a Soviet slave labor camp for ten years, because in 1948 when Israel became a nation he began telling all the Jews in Russia that it was time to go home. Early on, before the current movement of aliyah (return) Shifrin got out of Russia and came to live in Israel, first at Zichron Yaakov and now in the Holy City of Jerusalem. He has been our dear friend for many years now. He and his lovely wife Elenora sat rejoicing with us about the great things that God has wrought.

On another evening in August, 1991 we spent about two hours with General Ariel Sharon who heads up a government agency assisting the Soviet Jews. In his Knesset (Parliament) office we sat in deep discussion. He also spoke of the Divine assistance Israel receives. He also spoke of the problems the huge increase in population was bringing to the beleaguered nation of Israel. He also spoke of absolute confidence that the Lord would come to the aid of Israel once again. Our party was

Russian Jews, recent immigrants to Israel. An ancient Hebrew prophet declared, "Therefore, behold, the days come, saith the Lord that it shall no more be said, the Lord liveth, that brought up the children of Israel out of the land of Egypt; But, the Lord liveth, that brought up the children of Israel from the land of the north, and from all the lands whither he had driven them: and I will bring them again into their land that I gave unto their fathers" (Jer. 16:14, 15).

the last to leave the Knesset Building late that night in December. The only ones remaining behind as we exited with General Sharon were the security guards.

NCLCI

When the executive council of NCLCI had the meeting with Mr. Shamir in January, 1992, he spoke again of the miracle of the return of the Russian Jews. The room was filled with TV camera crews, newspaper photographers and representatives from the Government Press Office (Beit Agron). It was recalled that he and I had previously discussed the prophecies of this from the Bible.

WHITHER, U.S.A.?

It has been the policy of the U.S. government to pressure the Soviet leaders for the release of the Russian Jews. We are not willing to receive them into this country in any large numbers. The only place for them to go is to Israel. Israel needs loan guarantees to be able to obtain loans for the purpose of supplying for the incoming Russian Jews. The money will provide housing, employment, and will be used to expand the scientific and industrial infrastructure to create conditions where further loans will not be needed. Much of the money borrowed will be spent by Israel in the U.S.A. for the goods and equipment that will be used.

Israel has asked for a ten billion dollar loan guarantee so they can borrow from private U.S. lending institutions at a favorable rate of interest. Our cost will be minimal or non existent. Israel has a perfect record in paying back loans, matched only by Norway. The U.S.A. guaranteed loans amounting to two hundred billion dollars for various domestic projects (like student loans) and for foreign nations. Asking for loan guarantees is not so unusual. Israel asks for the guarantees to be administered at two billion dollars a year. What is requested is only one percent of the total figure of our loan guarantees. I was asked to make a statement at a press conference in Washington, DC. My statement on the loan guarantees follows:

THE LOAN GUARANTEES
Friends of Jerusalem Press Conference

National Press Club
Washington, DC October 28, 1991

Statement by David Allen Lewis
Chairman of the Board, Nat. Christian Leadership Conference
for Israel.

I have recently returned from Israel where on this and other occasions, I have had the opportunity to observe first hand the wrenching need which the State of Israel has in providing for her persecuted exiles from Russia, Eastern Europe, and Ethiopia.

In spite of the tortured mathematical Rubic twists of the opponents of loan guarantees to Israel, and the quoting of dubious sources of information about Israel's ability to repay the loans, as an Evangelical leader, and as the chairman of the board of the National Christian Leadership Conference for Israel, I urge our president and other leaders to move forward with these loans to enable Israel to borrow money from private lending institutions at favorable rates for the following reasons:

1. Israel's record of repaying loans in a timely manner is impeccable and unique among nations who have received such guarantees from us. Let the record be clear, this is not foreign aid. This is a business deal with one of our best customers.

2. A strong argument can be put forth for Israel's ability to repay these loans enhanced by the fact that much of the money will go into self amortizing ventures in Israel's private sector into which repayment is factored.

3. Much of the money will be spent to purchase products in the U.S., and interest will be paid to American lending institutions to the benefit of our own economy.

4. As U.S. Senator Robert W. Kasten, Jr. indicated on September 10, the loan guarantees will cost the American taxpayers nothing. Even the substantial "origination fee" will be prepaid by Israel.

5. Furthermore the $1.6 billion dollar deposit which the U.S. will put in trust as a guarantee will be the source of considerable earnings for our economy in the form of interest.

6. Not only will these funds be used to meet enormous humanitarian needs, they will contribute immensely to Israel's economy and increase her already significant role as a U.S. client. Israel is one of our best trading partners, spending over $1.5 billion dollars in forty-two states in 1989-1990 alone.

7. Finally, I have serious concerns about the moral ground on

which the needs of refugees whose flight from persecution we have encouraged, are held hostage to preserving some "delicate balance" with Arab countries in whose streets we hear the cry "DEATH TO AMERICANS, DEATH TO ISRAEL." On the other hand Arab countries such as Syria, the world's biggest drug dealer and money launderer, sell drugs on our streets, (see "Narco Terrorism," Rachel Ehrenfield) used their "bonuses" for participating in the Gulf War, to purchase Scud C missiles and other sophisticated weaponry and build plants to manufacture such weapons to be aimed solely at Israel as in the case of Egypt, and Syria.

Mr. President, Mr. Baker, Israel was asked to wait six months before applying. When they did apply in September, they were asked to wait an additional four months while the need mounts and the hurting continues. Is this any way to treat a friend?

I AM CONCERNED

Does it seem to you that our government is turning away from Israel? This is the way it appears to me and I am deeply concerned. God will not overlook this. He will bless those who bless Israel . . . The return of the Russian Jews is a fulfillment of prophecy. Should we be aiding that fulfillment or obstructing it as a nation? I think the answer is obvious. I have no doubt that the prophecy will be fulfilled, regardless of what the U.S.A. does. However, we will give account of our actions to the Almighty. He will raise up someone else to take our place and receive the blessing if we fail!

The whole story is not written. There are still over two-and-a-half million Jews to come out of Russia. Our son-in-law, Tom Brimmer, has just come back from ministering in Russia. The team gave out over twelve thousand Bibles in two weeks. Their work was a blessing to the churches in the C.I.S.

In addition Tom made contact with Jewish leadership and helped with plans to get more Russian Jews to Israel. He is working with a project to fund the passage of poor Jews who cannot afford to get out. Some were recently in slave labor camps, many of which still exist and operate in the C.I.S. These unfortunates have come to Israel hurting and needing healing.

Last week I was in Jerusalem and Tom told me that he plans to go on the next ship leaving Haifa for Odessa, from whence a shipload of hundreds of Russian immigrants will be brought back to Israel. Tom will assist with this transfer and help get the newcomers established in Israel. Please pray for our work.

Exodus Shipping Line. Lightle & Sheller have leased this ship to carry Russian Jews from Odessa to Haifa. Tom Brimmer will accompany the next trip as a volunteer.

Meridel Rawlings lives in Mevesserit Zion, Israel with Jay and their children. Gracious hostess to pilgrims from all over the world, she is well-known as author of the best-selling book, *Hunters and Fishers,* which is about the plight, prospects, and prophecies of the Jews of the North.

Jay Rawlings head of Vistas of Jerusalem; publisher and film producer, a Christian involved for many years in helping the Russian Jews. His story is told in the *Jerusalem Courier,* 1984, Vol. 4, #1. Tom and Becky Brimmer are associate editors of their world-renowned magazine.

Mordachai Outcry Christian demonstration at the Soviet Embassy, Washington, DC, circa 1986. Christians demand release of the Soviet "Refusenik" Jews (refused permission to leave). Jan William Van Der Hoeven, chief spokesperson of the International Christian Embassy of Jerusalem is seen speaking in this photo.

Problems that distress and gladden the heart. Israel rejoices that the prophecies about the Jews of the North (Russia) coming home to Eretz, Israel are being fulfilled. Prime Minister Shamir expressed this to me over and over in our recent forty-five-minute conversation with him in Jerusalem. However, terrible housing and employment problems have to be solved! This is a tent "city" in a park in downtown Tel Aviv.

Dr. Lewis speaks a prophetic word to young Russian immigrants. It was a powerful moment.

29

Don't Lose the Heavenly Vision

A lot of preachers are talking about reforming the world and ushering in the Kingdom before Jesus comes back. While we work to make the world a better place, we understand that it is the coming of Christ that is our final and real hope. Thank God we don't have to put our ultimate hope in the feeble efforts of man. Anyone who thinks the world is getting better is just plain blind.

There are riots in the streets of our cities. Every village and hamlet trembles at the thought of ritual killings, sacrifices of children, and satanic rituals. Hooligans may rampage your quiet suburb next. In my peaceful hometown women are raped, sodomized, and brutalized in their homes in "nice" neighborhoods, murderers strike down innocent victims, drugs are sold openly on the streets, witch covens and satanist cults practice their dark and esoteric rituals.

Drug lords seem to have more power than politicians and law officers. Heavy duty attack weapons are now used to gun down innocents on the city streets.

America is now on the verge of revolution. In 1965 the American intefada began with Watts riots in Los Angeles. Rioters rampaged, buildings burned, looting was widespread, and many were killed. The police could not control the situation so the National Guard was called in. For twenty-seven years South Central Los Angeles has been a war zone. Murders and gang wars are so common that they hardly make the news. Only when the violence is stepped up, as it was in response to the verdict in the Rodney King case, do the TV vultures descend on the scene again. Once again the National Guard and the Marines are called to restore order. The gangs regroup, the drug pushers continue, violence is perpetuated. The poor and the downtrodden suffer. Moloch gloats. His funeral pyre burns higher and higher, but is appetite is insatiable.

One day riots will break out in forty cities. Violence and looting in the suburbs and bombing the homes of baby boomers and yuppies will create a demand for extraordinary measures. We want law and order now! The armed forces must be movilized nationwide to quell this civil disobedience. Martial law will be declared and welcomed. Normal governmental processes will be canceled. Jackbooted troops will stand at every corner. A president could become a military dictator over such a junta. Executive orders already signed into law make legal provision for such a harsh takeover in the event of internal violence.

Is America on the verge of a revolution? The Los Angeles riots are a small picture of what will yet develop on a nationwide scale. Commotion, havoc, chaos, and upheaval will prepare the way for the governmental structure that will bow to, and cooperate with, the Antichrist.

All of this could happen before the Rapture, or it may be after, during the Tribulation, but it will happen!

NEW YORK, NEW YORK

I was recently in New York City, once again. It is a jungle. Worse than I ever remember it being before. There is my old college classmate, David Wilkerson, holding church in an old theater off Times Square, in the very pit of that man-made hell. Some are so hungry for God they come an hour early to get a seat. The place is always packed. How I admire David for his courageous work. You take your life in your hands to walk the streets of the big rotten apple. No longer can one safely take a stroll in the city parks. People acting more like animals than human beings prowl the streets looking for drugs, thrills and victims.

David Wilkerson's dear wife Gwen has battled cancer for years and his married daughter also seeks healing from this dread disease. All of hell's fury is unleashed against those who stand on the front lines to rescue the perishing. David works day and night for the Kingdom. He believes in the Rapture. He has not lost the heavenly vision. Nor is he an escapist. If you say David Wilkerson is an escapist I charge you with being the vilest of liars. I declare that you will stand in the judgment and give account of your slanderous and evil vilification of a man of God.

WE ARE PILGRIMS
Songs of Heaven

This world is not my home, I'm just a passing through
My treasures are laid up somewhere beyond the blue.
The angels beckon me from heaven's open door
And I can't feel at home in this world any more.

Some who do not share our prophetic vision make fun of us for singing songs about heaven. But the words heaven and heavens appear in the Bible 738 times. That should be enough to justify a song or two about it. Let our churchly unbelievers gnash their teeth — we will sing it anyway.

I might as well really stick my neck out, now that I've antagonized them thus far. Remember the old country church song?

Some glad morning when this life is o'er, I'll fly away
To a place on heaven's blessed shore, I'll fly away.
I'll fly away, Oh glory, I'll fly away
When I die, Hallelujah bye and bye,
I'll fly away.

Go ahead and sing it, saint. Don't let the worldlings in the pulpit rob you of your heavenly vision. If your pastor makes fun of you, ask God where you should go for real spiritual food. Anyway, the phrase "I'll fly away" is taken straight from the Bible.

The psalmist David expressed the longing of his soul: "And I said, Oh that I had wings like a dove! for **then would I fly away, and be at rest**" (Ps. 55:6).

The days of our years are threescore years and ten; and if by reason of strength they be fourscore years, yet is their strength labour and sorrow; for it is soon cut off, and **we fly away** (Ps. 90:10).

WE ARE PILGRIMS AND WAYFARERS ON THIS EARTH

Open thou mine eyes, that I may behold wondrous things out

of thy law. **I am a stranger in the earth:** hide not thy commandments from me. Thy word [is] a lamp unto my feet, and a light unto my path (Ps. 119:18,19,105).

These all died in faith, not having received the promises, but having seen them afar off, and were persuaded of them, and embraced [them], and **confessed that they were strangers and pilgrims on the earth** (Heb. 11:13).

Dearly beloved, I beseech you as **strangers and pilgrims**, abstain from fleshly lusts, which war against the soul (1 Pet. 2:11).

And I have also established my covenant with them, to give them the land of Canaan, **the land of their pilgrimage, wherein they were strangers** (Exod. 6:4).

Thy statutes have been my songs in the house of my pilgrimage (Ps. 119:54).

In making his defense and appeal before the king, the apostle Paul said, "Whereupon, O king Agrippa, I was not disobedient unto the **heavenly vision**" (Acts 26:19). Paul had his heart set on his earthly mission, but never lost the heavenly vision.

ABRAHAM LOOKED FOR A HEAVENLY CITY WHILE HE SOJOURNED ON EARTH

By faith Abraham, when he was called to go out into a place which he should after receive for an inheritance, obeyed; and he went out, not knowing whither he went. By faith he sojourned in the land of promise, **as in a strange country**, dwelling in tabernacles with Isaac and Jacob, the heirs with him of the same promise: **For he looked for a city which hath foundations, whose builder and maker is God** (Heb. 11:8-10).

OUR HOPE NOT IN THE THINGS OF THIS WORLD

Paul wrote to the Corinthian Church: "And if Christ be not raised, your faith is vain; ye are yet in your sins. Then they also which are fallen asleep in Christ are perished. **If in this life only we have hope in Christ, we are of all men most miserable**" (1 Cor. 15:17-19).

Now this I say, brethren, that flesh and blood cannot inherit the kingdom of God; neither doth corruption inherit incorruption.

Behold, I shew you a mystery; We shall not all sleep, but we shall all be changed,

In a moment, in the twinkling of an eye, at the last trump: for the trumpet shall sound, and the dead shall be raised incorruptible, and we shall be changed.

For this corruptible must put on incorruption, and this mortal must put on immortality.

Therefore, my beloved brethren, be ye stedfast, unmoveable, always abounding in the work of the Lord, forasmuch as ye know that your labour is not in vain in the Lord (1 Cor. 15:50-58).

Maintaining the heavenly hope does not cut us off from practical daily realities of living in this world. Paul's very next words are, "Now concerning the collection . . ." (1 Cor. 16:1).

Let the words of Jesus, uttered in the Sermon on the Mount be our final admonition. Practical Christian stewardship is a theme elucidated by Jesus in the Sermon on the Mount.

Lay not up for yourselves treasures upon earth, where moth and rust doth corrupt, and where thieves break through and steal:

But lay up for yourselves treasures in heaven, where neither moth nor rust doth corrupt, and where thieves do not break through nor steal: **For where your treasure is, there will your heart be also** (Matt. 6:19-21).

AN APPEAL TO BIBLE COLLEGES AND SEMINARIES

Professor Robert Lundstrom (Zion Bible College, Providence, RI) speaks frequently on why our Bible colleges and seminaries put so little emphasis on eschatology. He asks what it will take to get a full restoration of church doctrine back into our church schools. We are so concerned about getting the Bible into public schools, while we should be concerned about getting the (whole) Bible back into the Bible schools! Why are our evangelical schools embarrassed by these biblical truths? Some of our Bible college and seminary professors are making an honest effort to see a restoration of Bible emphasis and interpretation, but they have a hard job. We have slipped so far from our moorings in the faith.

I call on our educational leaders to reexamine the curricula of our schools and help to bring a healing to our backsliding churches. If we turn out young pastoral candidates who have not received competent teaching in eschatology, what will they preach in these end times? Will they join the ranks of the scoffers, walking after their own desires, and saying, "Where is the promise of His coming?" I highly respect our Bible college and seminary presidents, and I hope they will look into our concerns. Certainly the task is not impossible. With God's help we can prevail.

We would be pleased to hear from any Bible college president whose school is offering significant courses about Daniel, Revelation, and prophecy. We also wish to hear from individual teachers who are involved in teaching a pre-millennial point of view. Send us a list of the courses offered, denominational affiliation (if any), and the name and address of your school. We need to compile a list for referral. We are constantly asked where people can go for training in these areas — especially for these last days. If you have ideas as to why our schools have almost stopped teaching the prophetic portions of the Bible, please communicate with us. Also send any ideas you have on how we can solve these problems and get the message of prophecy back in our schools. Write: David Allen Lewis; P.O. Box 11115; Springfield, Missouri 65810; U.S.A.

GOING TO THE DOGS

Recently a university president who heads up an evangelical inter-denominational seminary remarked that last night his Bible must have fallen to the floor in his home. In the morning he found that the dog had eaten the book of Revelation. He remarked that he wished everybody's dogs would eat all the Books of Revelation out of the Bibles.

SOME NEW FRIENDS

One of my late dear friends in Canada was sick in bed. Some Catholic charismatics heard about it and came to pray for him. In the course of the conversation the leader asked, "Have you ever read the *Jerusalem Courier* published by David Lewis who heads up Christians United for Israel? It is such a wonderful paper. Such an inspiration. We just got the latest issue and have enjoyed it so much." My friend rejoiced with them. While some are abandoning the heavenly vision, others are embracing it.

NOT AN ESCAPIST

I know some accuse us of escapism. So be it! We are here for threescore and ten, and then eternity. Don't abandon the heavenly vision. I deny the charge of escapism.

I have marched with the anti-abortionists, 14,000 strong, in Washington, DC. I have conferred with ambassadors, prime ministers, senators, and members of the house of representatives. I have prayed with many of them. I have testified before the Senate Foreign Relations Committee. As chairman of the board of the National Christian Leadership Conference for Israel, I put forth continuous action with my colleagues. I am involved in world evangelism, missions, literature distribution in Russia, and the Commonwealth of Independent States.

As a member of the Christian Committee of the United States Holocaust Memorial Council (A U.S. congressional appointed council) I make my contribution of time, effort and money in this great cause. You will be able to visit our museum of the Holocaust in the Spring of 1993 (D.V.). There it is, under construction, over two-thirds done, right on the Capitol Mall near the Smithsonian Institute. It has cost us dearly to take the stand we take for Israel. But I love my Lord and His Chosen people and so I gladly pay the price.

We went into the war zone of Lebanon with bombs falling and artillery firing in Beruit — we were there on a fact finding mission in 1982 during the heat of battle. (See my book *Magog 1982 Canceled.*) Still some say we are escapists.

I called for a prayer demonstration in front of the White House on two different occasions. We were joined by many concerned Christians on both occasions. Yet I am called an escapist because I believe in the premillennial coming of Jesus Christ and because I believe in the outgathering of the saints (the rapture). If I go any further I may be accused of boasting. (2 Cor. 10). But in spite of all the slanderous charges against all of us premillennialists, we stand firm in our faith.

"ESCAPISTS" WHO HAVE GOALS?
An Oxymoron

An oxymoron is a figure of speech in which contradictory ideas or terms are combined. Escapists don't set long range goals. To speak of a goal-setting escapist is a good example of an oxymoron. The church I am ordained in has set a goal of establishing 5,000 new churches by the year 2000 (D.V.). We have already enlisted over 1 million prayer partners. We plan to train 20,000 new workers for the ministry and win at least 5 million souls to Christ in the USA by the year 2000. The stated doctrine of my church is premillennial. We hope that Jesus comes soon, but if He has not come by 2001, it will not change one thing — we will keep on working and setting goals. Yet, in the eyes of some we are escapists. It is time for our accusers to do a reevaluation.

Our faith is strong and not weak. We cast our all in with Jesus. We will labor, watch, and pray while we are here. We know we will be evaluated for our works and our words. We are ready, by the grace of God, to stand in the Bema Judgment and face our accusers. We welcome the day when God will settle the accounts. We just believe the Word of God, and act upon and live by its precepts. We could do no better than to emulate the words of Jesus who said, "I must work the works of him that sent me, while it is day: the night cometh, when no man can work" (John 9:4).

> Life's evening sun is sinking low.
> Just a few more days and I must go
> To meet the deeds that I have done,
> Where there will be no setting sun.
> (Gospel chorus, anon.)

FREE SUBSCRIPTION

The price of this book includes a complimentary subscription to **Prophecy 2000** quarterly newspaper, published by David Allen Lewis. This will keep you updated on many of the subjects in this book.

PROPHECY 2000

Synagogue of Satan!
By Rev. Robert Shreckhise
Startling Explanation of
Difficult Passages in
Revelation 2 & 3

ALAS BABYLON!
Depression in 1990s?
How to Protect
Yourself
The Mark - 666?
New World Economy
The Manipulators

Eliazer Ben Yehuvda Revival - Hebrew Language

8, No. 1   The Prophecy Intelligence Digest   ©1990 David A. Lewis Ministries, Inc.   Price $2.00

The World Economy– Your Financial Future

OPINION

By David A. Lewis
I do not have to be a mind reader know that sometime today you ught about money. You put a rter in the parking meter, or paid 39 for a hamburger at McDonalds. ney was paid out for groceries, , car payments, repairs, clothing, he telephone bill.

Why is gold precious? Because of its rarity. If all the gold that has ever been mined out of the earth were gathered and formed into a cube, then placed beside the Washington Monument it would look like an ice

Thursday, August 17, 1980

OUR EDITORIALS

S&L blunder bodes ill for futures

THOMAS EAGLETON

Depression.

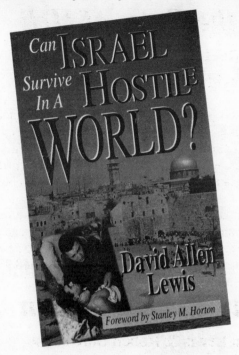

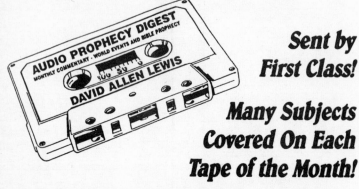